D0498514

UNHOLY

UNHOLY

WHY WHITE EVANGELICALS
WORSHIP AT THE ALTAR
OF DONALD TRUMP

———

SARAH POSNER

RANDOM HOUSE
NEW YORK

Published in the United States by Random House,
an imprint and division of Penguin Random House LLC, New York.

RANDOM HOUSE and the HOUSE colophon are registered trademarks of
Penguin Random House LLC.

LIBRARY OF CONGRESS CATALOGING-IN-PUBLICATION DATA
Names: Posner, Sarah, author.
Title: Unholy : why white evangelicals worship at the altar
of Donald Trump / by Sarah Posner.
Description: New York : Random House, [2020] |
Includes bibliographical references and index.
Identifiers: LCCN 2019044820 (print) | LCCN 2019044821 (ebook) |
ISBN 9781984820426 (hardcover) | ISBN 9781984820433 (ebook)
Subjects: LCSH: Trump, Donald, 1946– —Influence. | Religious right—
United States—History. | Christianity and politics—United States. |
Christians—Political activity—United States. | Evangelicalism—
Political aspects—United States. | White supremacy movements—
Religious aspects—Christianity. | Political culture—United States. |
United States—Politics and government.
Classification: LCC BR526 .P67 2020 (print) | LCC BR526 (ebook) |
DDC 320.520973/090512—dc23
LC record available at https://lccn.loc.gov/2019044820
LC ebook record available at https://lccn.loc.gov/2019044821

Printed in the United States of America on acid-free paper

randomhousebooks.com

2 4 6 8 9 7 5 3 1

First Edition

Book design by Susan Turner

For Doug

"We put God right at the center of the White House."

—*Paula White,* speaking at an Evangelicals for Trump campaign event at Solid Rock Church, Cincinnati, Ohio, March 6, 2020

CONTENTS

INTRODUCTION

Over the many months of covering the evangelical reaction to the presidential primary candidacy of Donald Trump in 2015 and 2016, I kept looking for the aha moment—the event, utterance, or handshake that might explain the seemingly improbable evangelical attraction to a biblically illiterate libertine. I had covered the Christian right for well over a decade, including the process, in two previous Republican primaries, that movement leaders had engaged in to decide which presidential candidate to bless. I attended countless church services and prayer gatherings, in venues ranging from megachurches to storefronts. I covered Christian conferences, the staples of which were mesmerizing Christian pop music, prophecies, spiritual warfare, and faith healings. I had hands laid on me, watched the casting out of demons, saw money change hands. I heard conspiracy theories about Barack Obama and Hillary Clinton, about secularism and feminism and the "gay agenda," about socialist and Muslim fifth columns on the cusp of bringing America to her knees. I heard myriad exhortations to Christians not to abandon politics, indeed to elevate their political engagement, to call their representatives in Washington, to vote. I wrote a book about the prosperity gospel, a quintessentially American theological invention exploited by televangelists to twist the arms of their flocks, teaching that God will bless them with health and riches if they fill their high-flying pastors' coffers with their hard-earned cash, even before they pay their rent.

In presidential politics, I covered the rise and fall of Baptist pastor-turned-politician Mike Huckabee in 2008, the tepid evangelical reaction to John McCain winning the Republican nomination that year, and the subsequent elation at his selection of Sarah Palin as his running mate—the first Pentecostal on a major party ticket. During the 2012 primaries, I spent days at prayer rallies and church services, the Iowa straw poll, the Iowa caucuses, and the primaries in South Carolina and Florida, where the candidates—many of whom had deep connections with the Christian right—competed to be the most pious, the most saved, the most committed to governing the country from a "biblical worldview," as the former congress-woman from Minnesota, Michele Bachmann, would often repeat. In the end, emerging from the pack of seven candidates was the disappointing, flip-flopping Mitt Romney, a member of the Church of Jesus Christ of Latter-Day Saints whom many evangelicals viewed with deep and bigoted suspicion. Robert Jeffress, the Southern Baptist pastor of a Dallas megachurch who went on to become one of Donald Trump's closest evangelical advisers, famously accused Romney of belonging to a cult.

By the time Trump ran for president, I had traveled to seventeen states, listening to campaign speeches, sermons, and theories about the second coming. I had seen everything from the buttoned-up Washington gatherings like the Values Voter Summit to the unbound, euphoric world of biblical prophecy and intercessory prayer. I took the Christian right leaders and voters I had immersed myself with over all those years at their word: in a presidential candidate, they were looking for a fellow Christian who had an unwavering track record of defending and promoting their core issues: opposition to abortion and LGBTQ rights and promotion of their "religious liberty."

When Donald Trump announced his candidacy in June 2015, I was deeply skeptical that he would be their man. He did not even try to tell a personal salvation story or display the most rudimentary Bible knowledge. Instead, he was enthralling the alt-right, a once-fringe movement of white supremacists and neo-Nazis that was, alarmingly, finding a foothold in mainstream politics as Trump buoyed them with his cruel nativism and casual racism. But as Trump energized this sordid faction, he simultaneously drew the attention of curious white evangelicals, many of whom also responded to his racist, anti-immigrant, and anti-Muslim rhetoric, cheering it as a brave assault on political correctness. As I watched it unfold and talked to white evangelical leaders and voters on both sides of the Trump Question, one thing became clear: as a "Christian," Trump was a work in progress. But God had a plan. Trump was a strong leader, a rich man, a successful real estate mogul. He could fix what was broken—politicians, even Republicans, who weakly gave in to the liberal ideas that had ruined America—and restore America's true redeemers to their rightful place in American political leadership. Trump might still be a "baby Christian" in the eyes of some of the evangelical leaders who decided to back him, but he was nonetheless anointed for this time and place.

The aha moment, then, was not something particular Trump said or did but the realization that Trump was the strongman the Christian right had long been waiting for. They had been waiting for a leader unbowed, one who wasn't afraid to attack, head-on, the legal, social, and cultural changes that had unleashed the racist grievances of the American right, beginning with *Brown v. Board of Education* and persisting through the 1960s and '70s in opposition to school desegregation and government policies to promote it—long before evangelicals made opposing abortion their top issue. Those grievances never went away; the conservative movement's right flank perpetually groused that the Republican "establishment" had too often made concessions to the liberal political order that had stolen away the rights of Christians, of parents, of whites, and of churches, even America's very foundation as a "Christian nation." Because of the feebleness of the Republican establishment, this thinking went, "political correctness" had made it taboo even to question that liberal order, much less destroy it. Trump might not be able to correctly cite a single Bible verse, but his fearless, impulsive campaign was, after years of spineless establishment Republicans, finally putting political correctness in its place.

Horse race political coverage is ill-equipped to tell this story, with its relentless focus on daily, or even hourly, tweets and spats, and its fixation with instant reactions and who trolled whom. The full story of this seemingly unlikely alliance between Trump and the Christian right spans decades of American political history, its contours shaped by the machinations of two generations of political organizers, lobbyists, and consultants, its possibility realized by the evolution of American Christianity in the age of prosperity, television, and later, the Internet. Understanding how the Trump presidency happened, and why conservative white Christians continue to guard it like loyal subjects of a besieged monarch, requires a thorough accounting not just of the Trump moment but also of the conditions that led to him, and that could lead to another Trump in the future.

I was born in 1964, the year the Civil Rights Act became law. I was nine when the Supreme Court struck down the criminalization of abortion. I was ten when Richard Nixon resigned the presidency in disgrace. I was raised to believe that despite the jagged trajectory of civil rights in the United States, there was a political consensus for advancing greater equality and good government. I believed our political system would put up guardrails against future Nixonian corruption. (Like everyone else, I couldn't conceive of Trump-level corruption.) As a college student, I never imagined that years later the country would be debating the morality of contraception, or that nominees to the federal bench would refuse to say whether *Brown* had been correctly decided.

In January 1986, I ditched my jeans and T-shirts and bought a conservative gray suit for a trip to Washington to meet the subjects of my senior thesis on the growing Washington political apparatus of the religious right. I visited the Heritage Foundation and collected books and pamphlets. Among my interviewees was the legislative director of the Eagle Forum, the stronghold of the indefatigable anti-feminist activist Phyllis Schlafly. Beverly LaHaye, the founder of Concerned Women for America, couldn't meet with me because of a bad back, but I learned from her assistant how the organization had, community by community, enlisted housewives outraged by moral decline—or by liberal feminist college students like me—to get involved in politics. Of the many pamphlets I collected in those days, "How to Lobby from Your Kitchen Table" is one of my favorites, and I still have it in my collection of religious right ephemera that has helped me understand the evolution of Trump's foremost promoters and defenders.

On that visit to Washington, I also met with the most important architect of the New Right and religious right, Paul Weyrich. As the middle chapters of this book detail, Weyrich came to Washington, much as Trump did so many years later, with the intention of breaking an "establishment" stranglehold on politics. Weyrich harbored a disdain for political and economic "elites" and maintained that an authentic America had been destroyed by liberalism, diversity, and the expansion of civil rights—all essential components of the Trump grievance list decades later. But unlike Trump, Weyrich was a detail-oriented and tireless political organizer. In 1974, to boost Republican electoral prospects in the wake of Watergate, Weyrich founded the Committee for the Survival of a Free Congress, later renamed the Free Congress Foundation, which he led until his death in 2008. Through Free Congress, Weyrich trained and promoted political candidates, analyzed and assessed legislation, pressured federal policy makers and lawmakers. Later, through his Coalitions for America, he brought together activists working on disparate issues to form a cohesive conservative coalition. Even today religious right activists keep up a tradition that Weyrich started—a weekly, off-the-record strategy lunch for movement leaders—citing his "rare combination of strategic vision, principle and entrepreneurial spirit."[1]

When I met him in his Capitol Hill office in 1986, he was polite but taciturn as he explained his project of organizing conservatives state by state, city by city, precinct by precinct, to realize conservative domination in politics. He described the challenges of making conservatives interested in what he called "family" issues—a broad term that included opposition to abortion but also embodied conservative fury over the government's role in a range of issues from childcare to school curricula. Reagan had been a disappointment, Weyrich told me, insufficiently dedicated to the cause. Even though Reagan today continues to be hailed as a conservative icon, Weyrich that day gave Reagan a grade of "barely passing." What did these political agitators want that Ronald Reagan couldn't deliver? I wondered.

I next saw Weyrich twenty years later, after I had gone to law school and practiced law for nearly a decade before becoming a journalist. In 2006, I covered the very first Values Voter Summit, now the premier Washington event where the Christian right and Republican politicians curried favor. Weyrich, by that time in declining health and wheelchair-bound after the amputation of both legs below the knee, was a diminished presence on the stage, his voice having lost the booming vigor I remembered. Like other speakers, he was gloomy (correctly, it turned out) about the prospects for Republicans to retain control of Congress in the upcoming midterm elections. They had, once again, lost faith in the "establishment" Republicans. Republicans would lose the next two presidential elections to Barack Obama. But thanks in no small part to the political infrastructure Weyrich had built, the GOP was able to regain control of Congress and later put Trump in the White House.

Over his decades in Washington, Weyrich was a looming presence with a volatile personality who inspired legions of activists and aspiring politicians to sign up both as foot soldiers and as battle commanders in his crusade against secular liberal enemies as well as what he perceived to be conservative elitism. Although Trump was partying at Studio 54 when the New Right mastermind was in the trenches of the capital, Weyrich did rouse the man who would become Trump's vice president, Mike Pence. "I want to be like Paul Weyrich when I grow up," Pence, then a congressman from Indiana, told attendees at a 2008 dinner celebrating Weyrich's career at the

Four Seasons Hotel in Georgetown.[2] Pence lauded Weyrich as "a mentor and a friend" who "encouraged me to stand on the foundation of my faith, to stand up for conservative values, and to pursue those with conviction and with an eye on the long view."[3] When in Congress in the 2000s, Pence led the Republican Study Committee, the conservative caucus co-founded by Weyrich in 1973, and he attended the weekly, off-the-record meetings with more than sixty conservative organizations, congressional Republicans, and Republican White House officials, held at Weyrich's Free Congress Foundation. The "main objective" of these regular meetings, according to Weyrich, was "to see to it that the inside and the outside sing from the same sheet of music."[4] That same coordinated action plan lies at the heart of Pence's current role as Trump's de facto policy liaison to the religious right.

Before Trump, few could have conceived of a candidate winning the Republican nomination without using the language of "faith" and "Christian values" that had become commonplace, even required, since the rise of Weyrich's religious right in the late 1970s. Instead, Trump spoke another lingua franca of the American right—the rhetoric of resentment, of lost domination, of grievances against "special" rights for others at the expense of white Christians. When Trump says he made it safe to say "Merry Christmas" again, it sounds insipid to outsiders, but to the Christian right it simply encapsulates how he is restoring their diminished power. Although Weyrich is best known for launching the modern religious right, my deep exploration of the historical record shows how he and his New Right allies laid the groundwork not just for Trump's union with the religious right but also for their attraction to his crude politics of white nationalist grievance.

Trump's ascent was not an ideological aberration, despite his deviations from Republican free market and foreign policy orthodoxies. For the Christian right, Trump is a culmination of five decades of political organizing. On the surface, the Christian right is saturated with rhetoric about "faith" and "values." Its real driving force, though, was not religion but grievances over school desegregation, women's rights, LGBTQ rights, affirmative action, and more. Trump became their hero despite being a thrice-married philanderer who talked about dating his daughter, paid off a porn star to keep quiet about an affair, and was terrible at God talk. He became their savior because he spoke the language that tied them and him—and the grievances of the alt-right—together against "political correctness," civil and human rights, and at its core, the entire arduous project of maintaining a pluralistic, secular, liberal democracy. The era of the "values voter" was over; the era of the Trump voter had begun.

UNHOLY

The Blueprint for an Assault on Civil Rights

L ess than two weeks into Trump's presidency, I was leaked an explosive document: a draft executive order "establishing a government-wide initiative to respect religious freedom" that was under White House consideration and that was being circulated inside federal agencies. As I digested the four-page draft, I saw in it an audacious attempt to end-run the democratic process to create, with the stroke of Trump's pen, rights for conservative Christians that exceeded what the courts, Congress, and nearly every state legislature had ever granted them. The draft envisioned giving any person or organization—including government employees, contractors, grantees, and not-for-profit and for-profit corporations—permission to refuse to transact virtually any type of business with someone based on their sexual orientation, gender identity, or marital status, or because they had had premarital sex or an abortion. It would have permitted such exemptions in nearly every facet of life, "when providing social services, education, or healthcare; earning a living, seeking a job, or employing others; receiving government grants or contracts; or otherwise participating in the marketplace, the public

square, or interfacing with Federal, State or local governments." The
document derided the government as the enemy, an arrogant tyrant
to religious people. "Americans and their religious organizations," the
draft read, "will not be coerced by the Federal Government into participating in activities that violate their conscience."[1]

Taken out of context, the draft executive order might have
seemed chock-full of legalese, perhaps paranoid and excessive, and
completely out of touch with mainstream twenty-first-century American social mores. It was not a fresh brainchild of the new Trump
administration; it represented the culmination of decades of Christian right legal and political advocacy for "religious freedom." The
draft's framing—that an imperious, secular government was bent on
stripping Christians of their rights—had been years in the making,
dating back to the 1970s. Then, in the religious right's formative
years, activists first formulated arguments that government policies
promoting school desegregation were an infringement on Christians'
freedom to educate their children. But this time the government
"social engineering" that was provoking the backlash was not school
desegregation and associated policies but reproductive rights and the
more recent, rapid advance of LGBTQ rights, including marriage
equality.

The draft executive order that I had in hand seemed to capture
every possible permutation of the ever-expanding list of wrongs that
religious right ideologues claimed, over several decades, had befallen
Christian America. Even though it bore no indication of its author or
authors, I knew it wasn't the work of a lone zealot taking the pulse of
a brand-new administration, spitballing in the hope of getting
Trump's attention. Having monitored the methods of Christian right
advocacy over the course of the preceding decade, I was well
acquainted with the warnings of pastors, pundits, and politicians—in
legislative hearings, Supreme Court arguments, political rallies, and
sermons—to their foot soldiers that the government was poised to
crush their religious liberty by making pharmacists fill prescriptions
for emergency contraception, by forcing Christian adoption agencies
to place children with same-sex couples, or by compelling Catholic

social service providers to refer clients who had been sexually assaulted for reproductive health care.

The draft executive order would allow a Christian adoption agency to refuse to place children with a non-Christian couple. It would allow a social services contractor with the federal government, one that received taxpayer funding, to turn away a client because it objected to her private sexual activity or because she was a lesbian. It would permit a psychologist to refuse to treat a patient based on their gender identity. It would allow a landlord to evict a tenant who had had an abortion, or an accountant to refuse to prepare a lesbian couple's tax return. It would enable every imitator of Kim Davis, the Kentucky county clerk who refused to issue a marriage license to a gay couple and became, in the process, a national Christian right hero. The draft order was the Christian right's wish list for the Trump presidency.

When I shared the draft with constitutional law experts and civil rights lawyers, they were astounded, using words like *sweeping, staggering,* and *blunderbuss* to describe it. And while they believed the document, as drafted, was an unconstitutional violation of the separation of church and state because it would give special privileges to a particular set of sectarian religious beliefs, they still feared its impact. The Trump presidency had already begun to test all customs and norms, including the rule of law, as never before. If Trump signed the executive order, the force of that act would expose some of the country's most vulnerable people—including children, immigrants, and LGBTQ youth—to religion-driven discrimination in social services like foster care and other settings where vindicating one's rights can be bewildering, challenging, and often impossible. "They would say this is a nondiscrimination order," Jenny Pizer, a lawyer at the LGBTQ rights organization Lambda Legal, told me. "We disagree. We would say being denied the ability to discriminate against others is not discrimination against you."

The disclosure of Trump's executive order draft rattled a civil rights community already on edge over Trump's election, but the controversy only energized Christian right leadership to press Trump to sign it. "Mr. President," the Heritage Foundation's news site *The Daily Signal* pleaded, "Don't Cave to Liberal Fear mongering. Protect Religious Freedom."[2] Leading conservatives on the powerful, agenda-setting Council for National Policy, pleaded with the president to sign the order to protect earnest, hardworking Christians. Religious humanitarian relief organizations, adoption placement agencies, schools, and small businesses with religious owners who claimed religious objections to LGBTQ rights, abortion, and contraception were suffering under the weight of "Obama era antireligious regulations," the letter read. They needed "protections that you can grant through an executive order to prevent federal discrimination against them for acting in accordance with their beliefs."[3] Fifty-two Republican members of the House and eighteen Republican senators also weighed in, pressing Trump to sign the order.[4] The House lawmakers' letter echoed the charges that an overbearing, coercive federal government under Obama had stolen away God-fearing Americans' religious freedom. "We look forward to coordinating with your administration," they wrote, "so that critical religious liberty and conscience protections may finally be restored to millions of Americans who have been harmed and unprotected for far too many years."[5]

Despite these appeals, Trump took months to make a decision. In the end, he opted for a more general edict, signed in a jubilant, sun-drenched Rose Garden ceremony on the National Day of Prayer, which falls each year on the first Thursday in May. He gathered a dependable entourage of Christians who would vouch for his piety and dedication. Jack Graham, pastor of Prestonwood Baptist, a Southern Baptist megachurch in Plano, Texas, delivered a prayer "in the dear name of Jesus."[6] Pence, in an unmistakable dig at Obama, pointed out that while every president, since Harry Truman instituted the National Day of Prayer in 1952, had issued a proclamation commemorating it, "not every president has done so in the Rose Garden at the White House." Pence then praised Trump's piety. "Our president is a believer," he said. "He loves his family, and he loves his country with an unshakable faith in God and the American people."

With his top spiritual adviser, the televangelist Paula White, standing behind him, smiling, nodding, and clapping with approval, Trump spoke about the importance of faith and religious tolerance—platitudes even more empty given his executive orders designed to ban Muslim refugees from entering the United States. "We will not allow people of faith to be targeted, bullied, or silenced anymore," he said to applause. "And we will never ever stand for religious discrimination. Never ever. Tolerance is the cornerstone of peace."[7] The president who, during his campaign, could not bring himself to condemn white nationalists and anti-Semites and regularly vilified Islam, consecrated an executive order granting legal protections specially crafted for his Christian right allies by inveighing about his commitment to religious tolerance.

The order Trump signed that day, unlike the draft that had circulated months earlier, did not specifically single out sexual orientation, gender identity, or marital status as grounds for discrimination, as the original draft had, reportedly because Ivanka Trump and Jared Kushner, the presidential daughter-son-in-law advising team, had talked Trump out of taking such an explicitly anti-LGBTQ stance. (Not long afterward, though, Trump would ban transgender troops from the military, via a tweet.) Some prominent Christian right advocates of the religious liberty agenda, like *National Review*'s David French and Princeton University's Robert George, even dismissed the signed order as "worse than useless," "meaningless," and even a "betrayal."[8] But its seemingly bland provision, overlooked by many, directing the attorney general to "issue guidance interpreting religious liberty protections in Federal law," was broad enough to carry out the scuttled order's objectives. Given this general instruction to Attorney General Jeff Sessions, one civil rights lawyer who had served in the Obama administration worried to me that "the breadth of what the AG could issue is virtually unchecked."

Five months later, Attorney General Sessions issued a twenty-five-page memorandum, entitled "Federal Law Protections for Religious Liberty," directing federal agencies, in every action they took—as employers, as policy makers, when disbursing grants, or when contracting with outside companies to provide taxpayer-funded government services—to protect the religious liberty of individuals and companies. "Religious liberty," the memorandum read, "is not merely a right to personal religious beliefs or even to worship in a sacred place. It also encompasses religious observance and practice." Therefore, "[e]xcept in the narrowest circumstances, no one should be forced to choose between living out his or her faith and complying with the law."

This had been a common argument for the Christian right when a health care worker did not want to provide reproductive health care, when a company did not want to cover contraception in its insurance plan, when a wedding photographer did not want to work at a gay wedding, or when any employer did not want to hire a lesbian employee. But Sessions's memo dramatically expanded the scope of these kinds of refusals across the federal government. "Therefore," the memo read, "to the greatest extent practicable and permitted by law, religious observance and practice should be reasonably accommodated in all government activity." Americans United for the Separation of Church and State called the document "a roadmap for how to discriminate against most anyone, including women, LGBTQ people and religious minorities." But it was more: it was a blueprint for creating not just new rights but new authority for conservative Christians, according them extraordinary preference so long as the federal government was administered by Donald Trump.

Trump, then, did not just deliver policy, in a quid pro quo with a voting bloc that fueled his election. He delivered power. And for that, he was not merely a reliable politician worthy of their praise. For the Christian right, Trump is no ordinary politician and no ordinary president. He is anointed, chosen, and sanctified by the movement as a divine leader, sent by God to save America.

2

God's Strongman

T he facile explanation for this apparently improbable union
between the proponents of "faith," "values," and "family" and
the profoundly impious real estate huckster and serial philanderer is that the Christian right hypocritically sacrificed its principles in exchange for raw political power. But this purely transactional
explanation for the Trump-evangelical merger elides the deeper bond
between Trump and his devoted flock. Although Trump is illiterate
in evangelicals' lexicon and spent his adult life flagrantly contraven-
ing their sexual mores, his evangelical supporters are nonetheless
starstruck. He may not be one of them, but they idolize how he
loudly and fearlessly articulates their shared grievances—that alien
anti-Christian, anti-American ideologies have taken over the government, judiciary, media, education, and even popular culture and
forced edicts upon a besieged white Christian majority, cowing them
into submission by invoking "political correctness" that aims to cen-
sor, silence, and oppress them.

The Trump-evangelical relationship represents an intense meeting of the minds, decades in the making, on the notion that America

lies in ruins after the sweep of historic changes since the mid-twentieth century, promising nondiscrimination and equal rights for those who had been historically disenfranchised—women, racial minorities, immigrants, refugees, and LGBTQ people—eroded the dominance of conservative white Christianity in American public life. Trump apparently has not cracked the binding on the Bible he waves in the air while speaking to evangelical audiences, but he fluently speaks the language of conservative white Christian backlash against the expansion of rights for previously disenfranchised and marginalized Americans. Trump not only gives voice to the Christian right's perceived loss of religious dominance; he pounds away at grievances over white people losing ground to black and brown people and immigrants, of men losing ground to women, of "originalist" judges under the sway of liberal intruders demanding "special" rights. Trump reassures white evangelical voters that he will restore the America they believe has been lost—the "Christian nation" that God intended America to be, governed by what they claim is "biblical law" or a "Christian worldview."

The evangelical adoration for Trump is rooted in far more than his willingness to keep a coveted list of campaign promises, like appointing anti-abortion judges or expanding religious exemptions for conservative Christians, such as bakers who refuse to make a cake for a gay wedding. Trump inspires this high regard because he is eager to use strongman tactics in order to carry out those promises. For decades, the Christian right has successfully used the mechanisms of democracy, such as voter registration and mobilization, citizen lobbying, and energetic recruitment of religious candidates to run for office, to advance its agenda. In these efforts, conservative evangelicals are driven not by a commitment to liberal democracy but rather by a politicized theology demanding that they seize control of government to protect it from the demonic influences of liberalism and secularism. Previous presidents pandered to evangelicals, but Donald Trump constitutes the culmination of a movement that has for decades searched for a leader willing to join forces in this battle without cowering to shifting political winds. In Trump, the

Christian right sees more than a politician who delivers on promises; they see a savior from the excesses of liberalism.

And for their purposes, Donald Trump arrived on the political scene not a moment too soon. He burst in at a critical moment, when top Christian right leaders were becoming painfully aware they were losing their demographic supremacy. In 2006, white evangelicals made up 23 percent of U.S. adults, a formidable segment of the population. A short decade later that number had dropped to 17 percent, owing to rising proportions of nonwhites and people unaffiliated with religion. But because white evangelicals are uniquely politicized and highly mobilized to vote, they can exert an outsize influence on our elections and political culture if they unify around a candidate or cause. In the 2016 election, white evangelicals made up 26 percent of voters and fully one-third of Republican voters. Eighty-one percent of those people voted for Donald Trump.

Although their overall numbers are dropping, Trump's presidency has given white evangelicals new life as the most influential political demographic in America. In office, he has been beyond solicitous to the Christian right leaders who support him. He has given them the political appointees and judges to implement their political agenda, delivering in ways that even they likely never imagined. As the veteran operative Ralph Reed, now head of the advocacy group Faith and Freedom Coalition, proudly told his annual conference in June 2019, "there are more Christians serving in the Cabinet, serving on the White House staff, in the subcabinet," than under "all previous presidents combined." When a decision needs to be made in the Trump White House, Reed went on, "the people who are writing memos and in the meeting advising the president are on our side, more than ever before."[1]

White evangelicals remain the most enthusiastic boosters of Trump's presidency, supporting him more than any other demographic group by significant margins. Two years into his term, when just 37 percent of all Americans approved of his job performance, 71 percent of white evangelicals did. Just 42 percent of all Americans agreed with Trump's demand to build a wall at the U.S.-Mexico border, compared to 76 percent of white evangelicals. While many Americans gasped and gaped at Trump's overt racism, 73 percent of white evangelicals believed he was doing a good or even excellent job on race relations.[2] Although evangelicals constitute far from a majority of Americans, the president's bottomless support for them has enabled the Christian right to dictate administration policy, creating a tyranny of the minority that they see as a divine assignment and a last chance to save America. Trump's white evangelical supporters, then, have chosen to see him not as a sinner but as a strongman, not as a con man but as a king who is courageously unshackling them from what they portray as liberal oppression.

That means that dissenters—including their own evangelical brothers and sisters—are demeaned, dismissed, and ostracized for their insufficient loyalty to Trump, the pagan king. Longtime evangelical insiders who raise objections to Trump's candidacy, or who question their brethren's eventual genuflection to him, have been cast aside by powerful players in the pro-Trump evangelical world, left struggling to understand exactly what has happened to a community that was once their spiritual, cultural, and political home. Mark DeMoss, a former chief of staff to Moral Majority founder Jerry Falwell, Sr., and a pioneer of the niche profession of Christian public relations, is one evangelical leader who now finds himself in that wilderness. "How do people who have spent their entire adult life preaching" religious piety, sexual purity, and so-called family values "just suddenly flip a switch and endorse a candidate who doesn't reflect what they've been preaching and telling their congregations they should be looking for?" he asked me. DeMoss formerly represented some of the most recognizable names in evangelicalism and served as an adviser to Mitt Romney's 2008 and 2012 presidential campaigns. His extended family has deep ties to Falwell's Liberty University, and he himself served on the executive committee of the university's board of trustees. But after publicly criticizing Jerry Falwell, Jr.'s, endorsement of Trump in the 2016 primaries, he was forced out of that position—foreshadowing the Trumpian use of power and authority to silence and ostracize critics. DeMoss and many others shared with me their bafflement and even anguish during the tumultuous months of the 2016 presidential campaign, when Trump marched ever closer to the nomination, their protests of his unfitness and immorality proving futile as he consolidated power among their ranks. Midway through Trump's first term, one of his most enthusiastic evangelical backers, Robert Jeffress, pastor of First Baptist, a Dallas megachurch, called anti-Trump evangelicals "spineless morons" on Fox News personality Todd Starnes's radio program. By that time, such disdain for Trump's evangelical detractors had become so entrenched that Jeffress's insult was barely noticed as anything unusual.

Just like Trump himself, contemporary evangelicalism has been profoundly shaped by celebrity and television. Trump's path to evangelical strongman was not paved by a career in politics talking about faith, family, and freedom, the playbook followed by his predecessors and many of his onetime rivals, like Texas senator Ted Cruz, or now-Housing and Urban Development secretary Ben Carson. It was paved by a career starring in reality television and, importantly, studying Christian television and befriending some of its biggest stars. Trump is more like a televangelist than a politician—which is exactly why he was able to break the politician mold for evangelical voters who had come to believe that other presidential candidates, for all their faith talk, had ultimately failed to deliver government guided by "Christian" or "biblical" values.

Previous Republican candidates cultivated relationships with televangelists in a quest for the votes of their considerable audiences. But more than any other Republican candidate, Trump's politics were defined by televangelism itself. Although televangelists operate out of tax-exempt churches, at their core their ministries are businesses, bringing in millions of unaccountable cash, used for enriching the pastor with extravagances like mansions portrayed as parsonages, or private jets held to be essential tools for spreading the gospel. Televangelism has created an audience, for both church and politics, that is enthralled with showmanship and captivated by powerful personalities and flamboyant tales of miracles and supernatural successes, from cancer healed by prayer to bank accounts suddenly flush with heaven-sent cash.

For Trump, cozying up to televangelists was not just election-year pandering. Trump was perfectly comfortable in a world of celebrity and supernatural wonders, in contrast to George H. W. Bush, who in 1987 gave a pained interview on the Trinity Broadcasting Network, home to the world's most influential televangelists, touting his commitment to God as a well-heeled Episcopalian. Trump didn't give stump speeches extolling, like George W. Bush, the virtues of "compassionate conservatism." Instead, his rallies were more like tent revivals, his speeches more like a televangelist's promises of miraculous success than considered policy prescriptions.

Since televangelism was popularized in the 1970s, it has propagated the prosperity gospel, a theology that its many Christian critics consider a heresy and a fraud, charging its proponents with distorting biblical teachings by claiming that God wants believers to be rich while pressuring congregants and viewers to line their pockets. The prosperity gospel, born in America in the mid-twentieth century, teaches that those who "sow a seed"—or give their money to their pastor or his ministry—will receive a supernatural, thousandfold blessing in return. The prosperity gospel thrives on powerful, charismatic authority figures who demand unquestioning "obedience" from their congregants. Some followers who extricated themselves from prosperity gospel churches have shared their stories with me—stories that sound as if they or their loved ones had been held hostage by faith. A single mom worried that if she didn't give the pastor her "first fruits"—the money she earned before she paid any of her own bills—God would curse her. A young woman refused to believe the open secret that the pastor had forced women in the congregation to have sex with him, telling them it was what God commanded. A man was forced out of his church and isolated from his friends because he had dared to question the pastor's authority. A woman found her dead mother's notebooks documenting the thousands of dollars she

had mailed to a televangelist who promised it would bring her miraculous healing from breast cancer. Prosperity preachers invoke Psalm
105:15, God's admonition to "touch not mine anointed ones, and do
my prophets no harm," transforming a reminder of God's covenant
with Abraham and his descendants into a tyrannical bludgeon against
criticism of a pastor's "authority," even when the pastor is enriching
himself with congregants' donations or engaging in sexual misconduct. Although there is no evidence Trump can cite this Bible verse,
there is plenty of evidence that he believes himself to be empowered
to degrade, berate, and ostracize his critics.

These "anointed" leaders present themselves as modern-day
prophets and apostles, able to receive revelations directly from God.
Revelation knowledge supersedes facts and reason. The authority
figure is then said to be imbued with supernatural powers—to heal
illnesses based on faith, to lift out of poverty a congregant who gives
him her last dime, to cast out the demons that are plaguing her with
a spirit of poverty, to declare victory over satanic forces. While previous Republican presidential candidates engaged in campaign outreach to televangelists in the hopes of garnering the votes of their
significant audiences, Trump is the first to act like one—making up
facts, promising magical success, pretending to solve complex problems with a tweet or an impetuous boast. He demands secrecy from
his employees and acolytes. He requires members of his cabinet to
publicly and submissively declare their loyalty. His pronouncements
are not to be questioned. And his followers believe he will—
supernaturally or otherwise—make America great again. They believe
Trump will achieve MAGA because God has anointed him to carry
out this mission. He may not actually be a Christian, but God has
chosen him to protect Christians and therefore America.

This thinking is a profound reversal of the Christian right's long-
standing playbook for presidential politics. For decades, top Christian right operatives like James Dobson, the founder of Focus on the
Family, and influential evangelical activists in early primary states
like Iowa and South Carolina, insisted that in order to win their support, a Republican presidential candidate must be a Christian, must

have a relatable salvation story, and must link that faith narrative to a way of governing according to Christian values. Trump largely snubbed these demands, instead constructing his faith story largely from the accounts of his longtime friend, the televangelist Paula White. According to White herself and other evangelicals who have helped spread this origin myth, in the early 2000s, Trump saw the popular, slim, well-coiffed blonde preach her message "The Value of Vision" on TV. Trump, the story goes, liked watching Christian TV and just happened on White's show while channel surfing. Johnnie Moore, another Christian public relations professional who became the spokesman for the Trump campaign's evangelical advisory board, packaged the story to me this way: White's message—that having "vision" is crucial for success in life—was easily digested by the businessman Trump, since she presented biblical ideas in a way that made sense in a business context. "You can take it as a business person, you could say I can apply this to my life today or this is how I think about things," Moore said, as he recalled how he later watched White deliver her "message" and realized it "wasn't just like preaching the Bible, it was the Bible meets practical life in a way a mega business person can relate to."[3] Trump liked what he heard—or perhaps, saw—called White up, and they have been friends ever since.[4] In the mid-2000s, Trump appeared on White's television show, *Paula White Today,* in which she was discussing "keys to successful living," to talk about his business success. He told her his father set a good example for him by doing "nothing but work" and rarely taking vacations.[5] More than a decade later a *New York Times* exposé showed that Trump and his father grew their wealth from "dubious tax schemes," including "instances of outright fraud."[6] But White, and the legend built around her relationship with Trump, helped portray him to evangelical audiences as a successful businessman who applied "biblical" values in his everyday life.

Like Trump's businesses, White's had come under scrutiny, and like Trump, she evaded transparency and accountability. In 2007, Sen. Charles Grassley, the Iowa Republican who was then the ranking member of the Senate Finance Committee, launched an inquiry

into whether White and five other televangelists—Kenneth Copeland, Eddie Long, Joyce Meyer, Creflo Dollar, and Benny Hinn—
had abused their tax-exempt status by using donations to their
ministries for personal gain. Grassley had been spurred to action by
the Trinity Foundation, a Dallas-based watchdog that had long investigated financial abuses of televangelists, and that delivered to Grassley's committee packages of material detailing self-enrichment and
self-dealing with tax-deductible donations. Grassley opened the
probe, he said, because Americans who give generously to religious
organizations "should be assured that their donations are being used
for the tax-exempt purposes of the organizations."[7] For many years,
televangelists had flaunted their wealth as a sign of God's favor—
a central tenet of the prosperity gospel that they preach—flying in
private jets, purchasing multiple homes and luxury cars, and traveling to exotic destinations. At first Grassley seemed determined to
find answers, but some of the six, including White, resisted providing
full documentation that would aid the investigation. Trump shares
this aversion to transparency in his business affairs and also behaves
as if Congress has no authority to probe them. As a citizen, Trump
long blocked transparency of his businesses, and as president, he has
stonewalled the public and investigators about his personal finances,
as well as the inner workings of his campaign and his White House.

Unlike secular nonprofits, churches are not required by law to
make their tax returns public, so the finances of these televangelists
remain hidden from public view. The public effectively subsidizes
them because donations to them are not taxed, and the donor receives
a tax deduction. Three years after launching the investigation, Grassley, under pressure from religious right groups protesting that it was
infringing on their religious liberty, shut it down without making any
recommendations for greater transparency or accountability. Senate
investigators opted instead to recommend "self-reform within the
community," a toothless result in keeping with the conservative
antagonism toward government regulation of business and, in particular, toward what evangelicals denounce as government interference in church affairs. Grassley's committee staff reached this

conclusion despite documenting its findings about some of the televangelists' finances. In White's case, her church had received more
than $35 million in tithes and offerings in 2006 alone. She had pur-
chased, with her then-husband, Randy White, a $3.5 million condo-
minium in Trump Tower in New York. They also owned a lavish
Tampa Bay, Florida, home and chartered a $1.2 million jet and other
private aircraft for personal trips. But the committee was unable to
probe the full extent of White's ministry's finances, because while
some former staffers "wanted to speak with Committee staff," they
had signed confidentiality agreements and "were afraid of being sued
by the church."[8]

Senate staff acknowledged that the refusal by White and three
other televangelists to provide information made it impossible "to
determine whether and the extent to which they are reporting and
paying taxes on income earned" by multiple business entities they
created, in addition to their churches. Despite these frustrations, the
committee did not recommend any tax law changes to require transparency or oversight of for-profit extensions of churches. Instead,
Grassley's committee did the opposite: it recommended the elimination or weakening of one provision of the tax code, the Johnson
Amendment,[9] that, since 1954, has conditioned the tax-exempt status of nonprofit organizations, including churches and other houses
of worship, on refraining from endorsing candidates for public office.
For years, politically powerful evangelicals had pointed to the Johnson Amendment as evidence of an oppressive government bent on
silencing the free speech of conservative Christians, even though the
rule does not prohibit speech but only guards against the use of those
tax-exempt dollars for electioneering. If it were repealed, evangelical
celebrities would be further emboldened to use their perches for
endorsements and even fund-raising, mightily strengthening their
political hand. The merger of church and state that the Christian
right has favored since arising as a force in Republican politics would
be one crucial step closer to reality.

Shortly after Grassley's staff recommended the rollback of the
Johnson Amendment in early 2011, Trump began publicly toying

with a presidential run. And just as White had introduced Trump to her television audience as a prosperous titan of real estate, another Christian television personality stepped in to offer a helping hand. In the spring of 2011, David Brody, the affable political correspondent for the Christian Broadcasting Network, approached Trump about doing an interview for his evangelical Christian audience. The network had been founded in 1960 by one of the pioneers of evangelical presidential politics, Pat Robertson, who later founded the Christian Coalition, an early training ground for evangelical political candidates and their supporters. Robertson, who challenged George H. W. Bush in the 1988 presidential primaries, was by the 2010s a relic of the 1980s heyday of the Christian right's old guard, hosting the network's daily *700 Club* program and drawing ridicule and condemnation for making statements like "there is a spiritual component" to multiple sclerosis, a "demonic" thing "that you literally have to cast out,"[10] and that black Americans were better off during the Jim Crow era because "it used to be, like in the '30s, that blacks were self-sustaining, they had wonderful families, they had homeownership, they were in business."[11] But Brody, his man in Washington, had a knack for cozying up to people in power and persuading them that reaching the network's considerable evangelical audience was a necessity for electoral success.

By the time he scored the Trump interview in April 2011, Brody, a baby-faced reporter with a credulous demeanor, was already known as the network's soothsayer of evangelicals' role in Washington and national politics. His blog, *The Brody File,* was widely read by political reporters for little scoops into the thinking or strategy of Republican candidates or evangelical voters, and he appeared frequently on secular network and cable television political shows to offer his insights. In Trump, he saw a student in need of guidance. "My pitch at the time was something along the lines of 'If you're going to run, you are going to need evangelicals behind you, so you might want to get out in front of an evangelical audience,'" Brody recalled to me in 2016, in CBN's downtown Washington, D.C., studios.[12] Although Trump had ultimately decided against running in 2012, this early

testing of the waters is evidence that many of the people who ultimately got on board were at least willing to entertain his political
prospects and were even early promoters of him.

In his Trump Tower interview, Brody made awkward efforts to
get Trump to open up about religion, only to be met with trademark
Trump ramblings—none of which seemed to diminish Trump's lus-
ter among evangelicals. "Talk to me a little bit about how you see
God?" asked Brody, a question for which any other Republican would
have been ready with a well-rehearsed response, but Trump
responded with a vague disquisition on Christianity and praise of the
Bible as "the book, it is the thing." Trump claimed to attend church
"as much as I can." He recounted his conversion from being pro-
choice to pro-life, after, he said, a friend had contemplated abortion
for his wife, but ultimately considered his baby "the apple of his eye."
Brody helped Trump tap into evangelical anxieties, asking him about
what he called "the Muslim problem," noting that evangelicals have
"some concern about the teachings of the Koran." The Koran, Trump
replied in a prelude to the Islamophobia that marked his 2016 campaign and his presidency, teaches "some very negative vibe."[13] All the
questions were neatly queued up, and even the most casual observer
of evangelical politics could easily have been prepared to deliver any
number of foolproof paeans to God and country. Trump didn't seem
to get it—yet Brody and other important guests on his program were
strenuously signaling to viewers that Trump could probably pass
their tests anyway.

Brody capped off the interview with a Times Square chat with
Kellyanne Conway, who would in 2016 become Trump's campaign
manager and, after he was elected, one of his closest White House
advisers. Conway, well known to evangelical viewers because of her
work as a pollster and frequent public speaker who offered insights
on public opinion on conservative issues, laid out reasons why evangelicals would be intrigued with a Trump candidacy. She expressed
bullishness on Trump because of his declared opposition to same-
sex marriage and abortion—even though these appeared to be
dreaded "flip-flops" from prior positions—and, crucially, his ability to

"talk very forcefully" on foreign policy. "I doubt Donald Trump would bow to foreign leaders," Conway said admiringly.

Brody then enlisted influential evangelicals for their views. Tony Perkins, the Family Research Council president, told him, "Donald Trump is not talking like a typical politician," and he has "gotten the attention of social conservative voters." Ralph Reed, a onetime aco-lyte of Robertson who now heads the Faith and Freedom Coalition, which promotes political engagement by conservative Christian vot-ers, spoke of a "nascent and growing curiosity in the faith community about Trump." In April 2011, Trump was already being marketed as a bold, iconoclastic leader who didn't really fit the mold—but might well just be the man evangelicals were looking for. It would be suf-ficient for him to pay lip service to their issues if he could enthrall them with his other qualities—his purported success as a business-man, his "outsider" status, and his willingness to "tell it like it is."

The next month Brody got an "exclusive" scoop from Trump's personal lawyer, Michael Cohen.[14] Trump would be meeting with "top" evangelical pastors in Trump Tower, an event organized by his friend Paula White. White has described the meeting as something Trump asked her to set up, because he was considering running for president and "I need to hear from God." Preaching in a Florida church just days after Trump was inaugurated in 2017, White recalled how twenty or thirty pastors spent six hours with Trump, praying and speaking with him. The next day, though, White claimed Trump told her, "I just don't feel it's God's timing."[15]

Trump would go on to make repeal of the Johnson Amendment—which could open up churches to limitless electioneering and the pos-sible flow of unaccountable campaign cash through their coffers—a centerpiece of his outreach to the Christian right. Jerry Falwell, Jr., the president of Liberty University who was one of the first evangelical leaders to endorse Trump in the 2016 primary, told me that Trump had privately discussed his support for repealing the law. Falwell said Trump spoke to him about "how it needed to be repealed, and how it pretty much silenced people of faith because it scares pastors and leaders of nonprofit organizations like Liberty University and others from taking a political position because they're afraid of losing their tax exempt status."[16] This characterization was not true; the Johnson Amendment does not prohibit pastors or nonprofits from taking positions on political issues, only from using tax-exempt resources to endorse a candidate in an election. At his pivotal June 2016 meeting with one thousand evangelical leaders in Manhattan, which cemented evangelical support for his candidacy, Trump bragged that "I think maybe it will be my greatest contribution to Christianity and other religions is to allow you to go and speak openly, if you like somebody."[17] With Trump's blessing, at the 2016 Republican convention, the party added a plank to its platform calling for repeal of the Johnson Amendment. "Republicans believe," the platform now reads, "the federal government, specifically the IRS, is constitutionally prohibited from policing or censoring speech based on religious convictions or beliefs."[18] At the convention in Cleveland, Ralph Reed told a luncheon gathering of Christian right activists that the platform change was made at Trump's "insistence." The role of the Johnson Amendment, Reed said in a familiar warning, was to "harass and persecute the conservative faith community," as it "puts a gun to the head of every church," such that "if you so much as utter a word about politics, we will revoke your tax-exempt status."[19]

Once in office, Trump signed an executive order directing the IRS to stop enforcing the Johnson Amendment. He later bragged, falsely, that his White House had repealed it, even though repealing it would require an act of Congress. Nonetheless, Trump's promises, and the lack of enforcement of the rule, have worried campaign finance watchdogs like the Campaign Legal Center, which argues that "in the wake of U.S. Supreme Court decisions like *Citizens United,* there is every reason to believe that any effort to loosen the Johnson Amendment's strictures would lead to a new flood of dark, unaccountable and tax-deductible campaign funds into our elections."[20] As much as Trump displays little interest in the details of policy, the Johnson Amendment is one he has consistently focused on.

. . .

Despite the friendly entrée into the world of evangelical politics in 2011, when Trump finally did launch a presidential bid in mid-2015, few believed that a twice-divorced, proudly philandering casino mogul could win over evangelical voters. In the opening months of his campaign, Trump spent his time lambasting "political correctness" and "globalism," casting Mexicans as "rapists" and "criminals," promoting a border wall, and intensifying his calls for restrictions on immigration, even legal immigration. Other candidates, like Florida senator Marco Rubio, focused on religious liberty or, like Wisconsin governor Scott Walker and Texas senator Ted Cruz, honed their cadence as preachers' kids, a signal instantly recognizable to evangelical voters that goes mostly unnoticed by outsiders. But as it turned out, Trump's hard-line message was precisely what many white evangelicals had been waiting to hear. Even voters who supported another candidate in the primaries were grateful for his role in defining the terms of the coming election. Trump "shook things up and freed the other candidates" to speak more freely, Ann Cortes, a Ted Cruz supporter in South Carolina, told me. Trump "has energized" the entire party with this boldness, said Lois Stratos, another voter I met at a Charleston rally for Cruz—an evangelical insider fluent with the movement's politics and rhetoric and who ended up capitulating to Trump.

Even in the early stages of the primary season, Trump had, in many ways, already won: he was seen as the party's new standard-bearer, its fearless truth-teller standing up to the shadowy forces that were eroding America's greatness by forcing it to consider the historical marginalization of out-groups like immigrants, women, religious minorities, nonwhites, and LGBTQ people. "Everyone is tired of political correctness," Cortes told me.

The multiple passes that the Christian right gave to Trump, who couldn't cite a Bible verse or articulate even the most basic tenets of Christianity, was a sharp break from its litmus tests for other presidential candidates. In previous election cycles, candidates were put through the rigors of forums and debates where they were pressed about their commitment to opposing abortion, same-sex marriage, or federal funding for Planned Parenthood, and they vied for valuable endorsements from powerful leaders. Trump steamrolled into the Oval Office after paying only minimal lip service to these dictates.

Throughout the primaries, Trump galloped ahead of other Republican candidates, even ones with strong evangelical reputations like Cruz, Rubio, Walker, and Ben Carson. The more he called for a wall or for banning Muslims, or lambasted "elites" and "political correctness," the more he cemented his standing with white evangelical voters. Finally evangelical leaders relented and acknowledged what the voters they had so carefully groomed to be "values voters" apparently wanted: a wall builder, a rule breaker, and most important, a strongman. The evangelical publisher Stephen Strang, who owns the widely read *Charisma* magazine, which promotes the careers of televangelists like White and a widening circle of self-styled prophets and revivalists, wrote in his hagiography, *God and Donald Trump*, that Christian leaders believe Trump is a "chosen vessel used by God despite his flaws." Strang even compared him to General George Patton, "a man with a heaven-sent mission, and the rough edges, crusty language, and arrogance are essential aspects of his character and force of will."[21]

Trump was a slow learner—and in fact today could still be described as a remedial student—but the Christian right has nonetheless cast his lax learning curve as a delightful asset. That June 2016 meeting at a Manhattan hotel, attended by nearly a thousand evangelical leaders, was crucial for selling Trump to skeptical pastors and activists. But even with Trump's lack of fluency with evangelical rhetoric, "the evangelicals that came into that meeting maybe leery of Trump went out of that meeting one hundred percent confident and persuaded that Trump was the right guy," said Jared Woodfill, a Houston lawyer and activist who has spearheaded efforts to scale back gains in LGBTQ rights in his state and around the country. "I mean, the way he was humble, he addressed the issues with clarity," Woodfill told me enthusiastically, and "I came out of that meeting [thinking that] this is someone I could work with, this is someone I could help, this is someone who could make a difference." As president, "in Donald Trump you see someone who has engaged in more ways than any president I'm aware of on issues that are important to evangelical Christians."[22]

Trump's lack of a salvation story proved to be little more than a hiccup. Religious right icon James Dobson, founder of Focus on the Family, told an interviewer he had heard that Trump "did accept a relationship with Christ, I know the person who led him to Christ." It was fairly recent, Dobson added, "and I believe he really made a commitment, but he's a baby Christian, we all need to be praying for him." Dobson acknowledged, though, that Trump "doesn't know our language," noting that he "said hell four or five times" during the meeting. Paula White, who Dobson later confirmed was the person who led him to Jesus, vouched for Trump, telling *The Christian Post*, "I can tell you with confidence that I have heard Mr. Trump verbally acknowledge his faith in Jesus Christ for the forgiveness of his sins through prayer, and I absolutely believe he is a Christian who is growing like the rest of us."

Over the course of his campaign and his presidency, Trump has had so many meetings with Christian right figures that it is astonishing that he hasn't made more progress in speaking their evangelical language—and perhaps even more stunning that he is consistently and repeatedly forgiven for these lapses. As Tony Perkins, the Family Research Council president, put it, evangelicals have repeatedly given Trump a "mulligan" for his past behavior, including his affair with porn star Stormy Daniels, and they will continue to do so as long as he continues to deliver on policy.[23] Trump is the first Republican to be treated with such leniency—and it's because, unlike his predecessors, he has exhibited no compunction about flexing his executive power in unprecedented ways to implement long-sought Christian right policy and stacking the federal courts with conservative judges, in ways that will endure over generations.

This deference to Trump is a break with the past, when leaders did not hesitate to use their bully pulpits to lambaste Republicans resistant to their demands. In 1998, speaking to the influential Council for National Policy, Dobson threatened to form a third party because Republican leaders, "when they moved into power, moved to immediately insult" their conservative Christian supporters and abandon their priorities.[24] In 2007, conservative Christians, again gathered at a CNP meeting, revived the third party threat because they feared former New York mayor Rudy Giuliani would win the Republican nomination.[25] (These same conservatives have not publicly complained that Giuliani went on to become one of President Trump's personal lawyers and advisers.) John McCain ended up getting the nomination, also a disappointment to movement leaders who later lamented that they had not done more to promote the candidacy of former Arkansas governor Mike Huckabee, a Baptist pastor. Huckabee had told the 2007 Values Voter Summit—the annual gathering of Christian conservatives where Republican leaders seek to supercharge their party's most dependable get-out-the-vote machinery, especially in election years—that "the other candidates come to you," but "I come from you." Among the 2008 contenders, McCain was excoriated for failing to adequately talk about his faith, and Mitt Romney was considered a "flip-flopper" because he had reversed his position on abortion. Although Trump committed both of these sins as well, he was forgiven and even lauded for his Christian baby steps as well as for his change of heart on abortion. The difference was that evangelical leaders saw both McCain and Romney as insufficiently tough to fight liberalism—and consequently not the strongman America needed.

This loyal rear guard stands ready to defend Trump precisely because they see him as a strongman whose authority is being questioned by secular and liberal forces. In advance of the 2018 midterms, Trump's evangelical base resolved to get behind their leader, a preview of how they will likely close ranks in 2020. That September I met Vicki Stahl, who was wearing a Trump 2020 T-shirt and had come to Washington for her first Values Voter Summit. Stahl had been convinced to make the trip from Highlands, North Carolina, after receiving a flyer about the conference from the American Family Association

(AFA), the Mississippi-based Christian right advocacy group that co-sponsors the Values Voter Summit with the more powerful, Washington-based Family Research Council (FRC). The FRC is best known for its muscular presence on Capitol Hill and now, inside the Trump administration, for opposing abortion, Planned Parenthood, LGBTQ rights, and church-state separation. The AFA is best known for its boycotts of companies with LGBTQ-friendly policies and its annual campaign maintaining that a "war on Christmas" is being waged by department stores that wish customers "happy holidays"—a claim often repeated by Trump himself. Both organizations were founded in the early days of the modern religious right—the AFA in 1977, the FRC in 1983—and their longevity and continuing influence demonstrate that, despite frequent obituaries written by political observers, the religious right remains a potent and enduring fixture in American politics.

These organizations and a host of others have only become more powerful under Trump's presidency. Movement leaders meet with the president regularly at the White House, and some of them have open invitations to call his cell phone, no appointment necessary. Trump's growing intimacy with the religious right has had the effect of elevating the status of elected officials who had long been religious right favorites but were fringe figures in the pre-Trump GOP. He has enhanced the reputations of his most ardent defenders and enablers, elevating North Carolina congressman Mark Meadows, chair of the far-right House Freedom Caucus, to be his chief of staff. Meadows, who attends the same evangelical church as Stahl, was known as one of Trump's most loyal "pit bulls" on Capitol Hill.[26] Meadows is also a fellow traveler with leading figures in the Christian right and a frequent guest on Fox News. He's been praised by his friend Tony Perkins, the FRC's president, as a "counselor" to Trump whom God is using "in remarkable ways." Meadows believed that as a congressman he was locked in a "spiritual battle" with dark forces, and that prayer took place more frequently in his Capitol Hill office than in those of other lawmakers because he understands the nature of the enemy and "the attacks are real."[27]

The 2018 Values Voter Summit gave Meadows a hero's welcome, as he roused the audience gathered in the basement ballroom of Washington's Omni Shoreham Hotel by greeting them, tongue in cheek, as "deplorables"—a well-worn dig at Hillary Clinton, who, in a now-infamous 2016 campaign speech, said that half of Trump's supporters were from "the basket of deplorables," people who were "racist, sexist, homophobic, xenophobic, Islamophobic, you name it." Even though it was evident that Clinton had been referring to the racist, white supremacist alt-right that Trump was embracing with increasing visibility, the Christian right likes to own the "deplorables" moniker, as a demonstration of their disdain not just for Clinton but for elites who look down their noses, as conservatives insist Barack Obama did, at voters who "cling to their guns and religion."

I met Stahl in the hallway outside the ballroom in the Omni Shoreham, as attendees milled about after hearing the morning lineup of speakers, including Senate Majority Leader Mitch McConnell, who urged the audience not to get "rattled" by the accusation made by Christine Blasey Ford that Trump's Supreme Court nominee Brett Kavanaugh had drunkenly sexually assaulted her in high school. He would, McConnell pledged to a grateful crowd, see to it that Kavanaugh was confirmed. McConnell reminded that audience that as much as they appreciated his efforts to stack the federal bench with conservatives, the gratitude was mutual. "It's your ideas and values that are turning this country around," he said. In turn, Stahl was impressed with McConnell. Even though he made only a glancing reference to religion and values and focused much of his speech on his satisfaction at his pace of judicial confirmations, Stahl declared him to be "so powerfully faithful."

Stahl, a slight woman with long light brown hair, looks younger than her sixty-seven years, clad in jeans and a Trump 2020 T-shirt. She hesitates a split second when I introduce myself as a reporter. She's reticent because she is "a bit shy," but it quickly becomes evident she is eager to share her views on what ails the nation, and what can be done to fix it. Her shoulders soften a bit as she settles into recounting her path to becoming a Trump enthusiast. In 2016, she originally supported Ben Carson and "never" thought she would get behind Trump. But she prayed about it and came to see that God had deliberately picked Trump, an unlikely warrior, as a message to the faithful: "God uses the unusual to get people like me that are grounded in faith to realize He can use whatever he wants to use. And then he can appeal to you from a godly standpoint in a man who we don't even think is personally godly."

Stahl's cadence accelerates as she talks about how God used Trump to save America from Hillary Clinton. Because she has scrutinized Clinton's past so thoroughly, Stahl knows "she's not up to any good." And even though it might "sound weird because of being a Christian," she admired the way Trump "stood up to" Clinton. If Clinton had been elected, Stahl believes it would have been "Armageddon."

For regular Fox News viewers and consumers of other conservative media, Christian and otherwise, Clinton and her allies are underhanded, diabolical, and imperious. For evangelical Trump supporters, the fact that he vanquished her while spurning political customs of probity suggests a supernatural force must be behind his improbable rise—because only by a divine hand could the rigid conventions of politics and the satanic machinations of the powerful have been so decisively shattered. Stahl, an evangelical and a self-identified "news junkie," gets her news from Tucker Carlson and Sean Hannity, whom she believes "are fighting for freedom for the American people, and they're standing in the gap for the media which has totally gone wild."[28] The phrase "stand in the gap" is common among politically active conservative evangelicals, used to implore grassroots activists to enlist as spiritual warriors, protecting the nation from divine retribution for its sins. It comes from the Book of Ezekiel, in which the prophet warns that God's fury will rain down on Jerusalem if the righteous do not rise up in response to God's command to stand up against corruption and sin. To the Christian right, America is a new Jerusalem—and risks the "fire of His wrath" because of its departure from what movement ideologues believe are its Christian ideals. For these activists, most of America's sins spring from secularism, feminism, abortion, and "gender ideology"—a derisive and increasingly popular catchphrase among conservative Christian activists, intended to vilify LGBTQ rights as a dark movement forcing anti-LGBTQ Christians to accept a radical, fringe set of norms about gender and sexuality, in violation of their religious freedom.

While the prophet Ezekiel did rebuke sexual sin, he condemned an array of other sins as well, including financial malfeasance and political corruption—two transgressions that Trump and his admin- istration are routinely accused of, but to which the Christian right turns a blind eye, chalking them up to "fake news" peddled by an enemy-of-the-people media. Even more revealing, one of the several sins provoking God's fury, in Ezekiel's telling, is mistreatment of for- eigners, in contravention of repeated biblical mandates to welcome the stranger. Despite the dozens of times welcoming the stranger is mentioned in the Bible, this directive falls on deaf ears for many evangelical Trump followers. Instead of finding more than twenty references to welcoming the stranger in the Bible, Stahl, like other evangelicals who support Trump's proposed border wall, believes "walls are biblical." Trump's pledge to build the wall is proof of his resolve to stand strong against enemy infiltrators, proof that he loves America so profoundly that he would never surrender to any "politi- cally correct" interpretation of God's word that liberal Christians or Jews might support.

To Trump's religious devotees, God specially prepared him for this role. Rose Troyer, who traveled to the Values Voter Summit with her husband, Mark, from Lititz, Pennsylvania, tells me she began to see that Trump was a leader prophesied in the Bible during the 2016 Republican primaries, after listening to evangelist Lance Wallnau and author and Fox News personality Jonathan Cahn, both of whom claim to have received divine prophecies about Trump's victory. Troyer was familiar with a book Cahn wrote comparing Bill and Hil- lary Clinton to the biblical figures King Ahab and his wife Jezebel, and Trump to Jehu, who succeeded Ahab as king. Sitting in the Omni Shoreham lobby while she finished her lunch, Troyer, a soft-spoken woman, paused briefly to amplify the Jehu analogy: he was a "wild man," just like Trump. Troyer didn't detail the comparison further, but in 2 Kings, Jehu is anointed to succeed Ahab after he orders Jezebel thrown from her palace window, after which his horses trample her to death, leaving her body to be ravished by dogs. "Lock her up" chants seem tame in comparison.

The prophecy promoted by Wallnau, an evangelist whose popularity and visibility have skyrocketed in the Trump era, is far less violent than Hillary as Jezebel, but it just as forcefully imbues Trump with divine power. Trump, Wallnau claims, is like King Cyrus—the Persian king described in the Book of Isaiah as anointed by God to liberate the Jews from Babylonian exile and to help them return to Jerusalem to rebuild their destroyed temple. (Wallnau has also claimed a numerical significance to his prophecy, since Cyrus's reign is described in the forty-fifth chapter of Isaiah, and Trump would become America's forty-fifth president.) In this interpretation, God chooses an outsider to restore the holy city and the Jews' rightful place in it—just as God could choose a political outsider to restore America to be the Christian nation it was founded to be, before it was overrun by secularism, feminism, and other ills associated with a pluralistic liberal democracy that has, in the minds of religious right activists, spurned its Christian heritage.

Wallnau was on hand at the Values Voter Summit to give a crash course in his Cyrus theory of the Trump presidency. That afternoon he advised the audience to stop worrying about whether a politician was a Christian, as long as he was, like Trump, a Cyrus. "Sometimes," said Wallnau to cheers and applause, "God can anoint a wrecking ball."[29] Foretelling that Trump would be a "wrecking ball" president is one of eleven prophecies Wallnau claims to have made about Trump that have come true, all proving his victory in a spiritual battle between satanic and godly forces. Wallnau has said Trump "has broken up a demonic cartel of political correctness and now it is up to you and me, each of us to move forward in our own sphere and knock down the obstacles that are silencing us and holding us back from what we are called to say and do."[30]

For Troyer, these tumultuous qualities are virtues in the service of Trump's nationalistic Make America Great Again ideal, and a counterpoint to the Obama years when the president promoted a "one-world government"—a phrase familiar to evangelicals who follow popularized end-times theology as a sign of the Antichrist's reign, oppressing the world with his globalist government that respects no nation's borders or sovereignty. Trump, in contrast to the nefarious, globalist Obama, shoves "one-world government" aside in favor of the way God wants things—for nations to each have their own cultures, governments, and people—because God wants these individual nations, not a universalist "one world," to worship him. Immigration is fine, but "we want people that want to come to be part of us, to have the American dream, we don't want to be invaded by a foreign entity that wants to change us." Trump understands evangelical Christians because he rejects "politically correct terminology" and is instead "down to earth with us." Trump's ascent is no accident of history, nor the result of a perfect storm of political conditions and the American zeitgeist. God has been preparing Trump "since birth" for this role.

Voters like Stahl and Troyer regard Trump as a savior anointed for this moment in history—and his unlikely ascent is, for them, only further proof that God's hand was at work in his election, making 2020, like 2016, yet another tipping-point election, one where America teeters on the brink. Once again God needs patriots to stand in the gap. There have been other elections that the religious right has portrayed as tipping-point elections, but never has the movement so unreservedly backed a candidate—not even Ronald Reagan or George W. Bush—with the messianic zeal with which it has enveloped Trump. Never has another political figure been seen as the locus of so much prophecy, and never have so many political leaders openly given themselves over to believing in such things. Although Stahl admires Vice President Mike Pence and considers him one of "the right people" Trump has chosen to "encourage," her shirt makes no mention of him. "Make America Great Again," the shirt says, omitting any mention of the running mate who in 2016 had served as such a crucial bridge between the apostate nominee and any evangelicals who were, like Stahl, once skeptical of Trump. Even someone as powerful and admired as Pence is subsumed by Trump.

Pence portrays himself as a dutiful servant to Trump in his role as vice president. With a vivid recounting of his deference to the president, Pence had thrilled a smaller audience assembled by the Family Research Council, its "Watchmen on the Wall" conference for politically active pastors, just before Memorial Day 2018. (Again, "watchmen on the wall" is a biblical allusion to God-ordained sentries at the holy city—or America.) Making a "surprise" appearance to speak to about five hundred pastors chanting "USA, USA"—unannounced and unacknowledged in his public schedule released by the White House—Pence paid homage both to Trump's boldness and to his piety. Trump's presidency, Pence proudly implied, has erased the separation of powers between the executive, legislative, and judicial branches, as Trump heroically carried out the Christian right agenda. "Last year, with the strong support of our partners in the Senate, this president appointed and saw confirmed more conservative judges to our federal courts of appeals than any single president in American history," Pence boasted. "And that doesn't even count Justice Neil Gorsuch on the Supreme Court of the United States of America." For Pence, the Senate and the judiciary serve not as a check on the executive but rather as Trump's "partners" in achieving his objectives, which are in lockstep with the objectives of the Christian right.

Since Trump named him as his running mate, Pence has served as his Christian right seal of approval, a standing he earned because of his long history of dedication to the movement, first as a radio host in his native Indiana, then as one of the most conservative Republicans to serve in the House of Representatives, and then as governor of his state. Because Pence both vouches for Trump's devotion to God and claims to provide the president with regular spiritual guidance, Trump is relieved of being forced to engage in genuine public demonstrations of piety himself. His role as Trump's deferential attendant and spiritual protector in the raging spiritual battle has only elevated Pence's standing with the movement's grassroots.

Longtime evangelical activists who have known Pence for years see him as a paragon of righteousness aiding Trump in carrying out God's divine plan, an exemplary leader for America and the world. In September 2018, I traveled to Chişinău, the capital of the former Soviet republic of Moldova, where the International Organization for the Family, an Illinois-based Christian right advocacy group, had organized the twelfth World Congress of Families (WCF). The WCF is an annual international gathering of politicians, clergy, lawmakers, and academics who peddle a panic that white Christian Europe is experiencing a "demographic winter" that must be combated by fighting against reproductive and LGBTQ rights and incentivizing Christian Europeans to have bigger families. In recent years, the conference has been welcomed and even co-hosted by top political leaders in Europe's rising nationalist, pro-Trump far right, including Hungarian prime minister Viktor Orbán, Italian deputy prime minister Matteo Salvini, and in Moldova, its then-president Igor Dodon.

In Chişinău's Soviet-era Palace of the Republic, as attendees mingled over a buffet breakfast in the expansive second-floor marble foyer, I found myself, after setting down my cup of coffee on a high table covered in white linen, in conversation with Thomas Jacobson, an American anti-abortion activist who had traveled from Ohio to speak on the panel "Human Life: The Challenges Facing the Sanctity of Life, and the Strategies to Confront Them." For many years, Jacobson had represented Focus on the Family in its anti-abortion advocacy efforts at the United Nations, until moving to Ohio, where he launched an organization called the Global Life Campaign, whose mission, according to its website, is "to be ambassadors of Jesus Christ and the Word of God, especially on behalf of unborn and pre-born children, and be international experts in abortion history, policy and data," so that they can "[a]waken people, especially God's people, to the reality that God is deeply concerned about abortion, innocent bloodshed, and the Greatest Genocide in history that is occurring in our time."[31]

Jacobson, a middle-aged man with close-cropped hair and glasses, sees Trump's presidency as carrying that same God-directed, anti-abortion agenda. Because Trump is imposing anti-abortion policies, he is governing in a godly way. "The divine authorization for civil government given by the Creator God, in Genesis 9, was to protect human life, inseparable from the duty to protect human life," Jacobson intoned mechanically, by way of explanation for why Trump was doing a "fantastic" job as president. Trump might not realize he's exercising divine authority, but Jacobson knows he is because he has researched the Bible and has been involved in public policy for decades. Like Vicki Stahl, Jacobson trusts that God would lead the American people to follow even an improbable savior: "Of every head of state I've ever known, he's been extremely open to receiving input from pastors, clergy, lots of times. But particularly pastors and Christian leaders and to listen to them, to listen to their wise counsel, and do what is pleasing to God and is good for the people." It is not pleasing to God if a country rebels against His authority, and it is therefore rebellious, even dangerous to the country, for Trump's critics to question him when he is exercising his God-given authority.[32]

Although Trump and his followers revel in the idea of his divine authority, in addressing the Watchmen on the Wall pastors, Pence also took pains to portray Trump as a relatable everyman who, like them, has a profound spiritual life. There he recounted how he personally secured one of the president's Bibles for display at the Museum of the Bible, which opened near the National Mall a year after Trump took office and is a major evangelical tourist attraction and a popular meeting place for Republican and Christian right gatherings.[33] Even before the museum opened, its top brass—led by Steve Green, the CEO of Hobby Lobby Stores, which won a 2014 Supreme Court case holding that a corporation's religious rights were violated by a federal requirement that its health insurance plan cover contraception—was already currying favor with the new president. Less than four months into Trump's presidency, during a White House dinner for evangelical leaders, Trump's friend and adviser Paula White presented him with a gift from the museum. It was a single page from an original King James Bible, given to Trump "for all you've done and will continue to do for us."[34] Us—again signaling that Trump's principal constituents are the evangelicals who have so carefully crafted his rise and have been his most reliable cheering section on his march to dismantling Americans' shared conception of a pluralistic democracy.

Green, in turn, wanted a Bible belonging to Trump for his museum. In Pence's telling, while at an event at the museum, he promised Green he could help him skip any paperwork required to procure such an item from the White House. That night he spoke by phone with the president, who, by Pence's account, was more than happy to oblige. The next day, Pence recalled, when he was in the Oval Office for the daily intelligence briefing, Trump slid the book to him across the Resolute Desk. Pence's demeanor turned sober, vouching for Trump's reverence by assuring the pastors, "You could see the tenderness and the care he had for it." The Bible, inscribed by Trump's mother, remains on display at the museum "until some-day, after six and a half years, when they start building the Trump presidential library." Pence paused briefly to let the audience bask in the prospect of a two-term Trump presidency.

In these settings, Pence injects his words with a studied self-effacement, presenting himself as a mere mortal, a humble Christian who can scarcely believe that God has placed him at the right hand of the greatest leader in recent memory, perhaps in history. When Pence finished his homage to Trump, Perkins laid hands on him and prayed that God would "give him wisdom as he counsels with the president," noting "that he speaks to the president with an under-standing that supersedes the understanding of man," and asking God "to continue to give him favor as he serves, humbly, the President of the United States and the people of this great country called America."[35]

3

Race Rules

In defending Trump from criticism, religious right leaders have given moral cover to the president's racism and white nationalism. With each tweet excused or rationalized, with each racist utterance waved off as misunderstood or manipulated by "fake news" to make Trump look bad, with each rejoinder that it is Trump's critics who are fomenting divisiveness, Trump's evangelical loyalists have helped make the unthinkable—an overtly racist American president—a reality.

Trump's white evangelical supporters have stood by him, even as he has refused to convincingly denounce white nationalism or the alt-right, and as he demonizes immigrants and people of color and implements brutal policies stripping migrants, even children, of their most basic rights. They support him not in spite of these stances but because of them—and they are keen to shield the president by questioning the motives of his critics and attacking their integrity.

This defensive strategy did not materialize only after Trump agreed to carry out their policy agenda on issues like abortion, LGBTQ rights, or Israel. It dates back to white evangelical support

for his presidential candidacy, when issues of race and immigration—
not the Christian right's priorities of opposing abortion and LGBTQ
rights—were the centerpiece of his campaign. As their bond solidified over the course of his presidency, Trump's white evangelical
advisers became some of the most prominent defenders of his immigration policies.

When I met Robert Jeffress at ten o'clock on a Saturday morning in
June 2019, he needed coffee. He had already been up for hours, for
an early hit on *Fox & Friends,* and then to deliver a prayer and a
speech at the "Road to Majority" conference, an annual event hosted
by the Faith and Freedom Coalition, a leading Christian right political organization and an unyielding Trump booster. In his Fox appearance, Jeffress joined the anchors in disparaging Democratic
presidential hopeful Pete Buttigieg, who that week had condemned
Republican support for family separations and detentions as "hypocrisy" for a party "that associates itself with Christianity." After playing
video of Buttigieg's remarks, the Fox anchors groaned in disgust,
then turned to Jeffress for his expertise. "One thing the Bible is clear
about," Jeffress said, "God has given government the right and the
responsibility to establish laws, enforce those laws in order to protect
citizens. There's nothing un-Christian about government protecting
its borders."[1] A few hours later, fresh off his Fox appearance, which
he promptly shared with his more than 200,000 Facebook followers,
Jeffress was onstage in the Omni Shoreham ballroom, taking in
standing ovations for his uncompromising intertwining of his conservative evangelical faith with the presidency of Donald Trump.

Jeffress, the senior pastor of First Baptist, a 151-year-old Southern Baptist megachurch in Dallas, which boasts a membership of
thirteen thousand people, is known for his forays into Republican
presidential politics well before Trump. In 2011, he famously refused
to endorse Mitt Romney in the presidential primary because he
believed Mormonism to be a "cult," instead throwing his weight
behind then–Texas governor Rick Perry, "a candidate who is a proven

leader, a true conservative, and a committed follower of Christ." That was the first time I met Jeffress, when he told me "Mormons embrace another gospel," which is why "they have never been considered by evangelical Christians to be part of the Christian family."[2] Since then, and since jumping on the Trump bandwagon in 2015, Jeffress's star has risen even more. Beyond his church, Jeffress is widely known for his regular appearances on Fox. His daily program, *Pathway to Victory,* seen for years on Christian television, has been adapted for Fox's streaming service, Fox Nation.

In introducing Jeffress to the audience—although it seemed evident he did not really need an introduction—Faith and Freedom Coalition chairman Ralph Reed lauded him as "somebody that the president regards as a good friend, as a dear friend, as a trusted advisor." Reed also took note of Jeffress's role on Trump's chosen cable news network and offered the highest praise for his appearances: "There has never been a time when I have seen him representing us on television when he has failed to stand up for the Gospel of Jesus Christ." Jeffress's speech was filled with exhortations to conservative Christians to carry out their biblical duty to engage in us-versus-them politics. The "Democrat party," Jeffress said, had "truly become a godless party" that has promoted "policies and values that are completely antithetical to the Christian faith." Liberal Christians, he went on, talk about "an imaginary God they have created in their own minds, a God who loves abortion and hates Israel." Jeffress's voice rose angrily. "Ladies and gentlemen, the true God of the Bible is one who hates abortion and loves Israel!" The crowd leaped to its feet, applauding and cheering.

Jeffress and I had arranged to meet promptly after his speech concluded in the west promenade of the Omni Shoreham lobby. I arrived first and staked out a table for two outside a coffee shop and snack bar popular with conference-goers. When I spotted him, a slender man with blandly styled gray hair, dressed in a blue suit, white shirt, and red tie, strolling through the hallway bustling with people, it struck me that on any other day, he would have blended in anonymously in virtually any downtown Washington scene. But that day, with attendees at the Faith and Freedom Coalition milling about, he was recognized as a star, and admirers stopped to greet him and pay their respects. As we sat talking, passersby approached to say hello. One, Craig Huey, owner of a direct marketing firm, name-dropped Dana Rohrabacher, the former Republican congressman known for his connections in Putin's Russia. Another introduced herself as an aide to Mark Walker, the North Carolina Republican who was a pastor before running for Congress.

Jeffress, despite his derisive television invective against Democrats, liberals, and pretty much anyone who doesn't fall into line with him, is conspicuously courteous in person. "I feel bad having this without you," he said, gesturing to the large coffee he purchased from the snack bar, even though I didn't want any coffee. He told me about his mother, who taught journalism, and about his "great respect for the press," as if to establish that his mind was more open than that of the "fake news" president he so diligently protects. But he nonetheless claimed to have his finger on the pulse of "a lot of people" who "are so believing they [the press] are out to get Trump, they just discount everything you all say, even if it shouldn't be discounted." As a result, on a host of issues—ranging from the sexual assault allegations against Trump, the family separation policy, Russian election meddling—Trump is untouchable. "I've said to the president several times," he said confidently, "unless Bob Mueller can produce a photograph of you holding the flashlight while the Russians were breaking into a voting machine—anything short of that he won't need to worry about."

On the family separation issue—the topic that led to Jeffress's umbrage at Buttigieg's charges of Christian hypocrisy—Jeffress repeatedly shifted blame from Trump and, notably, presented a series of rationalizations that portrayed immigrants and refugees as suspect and possibly criminal. No evangelicals, he claimed, are "sympathetic to depriving children of toothpaste and soap. Nobody wants children mistreated in that way or not cared for." But, he went on, "most thinking people don't believe Mr. Trump is responsible for the immigration crisis. It's something that precedes him by decades." When I pointed out that Trump started the family separation policy, Jeffress retorted, "any citizen who commits a crime and goes to prison is automatically separated from his children," although he conveniently omitted that they have a trial first, and conviction doesn't mean that the person's child is incarcerated as well. When I pointed out that seeking asylum is not a crime, Jeffress conceded that point but quickly added, "You can't rent babies to do that with, that's being reported as being done, you can't kidnap children and use them as pawns." This is the heart of the evangelical Trump defense on immigration: Trump is not at fault for an enormous problem that's caused, at its core, by the criminality of immigrants—an assertion they make, like Trump does, based on baseless claims and innuendo.

Early in his primary campaign, when Trump was gaining ground with white evangelical voters, he had few big-name evangelical endorsements. Jeffress, though, offered a hometown helping hand at a September 2015 rally held at the American Airlines Center in Dallas, the arena where the city's professional hockey and basketball teams play, with a capacity of twenty thousand. At the time, Jeffress claimed his invocation to open the rally wasn't an official endorsement, but it was hard to see it as anything but that. "Tonight we come before You thanking You for Donald Trump, who along with others is willing to selflessly offer himself for service to this nation, for no other reason than he desires to make America great again," Jeffress prayed, moments before Trump made a grand entrance. Later, during his characteristically meandering speech, Trump called out for Jeffress to join him back onstage. "Where is Pastor Jeffress, he's around here someplace. What a good guy, where is he? I love this guy, come here! I shouldn't say this, I should not say this, pastor, but I need all the help I can get." Trump placed his hand on Jeffress's shoulder as he loomed over Jeffress's much smaller frame. "I'm leading with the evangelicals, big league, and I really want to thank you, you've been so good." The two men briefly embraced, and Trump resumed his speech, which included a nearly ten-minute diatribe against illegal immigration, focused on his false, racist claim that illegal immigrants are violent criminals. He paid homage to families that he claims "were decimated, their families were decimated, their sons, their daughters, killed, by illegal immigrants. And it's a massive problem." In cities, Trump went on, "you look at crime in so many different places, and you see gangs, many of these gang members are illegal immigrants, they're rough dudes. They will be out of here so frickin' fast." The audience cheered.

Jeffress's endorsement came as few evangelical leaders put themselves in the Trump camp, and as the white supremacist alt-right was becoming entranced with his candidacy. The shock troops of the alt-right seethe with angry conspiracy theories, spurred on by YouTube propagandists and Reddit forums that say white people are oppressed by constant demands—from purveyors of "political correctness," "cultural Marxists," or "social justice warriors"—that they apologize for slavery or acknowledge the Holocaust. They obsess over tropes that they face extinction in their own country owing to immigration and civil rights for minorities. They thrilled to Trump's calls for mass deportations of undocumented immigrants, for an end to citizenship for children born in the United States to undocumented parents, and for a ban on Muslims entering the country. They applauded when he demeaned Black Lives Matters protesters at his rallies, and even called for violence against them. Alt-right provocateurs, often cravenly using pseudonyms online, were entranced by Trump's use of social media to amplify their racist memes.

Over the course of the 2016 campaign, Trump's utterances, whether on Twitter, at rallies, or on television, constituted evidence for the alt-right that he was a white knight rescuing them from repressive liberals and demographic doom. A retweet of a cartoon or doctored photo or mash-up of images or statistics could, with Trump's help, transform a crackpot theory on the margins into a powerful current of political discourse, disseminated far and wide. When pressed to condemn racist memes or reverse any of his endorsements of them, Trump never backed down, further evidence of his love of white people and resolve to stand up to the tyranny of political correctness.

This pattern developed during the manic early days of his campaign. In November 2015, as most political observers continued to doubt that he could win the nomination, Trump retweeted a white supremacist Twitter account that falsely claimed that blacks were responsible for 81 percent of white homicide victims. Falsifying statistics and stories of "black on white crime" is a staple of white supremacist propaganda, a tool that works simultaneously to depict blacks as inherently criminal and whites as their innocent victims. The fake statistic that was blasted from the future president's Twitter account was awarded the most egregious "pants on fire" rating from the fact-checking site *PolitiFact*—and served as a chilling prelude to Trump's daily lies from the White House.[3] After even Fox News' Bill O'Reilly urged him not to "put your name on stuff like this," Trump claimed on-air that his sources for the statistic were "very credible."[4] That same month, after supporters attacked a black protester at a rally in Birmingham, Alabama, Trump demanded, "Get him the hell out of here." The next day, on Fox News, Trump said the man was "so obnoxious and so loud" that "maybe he should have been roughed up." He reveled in graphic descriptions of violence perpetrated by undocumented immigrants, in service of his false claim that they commit more crimes than other people. He called for the surveillance of mosques in the United States and for possibly shutting some of them down. He advocated a "total ban" on Muslims entering the country—surely something that would resonate with the three-quarters of white evangelicals who told pollsters at the Public Religion Research Institute they agreed with the statement that the values of Islam were "at odds with American values and way of life." As Trump amped up his rhetoric, white evangelical voters were becoming increasingly enthusiastic about his candidacy. By the end of December 2015, one poll showed that 45 percent of white evangelical Republicans supported Trump over his sixteen primary rivals, putting him well ahead of second-place Ted Cruz, at 18 percent.[5]

These voters were catapulting Trump ahead of Cruz, who had spent his political career cultivating evangelical fidelity, and who, by December, had consolidated considerable financial and verbal backing from evangelical kingmakers and fund-raisers. Just after Christmas, Cruz met privately with three hundred evangelical leaders at the Texas ranch belonging to Farris Wilks, a reclusive billionaire evangelical donor who made his fortune in the fracking industry, and whose family bankrolled a super PAC backing Cruz.[6] Christian right leaders like the Family Research Council's Tony Perkins endorsed Cruz as "a constitutional conservative who will fight for faith, family and freedom." But these wealthy and influential leaders were lagging behind the base, which was increasingly moving in Trump's direction, at the same time as the alt-right was praising him as their "God Emperor."

In early January, three weeks before the Iowa caucuses, the fringe white nationalist American Freedom Party and the white supremacist "think tank" American Renaissance teamed up to push robocalls to Iowa voters, describing Trump as "the one candidate who points out that we should accept immigrants who are good for America. We don't need Muslims. We need smart, well-educated white people who will assimilate to our culture."[7] If the past were a reliable guide, political reporters had every expectation that a typical, well-worn sequence of events would follow this racist seal of approval: the candidate would be asked about this repugnant endorsement, he would unequivocally condemn it, and everyone would move on, satisfied that the candidate had firmly disassociated himself from white supremacists. But when CNN anchor Erin Burnett pressed Trump to distance himself from the extremists who had roundly endorsed him in the robocalls, Trump perfunctorily "disavowed" the calls but promptly interjected a defense of them: "People are angry, they're angry at what's going on. They're angry at the border, they're angry at the crime."[8] With those two sentences, Trump affirmed the central animating grievances and correlating conspiracy theories of the alt-right. There's something "going on" because of "the border" and, along with that, "the crime." And that's why it's understandable for (white) "people" to be "angry" and to look to Trump as a salve. Over time it became clear that incidents like this one, that the media saw as the "gaffes" or missteps of an inexperienced candidate, actually offered deep insights into who Trump was and who his advisers wanted him to be.

A few weeks later Trump made an even more explicit gesture to the alt-right, retweeting a Twitter account called @WhiteGenocideTM— "white genocide" being a central alt-right conspiracy theory that immigration, diversity, and civil rights were leading to the gradual extermination of the white race. The alt-right was thrilled by the affirmation and celebrated on Twitter. The next day, Jeffress flew to Iowa and spoke at a Trump campaign rally in Sioux Center. "I would not be here this morning if I were not absolutely convinced that Donald Trump would make a great president of the United States," he said. "Most Americans know we are in a mess, and as they look at Donald Trump, they believe he is the one leader who can reverse the downward death spiral of this nation we love so dearly." Three days later, Jerry Falwell, Jr., added his endorsement, calling Trump "a successful executive and entrepreneur, a wonderful father and a man who I believe can lead our country to greatness again." Although Cruz eked out a victory in the Iowa caucuses, Trump's big-name endorsements turned out to be the beginning of the end for Trump's Republican primary rivals.

There had been a time, during George W. Bush's and Barack Obama's presidencies, when the Christian right attempted to portray itself as a growing tent, eager to include immigrants and people of color in its ranks. Conferences were convened, and diversity was a big part of the show. At a summit held at Liberty University in 2010, the evangelist Lou Engle, the ardent crusader against abortion who was featured in the film *Jesus Camp,* emphasized to the students the role of "minorities" in a new "Moral Majority," using abortion as a metaphor for slavery. Earlier that year, on Martin Luther King, Jr.'s, birthday, Engle had promoted a protest of a Planned Parenthood facility in

Houston by accusing the organization of targeting African Americans and Latinos for abortion—depicted over and over, in films, at conferences, and at press conferences, as "black genocide." As part of the summit at Liberty, the Rev. Samuel Rodriguez, president of the National Hispanic Christian Leadership Conference, delivered the university's convocation speech to drive home the point that evangelicalism was ripe for a rebrand as part of a multicultural movement. "A Latino believer is when you take Billy Graham, Martin Luther King Jr., put them in a blender, and put salsa on top," Rodriguez said, telling the students that black and brown believers would challenge the liberal monopoly on advocating for civil rights. But for Engle and Rodriguez the unfinished project of full racial equality would have to take a back seat. "The civil rights issue of the 21st century," Rodriguez said bluntly, "is abortion."

In the wake of Obama's 2012 reelection, Reince Priebus, chair of the Republican National Committee who would go on to become Trump's short-lived chief of staff, presided over an "autopsy" that called for the party to adopt comprehensive immigration reform, temper its opposition to same-sex marriage, and cultivate better relationships with minority voters. The Christian right, which adamantly opposed the autopsy's suggestion to soften the party's focus on its core social issues, briefly flirted with the immigration reform bandwagon, and some evangelicals even backed a 2013 bill to overhaul the system. Those efforts proved temporary and, ultimately, hollow. Support for the bill collapsed, after which conservative evangelicals abandoned any pretense of supporting immigration reform that went beyond border security to include, potentially, a pathway to citizenship for undocumented immigrants, or citizenship for dreamers— the undocumented immigrants who were brought to the United States as children and know no other home.

Although conservative evangelical support for the 2013 immigration bill fizzled, a dedicated contingent of white evangelical reformers remained determined to press for systemic change on immigration that would do more than just tighten border security. They also sought to focus evangelicals on their own relationships with immigrants, pointing out that they might be worshipping side by side with them at church, and that all people were made in the image of God. When Trump burst on the scene, Russell Moore, the Southern Baptist Convention's point man in Washington, was at the center of these efforts and quickly spearheaded the evangelical opposition to Trump's racist anti-immigrant rhetoric and policy proposals. But in the battle of Moore versus Trump, the future president, with the help of Moore's evangelical brethren, emerged the victor.

Moore, a theologian and once the dean of the Southern Baptist Convention's leading seminary, in Louisville, Kentucky, had been elected president of the denomination's Washington policy office, the Ethics and Religious Liberty Commission (ERLC), in 2013. Moore, known as a critic of the divisive culture wars waged by the religious right's old guard, arrived in Washington with an apparent mandate from his denomination to bring fresh leadership and, importantly, to package its public face for a new generation. Moore's elevation was viewed as a pointed rebuke to the old guard particularly because the man he was tapped to replace, Richard Land, had been a religious right stalwart who had steered the Southern Baptist Convention's political presence through the period known as the conservative resurgence. The denomination underwent a purge of its more liberal wing, solidifying its positions against abortion and church-state separation, two issues on which it had previously taken more liberal stances, and cemented its alliance with the Republican Party.

Land had led the ERLC since the Southern Baptist Convention set down its Washington presence in 1988, becoming a dominant fixture in both evangelical and political circles. If reporters wanted to know "what evangelicals think" about virtually any subject, they would call Land, who was always happy to oblige. As a result, Land evolved into the de facto mouthpiece for all evangelicals, always eager to offer quotable pronouncements. But Land's omnipresence eventually turned into a liability when, in 2012, he made racist remarks on his radio program about the murder of Florida teenager Trayvon Martin and it was discovered that the offensive comments hadn't even been original—Land had lifted them from someone else's writing.

In one set of comments, Land called then-president Barack Obama and the Revs. Al Sharpton and Jesse Jackson "racial demagogues" for their public statements about George Zimmerman, the man who had shot and killed the unarmed teenager, claiming he had done it in self-defense. "Instead of letting the legal process take its independent course, race mongers are anointing themselves judge, jury and executioners," Land said. "The rule of law is being assaulted by racial demagogues, and it's disgusting, and it should stop." He accused Obama and black leaders of trying to "gin up the black vote."

That wasn't the only racist remark Land made about the Martin murder. Aaron Weaver, at the time a doctoral student in religion and politics at Baylor University, a Baptist institution, discovered that Land had also read liberally on the air, and without attribution, from talk radio host Jeffrey Kuhner's *Washington Times* column, which included an accusation that Obama had "poured gasoline on the racialist fires" by acting "under pressure from the Congressional Black Caucus" to "put the presidential spotlight on Trayvon Martin's death—and thereby bolstered the burgeoning protests." Land claimed "race hustlers" were "fomenting racial grievance and demonizing the 'white power structure.'"[9] Land issued an apology, claiming that he had been "committed to the cause of racial reconciliation my entire ministry." But Weaver, a scholar of Southern Baptist history, told me he saw it as "a nonapology apology," noting that Land had been involved in a 1995 resolution on racial reconciliation on the 150th anniversary of the Southern Baptist Convention, but not much more.[10]

On the surface, Moore's ascension looked like a new day could be on the horizon, as a new face representing a more inclusive Southern Baptist Convention, and inclusive evangelicalism, was coming to town. He took it as his mission to rebrand the evangelical movement and create a new generation of leaders who would be more relatable than the previous one. But his elevation to the Ethics and Religious Liberty Commission's leadership was met with a tepid reaction from the religious right's top brass. "I don't have that relationship with Russell that I had with Richard," the Family Research Council's Tony

Perkins told the *National Journal* in 2014. "I don't know Russell that
well. I think he's still trying to find his way."[11]

Moore is hardly a raging liberal; he's an ardent foe of abortion
and same-sex marriage, placing him squarely in the same camp as his
fellow evangelicals that he believed had gotten lost in the vulgar
thicket of partisan politics. Despite his ideological affinity with the
religious right, Moore had criticized its performative homages to
America's supposed founding as a "Christian nation," and most
pointedly, he had spoken out against the racism and xenophobia that
had long infected white evangelicalism. The "next wave of engagement," he promised, "will be gospel-centered."

Once in Washington, Moore forged ahead with his new approach.
Six months into his tenure, he criticized George Zimmerman's
acquittal in the killing of Trayvon Martin, saying, "When you add this
to the larger context of racial profiling and a legal system that does
seem to have systemic injustices as it relates to African Americans,
with arrests and sentencing, I think that makes for a huge crisis."[12]
He expressed outrage and grief after the police killing of another
unarmed black man, Eric Garner, in New York. "We have a group of
people—a small group of people, not a lot of people—some unrecon-
structed racists in American society and we have some who continue
to come and to sit in pews of churches and pretend as though they
are disciples of Jesus Christ," he said on an ERLC podcast. "And we
have some other people who are willing to speak to any possible
issue, from the framework of Scripture that goes on in the world,
until it comes to the question of whether or not we maybe do have
some legitimate problems being faced by our African-American
brothers and sisters in Christ. And then at that point they become
completely silent and say the gospel doesn't speak to this. I think
that's wrong."[13]

A Mississippi native, Moore even tilted at southern white evangelicalism's sacred cow. Two days after white supremacist Dylann
Roof murdered nine worshippers at Mother Emanuel AME Church
in Charleston, South Carolina, in June 2015, Moore took to his blog
to write that it was time to stop flying the Confederate flag. Moore

rejected claims the flag was merely a symbol of southern heritage, calling it "the emblem of Jim Crow defiance to the civil rights movement, of the Dixiecrat opposition to integration, and of the domestic terrorism of the Ku Klux Klan and the White Citizens' Councils of our all too recent, all too awful history."[14]

Trump, who had announced his presidential candidacy just one day before the massacre, would go on to become a hero to white supremacists for standing behind the preservation of Confederate symbols. Opposition to the removal of monuments—like the statue of Confederate general Robert E. Lee in downtown Charlottesville— often became the pretext for the white supremacist rallies that would escalate during Trump's presidency.

In late August 2015, as Trump's star was unexpectedly rising, Moore was promoting his new book, *Onward: Engaging the Culture Without Losing the Gospel,* to a gathering of religion reporters in a hotel ballroom in Philadelphia. As the silverware was still clinking over the journalists' buffet breakfast, Moore sat onstage, patiently expounding on his book's central thesis: that evangelicals should not promote a politicized version of their faith that only "confirmed a common secular caricature of Christianity as Elmer Gantry meets Yosemite Sam." For decades, Moore wrote, by emphasizing "'values' over gospel," with surprising air quotes around the religious right's essential catchword, evangelicals had "exported throughout the nation some of the worst aspects of southern Christendom."

The trend lines, though, were not in Moore's favor. A *Washington Post* poll taken just one month after Trump announced his candidacy showed that 20 percent of white evangelicals already supported him—putting him atop the crowded seventeen-person field.[15] When I asked Moore about this, he pronounced himself "disturbed" that evangelicals, who should see immigrants as "your brothers and sisters in Christ," were supporting the cruelly nativist Trump. While it was acceptable for evangelicals to have policy differences over how to fix the nation's immigration system, Moore said, "Where we should not have any differences is our opinion about immigrants themselves." Without naming Trump, Moore added, "That's what we're seeing right now so often in American culture, a demonizing of immigrants themselves, and using distancing language to speak of immigrants at worst along the lines of parasites, and then all the way over to the language of anchor babies that tends to depersonalize children created in the image of God." Moore promised that his "first priority" was "to deal with that issue, and to say you're dealing with people created in the image of God."

Presenting himself as the fresh new face of conservative evangelicalism to an audience of religion reporters was the perfect venue for Moore. He would, over the coming year, become a go-to pundit for both religion reporters and their counterparts on the politics beat, who were eager for affirmation that the religious right was in its death throes, teetering on the verge of displacement by a less angry and more affable "new" brand of evangelical, one who was more likely to read a book like Moore's than to get their news from Fox or *Breitbart*. These "new" evangelicals rejected the religious right's Bible-thumping Christian nationalism, the crass, heretical proof-texting of the prosperity televangelists, and the self-promoting prophesiers who were already beginning to coalesce around Trump. For reporters eager for a new story with an upbeat twist, Russell Moore was the latest emissary from this intriguing dissident front in the culture wars.

Moore seemed to have been sent from central casting for this role. As Trump marched toward the Republican nomination, Moore's handsome, boyish face graced the cover of the flagship evangelical magazine *Christianity Today,* and his op-eds—often stirring lamentations of evangelical support for the racist, xenophobic candidate —appeared in the country's leading newspapers. The winsome, telegenic southerner was tailor-made for the audiences of cable news, ever hungry for a final nail in the coffin of the religious right that for so long had dominated our politics with its bombastic moralizing wrapped in the flag. Moore was there to tell the news junkies of mainstream cable shows—an audience that couldn't quite fathom that such a retrograde movement persisted into the twenty-first century—that the religious right was indeed losing its grip. Evangelicals, Moore insisted, wanted a break from the religious right's presidential campaign playbook. They did not want, he predicted in early 2015, a presidential candidate who would "repeat clichés about appointing Supreme Court justices who will 'interpret the law, not make the law,'" or to use "'God and country' talk borrowed from a 1980s-era television evangelist."[16]

But in his crusade against Trump, Moore would be outmanned by forces beyond his control, including many of his own fellow Southern Baptists, along with the formidable spiritual army of self-styled prophets defending their own King Cyrus. Even though Trump has spawned what seems like an army of evangelical detractors, many occupying elite positions in Christian higher education, think tanks, and punditry, they never succeeded in bringing their brethren to a come-to-Jesus moment about him. Michael Gerson, the former George W. Bush speechwriter–turned–*Washington Post*–columnist, has written countless teeth-gnashing plaints about the ongoing evangelical genuflection to Trump. Evangelicals, he mourned around the one-year mark of Trump's presidency, had lost their "gag reflex."[17] Yet despite their prominent perches, Gerson and Moore are actually outliers among their fellow evangelicals.

As much as CNN viewers might have seen Moore pushing back on Trump, or might have read one of his scathing op-eds arguing that Trump "incites division, with slurs against Hispanic immigrants," peddling "ugly 'us versus them' identity politics,"[18] Trump's supporters in the movement conducted a barely concealed campaign questioning Moore's influence and motives. "Russell Moore is just one person," Jerry Falwell, Jr., told me in 2016. "If you call rank-and-file evangelicals, you'll find that they're concerned about their uncle or their father or their mother who had a job outsourced to some other country or who lost her job to illegal immigrants. I think those are the issues. I just don't think you'll find many evangelicals who say, 'Oh, you can't be a good Christian if your country doesn't protect itself or protect its borders.' I think it's a fundamental misunderstanding of the teachings of Jesus."[19] For Trump fans, then, Moore was not a top evangelical leader but an interloper who didn't understand the Bible. Instead of seeing Moore on secular television, or reading any of his prolific writings, they were reading Trump's Twitter feed, where he called Moore "truly a terrible representative of Evangelicals and all of the good they stand for" and "a nasty guy with no heart!"[20]

A well-connected religious right activist told me in 2016 that movement leaders regularly disparaged Moore behind his back. And even sympathetic fellow Southern Baptists believed Moore was galloping ahead of the rank and file with his views on immigration. Todd Littleton, a writer and Southern Baptist pastor in Tuttle, Oklahoma, said that Moore was "desperately trying to lead a younger group" of Southern Baptists toward his views on immigration, but that Trump and Ted Cruz, at the time Trump's closest competitor for the nomination, were tapping into evangelical fears about immigration and Islam. "It's an ironic move for a Christian person to be motivated by fear, when the very sacred text they say they believe actually says love casts out fear," Littleton told me. For a group, like evangelicals, who tend "to have an apocalyptic vision about everything," Littleton lamented, "You're probably going to side with someone who can use Christian discourse to say the same things Trump would say."[21]

As the 2016 GOP primaries were drawing to a close, and it was becoming increasingly clear that Moore was losing his lonely battle against Trump, he made a last-ditch appeal to what he clearly hoped were evangelicals' better instincts. The election, he wrote in a May *New York Times* op-ed, "has cast light on the darkness of pent-up nativism and bigotry all over the country." One prime example: how "those who have criticized Mr. Trump's vision for America have faced threats and intimidation from the 'alt-right' of white supremacists and nativists who hide behind avatars on social media."[22] Trump's victory, though, came amid the vile cacophony of white supremacists on social media that he relished—and never repudiated.

While Moore was casting his net for immigration-embracing evangelicals, white nationalists were cheering Trump's proposed immigration policies. His proposals for carrying out mass deportations of undocumented immigrants and ending birthright citizenship provoked white nationalist writer Kevin MacDonald to proclaim it "a revolution" that could "restore a White America." Other alt-right figures similarly praised Trump's apparent embrace of their trope that white people in America were being subjected to a "genocide" and "dispossession."[23] Trump, white nationalist leader Jared Taylor told me in an August 2016 interview about why he backed Trump, "is talking about policies that would slow the dispossession of whites. That is something that is very important to me and to all racially conscious white people."[24] But Trump spent more time condemning Russell Moore than any of these figures and nonetheless won the support of Moore's fellow evangelicals. After the pivotal June 2016 meeting with a thousand evangelical leaders at the Marriott Marquis Hotel in Times Square, multiple high-profile Southern Baptists joined Trump's Evangelical Executive Advisory Board—including Moore's predecessor who had lost his job in part because of his racist remarks, Richard Land.[25]

Other influential evangelicals used the occasion of the New York meeting to side with Trump. Eric Metaxas, a widely read evangelical author and popular radio host, who had been "agnostic" in the primary, described Trump to me as "kind of like your uncle who says stuff that makes you cringe, but you know that when push comes to shove, he's a decent guy." He rejected the concerns of some evangelical #NeverTrumpers who believed Trump to be "some kind of actual fascist who would disregard everything that they hold dear." Over time, Metaxas told me, "I did come to believe that, fundamentally, this is not a proto-fascist or someone who is going to upend the American system for his own nefarious or narcissistic designs."[26]

The union between the alt-right and religious right was cemented at the Republican National Convention in Cleveland, where the city was crawling with white men sporting the alt-right's signature "fashy haircut" and Trump's evangelical supporters were out in force to pray for his victory over Hillary Clinton, whose name was emblazoned on T-shirts worn all over town: "Hillary for Prison 2016." At a triumphalist alt-right celebration in a rented ballroom at Cleveland State University, the movement's éminence grise, Richard Spencer, who has since soured on Trump, at the time zealously embraced his candidacy. "Trump sincerely and genuinely cares about Americans, and white Americans in particular," Spencer told me. "And he expresses such nationalism and togetherness that no other candidate has expressed."[27]

On the steamy final day of the convention, hours before Trump accepted the party's nomination, at the English Oak Room in the Tower City Center, Stephen K. Bannon, then the executive chairman of the far-right news site *Breitbart,* was in a celebratory mood. He had just hosted the first U.S. screening of *Torchbearer,* a "Christian war film" that he co-wrote and directed with the backing of Citizens United, the conservative advocacy group known for its role in the 2010 Supreme Court campaign finance case that opened the floodgates for unprecedented amounts anonymous money flowing into elections. The film, Bannon's sixth with Citizens United, is a bizarre ninety-four-minute romp through Western history—from ancient Rome to contemporary America—purporting to make the argument that there is "an inevitable slide into darkness" when "societies shun God for secular vices." The spectacle had originally received an X rating from the Motion Picture Association of America for his excessive depictions of violence, Bannon said; even with its current R rating, it still brimmed with a grim, gratuitous brutality. When the lights came up at the film's conclusion, people in the audience were wiping away tears.

As we talked in the doorway to the dark wood-paneled reception area where guests mingled and munched on hors d'oeuvres, Bannon received greetings from appreciative attendees, including Miss Kay, the wife of the film's flamboyant narrator, Phil Robertson. The patriarch of the family portrayed in the hit A&E reality television show *Duck Dynasty,* Robertson had become a hero on the right for his brusque, Bible-inflected illiberalism. His star rose even higher after a 2013 profile in *GQ* that featured Robertson's crude homophobia on full display, along with his opining that black people in Jim Crow Louisiana, "pre-entitlement, pre-welfare," were "happy."[28] Calls for a *Duck Dynasty* boycott and for the network's temporary suspension of Robertson in the wake of the outcry over the piece only elevated his freedom warrior status on the right. In 2015, Bannon and his colleagues tapped Robertson to receive the Andrew Breitbart Defender of the First Amendment Award at the annual Conservative Political Action Conference just outside Washington, D.C. At the time, Bannon, one of the co-creators of the award, praised Robertson and his family for "taking their faith and conservative politics mainstream."[29] Robertson, Bannon told me, "went totally Old Testament on them, from the stage." He had found the star of his next film—one that he would use to bring the religious right and alt-right together.

Even though by this point in the campaign, the alt-right had already received extensive media coverage as a racist, anti-Semitic, Islamophobic movement, Bannon nonetheless proudly owned his leading role in it. *Breitbart,* Bannon boasted to me that day, is "the platform for the alt-right." He proceeded to try to dampen any perception of it as a racist movement. It's just a nationalist movement, not a white nationalist movement, he insisted. And while it might have elements of racists and anti-Semites, it's not a movement of racists and anti-Semites. Bannon pronounced Ben Shapiro, a former *Breitbart* editor and prominent Jewish conservative who had complained of the alt-right's anti-Semitism, a "whiner."[30] Bannon expressed his admiration for Europe's neofascist demagogues. "If you look at the identity movements over there in Europe, I think a lot of [them] are really 'Polish identity' or 'German identity,' not racial identity," he told me. "It's more identity toward a nation-state or their people as a nation."[31]

At the time, just a month before Trump tapped him to run his campaign, Bannon told me he knew the alt-right's numbers were too small to succeed electorally. That was why, he said, he aimed his film *Torchbearer* at another audience: conservative evangelicals and Catholics. The alt-right, Bannon said, would be nowhere as a political movement without religious conservatives. If those religious conservatives "just disassociated from the process," he said, "we'll never have a big enough coalition to ever compete against the progressive left." He had made *Torchbearer,* he went on, to appeal to that

Christian audience to tell the story of "the rise and fall of certain governments and empires within the Judeo-Christian West."[32]

At the convention, the Christian right fell into line, ensuring that Trump would consolidate that very coalition that Bannon dreamed of. Any dissenters either acquiesced or were banished. Cruz was booed out of the convention hall for a speech in which he refused to endorse Trump—a moment nearly forgotten after Cruz capitulated, like the rest of the Republican Party, to Trump. At the convention, it was already obvious that despite Cruz's tepid protest, the surrender to Trump was complete. Trump had satisfied many evangelicals by picking Pence as his running mate, and he lined up his final, crucial endorsements from important figures like Perkins and Dobson. "Donald Trump has committed to upholding and protecting the first freedom and therefore our ability as citizens to unite our nation once again under God," Perkins told the delegates. "Let us go forth from here and do that work."[33] As Perkins spoke, the work of uniting the alt-right and the Christian right had already begun and would become the centerpiece of Trump's general election campaign.

Later, in his appearance at the 2017 Values Voter Summit, the first of Trump's presidency, Bannon pointed to evangelical turnout as the pivotal factor in Trump's election victory, giving the religious right the affirmation it longed for from the GOP. In a speech invoking evangelical favorites from the Book of Ecclesiastes to *The Hobbit*, Bannon pronounced evangelical and conservative Catholic turnout as "the key that picked the lock in North Carolina, Florida, Pennsylvania, Ohio, Iowa, Michigan, and Wisconsin," making the difference for Trump's win. Bannon, who by this time had been forced out of the White House and had returned temporarily to his *Breitbart* perch, recounted a conversation with Jeff Sessions, then still the attorney general. "I asked him—any doubt in your mind that the hand of providence was critical for our victory?" Bannon, of course, would not be retelling this alleged conversation if the answer were not a resounding yes.[34]

• • •

While Trump was ostracizing Moore over his criticism of the alt-right, his campaign and especially his election victory made alt-right activists feel seen and legitimized. At a November 2016 Washington, D.C., gathering of white nationalists less than two weeks after he was elected, ringleader Richard Spencer infamously elicited Nazi salutes from the audience after shouting "Hail Trump! Hail our people! Hail victory!" He tried to pass it off as a playful joke ("in the spirit of fun," he told me later), but to attendees at the conference held at the Ronald Reagan Building, a federal-government-owned event venue on Pennsylvania Avenue two blocks from where Trump would soon open his luxury hotel, Nazism was admirable. Not long before Spencer gave his speech, in the corridor adjacent to the Atrium Ballroom, where other speeches were taking place, Emily Youcis, a round-faced twenty-six-year-old ballpark vendor from Philadelphia, was still breathless from what she said was a violent confrontation with antifascist protesters who had assembled all day outside the building. She ran her fingers through her straight dark hair, washed after those protesters—"commies," she called them—sprayed her with a white substance. Youcis, who was known online for her animated videos celebrating Hitler, mocked the protesters for calling her a Nazi. "I've never said I'm a Nazi," even though she had just recently been on *Radio 3Fourteen,* an online anti-Semitic program, discussing how she read *Mein Kampf* in high school and thought "Hitler was cool, I admired the way he spoke, I loved the parades, and the fashy aesthetic." She was drawn to the alt-right because "I hated myself my whole life because I was white, like ever since I was eleven years old, and the guilt just kept piling on." School, in particular, was a major source of her rage; she complained that night in Washington of being told that white people were responsible for slavery and for having to read *To Kill a Mockingbird.* The election motivated her. Trump might not be fully alt-right, but his nationalism was better than "the open borders hellhole that Hillary would have created, with importing all of the Somalians and Syrians, replace everyone with Somalians and that'll improve the country, right?"

It took Trump three days, and being pressed in a meeting with

New York Times reporters and editors, to grudgingly distance himself from Spencer's Nazi display, saying, "Of course I condemn. I disavow and condemn." It is hard to imagine any other president-elect, after having his name invoked in a Nazi chant, issuing such a belated and bland disclaimer. Spencer texted me the morning the *Times* ran a transcript of the interview, wanting to talk by phone. He previewed what would later become a staple of Trump's presidency: attack the press and insist that what you have seen with your own eyes and heard with your own ears is not actually true but rather a concoction of enemy news media. Trump had disavowed not the actual alt-right, Spencer insisted, but rather "this monster that the media has created about the alt-right. This idea that the alt-right is neo-Nazism, he's disavowing that." And in a forecast of Trump's own persistent attacks on the press as liars and fake news, Spencer added that the *"Lügenpresse"*—the German term for "lying press" used by the Nazis, revived by attendees at Trump rallies during the campaign, and invoked again by Spencer inside the Ronald Reagan Building—was "not exclusive to the Third Reich."

Trump's desultory reaction was not a random outlier but part of a pattern. He was not misspeaking or stumbling on words or misunderstanding what was happening. Trump had long been engaged in an ongoing rhetorical dance with the alt-right, starting early in his presidential campaign, eventually using his growing platform to elevate their odious ideas into the daily political conversation. During this whirlwind of racism and xenophobia that defined his campaign, Trump gathered strength with white evangelical voters, ultimately winning over a major swath of evangelical political leaders, pastors, and influencers and ascending to the White House owing to their support.

Trump's election only cemented Moore's isolation from Trump's core group of evangelicals, who found themselves enthralled with their extraordinary access to the Oval Office. Moore fell under fire, very publicly, from big-name Southern Baptist pastors who accused him of sowing divisiveness and threatened to withhold contributions to the ERLC. Jeffress warned that deacons in his church "do not

believe it [the ERLC] represents our church's beliefs"[35]—a remarkable accusation that was echoed by other Trump-aligned pastors.[36]
In response, Moore struck a conciliatory tone, writing a blogpost
apologizing to anyone who believed "I was criticizing anyone who
voted for Donald Trump"—which of course he had been.[37]

After the torrent of criticism over his "very fine people on both
sides" comment about the neo-Nazi violence in Charlottesville in
August 2017, Trump's white allies on his Evangelical Advisory Board
stood by him. After Charlottesville, a small group of evangelical leaders, including Moore, along with Steve Gaines, then president of the
Southern Baptist Convention, and the popular African-American
televangelist T. D. Jakes, pressed Trump to disavow the alt-right. In
an open letter, these leaders and about thirty others called on Trump
"to join with many other political and religious leaders to proclaim
with one voice that the 'alt-right' is racist, evil, and antithetical to a
well-ordered, peaceful society." The alt-right, they wrote, "does not
represent constitutional conservatism. The Constitution promotes
the dignity and equality of all people."[38] But like so many other things
that would have dominated the news in a normal presidency, the letter, titled a "Call for Unifying Leadership," did not register in the
public consciousness, lost in the maw of scandal and distraction.
The website that was registered to host publication of the letter—
www.unifyingleadership.org—is no longer live.

Only one member of his Evangelical Advisory Board—A. R. Ber-
nard, an African-American pastor and founder of the Christian Cultural Center, a Brooklyn megachurch—quit in protest after
Charlottesville. The rest stayed on, and some even praised him. Falwell tweeted, "Finally a leader in WH. Jobs returning, N Korea backing down, bold truthful stmt about #charlottesville tragedy. So proud
of @realdonaldtrump." Four months later, when Trump was reported
to have questioned why the United States offered protections to
immigrants from Haiti, El Salvador, and African countries—"shithole
countries," he called them—his evangelical defenders persisted in
taking his side. "I don't think there's anything racist about it at all,"
Jeffress told *The Washington Post*.[39] The president of the United

States was providing a megaphone for the core of the alt-right's ugly ideology: that white people are being "replaced" in their own country by alien outsiders destroying their "heritage." His evangelical supporters were cheering him on.

Just before the 2018 midterm elections, panic was escalating among Republicans that Democrats would regain control of the House of Representatives. Across the country, Christian right activists mobilized to rally voters to vote. In Washington, evangelical activists organized three days of conferences, all aimed at highlighting the critical need to get out and vote, so that Trump's agenda for America could be saved.

On the Saturday before the elections, Frank Amedia was serving as a pitchman for miracles at a Baptist church in northwest Washington, D.C. Amedia, an Ohio-based real estate developer and televangelist who was the Trump campaign's "liaison for Christian policy," had driven three hundred miles in his black pickup truck with Lorilee, his wife and co-pastor of their small church in the Youngstown suburb of Canfield. Amedia's crowning achievement as a self-described prophet, which had launched him from obscurity into national news coverage, was his claim that God had revealed to him, as early as the day Trump announced his candidacy in 2015, that he would become president. Amedia claims to have listened to God through every twist and turn of the Trump campaign, unwavering in his contention that he had to believe what God was telling him directly. Because Amedia travels in religious circles in which believers actually do believe God speaks directly to modern-day prophets, his claim to have accurately predicted Trump's improbable victory only elevated this minor televangelist's prophecy hustle.

After Trump was elected, Amedia claims to have heard again from the holy spirit, and he created POTUS Shield, a loose organization of Amedia's televangelism friends that purports to engage in intercessory prayer that protects Trump from demonic enemies. While its unpolished website looks like an amateur barely tinkered with kitschy patriotic templates, POTUS Shield has been embraced by leading figures of the religious right, including the Family Research Council executive vice president Lt. Gen. (Ret.) William "Jerry" Boykin, who serves on its "council." Amedia is also close friends with Stephen Strang, the influential charismatic Christian magazine and book publisher, who has further amplified Amedia's supposed prophetic abilities and advocacy on Trump's behalf in his two hagiographic books, *God and Donald Trump* and *Trump Aftershock*. POTUS Shield's leaders claim to possess a "divine mindset" through which each one "sees beyond what is obvious or natural and discerns the Will of God as inspired by Holy Scripture that is revealed with fresh revelation"—like when they discerned God's "breaker anointing upon Donald Trump to usher in a new era."[40] In the charismatic circles in which Amedia travels, a "breaker anointing" is the ability to ask Jesus to intervene and destroy any impediment to establishing "His purposes" on earth. Televangelists have a long history of perpetuating spiritual scams to serve their political—and financial—ends, but this particularly dangerous claim maintains that God has authorized the president of the United States to destroy his adversaries, in order to achieve what they claim are God's objectives.

Amedia, a tall, burly sixty-six-year-old convert from Judaism, says that before returning to his native Ohio to open the doors of Touch Heaven Church, he was for twelve years the senior pastor of "a large Spanish-speaking church" in Miami, Florida, making him perhaps an unlikely fan of Trump's nativist campaign. But that incongruity is how, he told me, he "knew it had to be God" telling him that Trump would win the presidency. Amedia, like many of the televangelists and pastors who found themselves catapulted to greater prominence owing to their subservience to Trump, was virtually unknown outside his own religious circles before a mutual friend in business, who he refused to name, introduced him to Trump. In a Trump Tower meeting, Amedia claims to have "prophesied to his face," and Trump granted him the ceremonial role in his campaign. At the time, Amedia told me, "it was very important for me to satisfy in my own heart and also personally that there are no racist beliefs with Mr. Trump."

After meeting with him, he concluded, "I don't believe that the man has absolutely any bias at all toward any race or color," because he had heard him say, "I love the Hispanic people," "I love the Asian people," and "I have many dear friends who are Muslims."[41]

Amedia boasts of his own relationships with black and Latino evangelicals and tries to provide cover for the president's racism. He refers to his relationship with Bishop Harry Jackson, one of the most prominent African-American pastors aligned with the Trump administration, and Alveda King, the late civil rights leader's niece and Christian right activist, as "the three amigos."

The District of Columbia, where only 4 percent[42] of voters chose Trump, and Prince George's County, the predominantly black and Democratic suburb where Jackson's church is located, seemed unlikely places for eleventh-hour campaigning for the Trump agenda, given that none of the local races were battlegrounds that could be tipped by a groundswell of evangelical turnout. But local get-out-the-vote was not the point. The action at the conferences was televised on Christian networks or livestreamed on the Internet, meaning that a broader audience could get swept up in the conferences' signs and wonders, including the miracle of Trump and the "Esther moment"— in which the believers, like the Persian queen in the Book of Esther, were poised, if they would only bravely act, to defeat America's, or rather Trump's, enemies. These performances, which included preaching, singing, dancing, and spiritual "gifts" like speaking in tongues and holy laughter, would show viewers that these fervent worshippers of both Jesus and Trump represented diverse gatherings of Jesus followers, crushing the impression created by Trump's nearly all-white MAGA rallies.

When I arrived that Saturday at Chevy Chase Baptist, a tidy red-brick church tucked around the corner from a bustling commercial strip in one of the bluest neighborhoods in America, Amedia was warming up the audience gathered for a conference called "Shift America." He was recounting his direct download from God about candidate Trump's presidential prospects, and how he stood by God's chosen one through each controversy that had threatened to strike a fatal blow to his candidacy. Only "unhinged faith," he said,[43] "gives you unhinged change" and "unhinged gifts," and he urged his audience into a crescendo of assents and amens and come ons and yeses and hoots and clapping and holy laughter. Anyone who doubted "the crazy things that God was having me prophesy in the election" of 2016, or who, unlike him, wobbled on supporting Trump, just wasn't radical enough. The rat-tat-tat and shabah-shabah of tongue-talking ricocheted around the modest sun-dappled sanctuary; the rising ecstasy seemed to spur Amedia to greater outrageousness. "I've raised three dead people!" he bragged, as the roughly one hundred congregants raised their arms in praise and cheered him on, as if his boasts were proof of how "unhinged faith" could achieve victory against satanic forces and even death itself. "Get up and walk!" he claimed he commanded a corpse in a funeral home in Girard, Ohio, just a little over a week after he "came out of the Jewish temple" and became a Christian. "What the demons hate the worst," Amedia pressed on, "are risk-taking overcomers"—like Trump, and like his "radical" Christian supporters. Trump, he added, would win even if Republicans lost in the midterms; in fact, Amedia contended, not having an enemy might well sap the president of his strength. Trump was a "street fighter," and "if there's no one to fight he's not potent." If the Democrats took over Congress, "bring it on."

As Amedia's sermon descended from its rhetorical apex and the euphoria began to settle, the sanctuary had the feel of a collective crash from a sugar high, or from something more powerful. Without missing a beat, Amedia pivoted to logistics and announcements. He urged the audience to attend Jackson's conference, "Rise Up 18," taking place in two days, on election eve. It was important, he cajoled them, to bring their "radical" faith, as there was "no time to play religion, Jesus is coming." In case anyone was hesitating, he threw in an additional incentive: they wouldn't have to pay the thirty-five-dollar conference fee if they said Pastor Frank sent them. Aping a stereotyped Jewish cadence, he added, to laughter, "You know I'm a Jew, I know how to make these things happen."

• • •

Amedia is part of an increasingly powerful network of televangelists, pastors, musicians, writers, and self-promoters who fuse elements of prosperity theology with the core beliefs of a more recent charismatic movement known as the New Apostolic Reformation (NAR). The NAR, which like the prosperity gospel is deeply controversial and even heretical to many conservative evangelicals, holds that modern-day prophets and apostles receive direct revelations from God. They are "anointed" to mobilize their followers to engage in spiritual warfare against demonic enemies, all aimed at enabling Christians to "transform" every one of America's communities and take dominion over the seven "mountains" or "spheres" of societal influence—religion, family, education, government, media, arts and entertainment, and business. Like the prosperity gospel, the NAR has had a ripple effect throughout charismatic and Pentecostal Christianity in America and around the world, drawing in followers through television, podcasts, magazines, conferences, social media, and the overlapping, mutually reinforcing marketing efforts of its most prominent adherents. Like the prosperity gospel, the NAR has elevated an ethnically diverse stable of leaders and attracted diverse followers. Many of its leaders, like *God's Chaos Candidate* author Lance Wallnau and Cindy Jacobs, an "apostle" from Texas who leads "generals" in a spiritual war, serve on the POTUS Shield council, are celebrities of the Christian right, and were on hand for the pre-midterm spectacles in Trump's Washington.

As a global movement whose top ideologues often boast of its multicultural following, this burgeoning charismatic Christian movement seems to be an unlikely fit with Trump's MAGA. But in many crucial ways, Trump and this fact-free, faith-based movement dovetail perfectly: their promotion of revelation over reality, spontaneous utterances over facts, baseless promises of wealth and success, and aggressive, accountability-free fund-raising. Perhaps most deviously, they provide him cover to assert that the black and brown constituencies of this corner of evangelicalism are living proof that charges of racism against him are, as his top "spiritual" adviser Paula White put it just before the midterms, "fake news" that comes "from the pit of hell."

The night after Amedia's stem-winder, the "Shift America" conference held its Freedom Gala at the Hyatt Regency, a high-end
hotel within view of the Capitol. About four hundred attendees paid
$200 apiece, dressed in sparkling cocktail dresses and tuxedos and
gathered in one of the hotel's ballrooms to dine on filet mignon and
sing and dance to praise and worship songs with earworm-inducing
riffs like "it may look like I'm surrounded, but I'm surrounded by
You"—meaning Jesus. They heard an "exhortation" from former
Republican congresswoman Michele Bachmann, who two months
earlier told the Values Voter Summit that under Trump, "we are living in an unparalleled golden time." Here she was introduced as "a
lioness" and "one of the key movers and shakers in the spirit realm."
Wearing a leopard print dress, Bachmann paced the stage like a well-
trained evangelist and boasted of her pride in her recent meeting,
along with other evangelical figures close to Trump, with Saudi Ara-
bia's crown prince Mohammed bin Salman, who had recently been
implicated by the CIA—now reviled by Trumpian circles as the
"deep state"—in the gruesome murder of journalist Jamal Khashoggi.
The audience cheered as Lou Sheldon, the octogenarian founder of
the religious right organization Traditional Values Coalition, created
in the early 1980s to advance a "moral code and behavior based upon
the Old and New Testaments," received a Lifetime Achievement
Award. Georgian Banov, the evangelist who hosted the "Shift America" conference, told of his lack of freedom under Communism in
his native Bulgaria and how he discovered true freedom in Jesus and
America. Money was raised for Banov's organization to halt child sex
trafficking—although it was not specified how, exactly, the money
would be used to achieve this purpose. The audience was pressured
into "obedience"—which was measured by whether they put money
in the envelopes on their tables. "Partnership is designed by God to
dramatically increase the abilities, resources, and rewards of every
believer" was the message printed on the envelopes' exterior.

The omnipresent Wallnau delivered a keynote address—a rushed
mash-up of Trumpian greatest hits, like political correctness "is just
another way of silencing Christians" and "journalism is completely

under the ideological and spiritual possession of a demonic force," and Trump's success is "supernatural." Despite his broadside against journalists, Wallnau, who was actually affable and chatty, was happy to talk with me after his speech when my tablemate, Lisa Plummer, an enthusiastic follower who had traveled to the conference from Delaware, introduced me to him.

As fans gathered around, hoping to get a selfie with this prophet, Wallnau energetically recounted to me how he was introduced to Trump by Paula White's PR agent in 2015, after he had prophesied that Trump was God's chosen candidate. He was worried, though, that after the *Access Hollywood* tape came out, his 2016 book, *God's Chaos Candidate,* would fall flat, should Trump lose the election and Wallnau be proven wrong. "I was trying to do damage control on my book," he admitted cheerfully, the scent of the mint in his mouth wafting toward me. He had filmed himself in his room at the Mount Zion Hotel in Jerusalem delivering an "explanation," that the "devil was exposing information in order to destroy a candidate," but that as a result, God was "humbling" Trump, making him "more qualified as a candidate than anyone else." The video, broadcast on Facebook, went viral, turning him into a social media star.[44] Now he regularly posted videos with the production values of FaceTime on Twitter, Facebook, and YouTube, and he has become one of the Christian right's most visible Trump promoters and perpetuators of right-wing conspiracy theories about the left. "I ended up building a following in media all on my own doing damage control," he chuckled—the same method deployed so effectively by Trump.

At the gala, Amedia closed the festivities by leading prayers for Trump, for the midterms, and "for the third Supreme Court appointee that will be coming forth very soon." He drew stark lines between Trump's allies and enemies, and he claimed that God had given Trump the authority to purge those enemies. He called for God to sow "confusion and chaos," to keep Trump strong, safe, and healthy, and to take "those away from his inner circle, Lord, that would detract [*sic*] him from the things that you would have him do and put those in place quickly that should do what they should do." He called

his amigos Jackson and King to the dais to pray. He did not specifically mention Robert Mueller, or the Russia investigation, or any of
the myriad controversies around Trump but rather positioned Trump
as an all-powerful, divinely guided leader who could "remove those
from the deep state, remove those from any state, remove those from
within and without, as his authority allows him, Father, without fear,
and without accountability to popular opinion, but only to you and
you only, oh God."

The next day, when I met Amedia in the lobby of Jackson's megachurch, he was limping. The man who claimed to have raised the
dead couldn't heal his bum knee; as we traversed the halls to Jackson's green room and then into his adjoining office for an interview,
Amedia was on his cell phone, trying to get an antibiotic for the
infection he said was causing the pain. In two days, he was traveling
to a revival in Isiola, Kenya, hosted by his Touch Heaven Ministries,
which promises yet more "miracles, signs and wonders." In the hallway, a young man stopped us to chat, telling Amedia he saw him on
Sid Roth's television program.

Roth, a friend of Amedia's, hosts the long-running talk show *It's
Supernatural*, filmed before a studio audience, during which Roth purports to "investigate" the "supernatural" reasons behind real-life occur-
rences. His show has helped promote the "breaker anointing" concept
that Amedia and his allies claim Trump possesses. Roth, like Amedia,
grew up Jewish and is now "a Jewish believer in Jesus" and an "ardent
Zionist." He had told me he visited Trump Tower with Amedia and
detected a "latent gift" in Trump. Once in office, Roth predicted,
"divine help" would cause that gift to "come to the surface and he will
be a great great patriot, a great leader of America like Abraham Lincoln
or George Washington." Roth, who told me in the interview he knew I
was Jewish, later mailed me a copy of his 2009 book, *They Thought for
Themselves: Ten Amazing Jews*, which profiles Jewish figures who converted to Christianity "to achieve their destiny."

As Amedia and I sat down in Jackson's spartan office, a suit and shirt draped across the desk, Amedia spoke of his certainty that God's hand was on Trump, and said he doesn't care whether Trump was a Christian as long as God chose him. He defended Trump from charges of anti-Semitism and racism. He pointed to Trump's Jewish daughter, Ivanka, who converted when she married Jared Kushner, his Jewish grandchildren, and his decision to move the American embassy in Israel from Tel Aviv to Jerusalem, a long-sought goal of Christian Zionists like Amedia. (Amedia claims to have helped Trump write his 2016 speech to the American Israel Public Affairs Committee, which was a turning point in Trump's campaign to win over right-wing Zionists, both Jewish and evangelical.) He spoke of a visit to the vice president's residence for a small dinner gathering, his respect for presidential adviser Kellyanne Conway, and his view that the hand of God was not on Steve Bannon "to be a transformer of destiny"—but that God's hand was on the president's son, Eric. "There's something very very deep in his genes," Amedia said admiringly.

During the campaign, Amedia served on the National Diversity Coalition for Trump, which had been assembled by Michael Cohen, Trump's then–fixer and lawyer. At the time, I was reporting both on this "diversity" coalition and on the growing adoration of Trump by white supremacists, who were, with Trump's validating winks, tweets, and signals, moving from the fringe of American politics into a visible position in the right-wing coalition assembled by Trump. I had been seeking comment from the Trump campaign about the glowing endorsements of nearly two dozen far-right figures—including white nationalists, neo-Nazis, Klansmen, and militia leaders—but had received no response. But my request for comment about the National Diversity Coalition was passed on to Cohen, who called me from a Trump Organization number, insisting that the coalition was separate from the campaign, in part "to dispel the notion that the mainstream liberal media portrays Mr. Trump as racist." He robotically recited, "Our mission statement is to support Donald Trump and his solutions that address economic disparity, foster job creation, support small business, preserve faith and family principles, and strengthen communities with conservative action, specifically, within the minority communities."[45]

I pressed him about statements that some of the coalition's advisers had made. Frances Rice, chairman of the National Black Republican Association, compared Democrats to the Klan and claimed the Democratic Party was racist and kept blacks in "virtual slavery." Dahlys Hamilton, chairman of Hispanic Patriots for Trump, had proudly told me she was a conspiracy theorist and suggested on social media that President Obama might be a secret ISIS agent and that Hillary Clinton aide Huma Abedin was a secret Saudi spy. Steve Parson, an African-American Pastor for Trump, had said, "The Jews are the wealthiest people in the world, because they have a higher percent of them that are business-owners." But when I asked Cohen about them, he waved me off. These individuals, he told me, don't represent the coalition, implying that neither he nor the group was responsible for their bizarre or racist statements. Instead, he repeated, all the coalition members were there to represent other members of their ethnic group who supported Trump.[46] Cohen's effort, which he consistently portrayed as disengaged from the campaign apparatus, used the coalition members as props to try to deflect from Trump's racism. Meanwhile, any of them could have easily been the target of the racist mockery of Trump's white nationalist supporters, who routinely ridicule nonwhites as dumb and gullible—and worse.

Despite Cohen's role in elevating this "diversity" charade, nearly two years into Trump's presidency he became persona non grata among Trump allies, after flipping and cooperating with federal prosecutors investigating Trump and the Trump Organization. When Amedia and I spoke, Cohen had recently told *Vanity Fair* that Trump had, in private conversation, routinely made racist statements, including that "black people are too stupid to vote for me," and referring to an *Apprentice* contestant, he had said, "There's no way I can let this black f-g win."[47] Sitting in the office of his "amigo," a black pastor, Amedia shrugged it off. "I don't believe it," he said, even though many of Trump's documented public statements made these private slurs believable. But for Amedia, not only was Cohen suspect, the media was as well. "An exclusive article with *Vanity Fair*?" he asked incredulously. "Did they pay him?"[48]

Amedia was hardly alone in dismissing Trump's racism as overblown or a lie perpetrated by the media or his political opponents. "President Trump is absolutely not a racist," Paula White said on Kenneth Copeland's popular television show, *Believer's Voice of Victory*, in an episode titled "Addressing the Spirit of Racism," one of ten aimed at mobilizing evangelical voters for the 2018 midterms. Calling the president a "blue collar billionaire," she noted that she has lived in Trump Tower, and "there's diversity of every faith, there's diversity of every ethnicity." Of accusations that "he's a racist," White added, "that's been the narrative of the Democratic platform."[49] By shielding Trump from criticism over his rhetoric and policies that most delighted the alt-right—casually racist tweets or statements, policies that banned immigrants and refugees, deported them, detained them, or otherwise mistreated them, including children and babies—Trump's evangelical defenders were effectively solidifying the Republican base as committed to both Christian and white nationalism.

Trump won over white evangelicals because they shared his vision of America and, fatefully, in spite of Russell Moore's role as the evangelical anti-alt-right Cassandra. Trump succeeded not only by embracing the Christian right and the alt-right but also by brazenly scorning the "new" evangelicals like Moore. Throughout his presidency, Trump's evangelical allies have made deliberate efforts to lend a religious sheen to his most abominable policies. They have tried to portray him as a unifying, benevolent strongman who loves all Americans and seeks to protect them from "invasions," and as a victim of Democratic and media machinations to unfairly portray him as a racist. As Trump's policy of separating refugee families at the southern border was the subject of increasing media scrutiny, Paula White made a show of visiting a detention facility operated—with taxpayer-funded grants—by Youth for Tomorrow, a Christian nonprofit, to counter the negative narrative emerging about the administration holding children in cages at the Texas border, and being ferried to secret detention centers around the country. Appearing on CBN, White declared the Youth for Tomorrow center in Bristow, Virginia, to be "beyond phenomenal," claiming it provided "three square meals, psychiatric care, clinician [sic], medical care, chapel, events, schooling, language, and love."[50]

Trump's favorite pastor's televised sanitizing of a policy that had drawn condemnation from around the world, and sparked comparisons to American internment of the Japanese in the 1940s and even to Nazi Germany, didn't end with her cheery endorsement of the virtues of one facility. Asked by CBN's national security correspondent, Erik Rosales, to cite the biblical scriptures that came to mind when she saw the facility, White protested, "So many people have taken biblical scriptures out of context on this, to say stuff like well, Jesus was a refugee. Yes, he did live in Egypt for three and a half years, but it was not illegal. If he had broke the law, then he would have been sinful, and he would not have been our messiah."[51]

Other religious leaders were aghast. Matthew Soerens, U.S. director of church mobilization for World Relief, the humanitarian arm of the National Association of Evangelicals and a visible evangelical advocate for immigrants, argued that "various biblical examples of civil disobedience quickly make any such claim untenable," and "for those who follow Jesus today, we can insist that our government respond to the plight of vulnerable people in ways that both extend compassion and honor the law."[52] Even the generally pro-Trump Russian government propaganda site RT wryly noted, "Whether breaking laws disqualifies a person from being a messiah is a debatable question."[53]

But White reacted in quintessential Trumpian fashion—spurning the possibility of either a clarification or an apology, and instead attacking her critics. In a column for The Christian Post, she accused her critics of being "less offended by what I said [than] they were excited to criticize someone associated with the Trump administration. They weren't just inferring I lacked compassion, they were calling me dumb, and by extension, all evangelicals who support the president." These critics, she added, were just seeking "to shame the 81% of us who did vote for President Trump into believing we're dumb, cruel and unsophisticated—and they would love nothing more than to use the Bible to do it."[54]

With the help of his evangelical entourage, Trump has diminished not only Russell Moore the man but, more important, the wing of evangelicalism that he represents. He has catapulted figures like Jeffress to greater stardom. There was a time when Moore claimed to represent rank-and-file evangelicals who were weary of polarizing figures like Jeffress, and who wanted to show compassion to immigrants and refugees. But that project has been eviscerated by the surrender to Trump, the strongman who cannot be questioned. "I think Russell made a big mistake in vilifying not just President Trump but those who supported him," Jeffress told me at the Faith and Freedom Coalition event in 2019. "I think he's backed off from some of that" due to pressure from "people in the pews," who were "highly offended" by his criticisms of Trump. Jeffress, who once complained to Fox's Sean Hannity about "namby-pamby, pantywaisted, weak-kneed Christians" who wouldn't vote for Trump, seemed satisfied that in the end, after all the op-eds and TV appearances and Twitter battles, Russell Moore had finally been put in his place.

4

The Alt-Right Out in the Open

The alt-right seemed to burst suddenly from the fringes into the 2016 election, propelled to the national stage by Trump's campaign. Everything about the mutual fascination between Trump and the alt-right looked alarmingly new and explosive—a major party candidate gaining momentum not in spite of energizing white supremacists but because of it. But even before the term *alternative right* came into vogue in the late 2000s and later provided fuel for Trump, white nationalists populated Washington, working for the government and conservative think tanks, writing for widely read conservative magazines, and crafting new ways to make their racism palatable to traditional conservatives. Major figures in conservative and Republican politics sought, episodically, to ostracize them from mainstream circles. But these inconsistent efforts to quell the implacable rancor were ultimately unsuccessful, and it grew into the force that eventually drove Trump's rise.

Energizing white nationalists was not an accident or a quirk of Trump's supposedly "anti-establishment" presidential run—it was the very center of his campaign strategy. Steve Bannon, seizing on the alt-right's propaganda, sought to test its currency with prospective voters well before Trump formally entered the race. In 2018, Christopher Wylie, a former employee of Cambridge Analytica, the data analytics company eventually hired by the Trump campaign, divulged that Bannon, while still at *Breitbart* but before formally joining the Trump campaign, worked with Cambridge Analytica to help it focus-group slogans and strategies. As early as 2014, the phrases "drain the swamp," "build the wall," "deep state," and, tellingly, "race realism" were tested. According to Wylie, these phrases, Bannon's researchers found, performed well among "young, white Americans with a conservative bent" who exhibited a "high level of alienation."[1] Cambridge Analytica's former CEO Alexander Nix was caught on video by the UK's Channel 4 bragging that he had met many times with Trump and that "our data informed all the strategy."[2] The firm then helped lay the groundwork for Trump's campaign by identifying and priming a base that would be receptive to his articulation of the grievances of white "dispossession." Trump and Bannon, the propagandist who took credit for giving the alt-right its platform, understood early on how to capitalize on the seething underbelly of the American far right. It was a force that had been driven to the margins following progressive advancements of the twentieth century—the New Deal and Great Society and War on Poverty, the civil rights and women's rights and gay rights movements, to name just a few—but it was no less potent for its lack of mainstream acceptance and was poised to stage a backlash and break out into the open.

"Race realism," in particular, is a common term used among the alt-right as a euphemism for racism, to conceal their white supremacy with a thin layer of pseudo-intellectualism. Jared Taylor, who had glorified Trump in robocalls to Iowa voters advocating for restricting immigration to "smart, well-educated white people," uses the term "race realism" as a "philosophy" that "race is an important aspect of individual and group identity, that different races build different societies that reflect their natures, and that it is entirely normal for whites (or for people of any other race) to want to be the majority race in their own homeland." Taylor's *American Renaissance* website

warns that if "whites permit themselves to become a minority population, they will lose their civilization, their heritage, and even their
existence as a distinct people."[3]

Once Trump secured the Republican nomination, Taylor was
one of the alt-right's top ideologues who were emboldened to be even
more public and visible, speaking on behalf of many others who he
claimed were forced to remain anonymous because of "this soft
totalitarian environment" in which "not very many of us can afford to
be out of the closet on this." Taylor was speaking on a sweltering late
summer day two months before the 2016 presidential election at
Washington's storied Willard Hotel, where he hosted, with Richard
Spencer, a press conference that they billed as "What Is the Alt-
Right?" At the time, the presidential campaign was simmering with
hate and dread; Trump had recently hired Bannon, and Hillary Clinton had just delivered a scathing campaign speech at Truckee Meadows Community College in Reno, Nevada, calling "the de facto
merger" of *Breitbart* and the Trump campaign "a landmark achievement for the 'Alt-Right,'" a "fringe" movement that "has effectively
taken over the Republican Party."[4]

Rather than retreating, the alt-right was elated by the attention
from its leading bête noire. It had finally poked the bear, and in so
doing had been made manifest. Drawing attention from a reviled
political enemy was an empowering development, proof that snow-
flake feminists and other Clinton supporters had been "triggered" by
the alt-right's rising notoriety and by its virile champion Trump. The
Republican nominee might not have been reading white nationalist
literature, Taylor had told me in an interview a few weeks earlier
about why he was backing Trump, but he saw that Trump "reacts in
an instinctive way," similarly to the "many Americans who feel as
though their country is slipping through their fingers."[5] Trump spoke
for these people Taylor insisted had been kept down. "I have been
criticized many times for saying that I want my grandchildren to look
like my grandparents, not like Fu Man Chu or Whoopi Goldberg or
Anwar Sadat," Taylor told reporters and supporters at the Willard.
"That, apparently, is a horrible thing for whites to say." He blamed

"the current egalitarian zeitgeist, that to wish to maintain one's heritage, so long as one is white, is a bigoted thing."

Spencer and his cronies landed at the Willard after getting the boot from the National Press Club, which turned him away after discovering what his blandly named National Policy Institute truly was—more evidence, to Spencer, that politically correct thought police were oppressing them. In a last-minute scramble, Spencer had secured the Peacock Lounge at the Willard, an even posher venue around the corner from the press club, a few blocks from the White House, and across the street from the soon-to-be-opened Trump International Hotel. Spencer, overdressed for a Washington summer day in a brown wool tweed jacket, was sweating but ebullient. He didn't mince words or try to euphemize his goals. "We want something heroic. We want something that is not defined by liberalism, or individual rights, or bourgeois norms. We want something that is truly European and truly heroic," he told the assembled media and alt-right acolytes in attendance, some streaming the event with their phones. "Race matters," he went on, "and race is the foundation of identity."[6] With this, Spencer was trying to brand the alt-right, not as the nameless Pepe-the-frog-saluting cartoon demagogues of Twitter, but as highbrow, suit-wearing iconoclasts standing up to elite gatekeepers who had for too long bowed to politically correct antiracism.

Joining Spencer and Taylor at the podium was the anti-immigrant demagogue Peter Brimelow. Once an admired figure in mainstream conservatism, for the past twenty years he had been in exile from what he derisively called "Conservatism, Inc." Brimelow, an immigrant from England, is the founder and editor of the website *VDare .com*, a hotbed for virulently anti-immigrant and white nationalist writers, many of whom believe themselves to have been wrongly ostracized from "Conservatism, Inc.," over their racist and xenophobic writings. Brimelow, who founded *VDare* after losing his position at the leading conservative magazine *National Review* in the late 1990s, named the site after Virginia Dare, the mythical first child born to white settlers of the American colonies, and the subject of white nationalist folklore for nearly two centuries.[7] At *VDare*, Brimelow oversees a lineup of writers and polemicists who produce a daily menu of nativist and white nationalist articles, blogposts, podcasts, and videos. The site regularly features gory, conspiratorial tales of "anti-white hate crimes" and the supposed epidemic of "immigrant mass murder syndrome."

In *VDare*'s pages, the supposed criminal hordes hail from all over the world, not just from the Mexico and Central America of Trump's fever dreams. *VDare* has been tracking this supposed "trend" since 2007, after the mass shooting at Virginia Tech, where the gunman was Korean American. Although no immigrant group escapes *VDare*'s notice ("Asians appear to be especially vulnerable" to committing crimes), the site does single out Muslims for particular vitriol. "It is now indisputable that mass Muslim immigration is incompatible with Western society," *VDare*'s page on "Immigrant Mass Murder Syndrome" reads. "It should be halted, and the Muslim communities that have established themselves expelled."[8] At one time, though, Brimelow was the toast of the town and deeply connected to the top figures in the conservative aristocracy, the editor and publisher of *National Review*, William F. Buckley and William Rusher.

During the Willard press conference, Spencer, Taylor, and Brimelow expressed confidence that their movement's ambitions—and its wherewithal to carry them out—far exceeded its ragtag reputation online. I asked Spencer if the movement had any funders akin to the Koch Brothers, the powerful energy barons whose dark money has bankrolled the antiregulatory agenda of the conservative movement. "Vlad," Spencer replied, quickly claiming he was being tongue-in-cheek. "I admire Putin," Spencer told me later over drinks at the hotel bar. "Who wouldn't?" Spencer's battle, though, was not for cash but for hearts and minds, for ideology—and like Europe's far-right "identitarians," the continent's new fascist philosophers, he's playing a long game.

Brimelow quietly hinted at exactly that kind of influence—gradually changing minds by relentlessly injecting its ideas into the political discourse, eventually eroding their shock value, and pulling the political discourse to the right. During the back-and-forth at the press conference over how the alt-right could amass the funding to "professionalize" and build a presence in Washington, Brimelow, a white-haired septuagenarian who speaks in a low-volume mumble, piped in, "Alt-right people do tend to live in D.C., do tend to do conservative think tank jobs."

The almost offhand comment got lost as the speakers moved on. After the press conference ended, as a handful of reporters lingered, preparing to take Spencer up on his invitation to decamp to the hotel bar, I stopped Brimelow in the hallway. Spencer hovered, meddling by cracking jokes about the MSNBC star anchor Rachel Maddow. "My key alt-right writers all live here, in the belly of the beast," Brimelow said, declining to provide more details about other under-the-radar, inside-the-Beltway allies. "They work in politics and elsewhere," he said, remaining purposely vague about whether they worked on the Hill, inside government, or as lobbyists, allowing only that they work in "the government industry." He refused to say more but added, "They keep a low profile."[9] Brimelow would know—he was no neophyte to the D.C. political scene, or to the inner workings of the conservative movement from which he had been exiled. His career, more than Spencer's or Taylor's, contained all the warning signs of a festering movement that would culminate in Trump. It also shows how Trump was a catalyst, not a cause.

After earning an M.B.A. from Stanford Business School in 1972, Brimelow was living in Canada, working as a financial analyst and later as a financial journalist. But he longed to go to New York or Washington. In the mid-1970s, he struck up a friendship with William Rusher, publisher of *National Review* from 1957 through 1988 who, in a largely underappreciated way, was a major figure in shaping the grievance-driven, anti-establishment core of the modern conservative movement.[10] In their correspondence, tucked away in Rusher's extensive papers housed at the Library of Congress in Washington, D.C., was the story of Brimelow's ascent within "respectable" conservative circles, and how the nativist views he so openly espoused for twenty years led to his banishment from "Conservatism, Inc." Yet these very same views, another twenty years later, would be espoused by the president of the United States.

After Brimelow met Rusher while writing about his 1975 book, *The Making of the New Majority Party,* the pair kept up an avid epistolary relationship, frequently documenting and effusively thanking each other for fine dinners and lunches and outings to the opera during Brimelow's visits to New York. In 1978, Brimelow spent the summer in Manhattan, working as a guest editorial writer for *The Wall Street Journal*—a post Brimelow believes Rusher had recommended him for. It was a plum assignment for someone with Brimelow's aspirations, yet he had a litany of complaints. Chief among them was living in New York City, which was—to put it bluntly—not white enough for him. In his column for the Canadian *Financial Post,* headlined "Summer in the Big Apple Far from Rosy," Brimelow laid out eight numbered paragraphs, each summarizing his grievances about spending the summer months in a "hot, filthy" liberal urban nightmare. In one, he predicted that an underground cult novel might well tell us something significant about New York City's—and America's—future.

The book was French writer Jean Raspail's 1973 novel *The Camp of the Saints,* a racist celebration of a bloody race war resulting from immigrant "invasions" that would later become a must-read, even "prophetic," text for the alt-right and a favorite of Steve Bannon's. In his column, Brimelow wrote about how Raspail depicted "an effete West unable to prevent itself from being overwhelmed by an unarmed invasion of third world immigrants." Such a scenario was already underway here, Brimelow maintained, with "one million Mexicans alone" arriving illegally every year and now Haitians "showing up in open boats demanding political asylum." As a result, New York City, for Brimelow, was already a microcosm of the threat to America's future. Whites, he lamented, "have been a minority in the school system since 1967."

Brimelow was far from alone in his admiration for Raspail's work. John Tanton, the Michigan ophthalmologist behind many of the leading anti-immigrant think tanks and advocacy groups, including the Federation for American Immigration Reform, cited the novel as one of his inspirations. In a 1996 television appearance, Tanton said it raised "a cultural question, the difference between the people who lived in France, and the people who were coming, it raises questions of guilt, the people in France wondering if they had any right to deny these people to come in, and really the future of the civilization of the developed world in response to these enormous pressures that are building out there."[11] Even conservatives who are Trump critics see the novel's value. "The book is a kind of alt-right pornography, and I found it frequently repulsive to read," *The American Conservative*'s Rod Dreher wrote in 2018 when Trump was stoking a nativist panic about the caravan "invasions" from Central America ahead of the midterm elections. "Yet looking at that migrant caravan heading north, that 'numberless disinherited people of the South' who like a tidal wave, are marching north toward our fortunate country's wide-gaping frontier—it's impossible not to think about Raspail's ugly prophetic work."[12]

Both Tanton and Brimelow dressed up their nativism with facts and figures and claims that they were merely concerned about population growth and economics. When he wrote that column, Brimelow was just embarking on a career based on depicting the "civilization of the developed world" as facing an existential threat from a virtual pressure cooker of invaders—the same themes Trump would revive decades later. Trump, though, dispensed with any pretense of relying on data or the language of social science. He translated the existential argument into a simple, three-word, mass movement battle cry—Build the Wall—that resonated to a base for whom the foreign invaders were so determined and wily that only a physical barrier could save America from them.

Bannon, too, was a fan of *The Camp of the Saints*, making numerous references to it over the years at *Breitbart*.[13] When Trump brought Bannon onto his campaign in August 2016, the press treated the new campaign chief as a savant who had astutely selected obscure texts to bring edgy new ideas into American political discourse. In the months after Bannon joined the campaign, political journalists excitedly began looking into the books Bannon was reading, trying to discern the intellectual influences on the operation's new mastermind. According to *Politico,* he was said by "an associate" to be "the most well-read person in Washington,"[14] a quite obviously self-serving exaggeration of his supposed intellectualism. On the same day, *The Washington Post* published summaries of five books "to understand Stephen K. Bannon," all of them nonfiction.[15] He reportedly had read the Russian writer Aleksandr Dugin, an influential far-right political theorist in Russia, Europe, and the American alt-right, as well as the Italian fascist Julius Evola. But Bannon was no savant—his supposed genius owed much to the white nationalists who came before him. Long before Bannon was on the political scene, Brimelow was citing Raspail and other far-right writers now in vogue in the alt-right, using both fiction and agitprop to raise the alarm about America's white "ethnic core" being ravaged by immigration.

Brimelow now considers Rusher to have been a "nursemaid" to the conservative movement, telling me, "Rusher's role was nurturing and organizational rather than explicit and visible leadership. But he was on the right side of everything, from Draft Goldwater to Reagan in 1980, whereas Buckley, contrary to hagiography, was not." Rusher, Brimelow said, "did a great deal of detailed hard work, much of it helping other people, of which Buckley was quite incapable."

Brimelow even delivered volumes of cherished poetry to his friend. In a March 1978 missive—thanking Rusher for a "tremendous" dinner and a discussion of *Rigoletto* when he last visited New York—Brimelow enclosed a book of poems by the British politician Enoch Powell. "It is weird," he wrote, "but I like e.g. Alexander, p. 37."[16] Rusher responded with gratitude. "I've already looked at 'Alexander,'" he wrote back about Powell's four-stanza poem glorifying Alexander the Great, "and share your pleasure in it; I certainly look forward to reading the rest."[17]

The poet-politician, too, would later become a hero to the alt-right. Powell was infamous for his 1968 "Rivers of Blood" speech to Conservative Party members in Birmingham, England, as Parliament was considering the Race Relations Bill, which made it illegal to

discriminate based on race in housing, employment, and public services. In addition to opposing the nondiscrimination bill, Powell's
speech was an incendiary denunciation of immigration, quoting a
Virgil prophecy of civil war warning of "'the River Tiber foaming with
much blood.'" In the speech, which set off a firestorm in British politics, Powell claimed to recount a conversation with a constituent,
horrified at an influx of outsiders, who told him, "In this country in
15 or 20 years' time the black man will have the whip hand over the
white man." Powell endorsed this nameless everyman, warning, "We
must be mad, literally mad, as a nation to be permitting the annual
inflow of some 50,000 dependents, who are for the most part the
material of the future growth of the immigrant descended population." It was, Powell continued ominously, "like watching a nation
busily engaged in heaping up its own funeral pyre."[18]

Five decades later alt-right circles commemorated the anniversary of the speech and even used it as a fund-raising pitch on
Brimelow's *VDare.* "My own views about immigration and the nation-
state were profoundly shaped, when I was a student in England, by
Enoch Powell's great speech on the unprecedented immigrant influx
into Britain," Brimelow wrote.[19] Figures on the alt-right so admire
Powell that one, the virulently anti-Semitic podcaster Mike Peinovich, adopted his name as a pseudonym. Until rival alt-righters outed
him, also revealing that his wife had Jewish ancestry, Peinovich used
"Mike Enoch" as his *nom d'Internet* for his *The Right Stuff* website
and *Daily Shoah* podcast, a repulsive display of unbridled anti-
Semitism and Holocaust denial that popularized the "echoes" or
three parentheses around someone's name to indicate their Jewish-
ness. Adopting the name of a European fascist as a pseudonym was
not unique to Peinovich; a onetime lieutenant of Spencer's, Elliot
Kline, used the pseudonym "Eli Mosley," after the British politician
Oswald Mosley, who, inspired by Mussolini, founded the British
Union of Fascists in 1932.

In the late 1970s and '80s, Brimelow continued to ascend within
American conservatism. He worked as a policy aide and speechwriter for Utah senator Orrin Hatch from 1979 through 1981, while

still writing a column for the *Toronto Sun*.[20] Buckley even recommended Brimelow to Rupert Murdoch, the conservative media tycoon who would, in 1996, launch Fox News. In the mid-1980s, Murdoch's News America Publishing owned the *New York Post,* and Buckley had provided his imprimatur for Brimelow's application to be its editorial page editor. "I think it is clear," Buckley wrote to Murdoch, "that Peter is a formidably credentialed man, and both Bill Rusher and I can vouch for his solid conservatism." Murdoch sent his regrets after he selected another candidate, noting, "I was very taken with Peter and hope that we can work something out in the future."[21]

That didn't happen—but Brimelow's career didn't suffer, as he went on to write regularly for Buckley's own publication beginning in 1988. Then in 1995, he published *Alien Nation: Common Sense About America's Immigration Disaster*. The book was a culmination of Brimelow's writings in *National Review* and elsewhere—in the 1990s, he served as an editor there. At *Forbes* he had been viciously critical of U.S. immigration policy, claiming it "discriminated against Europeans," had "opened the Third World floodgates," and thereby "upset" the "ethnic mix" of the country. In a 1992 *National Review* cover story, Brimelow issued the dire warning that by 2020 "the proportion of whites could fall as low as 61 percent."[22] In *Alien Nation,* Brimelow tried to deflect the charges of racism his earlier articles had provoked. "Because the term 'racist' is now so debased," he wrote, "I usually shrug such smears off by pointing to its new definition: anyone who is winning an argument with a liberal."[23] (Conservative pundits like Ann Coulter still relish echoing this snide formulation.) Not surprisingly, Brimelow failed to deter negative reviews, and some prominent publications pilloried the book. *Business Week* called it an "ugly jeremiad." The headline in *The Wall Street Journal* read, "Natterings of a Neo-Nativist," and the reviewer called the book, presciently, "a blueprint for a resurgent isolationism, for the return of a fortress mentality."[24]

Brimelow's well-documented views were hardly an impediment to his rise within conservative media. Buckley, after *Alien Nation* was published, wrote to Brimelow to tell him he was "absolutely delighted by the attention your important book is getting."[25] Buckley was delighted until Brimelow's nativist views became inconvenient for *National Review*, which let him go in 1997, nine years after his friend Rusher had retired. Rusher, Brimelow lamented to me, "just didn't want to confront the cuckservatives who got control of *National Review*."[26] Although he still remembers Rusher fondly, Brimelow held a grudge against Buckley for years; when Buckley died in 2008, Brimelow eulogized him ("RIP—Sort of") on *VDare* by accusing him of having been "effeminate," "vicious," and "deeply insecure," as well as having "broken" the conservative movement he helped found by eventually supporting immigration policies Brimelow had dedicated his life to destroying.[27] That internecine battle within conservatism over immigration policy would simmer for another two decades before Trump made it the defining issue of his presidential campaign.

One of Trump's longest-serving policy advisers and speechwriters, Stephen Miller, is the cold heart of his administration's white nationalist policies. Miller's role in crafting Trump's Muslim ban, restrictions on refugees seeking asylum, family separation policies, and other hard-right anti-immigrant initiatives have made him a figure of intense interest. Much has been said and written about his unlikely turn, as the son of a liberal Jewish family growing up in Santa Monica, into right-wing politics, and his ascent to the White House by way of the Capitol Hill offices of Rep. Michele Bachmann and Sen. Jeff Sessions, and then the Trump campaign. He has masterminded many of Trump's most cruel and extreme policies and been the architect of his most nationalistic speeches. But before coming to Washington, and before the alt-right even adopted that moniker, Miller had begun forging relationships with some of its leading figures.

In 2007, then a Duke undergraduate and member of the Duke Conservative Union, Miller had worked with Richard Spencer, then a Duke graduate student, to bring Brimelow to campus for a speech on "Globalization and National Identity."[28] Recalling his Duke days more than a decade later, Spencer claimed that he and Miller hadn't spoken for seven years. But his admiration for the rising star he had first known as a campus activist only blossomed while Miller was in the Trump White House. Even though Bannon had ostentatiously claimed the alt-right mantle, Spencer derided him for having only "elective affinities" with the movement. Miller, though, was a hero.

In February 2018, months after the neo-Nazi violence that Spencer and his minions wrought in Charlottesville, I met with Spencer and his allies at the Alexandria, Virginia, town house where they were holed up. I arrived on a bitterly cold morning, and Spencer was late to escort me to the second-floor entrance in the alley behind the building, where a "no trespassing" sign hung on a chain. Via text, he apologized for his tardiness, then ambled down the stairs to let me in. He appeared to have just woken up, and as we walked through the small kitchen into the living area, bottles of liquor were still out, and a half-smoked cigar rested in an ashtray.

Spencer's lieutenants cycled in and out of the room while we talked. Evan McLaren, a young lawyer who was executive director of Spencer's National Policy Institute, shuffled in wearing jeans, a blue hoodie, and slippers. When Spencer stepped out to take a Skype call from Daniel Friberg, a Swedish far-right white nationalist who was Spencer's "man in Budapest"—a hub of international alt-right activity—I talked with Greg Conte, his twenty-nine-year-old bodyguard. Conte had been drawn to the alt-right through Spencer's National Policy Institute conference in 2015. Conte began writing for Spencer's website, initially using the pseudonym "Gregory Ritter," and eventually provided security for Spencer.

Conte, who "grew up with a pretty normal childhood," attended Quince Orchard High School, a public school in the affluent and diverse Washington, D.C., suburb of Montgomery County, Maryland. There, he complained, he had to read "third-rate books" like Zora Neale Hurston's *Their Eyes Were Watching God* "that are chosen because they are written by blacks." In 2012, he graduated from Georgetown University with a degree in Russian. While there, he was kicked out of the ROTC "because some kid reported me for being a Nazi, even though I wasn't." Conte told me the accusation arose after he got drunk and drew, on a chalkboard, a picture of Hitler with swastika eyes, and the words, in German, "I'm the führer," which was "obviously meant incredibly ironically." To retrospectively say something like that was "obviously ironic" is a staple of alt-right deflection of charges of, especially, neo-Nazism. Conte, who portrays himself as a language and history buff, complained that his German classes at Georgetown were "heavily politicized" with "constant guilt-tripping" about the Holocaust.

Although Spencer's movement is rife with such open and casual anti-Semitism, there is at least one Jew he sees as a preeminent ally. Sitting in the town house living room on a leather couch beneath a gold-framed portrait of Napoleon—someone who Spencer once told me gave him a "boner" because of his own gusto for imperialism—Spencer lavished praise on his old friend Stephen Miller. He said Miller had dared to do what Spencer had long called for: radically restrict even legal immigration. Although Spencer's enthusiasm for the erratic Trump waned over the first chaotic year of his presidency, Miller zeroed in on the right policies rather than merely throwing rhetorical firebombs. In particular, Spencer said approvingly, Miller reenergized the far-right talking point of ending "chain migration"— a nativist term for the family reunification that has long been part of the American legal immigration system that the right used as a pejorative to refer to the arrival of "millions of foreigners that threatens our survival as a united, free, and prosperous nation."[29] In February 2019, when Trump declared a "national emergency" at the southern border, he falsely cited "chain migration" as a reason: "Where a bad person comes in, brings 22 or 23 or 35 of his family members— because he has his mother, his grandmother, his sister, his cousin, his uncle—they're all in."[30]

For Spencer, Miller had fearlessly embarked on a project that weak-kneed conservatives had been too cowed by public opinion to attempt. Conservatives, he complained, had focused too much on ending illegal immigration and preventing "amnesty" for those here illegally. But for Spencer, legal immigration is just as much, if not more, of a demographic threat to whites, and Miller was a "singular person" in championing its end. "We would not even be talking chain migration if not for Stephen Miller," Spencer told me admiringly. Miller, he said, had laid out the numbers on the official White House website that showed, to Spencer, that ending chain migration would reverse America's declining white demographic. "Every hour," the graphic warned, "the U.S. permanently resettles enough migrants on the basis of family ties to fill a small auditorium," and "every day, the U.S. resettles enough migrants on the basis of family ties to fill a large high school." Every year, it concluded, the country "resettles an immigrant population larger than the size of Washington, D.C."[31] Miller had been pushing the envelope beyond typical Republican anti-immigration talking points, which focused on deporting undocumented immigrants and ending illegal immigration—but not on restricting legal immigration. "You could see talk like that from FAIR or Numbers USA or *VDare*," said Spencer, referring to far-right anti-immigration advocacy groups and Brimelow's site, "but did you ever hear a mainstream Republican talk about that?"[32]

Despite his esteem for Miller, Spencer said he would go many steps further than merely ending immigration to reverse demographic changes. In the past, he had called it "peaceful ethnic cleansing." To me, he advocated "reimmigration"—meaning sending people who were not "European," including U.S. citizens, back to where their ancestors had immigrated from. (Trump seemed to share this view when he tweeted, in July 2019, that four Democratic congresswomen of color, three of whom had been born in the United States, should "go back" to the "totally broken and crime infested places from which they came.")[33] Spencer would even not rule out that Miller, an American Jew, could be "reimmigrated" as part of his scheme. "Jewish people are not white. Ashkenazis have white skin color," he said, but they would not be part of Spencer's imagined ethno-state, because "the story they have about themselves is just different, different from the story we would tell, that a white person, a European would tell."[34] Even though Spencer theorizes about a future white "homeland," he calls himself not a "white nationalist" but an "identitarian," drawing the term from far-right movements in Europe that, too, have tried to stop immigration, and whose members claim cultural superiority over people they denigrate as culturally inferior interlopers.

Spencer pointed to his and Miller's efforts to bring Brimelow to Duke as possibly his own most formative influence on the future White House strategist. "I don't think I created this for Stephen Miller. Even if fates had not brought us together at Duke, he probably would have ended up in the same place," Spencer told me. "That being said, we did bring Peter Brimelow to campus in 2007, that's something."[35]

While Trump has kept Miller on as one of his most trusted aides, occasionally, for impenetrable reasons, the White House will turn away others with alt-right ties. On a Friday night in August 2018, nineteen months into Trump's presidency, as the House was in recess and the Senate was gearing up for Supreme Court nominee Brett Kavanaugh's confirmation hearings, the White House quietly fired Darren Beattie, a little-known policy development aide and speechwriter.[36] The abrupt dismissal was prompted by a CNN report that had appeared a few days earlier, revealing that in 2016, Beattie had given a speech at the H. L. Mencken Club, a conference of far-right activists and academics, many of whom promote white nationalism, on a panel alongside Brimelow.

The Mencken Club was founded in the mid-2000s by Paul Gottfried, known as the godfather of paleoconservatism—a movement of "traditionalists" in the mold of the nativist, isolationalist Pat Buchanan, who, according to Gottfried, "opposed immigration because they thought it would reduce the moral and cultural cohesion of American society."[37] Gottfried has claimed that he developed the term *alternative right* with Spencer in 2010, but he has since distanced himself from the alt-right's explicitly Nazi spectacles.[38] The Mencken Club's denizens consider themselves to be on the vanguard of the American right, fearless truth-tellers of what the right flank of Americans believes about race, immigration, and the American experiment itself. They deride the mainstream conservative movement as ineffectual, outdated, and intellectually moribund, accusing it of having "suppressed open discussion" and being "entirely beholden to corporate donors and Republican Party bosses."

When he spoke to the Mencken Club, Beattie had recently earned his doctorate at Duke University, writing his dissertation on the early-twentieth-century German philosopher Martin Heidegger's "diagnosis of modernity." Heidegger, who was a member of the Nazi Party, nonetheless remained one of the most influential European philosophers of his era. But the 2014 publication of his "black notebooks" provoked a reevaluation of his legacy, after his private writings laid bare how his virulent anti-Semitism undergirded his central philosophical ideas. The notebooks showed Heidegger's fixation on the conspiracy theory propagated by the forgery *The Protocols of the Elders of Zion*—that a cabal of conniving Jews secretly controls the world—and his failure "to immunize his thinking from such tendencies," according to the collection's editor, Peter Trawney.[39] Heidegger continues to fascinate many alt-right writers and far-right political theorists in the United States and Europe.

Beattie's Mencken Club speech, "Intelligentsia and the Right," was an arcane treatise—"nothing objectionable," he protested after his firing—in which he declared the conservative movement bereft of coherent ideas and argued for the ascent of an intellectual movement opposed to globalization and the "errors" associated with it, "particularly those associated with immigration and monetary policy."[40] That he gave a speech opposed to the conservative "establishment" was unsurprising; Beattie was, after all, a rare early academic endorser of Trump's candidacy, having decided just one month into his primary campaign to support him.[41] Beattie admired Trump's "willingness to take a position on immigration that was so antithetical to corporate Republican donors and then not be cowed by the usual shaming tactics."[42] (In 2019, Beattie was hired by Republican congressman Matt Gaetz, one of Trump's most loyal defenders on the Hill, who is known for his friendly ties to the alt-right.)

At Brimelow's *VDare*, writer James Kirkpatrick denounced the Beattie firing as a "shameless" caving to the "enemy of the people" (the media) and called for Trump to show greater "loyalty" to the base that had elected him.[43] But apart from letting Beattie go, there hadn't actually been that much caving. John Ullyot, a top communications official at the Department of Veterans Affairs, kept his job even after revelations that he had shut down department efforts to issue a statement condemning white nationalism after Charlottesville.[44] Another top communications aide at the Corporation for National and Community Service, Carl Higbie, was forced out after a raft of his racist, homophobic, and Islamophobic statements came to light;[45] he quickly found new employment at America First Policies, which advocates for Trump's policy agenda, and was fired from that position only after corporate donors began withholding contributions. At the Department of Homeland Security, one top official, Frank Wuco, kept his job despite an extended history of Islamophobic comments, while the Rev. Jamie Johnson, the head of the department's faith office, who was discovered to have said, in 2008, that the black community was responsible for turning "America's major cities into slums because of laziness, drug use and sexual promiscuity," was forced out.[46]

In most administrations, the insinuation of any one of these figures into a vital policy-making role would have presented an enormous scandal; in Trump's, it has become a ho-hum part of the news cycle. Most critically, Miller has remained one of Trump's top lieutenants, providing the intellectual energy for Trump's defining policies, despite his avowed white nationalism.[47]

Miller was not the only Trump administration official with ties to Brimelow's world. The day after Beattie was let go, *The Washington Post* reported that Brimelow had attended National Economic Council director Larry Kudlow's seventy-first birthday party at his Connecticut home. The birthday celebration was far from a one-off: Kudlow had been hosting Brimelow, a contemporary and fellow financial journalist, for dinner parties in his home for years. Despite Brimelow's very public profile in the white nationalist circles made more prominent by Trump, Kudlow, when confronted with the evidence, claimed bewilderment that Brimelow, with whom he had been friends "forever," held offensive views. He pleaded ignorance about "a side of Peter that I don't know, and I totally, utterly disagree with that point of view and have my whole life."[48]

It seemed implausible that Kudlow was unfamiliar with his long-time friend's job at the helm of a website that had served as a hub for the anti-immigrant far right for nearly two decades, and whose 1995 book had received considerable attention in conservative circles and in the mainstream press. Brimelow, like others in the Mencken Club and alt-right circles, had been loudly cheering Trump's anti-immigrant rhetoric since the early days of his presidential campaign, when he portrayed Mexican immigrants as rapists and criminals, and demanded a border wall to keep them out. Trump's call, in August 2015, to end birthright citizenship marked a particularly "stunning" turning point[49] for the silver-haired British immigrant whose own son, born in 1991 in New York before either Brimelow or his wife were citizens, bene-fited from the privilege.[50]

Brimelow had even written about Kudlow in *VDare*'s pages, expressing optimism, after Trump tapped him for the top economic job in March 2018, that under the wing of "a strong President," he would develop into a fellow traveler on immigration issues. "No-one is better equipped to emerge as a leading spokesman for immigration patriotism"—the site's euphemism for its anti-immigrant ideology— "particularly as he familiarizes himself with the powerful arguments and his ingenious mind sees the polemical opportunities,"[51] Brimelow wrote. In the wake of the revelations about his relationship with Kud-low, Brimelow turned his ire to Trump's critics, accusing Paul Krug-man of "ethnic hysteria"[52] after the *New York Times* columnist criticized White House officials like Kudlow "who are running cover for Trump policies, and imagine they can avoid association with the racism." Kudlow did avoid the association, though: he kept his job, and the episode turned out to be little more than a blip. Not everyone associ-ated with Peter Brimelow gets the Brimelow treatment in Trump's Washington.

• • •

As much as the aggrieved white men of the alt-right despise "Conservatism, Inc."—the well-heeled organizers of annual events like the American Conservative Union's Conservative Political Action Conference, or CPAC—many of them show up at these conferences anyway, hoping to find fellow alt-right travelers and together insinuate themselves into the conservative movement they revile. Held each year at the opulent Gaylord Hotel and Conference Center along the Potomac River outside Washington, CPAC has always sought to portray conservatism as the tax-slashing, fiscal conservative variety and to quell the racist and xenophobic elements in its ranks. Yet the presence of these elements has been a persistent problem. Between 2009 and 2011, Youth for Western Civilization, a short-lived campus organization that launched the careers of some figures who went on to the alt-right, maintained a presence there. Brimelow made waves at the 2012 conference, speaking on a panel titled "The Failure of Multiculturalism: How the Pursuit of Diversity Is Weakening American Identity."

Since Trump took office, though, the conference has become even more firmly oriented toward the alt-right. By 2018, the takeover appeared complete. Speakers who suggested that immigrants from Mexico had more in common with conservatives than liberals, and that they should be courted as Republican voters, were booed and shouted down.[53] At the conference's Ronald Reagan Dinner, Ian Walters, the ACU's communications director, said the Republican National Committee had elected Michael Steele its chair in 2009 "because he's a black guy. That was the wrong thing to do."[54] (Walters later apologized.) The conservative writer Mona Charen, a pillar of mainstream conservatism, was loudly jeered when she criticized the sexism and racism of the Trump era; security guards had to usher her out of the building.[55]

CPAC also has increasingly opened its arms to the rightward shift across the Atlantic, welcoming nationalistic and even neofascist elements. In 2017, CPAC hosted in its exhibit hall the Europe of Nations and Freedom (ENF), a coalition of far-right nationalist groups in the European Parliament that includes Marine Le Pen's

National Front in France, Geert Wilders's Netherlands Party for Freedom, and the Freedom Party of Austria, which was founded in the 1950s by ex-Nazis and whose leader, Heinz-Christian Strache, advocated a Muslim ban, claiming Islam has a "fascistic worldview." (In late 2017, Strache became vice-chancellor of Austria, and in May 2019 he was forced to resign after publication of a video in which he was drunkenly discussing lucrative government contracts with a woman claiming to be the niece of a wealthy Russian oligarch poised to invest in a German media company, in exchange for positive coverage of his party.) ENF literature claims that its members "base their political alliance on the preservation of the identity of the citizens and nations of Europe, in accordance with the specific characteristics of each population" through "the right to control and regulate immigration." A spokesman told me he hoped that ENF's presence at CPAC would produce a "harmonized cooperation between the United States and Europe."

The following year, as Charen was attacked and other mainstream figures were derided, CPAC gave prime speaking slots to the UK's Nigel Farage, the promoter of Brexit and an alt-right favorite, as well as Marion Maréchal–Le Pen, Marine Le Pen's niece and the granddaughter of National Front founder Jean-Marie Le Pen. Maréchal–Le Pen has described herself as the "heir" to her "visionary" grandfather, a notorious Holocaust denier fined multiple times for violating France's laws prohibiting denial of crimes against humanity. (Charen later said "the Le Pen name is a disgrace. Her grandfather is a racist and a Nazi," and she called the CPAC invitation to his granddaughter "a disgrace," drawing boos from the crowd.)[56] Because Marechal–Le Pen's appearance provoked a predictable stir, to guide attendees in speaking to the media, conference organizers distributed an email with "talking points" describing her as standing for "classical liberalism (i.e., conservatism)." The CPAC talking points portrayed her as a run-of-the-mill conservative, supportive of "school choice, private property, lower taxes, less government spending, market competition, and traditional marriage."[57]

But in her nationalistic speech to the group, Maréchal–Le Pen embraced Trump's "America First" rhetoric and anti-immigration policies, decrying "the development of an Islamic counter-society in France." Spencer cheered Maréchal–Le Pen as "utterly charming" and told me that in her speech "real identitarian themes were sounded, but enveloped in language that would appeal to her audience. The fact is, she's coming from a different place than movement 'conservatism.'" A few weeks after Maréchal–Le Pen thrilled American conservatives, Bannon, who by that time had left the White House but was selling his wares across the Atlantic, spoke to the National Front (now called National Rally) convention in Lille, France. "Let them call you racists. Let them call you xenophobes. Let them call you nativists," he said. "Wear it as a badge of honor."[58]

During what he affectionately called "LeCPAC," Spencer rented a ninth-floor room at the Gaylord as a meeting place, issuing a challenge, on Twitter, for mainstream CPAC-ers to come debate him. Spencer positioned himself on the room's small balcony, overlooking the interior courtyard of the hotel, guests milling about at the bars and restaurants below. He had an iPhone for livestreaming his performances, and his first, enthusiastic taker was Laura Sennett, an Antifa activist from Arlington, Virginia, who knew Spencer well. She brought him a bag of homemade cookies with both white and dark chocolate chips that, she said, were "made with love." Spencer humored her for a while—he ate a bit of cookie, and they talked about art—although he was clearly only minimally engaged and was just killing time.

Soon the room started to fill up with young people, many of whom came to get a selfie with Spencer rather than to argue with him. All the people had been screened in the lobby bar by Greg Conte, then Spencer's right-hand man, who had given out the room number to people "if they didn't seem crazy." After Conte ran interference in the lobby, Brian Brathovd, Spencer's pudgy blond bodyguard also known online as Caerulus Rex, screened people before allowing them onto the balcony to take selfies. Brathovd, once a member of the Army National Guard,[59] was the host of the anti-Semitic *Salting the Earth* podcast, part of Peinovich's (aka "Mike Enoch's") The Right Stuff network, and has co-hosted Peinovich's *Daily Shoah* podcast.[60] In Spencer's room at the Gaylord, he was gruff and officious, ordering people in and out, protecting both Spencer and the anonymity of his fans.

Most of the Spencer fans in the room were young white men, and none of them wanted to be shown on video, have their photo taken by a journalist, or reveal their real names. A college student from Missouri, who would identify himself only as "Chris" because "I have everything to lose by giving you my name," had come to see Spencer, not to argue with him. He told me "a sizable amount" of the college students at CPAC were, like him, fans of Spencer. "They may not necessarily completely agree with Richard's tactics," he said, "or how he phrases certain things, but we are part of a greater community called the alt-right." That greater community, he elaborated, included "extreme reactionary thought, so that could be Catholic monarchy, or monarchists, that could be radical traditionalists. White nationalism tends to be the greater, what is focused on, you could have white nationalism, you could have fascism." (He identified himself as a "radical traditionalist.") At CPAC, fellow travelers were able to identify one another by their language, outlook, and views on Trump, who was not alt-right, Chris said, but a "stepping-stone" to politicians who were.

Another college student, who would not even give me his first name but said that he was from Wisconsin, echoed Chris's observation about the presence of alt-righters at CPAC. "You'd be surprised how many, I'd say at least a quarter of the people that are downstairs are at least sympathetic to the alt-right." At his college, a "large, well-known public university," he claimed to know "lots of them." Before coming to Spencer's room, he had met Peter Brimelow downstairs. "I was talking to him, he was pretty happy to see young people taking up the cause of the movement." This boyish, garrulous nineteen-year-old had familiarized himself with the history of Brimelow and others who were "purged from the conservative movement for years. Because it used to be very normal for basically explicit racial nationalism to be in some form a part of the American political movement." But "when all of those people were kicked to the curb, what ends up happening is people become more radical because they're disassociated from normal politics." He wouldn't tell me more identifying features about himself, because "one day I do want to be a politician," he said.

Although this student from Wisconsin volunteered for the Trump campaign, and for Ron Paul's presidential campaign before that, winning elections was not his ultimate goal for the movement. The goal, he said, was "to create a new European homeland." The student proudly identified himself "pure German in terms of ancestry" and had thought about living there. But although "I fit in very well with Germans, the problem is you have people like Angela Merkel who have destroyed Germany." But all was not lost, he added upon reflection. "I have a very close relative who is very high up in the Alternative for Germany Party," he says, referring to the ascendant far-right xenophobic party, formed in 2013 in opposition to Merkel's liberal policies on migrants and refugees. Six months after this student told me of his affection for AfD, party leaders marched with far-right rioters in Chemnitz, Germany, who roamed the streets assaulting perceived migrants, displaying neo-Nazi banners, and even giving the Nazi salute, which is illegal in Germany.[61]

The riots shook Germany and made news around the world. Yet AfD has continued to make inroads with German voters. "Like any new party, breaking taboos is the AfD's lifeblood," wrote the German magazine *Der Spiegel*. For AfD, the conditions are ripe for "transforming the country," even as "its shift to the right has continued unabated."[62] It is now the third-largest party in Germany's Bundestag.[63] One of its trademark tactics is for one party member to break "a social taboo with an outlandish, offensive statement," after which a "'moderate' member" steps in "to qualify his or her colleague's remarks," according to the German news site Deutsche Welle.[64] Over time, the party's radicalism becomes obscured and more mainstreamed.

In the United States, too many observers of the alt-right have focused on the movement's short-term victories and losses rather than its long game. In the aftermath of Charlottesville, the alt-right was "deplatformed"—purged (temporarily and episodically, it turned out) from social media—denied access by web hosting companies, and stripped of the ability to use credit card processing for online fund-raising. It was beset by infighting and recriminations. Some media and close observers declared the movement dead and finished.[65] But as with the Christian right, those obituaries were premature. As Spencer had always hoped, even without the traditional tools of political organizing, the alt-right was still capable of virally spreading its ideologies and, as Brimelow's career attested, doing it underground.

Setting up "think tanks," using books, podcasts, media, and social media to spread its ideas, and gradually pulling the more mainstream right further to the fringe are hallmarks of the far right in Europe, which aims to "modify the dominant liberal-democratic political culture and make it more susceptible to a non-democratic mode of politics," the Ukrainian political analyst Anton Shekhovtsov has written. "Importantly, the European New Right has focused almost exclusively on the battle for hearts and minds rather than for immediate political power."[66] The American alt-right has used the European New Right as a model in this and other ways—such as when Spencer claimed that the torch-carrying rallies in Charlottesville in May and August 2017 were inspired not by the Klan but by the Greek far-right party Golden Dawn; he considered such displays "spectacular; it's theatrical and mystical and magical and religious, even."[67]

The far right in Europe served as a model for a new politics in which the American right—just as Brimelow had with Raspail and Powell—was looking abroad for its inspiration. The goal has not necessarily been immediate electoral victory but an erosion of confidence in liberal democracy itself and growing acceptance of the ideological messages of the far right. After CPAC 2018 was over, Spencer said he met many alt-right kids there, and "they're talking about immigration, they're talking about chain migration." This was a big change; CPAC kids, Spencer said, "weren't talking about this at all four or five years ago."[68] That spring, hundreds of miles away in the mostly white town of Balaboo, Wisconsin, in the home state of the young man I talked with in Spencer's CPAC hotel room, a group of high school boys were photographed in their prom clothes giving a Sieg Heil salute. From the White House to the heartland, taboos had been shattered.

5

The Origin Myths of the Christian Right

The well-worn foundation story of the modern religious right depicts Moral Majority founder Jerry Falwell, Sr., as roused to action as a direct result of the Supreme Court's 1973 *Roe v. Wade* decision legalizing abortion, driving previously apolitical evangelicals out of the pews with a moral imperative to protect babies from slaughter. This mythology has cast evangelicals as historic heroes leaping to the defense of the innocent, and their movement as a righteous guardian of faith and family. But as much as abortion is now, four decades later, the centerpiece of the religious right agenda, the real story of the formation of this movement was not about protecting babies, families, or morality. Instead, it was a story of racist backlash against school desegregation and other civil rights advances, all cloaked in the language of freedom and religion. If today it seems a mystery how the movement of "family values" came to deify the irreligious, womanizing Donald Trump, this largely buried history shines a bright light on how they were drawn together by shared tropes—caricatures of social justice warriors and an overbearing government—to save white Christian America.

At the center of this story is Paul Weyrich, the architect of the antiestablishment New Right that rose up in the 1970s, purporting to be a right-wing populist alternative to country club Republicanism. Weyrich, an experienced political reporter and talk radio personality in his native Wisconsin, arrived in Washington in 1967 to work as a press aide to Gordon Allott, a Republican senator from Colorado. Weyrich's early years in Washington convinced him that conservatives had failed to match what he believed to be liberalism's powerful institutions guiding policy making in Washington: ideological caucuses within Congress where like-minded lawmakers shared ideas and shaped legislation, and the Brookings Institution. Back then New Right organizers saw that think tank—now considered by the left to be a centrist den of conventional wisdom—as a hotbed of the far left. In 1973, Weyrich co-founded the Heritage Foundation, the powerful, agenda-setting conservative think tank that today boasts an annual budget of more than $80 million, and the American Legislative Exchange Council, which has transformed the legislative landscape at the state level, crafting and lobbying for its model legislation to beat back gun control, eviscerate unions, curtail voting rights, privatize prisons and education, and detain immigrants. With a Republican congressman from Illinois, Philip Crane, Weyrich co-founded the Republican Study Committee, a right-wing caucus that deemed fellow Republicans too moderate. In 1979, he co-founded the Moral Majority with Falwell, considered by many to mark the founding of the modern religious right. But in many ways, the Moral Majority was a culmination, not the beginning; the movement had in fact begun years earlier, as Weyrich and his New Right allies cultivated religious voters to join the cause against an "elite" secular political culture that had foisted unwelcome social and cultural changes on white Christians.

From his early days in Washington, Weyrich was well-versed in propagating the rhetoric of white grievance. One of his tasks while working for Senator Allott in the late 1960s was to produce a weekly *Washington Report* radio broadcast, for which Weyrich asked Allott canned questions about the issues of the day. In 1969, the scripts often turned toward topics like "campus unrest," the civil rights movement, and busing as a mechanism to achieve school desegregation. Weyrich's writings from this period teem with animosity toward the left. Like much of the right, Weyrich and Allott were vehemently opposed to busing—but twisted that opposition into an attempted defense of equality. In one script, Weyrich said, "Opposition to bussing does not mean opposition to civil rights," to which Allott replied, "Forced bussing is a step backward in the whole civil rights picture," while maintaining that his position did "not lessen my commitment to providing equality and justice, through law, for all citizens."[1] In their words were the seeds of later New Right and Christian right rhetoric—that ending racism was the sole province of individual actors, and any government efforts to promote equality for minorities was an infringement on the rights of the majority.

Once Weyrich left Capitol Hill to focus on his own political organizing—launching, in 1974, the Committee for the Survival of a Free Congress—his New Right sought to expand a conservative constituency beyond well-heeled "elites" interested more in economic and foreign policy than in defending "traditional" or "family" values. To Weyrich and his compatriots, the old guard of the conservative movement was too focused on free market economics and not enough on moral, cultural, and religious issues. More important to the New Right than laissez-faire economics, Weyrich wrote in a 1982 essay, are "culturally destructive government policies" like "racial hiring quotas and busing" because "the damage they can do is enormous and practically irremediable."[2]

Although he struggled to persuade evangelicals to join him, opposition to abortion had also been one of Weyrich's top priorities. A deeply conservative Catholic who joined and later became a deacon in an eastern rite Catholic Church because he felt the Roman Catholic Church had become too liberal, Weyrich maintained a life-long and vociferous opposition to abortion, and in Washington he sought to politicize it. Even before *Roe,* Weyrich began priming Republican politicians to get in line with his anti-abortion orthodoxy and publicly shaming evangelicals who would not. In 1971, writing in *The Wanderer*, a conservative Catholic magazine, Weyrich praised a statement that President Richard Nixon had recently made, that based on his "personal and religious beliefs," he considered abortion to be "an unacceptable form of population control" and that "unrestricted abortion policies, or abortion on demand, I cannot square with my personal belief in the sanctity of human life—including the life of the yet unborn."[3] Weyrich urged his readers to express "gratitude" to the president for his "surprise" statement, noting that some observers found it "remarkable" in light of his religious adviser and evangelical icon Billy Graham's "well-publicized statements on the subject."[4] Questioned by a reader, Weyrich assured him that "I have a great deal of respect for Mr. Graham," but noted that in a 1970 radio broadcast, Graham had "said that nowhere in the Bible was it indicated that abortion is wrong. While he did not endorse abortion on demand as such, he did clearly indicate that in his view abortion is permissible in some circumstances." Nixon's statement was "surprising," Weyrich went on, because "we are unaware of any *strong* anti-abortion input among his close associates," and it could be assumed that Graham "did not give Mr. Nixon strong counsel."[5] Many decades later, in 2009, the public would learn, via the release of audiotapes by the Nixon Presidential Library, that Nixon did believe there were circumstances in which abortion is "necessary," such as "when you have a black and a white," or rape.[6]

In the immediate aftermath of *Roe*, Weyrich carried on with anti-abortion activism without evangelical support, concentrating on fellow Catholics. In 1975, he advised Catholic bishops on a strategy to "adopt a program which will make the abortion issue a hot enough political question that it is viewed as a key issue by nearly every Congressman," and, ultimately, to persuade lawmakers to pass a constitutional amendment banning abortion.[7] In 1976, on the third anniversary of *Roe*, he gave his employees his "blessing" to attend a right-to-life rally at the Capitol because "all of us who feel deeply about this matter owe it to our nation to join with others who are similarly concerned" so that "permissive killing will not go unprotested."[8] But as much as he and other Catholics were energized to take on abortion as a political issue, Weyrich could not motivate evangelical pastors to join them.

At the time, there was no evangelical consensus against legalized abortion. The evangelical conversion to opposing legal abortion without exceptions took place later, over the course of the second half of the 1970s and '80s,[9] as the Southern Baptist Convention, at the time the country's largest Protestant denomination, underwent a takeover by its more hard-line fundamentalist wing. Albert Mohler, a prominent conservative Southern Baptist theologian, has described *Roe* as "the catalyst for the moral revolution within evangelicalism," but he acknowledged that in the early 1970s, the absence of a "pro-life consensus" among Southern Baptists was also "generally true of the larger world of evangelicalism."[10] The evangelical world underwent a gradual change, convinced over time by the pastor and missionary Francis Schaeffer and his graphic anti-abortion films, that they should be outraged by *Roe* and fight for its demise. At the beginning, though, evangelicals "didn't want to know" about the issue, according to Schaeffer's son Frank, who, before leaving the fold, was his father's trusted partner in their antichoice activism. "It was a Roman Catholic issue, not a Protestant issue, and Dad had to go around basically twisting arms. In fact, he was the one who talked Jerry Falwell personally into taking a stand on abortion," Schaeffer has recounted.[11]

The resolutions of the Southern Baptist Convention (SBC) over this period show how evangelicals, pre-*Roe,* were in favor of legal abortion, gradually shifting into a more radical opposition as the religious right was being organized in the 1970s. In other words, the hard-line opposition to abortion followed the organization of the religious right, rather than serving as the impetus for it. Just two years before *Roe*—the same year Nixon announced his opposition to abortion—the SBC approved a resolution calling for legal abortion "under such circumstances as rape, incest, clear evidence of fetal abnormality, and carefully ascertained evidence of the likelihood of damage to the emotional, mental, and physical health of the mother." A call to legalize abortion in this range of circumstances would today be considered radically leftist by current Southern Baptist leaders, who oppose abortion with no exceptions, or perhaps with the sole exception to save the woman's life. In 1976, three years after *Roe*, the SBC adopted another abortion-tolerant resolution that called on citizens "to work to change those attitudes and conditions which encourage many people to turn to abortion as a means of birth control," but "also affirm[ed] our conviction about the limited role of government in dealing with matters relating to abortion, and support the right of expectant mothers to the full range of medical services and personal counseling for the preservation of life and health."[12] The following year the body was forced to issue a statement in light of "confusion" caused by the 1976 resolution—meaning it received pushback for sounding too liberal—stating, "we confirm our strong opposition to abortion on demand and all governmental policies and actions which permit this."[13] The SBC reaffirmed that resolution annually until 1980, when it finally adopted a more full-throated statement supporting making abortion illegal again. "Our national laws permit a policy commonly referred to as 'abortion on demand,'" the resolution read, and "we favor appropriate legislation and/or a constitutional amendment prohibiting abortion except to save the life of the mother."[14]

It is a testament to the religious right's powerful marketing machinery that the abortion trigger became the accepted conventional wisdom of the movement's founding. Overturning *Roe*—something now within reach from Trump's stacked Supreme Court—was its ultimate quest, while eroding abortion access, and even physically blocking women from clinics, were its incremental steps in the interim. No religious right conference or rally would omit mention of this modern-day "Holocaust," the most urgent "civil rights" cause on behalf of unborn innocents. In the decades after Ronald Reagan's first election, abortion gradually became a litmus test for Republican candidates that drove a hardening radicalism of the party's position and made "pro-choice Republican" a virtually extinct species. More than any other issue, even opposition to LGBTQ rights, abortion defined the religious right from the 1980s onward. Even if opposition to abortion had not exactly been the motivation for the political mobilization of the religious right, it seemed true in retrospect, since abortion had become so central to the movement's identity.

For years, movement leaders would retell the tale of how the Court's 1973 decision in *Roe* had triggered a swift holy war waged by the scandalized Falwell. His widow Macel wrote in her biography of her husband that reading about the case in the newspaper the day after the Court's decision caused him "to push away his coffee in dismay."[15] Richard Viguerie, an ally and collaborator of Weyrich's, described the preacher's message as always "entirely nonpolitical— until that 1973 *Roe v. Wade* decision."[16] When Falwell died in 2007, obituaries made clear that the media had also largely accepted the legend that Falwell had been propelled into politics by the moral outrage of *Roe; The New York Times* reported that Falwell had said *Roe* "produced an enormous change in him. Soon he began preaching against the ruling and calling for Christians to become involved in political action."[17]

These characterizations are a myth. The unchallenged consensus of contemporaneous reporting on Falwell's rise in the early 1980s made clear that abortion was not his or other evangelicals' immediate spark for political engagement. According to the journalist Frances FitzGerald, who profiled Falwell for *The New Yorker* in 1981, Falwell didn't say much publicly about abortion in the immediate aftermath of *Roe,* and he admitted that he and other evangelicals had not paid much attention to the abortion issue until at least three years after *Roe.*[18] In 1976, three years after the Court's decision, Falwell included abortion in a list of "America's sins" in sermons and writings, but it was just part of a laundry list, not a lightning rod. He did not speak in any detail about abortion until 1978 or write at length about it until 1981.[19]

The origin myth promoted by contemporary evangelicals also portrays their forebears as political naïfs, summoned out of their previous reticence to enter the political fray by the urgency of the national moral lapse that *Roe* represented. But just as the abortion spark is a myth, so is the claim that evangelicals were not political before the Supreme Court's landmark ruling. Fifteen years before founding the Moral Majority, Falwell had had no hesitation in opposing the 1964 Civil Rights Act, calling it a "terrible violation of human and private property rights." The bill, he sermonized, "should be considered civil wrongs rather than civil rights."[20] He helped distribute literature disparaging Martin Luther King, Jr., by then–FBI director J. Edgar Hoover, who oversaw agency surveillance, including wiretaps, on the civil rights icon, who he claimed was a Communist and "the most notorious liar in the country."[21] Falwell delivered an infamous 1965 sermon, "Ministers and Marches," just weeks after the Selma-to-Montgomery civil rights marches, during which state troopers, sheriff's deputies, and a white civilian posse brutally beat and teargassed marchers on what became known as Bloody Sunday. Falwell said, "I do question the sincerity and non-violent intentions of" King and other civil rights leaders, "who are known to have left-wing associations"[22]—a familiar imputation frequently made by both Falwell and Hoover. In her memoir, his widow Macel described that sermon quite differently, focusing on her husband's assertion that it was more important for ministers to preach the gospel than to get involved in the politics of civil rights. But when *Roe* came down, she claimed, it "threw Jerry into a dilemma of epic proportions, far greater even than the struggle against segregation"[23]—implying that he had been involved in the struggle against segregation, rather than opposing its end. But the historical record clearly shows it is fanciful revisionism to claim that Jerry Falwell ever privately or publicly struggled against segregation.

In 1968, Falwell invited segregationist George Wallace, the former governor of Alabama who had launched a third-party run for president, to give a campaign speech from the pulpit of his church.[24] And despite repudiating the "Ministers and Marches" speech in 1980,[25] just three years later Falwell was on television opposing the creation of a federal holiday commemorating King. He said on CNN, "I just feel that there are other Black Americans and the corporate body of Black Americans who are due honor more than one recent individual about whom there is a great question mark even to this moment," insisting that we don't know enough about King's character and morality because "the records are sealed," an apparent reference to Hoover's still-secret surveillance of King.[26] In fact, as evidence of the Hoover-led surveillance came to light many years later, it showed that Hoover spread numerous falsehoods about King and was obsessed with his sex life and with painting him as a national security threat with Communist ties.[27] Later birther smears against Barack Obama, many of which were perpetuated by Trump—that he might have been born in Kenya, that he was not a loyal American, and that he hid his college transcripts—echoed Falwell's insinuation, which other right-wingers frequently made during King's life, that King had a secret past he kept hidden from the public.

These kinds of tropes animated the untapped resource that Weyrich sought for his New Right coalition: white fundamentalists and evangelicals. In a 1981 lecture that he delivered at Harvard University, Weyrich described the religious right—a "thoroughly potent political force"—as comprising different segments of religious voters, with white evangelicals being the late adopters. Before them, Catholics had been outraged by abortion even before *Roe* struck down laws criminalizing abortion nationwide. (Weyrich once observed that the early Catholic activists of the New Right shared a common thread in that their parents had listened to the radio broadcasts of the virulently anti-Semitic Father Coughlin—whom Weyrich described mildly as "the noted political commentator.")[28] Second, amorphously religious "parents' rights" activists were motivated by their opposition to a 1971 comprehensive federal childcare bill that activists objected to because it "was aimed at giving the Federal Government enormous power and authority in the area of childcare and, in consequence, many of us felt it was dangerous, and, yes, immoral."[29] (In fact, it would have created federally funded childcare centers that provided educational, nutritional, and medical services.)[30] After Congress passed the bill, these "parents' rights" groups organized a massive and successful letter-writing campaign to the White House, pressuring Nixon into vetoing the bill. "The experience provided the key to the future," Weyrich said at Harvard—meaning that the activism of parents' rights groups offered a blueprint for the future mobilization of grassroots activists who contended that the government was imposing liberal ideology on them and their families.

But it was another issue that "catapulted" evangelicals "into a final awareness," Weyrich told the Harvard audience. "The Commissioner of the Internal Revenue Service attempted to close some Christian schools on the basis that they were discriminating against minorities." Ministers and other religious leaders were so angry, Weyrich said, that "they were ready to do whatever was necessary" to fight back.[31] In fact, the IRS did not threaten to close the schools—the agency had, in compliance with federal court rulings, merely developed policy that would deny tax exemptions to private schools that discriminated against students on the basis of race. But in casting progressive government action as the enemy of Christian freedom, Weyrich helped lay the groundwork for the central animating principle of the Trump-evangelical alliance: that the government, unfettered, would take away Christians' freedom, and only a strong hand like Trump's could save them.

Weyrich consistently repeated this racial backlash foundation story through the 1990s, recounting to historians and interviewers the difficulties he had persuading evangelicals to join his anti-abortion cause. He told the historian Randall Balmer that it was the IRS action regarding schools, not abortion, that "enraged the Christian community." According to Balmer, Ed Dobson, a close associate of Falwell's, corroborated his account.[32] Weyrich had similarly told the historian William Martin in 1996 that evangelicals were "galvanized" not by *Roe* but rather by the government "intervention against the Christian schools, trying to deny them tax-exempt status on the basis of so-called de facto segregation."[33] After white evangelical support propelled Trump into the White House in 2016, Balmer told me it showed the religious right had come "full circle to embrace its roots in racism" and had "finally dispensed with the fiction that it was concerned about abortion or 'family values.'"[34]

• • •

Although Falwell has long received the credit for founding the Moral Majority and driving white evangelicals into coalition with the Republican Party, at the time, Weyrich's top ally was not so much Falwell as the lesser-known Rev. Bob Billings, another fundamentalist Baptist preacher whose role in shaping the religious right has, for decades, been eclipsed by Falwell. Billings and Weyrich were well-acquainted by 1976, when Weyrich's Committee for the Survival of a Free Congress supported the pastor's quixotic congressional campaign in a heavily Democratic district in Indiana.[35] Before his failed run for Congress, Billings, a graduate of Bob Jones University and a former missionary, was a central figure in the Christian school movement—making him a vital player in the organized backlash against government efforts to ensure that tax-exempt private schools were not segregated.

When public schools were undergoing court-mandated desegregation in the 1960s, Billings was a leader in conceiving of, advising, and leading the nascent fundamentalist Christian school movement. A number of factors, along with school desegregation, converged to drive this effort to craft a religious public school alternative: fundamentalist suspicions about "government" schools; conspiracy theories that the secular humanist underpinnings of public schools were part of a Communist plot; and fears that a judicially engineered separation of church and state—most notably the Supreme Court's decisions in the early 1960s striking down mandatory public school prayer and Bible reading—would destroy Christian America. But the backlash against the federal government's moves to desegregate private schools became the spark that thrust Billings into national politics, as he crafted campaigns intended to bring rank-and-file churchgoers into his antigovernment crusade. Billings portrayed his Christian schools as an antidote to everything about the 1960s that conservatives despised: the moral laxity, the secularism, and most critically, the heavy hand of the federal government in public education and, particularly, desegregation.

In 1968, Christian school organizers in Hagerstown, Maryland, an industrial town on the state's western edge, drew Billings away from a position as principal of a Christian school near Akron, Ohio, to serve as the administrator of the brand-new Heritage Academy. The town had a long and deep history of racism and segregation; slaves were once sold in its downtown, which remained sharply segregated through the Jim Crow era. In 1950, baseball legend Willie Mays, making his professional debut with the New York Giants minor league team, was forced to stay in the all-black Harmon Hotel because he was barred from staying in the hotel with his teammates— something Mays later recalled as remarkable because he was able to stay at hotels with his white teammates in nearby Washington, D.C., and Baltimore. During the game, local fans yelled racist slurs, calling him "nigger," "watermelon man," and "crapshooter."[36] Washington County, where Hagerstown is located, had begun desegregation of its high schools in the 1956–57 school year,[37] and it completed its desegregation plan in the 1964–65 school year, when it moved 130 black elementary-age children from segregated to newly integrated schools.[38] In 1968, trying to persuade parents to support a Christian school, Billings turned to tropes about leftists, rather than explicit racial appeals. "We're not about to turn our young people into a bunch of draft dodgers, flag burners, draft card burners, hippies, yippies and beatniks," Billings promised at a fund-raising dinner for the school. The town's mayor, Herman L. Mills, praised Billings's efforts, telling the audience, "We'll keep our freedom and liberty because of people like you." Billings promised the school would teach creationism and impose strict discipline, saying, "We believe in using the other side of the hairbrush," citing the verse from Proverbs that "the rod of correction" would drive "foolishness" out of a child.[39] Billings was hired as the school's first headmaster; the IRS granted the school tax-exempt status in 1969.

Billings did not spare anyone in Hagerstown his views on race, or his belief that the majority was besieged by minority rights. In an April 1969 letter to the editor of the local newspaper, Billings complained that, at a ball game, another spectator spilled part of a "spiked" drink on him and didn't apologize. Billings raged that he was getting "an earache from listening to the pampering minorities who shout 'We want our rights!' Don't the rest of us have rights?" He segued into a diatribe about "false philosophies" in the classroom, while "old fashioned Americanism and Christianity are to be kept out. Is this freedom? Do we have freedom OF religion or freedom FROM religion?"[40]

From Hagerstown, Billings continued his itinerant pursuit of Christian schools. He became the administrator of a Christian school in Elmira, New York, and then in 1970, he was the principal of the new Hammond Baptist High School in Hammond, Indiana, which was affiliated with First Baptist Church, a fundamentalist independent Baptist church that at the time was considered one of the largest churches in the country.[41] Its pastor, Jack Hyles, co-founded Hyles-Anderson College in 1972, part of his flagship fundamentalist complex he named Baptist City, and he made Billings its first president.[42] In the late 1960s, Hyles, known as a "fundamentalist Baptist power-broker"[43] and "the Baptist Pope,"[44] rejected civil rights laws, sermonizing that "You can no more legislate people to love Negroes than you can cut the moon in pieces and have it for lunch. The only way you're going to have the race problem solved is when people believe the truth, and know Him Who is the truth and get born again; then the love of Christ fills their hearts and they are compelled to love their neighbor."[45] Hyles ostentatiously depicted public schools as dens of "sordid, wicked, communist" infiltration, where Black Panther literature was for sale and hippies subverted all discipline. If students were to be exposed to Black Panther literature, Hyles said in one thunderous sermon, then the Ku Klux Klan should be permitted to distribute its literature as well. He urged his congregants to get a second job if they needed to in order to pay for their tuition at Hammond High so they could get their kids out of the "cesspool" and into a school where "clean-cut, dedicated kids sit at the feet of cultured, fine, educated, godly people who believe the Bible." He trained his ire on universities, too, telling his flock that he'd prefer his son to fight in Vietnam than attend Indiana University because

"I'd rather him die for freedom than be taught filth and rot by folks trying to destroy freedom."[46] At Christian schools like Hammond Baptist High School, authority—in particular, that of Billings—was taken seriously, Hyles boasted to his congregation. "When Dr. Billings decides to discipline your child and your child comes home some night and has to stand up while he eats," the preacher warned, "don't waste your time calling me on the telephone saying, 'Preacher, I want to talk to you about what Dr. Billings did to my boy.' Because, brother, I'm going to be sitting there counting them as he gives them—Amen one, Amen two, Amen three."[47]

Hyles, who died in 2001, was accused of sexual misconduct with a congregant, a charge he repeatedly denied. His protégé and successor, his son-in-law Jack Schaap, was sentenced to twelve years in prison in 2013 after he pleaded guilty to sexually abusing a teenage girl in the congregation.[48] Hyles's son Dave, also a pastor, has been embroiled in sprawling independent fundamental Baptist sex abuse scandals in which he is accused of serially sexually assaulting teenaged girls at multiple churches, as leadership moved him around to different positions each time a new allegation surfaced.[49]

Throughout the late 1960s and early 1970s, Billings—Hyles's respected authority figure—traveled the country promoting Christian schools, serving as a speaker and consultant to the fledgling movement. In 1971, he published *A Guide to the Christian School,* a detailed how-to manual for the aspiring Christian school administrator. In it, he advocated strict admissions requirements for students and high standards for hiring teachers. An IQ of at least 90 would be required for admission for a student, Billings wrote, and the student must demonstrate "Christian indoctrination." Those who "show by their clothes, language, actions, and hair-dos that they have left the way of righteousness, humility, and reverence" should not be selected, and "emotionally disturbed" children "should never be admitted to the Christian classroom unless the teacher has faith to believe that the disturbing emotions and their influences will quickly be nullified."[50] As it turned out, the book had its origins as Billings's dissertation for his doctorate from the Clarksville School of Theology in

Tennessee. A decade later, when he was serving in the Department of Education in the Reagan administration, it came out that Clarksville was a correspondence school that state authorities had shut down because the degrees it offered were "false and misleading educational credentials."[51] The champion of Christian education had a "doctorate" from a diploma mill.

Billings's rise as a national political figure was set in motion by the IRS's moves to desegregate tax-exempt private schools, an initiative that was triggered by a 1969 lawsuit brought in the federal court in Washington, D.C. Parents of black children attending public school in Mississippi asked the court for a legal ruling that private schools in the state, known as segregation academies because they had been set up in response to public school desegregation with the express purpose of being all-white private schools, should not be entitled to a tax exemption, nor should their donors receive a tax deduction for their contributions. In 1970, the court issued a preliminary injunction barring the IRS from granting tax exemptions to private schools with discriminatory policies,[52] after which the IRS, under President Richard Nixon, said it could "no longer legally justify" allowing those exemptions and deductions to "private schools which practice racial discrimination."[53] In its 1971 decision making the injunction permanent, the court reasoned that the purpose of the charitable deduction was "rooted in helping institutions because they serve the public good," and that these institutions should not be entitled to it if their operations "contravene Federal public policy." Less than a decade after Congress passed the Civil Rights Act of 1964, and less than two decades after *Brown v. Board of Education* ruled segregated schools unconstitutional, this court found that federal public policy includes "the promotion of a healthy pluralism," which "is often viewed as a prime social benefit."[54] After the court's ruling, the IRS issued an official policy that any private school that "does not have a racially nondiscriminatory policy as to students" was no longer entitled to the tax exemption.[55]

The IRS then began warning segregated private schools—including those that claimed their segregationist practices were rooted in their interpretation of the Bible—that their tax exemption was at stake. It denied tax-exempt status to the Goldsboro Christian Schools, formed in 1963 in North Carolina, which maintained an explicit all-white admissions policy. And it warned Bob Jones University, a fundamentalist college in South Carolina and Billings's undergraduate alma mater, that its tax exemption was under scrutiny. In 1975, as a result of a separate federal court ruling—in the Fourth Circuit Court of Appeals, which controls South Carolina—that it was illegal for private schools to discriminate in admissions on the basis of race, the university dropped its ban on black students. The university deemed the court ruling "ridiculous, unconstitutional, discriminatory, and a declaration of war against the right of the individual to maintain freedom of association." But Bob Jones kept its ban on interracial dating and marriage on the grounds that it refused to operate "contrary to our Bible conviction."[56] The interracial dating ban continued to draw the IRS's attention, and the agency officially revoked Bob Jones's tax exemption in 1976,[57] after years of warnings. The university sued, claiming that the action violated its religious freedom.

Although the Bob Jones case became a cause célèbre for the religious right overall, the IRS's denial of exemptions was not widespread. According to a 1979 U.S. Commission on Civil Rights estimate, out of 3,500 private schools launched or expanded after nearby local public schools were desegregated, only 110 had lost their tax exemption, and these were schools that refused to comply with the original IRS requirement that they simply file a statement of nondiscrimination.[58] In other words, the schools stripped of their tax exemption were the segregationist hard-liners who refused to adopt a nondiscrimination policy even on paper. But that didn't stop Weyrich and his new protégés from demonizing the government's supposedly heavy hand and, in the process, creating an enduring movement centered on the shibboleth that the federal government is the enemy of Christians' religious freedom—unless it is staffed by them.

Billings founded Christian School Action in 1977, according to Weyrich, "to oppose President Jimmy Carter's initiative against Christian schools. The position of Carter was that it didn't matter if a Christian school had a policy of accepting anyone regardless of race, religion or creed; unless the school was integrated with the average number of Blacks and Hispanics in the nation it was guilty of de facto segregation."[59] (In fact, the efforts had begun during Nixon's presidency, and none of the various iterations of the policies the IRS proposed required "the average number of Blacks and Hispanics in the nation.") Weyrich was an "ardent" supporter of Billings, crediting him with heightening his awareness of "the needs and problems of the Christian schools."[60]

But in the spring of 1978, Billings, freshly arrived in Washington, was struggling to keep his fledgling organization afloat. Weyrich came to the rescue, shocked to learn that his well-connected friend was experiencing fund-raising woes, and dismayed that the Christian community had not sufficiently supported him with the resources that he needed. He told Billings, "My only sorrow is that because the Christian community has not come through to the extent they should, you have not had the kind of support facilities you really need to be totally effective. I mean, it would be a good idea if you had a secretary to answer the phones when you are away so your good wife would have more time for homemaking."[61] Weyrich, who regularly relied on the same well of wealthy donors—often the billionaire conservative patron Richard Mellon Scaife and the beer magnate Joseph Coors—to keep his own organizations funded, made a personal donation to Billings's organization.

Developments in the lawsuit brought by the Mississippi parents would soon enable Billings to mobilize his nascent network and make his mark in Washington. After the plaintiffs in that lawsuit threatened to return to court to ensure the rules against segregated private schools were being sufficiently enforced, the IRS issued a new set of rules, in 1978, setting out standards by which the schools could establish that they had a nondiscriminatory policy. Billings later said he recognized that this IRS move "ignited the

dynamite that had been lying around for years."[62] The 1978 proposed rule change provoked the most coordinated and vociferous
outcry from fundamentalist and evangelical pastors and church
leaders, as they followed Billings's lead.[63]

Under the proposed rule, any private school that a court found to
have racially discriminatory policies would not be entitled to an
exemption. In addition, any private school that had an "insignificant"
number of minority students and that had been formed or expanded
around the time of local school desegregation would similarly be
denied an exemption. The requirement for a not "insignificant" number of minority students was not particularly demanding—the school
would be deemed to have an "insignificant" number of minority students if it enrolled fewer than 20 percent of the percentage of minority school-aged children in its own community.[64] That meant, the
IRS explained, that in a community in which 50 percent of the
school-age population was minority, the school would need to have
only 10 percent of its student population be minority—or twenty
students out of two hundred. If the school failed to meet this standard, it could still retain its exemption if it could show to the IRS
that it was operating "in good faith on a racially nondiscriminatory
basis," such as giving scholarships to minority students, maintaining
active recruitment of minority students, demonstrating an increase
in the percentage of minority students enrolled, employing minority
teachers and staff, participating in sports and other activities with
integrated schools, and making other efforts to engage the minority
community.

Despite their light requirements, the opposition to the proposed
1978 rules was fevered and apocalyptic, portraying the very existence
of the budding private Christian school movement as under threat by
an overbearing, secular government. Billings hyperbolically portrayed
the proposed rule as "a gigantic leap by the IRS into complete control of Christian schools."[65] Assisted by Weyrich, the American Conservative Union, and others, Billings instigated a massive letter-writing
campaign in opposition. In his own letter to the IRS, Weyrich made
an argument that purported to denounce racism in a general sense,

but nonetheless insisted that Christians are entitled to their "religious" beliefs. "Racial discrimination is the pretext used to give the IRS this power to destroy private schools," he wrote, suggesting that the federal government's motive was not ending race discrimination but promoting discrimination against Christians—a theme that has persisted as an argument against policies prohibiting discrimination on the basis of sexual orientation and gender identity. Weyrich contended that the Committee for the Survival of a Free Congress "condemns racial discrimination, but we do not condemn those who may be misguided enough to believe in it simply because they do believe in it. Their private thoughts are their own, as far as we are concerned."[66] To Weyrich, racism was merely the "private thoughts" of individuals, not a systemic injustice, and therefore beyond the acceptable realm of government intervention. It is hardly a surprise, then, that even Weyrich admitted that his movement barely drew any nonwhite activists. As he acknowledged to *The New York Times* in 1980, "I'm not going to kid you that we have minorities running out of our ears. This is not a minority movement."[67]

After instigating the letter-writing campaign that deluged the IRS in opposition to the proposed 1978 rule, Billings and the American Conservative Union (ACU) held a press conference outside IRS headquarters in downtown Washington. Billings offered a parade of horribles that could befall private religious schools that had become "a vital part in the transmission of the morality and beliefs of our fathers down to our progeny." He laid out a "frightening" list of "potential consequences": the taxing of churches, particularly those with which "the government disagrees," and in the end, "nothing less than the destruction of religious freedom in the United States."[68]

IRS commissioner Jerome Kurtz, who was subjected to death threats during this period, tried to explain the proposed rule to Philip Crane, the arch-conservative Republican congressman from Illinois, who was also chair of the ACU and an ally of the budding Christian right. "The service is proposing to apply not a quota but a variety of standards to determine whether schools are racially discriminatory," Kurtz wrote in a letter to Crane, noting that there was no requirement of a specific percentage of minority students. Instead, the proposed rule "includes a numerical standard which, if met by the school, would generally close the matter. But schools that do not meet the numerical standard may establish that they are not discriminatory on the basis of other factors."[69] Even in the face of this reasonable and nonthreatening explanation, the Christian right and its allies in Congress continued to perpetuate the lie that the IRS was imposing quotas, and they continued to portray the minimal requirements for showing a nondiscriminatory school as a tremendous burden.

Despite these efforts by government officials to tamp down the firestorm with reason, the agitation continued. The IRS agreed to convene a four-day hearing at which opponents and supporters of the rule could testify. In his remarks, Billings protested to IRS officials that the Supreme Court decisions of 1962 and 1963, invalidating mandatory school prayer and Bible reading in public schools— when the court "threw God out of the classroom"—was "the impetus more than the '64 Civil Rights Act" for the Christian school movement. (If that was the case, he did not explain why he was so vehemently opposed to the IRS's efforts to desegregate tax-exempt private schools.) America, said Billings, "is a Christian nation, founded by Christian men, Christian people with Christian principles." These founders, he went on, did not think much of King George III "and the taxation without representation." Evincing his hostility to the government and his view—still echoed today—that federal government action amounts to tyranny, he concluded, "our opinion of, perhaps, IRS and other bureaucratic forms is as low as our forefathers' opinions were of George III in 1776."[70]

During a break in the proceedings, one of the pastors accompanying Billings, Roger Voegtlin, gave away the movement's biases. Asked by a reporter why these schools did not actually have more minority students, Voegtlin replied, "It's just two different cultures. We're old fashioned. We spank our kids. We salute the flag. Black kids—they're not used to discipline. They don't like what we have."[71]

As government officials explained to Congress and to the public, they had no choice but to craft a rule that would comply with federal court rulings on race discrimination and tax-exempt status. And the process by which a school that had an insignificant number of minority students could prove it was nondiscriminatory was consistent with the standards set forth in federal court rulings, James P. Turner, the deputy assistant attorney general for civil rights at the Justice Department, told a congressional committee. The rule, Turner said, is "unexceptionable and should be implemented as soon as possible."[72]

But Congressman Crane chose to ignore both the letter he received from Kurtz and Turner's testimony. Crane, who was a former private Christian academy headmaster himself, testified that the guidelines "would require private and religious schools to adopt an affirmative action program or forfeit their tax exemption. The linchpin in the IRS guideline is the racial quota." In spite of the fact that the rule imposed no racial quotas, Crane complained, "strict numerical quotas are not an accurate measure of the quality of education provided by tax-exempt schools. Moreover I fail to see [how] the IRS can infer racist intentions from statistics."[73]

For his efforts, Billings was praised in the pages of Falwell's Thomas Road Baptist Church's newspaper, the *Journal-Champion,* which admiringly noted that he was on a first-name basis with powerful legislators in the nation's capital.[74] Billings was laser-focused on government overreach into Christian affairs, and the need for Christians to fight back. "The cost of political negligence is slavery!" he told the *Journal-Champion,* an odd analogy given that the government action that had triggered the fundamentalists' objection was an effort to ameliorate the ongoing effects of slavery. "As our government increased its crippling pressure on the Christian home, school and church, the need for Christian action becomes increasingly critical. If Christians do not learn to master politics, we will, most certainly, be mastered by those who do," he said.[75] The same issue of Falwell's newspaper featured statements from Republican congressmen, including California's Robert Dornan and Crane, lambasting the IRS action as a "power grab." Dornan denounced it because "it simply cannot be assumed that a private school is guilty of racial discrimination when, in fact, such a school may well have been established simply to promote the inculcation of moral and religious value."

"I personally loathe discrimination on the basis of race," Crane claimed in a *Journal-Champion* column. "Accordingly, I have no sympathy whatever for the blatantly discriminatory recruitment guidelines proposed by the IRS. The guidelines, in effect, require quotas on the basis of race. They pit one citizen against another on the basis of artificial characteristics without regard for our longstanding belief in personal merit. In short, the IRS would promote the very discrimination it seeks to end."[76]

Falwell's newspaper regularly featured items that portrayed the IRS action as an immoral assault on Christians, while true sinners and wrongdoers got off scot-free. "Is the government harassing schools?" blared a headline on a column written by Tim LaHaye, the evangelical and Bircher best known for his co-authorship of the fictional *Left Behind* series, but who was also a major power player in the early religious right. "Doesn't it seem strange that the U.S. government is lenient on communists, criminals, drug pushers, illegal aliens, rapists, lesbians, homosexuals and almost anyone who violates the law, but is increasing its attacks on Christians?" LaHaye pondered.[77] An editorial charged the IRS had turned "quotas" into "an illegal test for integration." Perhaps, the editorial speculated, "the underlying strategy is to cripple the Christian school movement." After all, the editorial maintained, the Christian schools had embarrassed the public schools with their high level of education and godliness, so it must be the government's aim to suppress them. "The pupils from Christian schools are disciplined, respectful, and competative [sic]," the editorial read. "They are creative, but most of all, they are clean. They score higher on the standardized test. In essence, the Christian schools are an embarrassment to the public school."[78]

That spring Falwell implored pastors to join him in Washington for his "I Love America" rally, to let "our nation's capitol [sic] know that there are fundamentalists who will stand up and be counted. The issue is religious freedom." They would be crusading against abortion, pornography, and too much sex and violence on TV. "But I am especially concerned," he wrote, "about the IRS attempt to legislate regulations that will control Christian schools. If they do it, they will destroy the Christian school movement. Fundamental pastors are unalterably opposed to intrusion by bureaucracies into our religious freedom."[79]

Billings later claimed the conflict between Christian schools and the IRS did "more to bring Christians together than any man since the Apostle Paul."[80] He did not have the name recognition of Falwell, but he is credited with introducing Weyrich and other colleagues to Falwell and became the Moral Majority's first executive director in 1979. Later, he was tapped to be the Reagan campaign's religious liaison.[81] During the campaign, Reagan gave a speech at Bob Jones University, calling it a "great institution" and siding with the institution in its showdown with the IRS: "You do not alter the evil character of racial quotas simply by changing the color of the beneficiary."[82]

Once he was elected with the help of the religious right, Ronald Reagan vacillated between adopting a policy that would carry out the requirements of the court rulings on tax-exempt policy while also trying to appease its energized base.[83] Finally, in 1982, bowing to base pressure, his administration rescinded the IRS rule on discriminatory private schools, restoring the Bob Jones tax exemption. But the following year, the religious right was dealt a setback: the Supreme Court ruled that the IRS's denial of tax-exempt status to Bob Jones and Goldsboro Christian Schools was legal and did not violate their religious rights—a final defeat in the protracted case on whether the IRS had infringed on Christians' religious liberty. But the Reagan administration continued to side with other segregated private schools. In 1985, it restored the tax-exempt status of the Prince Edward Academy in Virginia,[84] which was one of the segregation academies that had lost its exemption years before. It had been founded, in 1959, at the height of Virginia's "massive resistance" against desegregation, when the Prince Edward County public school system chose to shut down for five years rather than integrate. As late as 1982, Robert Redd, the all-white school's headmaster, claimed the school did not discriminate in admissions, even though no black students had ever been accepted. That was because, Redd told the *Los Angeles Times,* blacks are less intelligent than whites.[85]

Billings, meanwhile, had made the transition from antigovernment gadfly to bureaucrat; Reagan had installed him at the Department of Education, where he became known around Washington as "the Christian Right's inside man."[86] His role at Education was to keep in touch with his nationwide network of Christian activists and school leaders. In 1983, he chaired the Committee on Education of the Council for National Policy, the secretive conservative umbrella group that, since its founding in 1981, has held quarterly meetings at posh hotels and resorts where political leaders and activists share ideas, network, and strategize. At an early 1983 gathering at the Loew's Anatole in Dallas, Billings presided over a presentation on "Lobbying the State Legislature for Churches and Christian Schools" by R. J. Rushdoony, the iconic leader of the Christian Reconstructionism, a harsh theocratic movement that advocates government according to strict "biblical" law.[87] Rushdoony, whose prolific writings profoundly influenced the religious right, was a key figure in the growth of the homeschooling movement. He believed that slavery was biblical, and that government should be dictated by biblical law (including, for example, the criminalization of homosexuality, with the possibility of the death penalty). Rushdoony maintained that both public education and any regulation of private education by the government was unbiblical and sought to supplant public education with Christian schools and homeschooling.[88]

As an Education Department official, Billings was no stranger to controversy. In 1983, the agency was forced to retract an issue of a publication distributed to college students, because it contained a column by Billings that denounced politicians, public educators, and the Supreme Court for being insufficiently pious. "Americans must make a decision," he wrote, "we can either succumb to the fickle ways of the pseudo-intellectuals and the humanists or we can become advocates of that which is holy and true." He suggested that the proclamation opening Supreme Court sessions—"God save the

United States and the Supreme Court"—be replaced with "God save the United States FROM the Supreme Court."[89] Later, he directed his staff to mail to private schools a copy of a speech he had given some years before, in which he cited the IRS actions against Christian schools and asked, "How can these things be happening in America, this land of freedom, this Christian nation?" A department staffer blamed the controversy on "hyper-sensitivity of certain elements in the Jewish community." The department was forced to apologize for the distribution of the speech.[90]

As much as the Christian right of the twenty-first century is now fixated on abortion and sexual politics, the backlash against the efforts of the federal government to desegregate tax-exempt private schools is embedded in the movement's DNA. The white evangelical attraction to Trump was not in spite of his extended birther crusade against Barack Obama, his racist outbursts in tweets and rallies, and his administration's plans to eviscerate federal protection of racial minorities from discrimination in housing and education by eliminating their ability to show discrimination based on the disparate impact of a policy, as opposed to having to prove discriminatory intent. The Christian right movement was born out of grievance against civil rights gains for blacks, and a backlash against the government's efforts to ensure those gains could endure. When Trump offers paeans to "religious freedom"—the very clarion call of the Bob Jones University defenders—or sloganeers "Make America Great Again," he is sending a message that rings true for a movement driven by the rhetoric and organizing pioneered by Weyrich and Billings. Trump's white evangelical admirers do not just see a leader who is making it safe to say Merry Christmas again, or holding the IRS back from penalizing pastors who endorse him from the pulpit. In Trump's words and deeds, they see an idealized white Christian America before civil rights for people of color—and a meddling government—ruined it.

6

The New Right and Racism

As the school tax-exemption controversy simmered in the 1970s, the early organizers of the New Right were simulta-neously stirring the antagonisms of white Christian voters over two other issues related to school desegregation: court-ordered busing and the changing content of public school textbooks. While Weyrich did not emphasize those two issues as specific inflection points in his later accounts of how he drew white evangelicals into the New Right, at the time busing and textbooks were generating as much acrimony from the New Right as the private school tax-exemption changes were.

The private school tax-exempt controversy involved parents who had already isolated themselves from the public schools because, Christian school leaders like Billings claimed, they saw all too clearly the totalizing, anti-Christian designs of the public school and gov-ernment "elites." As Billings told the Conservative Political Action Conference in 1979, "government schools distrust the private schools because they cannot 'control' them."[1] But countless prospective New Right voters still had children in those "government" schools—and the New Right had plans to turn those parents against their own public education system. An American Conservative Union fund-raising letter captured the tactic in a single sentence brimming with catchphrases designed to both terrify and incense its readers: "forced busing, if not stopped, will establish a deadly precedent for massive 'social engineering' control of American families."[2]

Both antibusing and antitextbook protests were directly aimed at impeding the process of desegregation of American education. Desegregation (a promise still unfulfilled, more than six decades after *Brown*) would not take place overnight and would require legal rulings, policy making, and social change from as far away as Washington and from as close to home as the local school board. The New Right played a key role in vilifying any government-led effort to address segregation in schools. Its propaganda maligned government functionaries as intent on subverting parents' authority over child-rearing with radical changes in public education, portraying these efforts as anti-American, anti-Christian, and subversive to the natural order of things. The New Right sought to agitate its grassroots with a message that desegregation amounted to nefarious bureaucratic tinkering with their comfortable status quo.

Organized opposition to busing, as well as to textbook changes that would finally broaden the classroom experience beyond an all-white canon and end the long erasure of the black experience from public school curricula, were early and defining battles for the New Right. In rhetoric foreshadowing today's Trump coalition and its derision for the institutions working to usher in a new era of non-discrimination and pluralism, the New Right stoked grassroots anxiety by portraying these changes as illegitimate exercises of "elite" power to impose "political correctness," infringing on the freedom of those whose lives had been unbothered by segregation and race discrimination.

In these confrontations with secularism, the fledgling Washington-based political apparatus of the New Right built a template for conflict that has endured through the decades: amplify a single local flare-up into a national issue emblematic of elite, liberal orthodoxy run amok. The religious right has adapted the tactic, first used by the New Right in its opposition to civil rights protections based on race, to its present-day attempts to roll back protections for LGBTQ people. Today a baker in Colorado who refuses to bake a cake for a gay couple becomes a martyr of conscience in the face of a supposed threat to his religious freedom; a local campaign against a nondiscrimination ordinance in Houston morphs into a national crusade portraying transgender bathroom access as a dark menace to the safety of women and girls across America. In both of these cases, people who were portrayed as pious or innocent—in Colorado, the baker, in Houston, the entire population of women and girls—became central characters in a melodrama, replayed on Fox News, the Christian Broadcasting Network, and social media, about the liberal oppression of Christians. This strategy has deep roots in the New Right's early organizing, when it first began to use the power of mass media, direct mail, and interlocking networks of political and religious organizations to create a continuous feedback loop of crisis to white Christians. This crisis was caused by liberalism's push to expand rights as broadly as possible in the United States—a quest that the New Right depicted as devastating to the core values on which the country had been founded. Just as the New Right of the 1970s had portrayed white parents and children as the victims of desegregation, today's religious right portrays Christians as the victims of civil rights advances for LGBTQ people.

In the 1970s, in two potent instances, one in Charleston, West Virginia, and the other in Boston, Massachusetts, outside organizers seized on powerfully symbolic local activists—white women and mothers who were held up as brave, feminine warriors standing against a dangerous liberal machine. In Charleston, Alice Moore led protests against "anti-American" and "anti-Christian" textbooks; in Boston, Louise Day Hicks led protests against busing. While the women served as the New Right's valiant symbols, a man, Robert Whitaker, a little-known organizer from Washington, D.C., helped to nationalize their protests in the service of a new, far-right populist agenda.

Along with other early New Right leaders, Whitaker is another example of the Brimelow thesis: that people associated with the alt-right (or before that moniker came into vogue, the New Right) have always been a seamless part of official Washington, often working anonymously in think tanks or for the government. Often their presence, and their impact on policy, has gone unnoticed. Sometimes they have attracted attention, their public statements have been deemed too fringe or embarrassing to their employers or movement leaders, and they have been dismissed, fired, or otherwise isolated. But years of this routine of purging the extremists only to discover—to much chagrin!—that there are always more of them has become *Groundhog Day* theater in the American right. These episodic banishments often came as a result of external pressure brought on by the embarrassment of fringe associations for mainstream conservatives—but the ostracized individuals would, time and again, turn out not to be outliers. Instead, they represented a potent and enduring strand of the American right, one that seethed with resentment over its exile from mainstream conservatism—making it primed to be activated when Trump came on the scene.

Trump, then, is not a shocking aberration who rose to power through a combination of celebrity, personality, Russian interference, and dumb luck. He is a New Right archetype reconditioned for the twenty-first century. He had predecessors—not in presidents but in activists, writers, policy makers, and legislators. "Mainstream" conservatism tried, occasionally, to expel them. As Trump exemplifies, they, and their odious ideas, never went away.

In 1974, Robert Whitaker was an otherwise anonymous economic analyst, working at the Civil Aeronautics Board in Washington, D.C., when, along with another far-right agitator, Robert Hoy, he created Populist Forum, a small and short-lived organization that helped local activists draw greater national media attention to their causes. Like Brimelow, in building his career Whitaker had the help of *National Review*'s Rusher, and played a small but consequential role in the rise of the New Right in the 1970s and '80s. He later drifted out of public view, only to resurface as a white supremacist hero around 2006, with the publication—on his blog, and on the neo-Nazi site *National Vanguard*—of his racist "mantra" that would become a rallying cry for the Trump-supporting alt-right during the 2016 election. The "mantra" began with a blatantly racist screed against immigration and segued to a cavil that white people were the real victims of racism. "But if I tell that obvious truth about the ongoing program of genocide against my race, the white race," Whitaker wrote, "Liberals and respectable conservatives agree that I am a naziwhowantstokillsixmillionjews. They say they are anti-racist. What they are is anti-white." The "mantra" closed with the line that would make Whitaker a megastar to white supremacists: "Anti-racist is a code word for anti-white."[3]

That phrase would later appear in spurious white supremacist petitions on the website Change.org, and on billboards in the South, part of what the Anti-Defamation League called "a strategy that has emerged in recent years on the part of white supremacists to try to reverse allegations of racism by implying that anybody who speaks out against racism is somehow therefore 'anti-white.'"[4] Whitaker has been lionized on racist websites, hailed as a visionary crusader against what white supremacists call "white genocide." He became an icon in the vilest corners of the Internet, on neo-Nazi and white supremacist sites and forums, where contributors shared ideas about how best to disseminate and repurpose his mantra in order to further propagandize the claim that there is a "white genocide" underway in America. The white supremacist Internet personality Horus the Avenger, host of the *White Rabbit* podcast, worked with Whitaker to bring his "consistent message" to white audiences.[5] "All the memes we use," according to the *Horus the Avenger* website, "come from the Mantra in one way shape manner or form."[6] In 2015, Whitaker joined the presidential ticket of the white supremacist American Freedom Party (AFP), which later ran the racist, pro-Trump campaign robocall in Iowa in early 2016 that alerted the country to the growing extremist support for his candidacy. Whitaker stepped down from the ticket after the party began supporting Trump,[7] but before his white nationalist party supported Trump, it placed a robocall on his behalf, targeting Idaho voters with a message opposing the resettlement of Syrian refugees there. The purpose of that robocall, according to Whitaker's website, was "to inform them that this non-white invasion of their state and ALL white areas constitutes white genocide and also to invite them to join the AFP, the only party standing up for white interests in America."[8]

When Whitaker died in 2017, he was widely mourned across the racist Internet. He "was a warrior for our people," wrote the white supremacist radio show host James Edwards, who had known Whitaker since 2004 and had featured him numerous times as a guest on his program.[9] Whitaker, according to the alt-right site *Counter-Currents,* gave "a voice to the dispossessed majority and turns the tables on the Leftist elites who would like to dispossess them into oblivion. Very few were talking about white genocide before Whitaker."[10] During his period as a white supremacist demigod, Whitaker's mantra and other writings were frequently featured on the website of David Duke, the former Grand Wizard of the Knights of the Ku Klux Klan. When Whitaker died, Duke promised on Twitter that "his Mantra lives on."[11]

Whitaker came to Washington in the early 1970s after studying for, but not completing, a Ph.D. in economics at the University of Virginia, where he studied under the economist James Buchanan, the creator of the public choice theory of economics. Buchanan's economic theory, deeply influential to the antiregulatory right, was based on his opposition to government by majority rule because, in his view, it infringed on the rights of those with a minority viewpoint.[12] When the Supreme Court ordered public schools desegregated, Buchanan was opposed; he described desegregation as a "whole mess" that should have been "worked out gradually and in accordance with local sentiment."[13] In 1956, two years after *Brown,* the Virginia legislature passed a set of laws, in response to segregationist

Sen. Harry J. Byrd's call for "massive resistance" to *Brown,* authorizing the state to shut down public schools that tried to integrate, and to provide tuition assistance to white students who refused to attend integrated schools. In 1959, after state and federal courts struck down these laws as unconstitutional, Buchanan and his colleague G. Warren Nutter developed a legislative proposal, building on the 1955 essay by free market economist Milton Friedman—considered by proponents of "school choice" to be the "father" of vouchers—to privatize the public schools by offering taxpayer-funded vouchers to attend segregated private schools.[14] Had the Virginia legislature adopted Buchanan's plan, it would have eviscerated the state's public school system.[15] Such animosity to public education became, and remains, the core of the right's attempts to subvert the civil rights revolution of the second half of the twentieth century: by portraying public schools and higher education as dens of anti-American "political correctness" or "cultural Marxism," the right aims to erode confidence in the educational system and its aspiration to make education the great equalizer in American society.

Whitaker claimed he never finished his Ph.D. because his dissertation readers, including Buchanan, were forced out of the University of Virginia in 1968—a step in the development of Whitaker's grievances against the education "establishment." In 1974, Whitaker was working as an economic analyst at the Civil Aeronautics Board in Washington, D.C.,[16] when the Kanawha County, West Virginia, school board adopted a new set of textbooks, in accordance with newly created federal guidelines that public school curricula include multiethnic writings by and about people of color, sparking acrimonious and even violent protests against the new textbooks. These Kanawha County protests, the National Education Association (NEA) wrote in a 1975 investigative report commissioned by the school board, posed a "threat to rights that have been newly won: the right of racial and ethnic minority groups to be included in the textbooks," as well as the right of all students to learn, among other things, that "the history of the United States is not one long, unblemished record of Christian benevolence and virtue."[17]

Alice Moore, who was then a member of the school board, an anti-sex-education activist, and the wife of a fundamentalist preacher, led the protests against the new textbooks, pointing a conspiratorial finger at the federal government for its "influence" over textbook publishers, charging that the government "promote[s] this stuff." Early on in the conflict, Moore's opponents clearly understood that "this stuff" referred primarily, although not exclusively, to the presence of black people in lessons and black people as authors of texts. Moore's initial targets were two language arts texts, one for eighth graders and another for eleventh graders, that included sections about dialect that Moore deemed contrary to "standard American speech." Those lessons amounted to teaching children "ghetto dialect," Moore contended, something she falsely claimed the NAACP opposed along with her. From the outset, reported historian Carol Mason in her 2009 account of the conflict, the local chapter of the NAACP "saw the textbook protest as a racist effort."[18] An unnamed citizen who spoke with a panel of experts, assembled by the NEA for its 1975 investigative report, saw the protests as "at least in part, 'a reaction to the black presence in America.'"[19] Moore's opposition to the dialect lessons, according to Mason, was triggered by "a fear of exposing Appalachian kids to black vernacular and coercing them to practice it."[20]

Moore similarly objected to the inclusion, as an optional, supplemental text for a high school Advanced Placement class, of former Black Panther leader Eldridge Cleaver's prison memoir, *Soul on Ice*. Cleaver, Moore contended in a repetition of the old racist trope, advocated black men raping white women.[21] A group of antitextbook parents in Moore's camp raised objections to the inclusion of other black writers as well, calling Langston Hughes's poems "A Toast to Harlem" and "Temptation" "anti-Christian" and the 1964 television film *My Childhood*, narrated by James Baldwin, "anti-white."[22] Several of the antitextbook protesters claimed they didn't object to all black writers, just those who were "convicted criminals"—but neither Hughes nor Baldwin was a convicted criminal. Some of them insisted to their black neighbors that they shouldn't want those texts either, as they represented a negative portrayal of their community. Again, being told what they should think by white parents understandably did not sit well with the black community. As a black minister told the NEA panel, "Racist notions like that—saying that not only do we decide certain things about what you do and where you go, but we also take the prerogative of choosing your heroes . . . I think those kinds of statements and the unacceptability of certain kinds of writings are an expression of a subtle racism."[23]

But the works of supposed "convicted criminals" were not the only source of anxiety for the antitextbook protesters. They even objected to an innocuous illustration on the cover of an elementary reading book that featured a white girl holding a bouquet of flowers, presenting them to a black boy so he could smell them. This image of interracial friendship, according to Nell Wood, who had chaired the school board's textbook selection committee, rankled textbook opponents as symbolic of integration, a process that had already taken place in Kanawha County in response to *Brown*.[24] Wood said several objectors pointed out the image to her, one of them even admitting, "This is what it's all about." That illustration of the white little girl and the black little boy, Wood recalled, was the inflection point for many of the antitextbook protesters.[25]

Throughout the early fall of 1974, after the school board approved the textbooks, the phrase "get the nigger books out" was heard and seen on graffiti and placards around Charleston.[26] The John Birch Society showed up, as did the Klan, with a cross burning; Nazi insignia were found in vandalized schools. Parents kept their kids home from school in protest; school buildings were burned and bombed; a school board building was dynamited. At one point the Kanawha County School Board closed all schools in the county for three days. Private Christian schools were formed in response. Eventually, the school board adopted most of the books, leaving only an elementary-level language arts series out of the curriculum. But the antitextbook protesters nonetheless scored a victory: the school board yielded to their demands that future textbooks must "encourage loyalty to the United States," "not encourage sedition or revolution against our government," and "not defame our nation's founders or misrepresent the ideals and causes for which they sacrificed and struggled."[27]

Connie Marshner, one of Weyrich's closest associates at the Committee for the Survival for a Free Congress who also had worked with the Heritage Foundation, traveled to Charleston to help train protesters. She later claimed the uprising gave her "the first inkling" of a "parents' rights movement" afoot in the heartland, and she used it as an example of a supposedly spontaneous uprising of concerned, pious citizens in the face of secular humanism, in her 1978 anti-public-education book, *Blackboard Tyranny*.[28] Bob Whitaker and James T. McKenna, a Heritage Foundation lawyer and veteran of the IRS private school tax-exempt wars, sought to continue the conflict, even after Kanawha County children settled into their school year and the protests dissipated. In November 1974, they worked with remaining local protesters, staging what they called a "national rally" in downtown Charleston.[29]

More than six months after most Kanawha County residents apparently lost interest in pressing the issue, McKenna published an article about Kanawha County in *Conservative Digest,* a leading New Right magazine published by direct mail trendsetter Richard Viguerie, part of the triumvirate, along with Weyrich and Conservative Caucus founder Howard Phillips, leading the organization of the New Right political apparatus in Washington. (Viguerie would later boast that the magazine "served as the transmission belt for New Right ideas and programs" and claimed that between 1975 and 1985 it received "more publicity than any other opinion magazine in America.")[30] McKenna's article cited and relied on "You Shall Not Do This to My Child!,"[31] a report from segregationist Bob Jones University, which had joined the antitextbook protests as part of the unified force of New Right and religious right opposition. The protests, McKenna wrote in language typical of *Conservative Digest*'s self-serving promotion of the New Right's successes, "may well have sounded the knell for compulsory public schooling and possibly destroyed the ability of government to make any realistic claim that its schooling is 'public' in the sense of being a true reflection of the people."[32] To *The New York Times,* McKenna stopped short of calling outright for the end of public education. "Parents are worried that the schools are turning into big, impersonal governmental bureaucracies that do not respond to pressure from the grass roots," he said. "People no longer automatically trust the Government to know what's best. In the case of the schools, they want to do something about changing things before it's too late."[33] By including the warning "before it's too late," McKenna was signaling to the New Right grassroots that their action was essential to prevent catastrophe—an apocalyptic motivational device characteristic of the New Right. Weyrich took these grievances directly to the Republican Party, telling the platform committee at the 1976 Republican National Convention in Kansas City, Missouri, that the Kanawha County parents, led by Alice Moore, recognized that the textbooks were "being used to denigrate their parental authority, to deride the values upon which this country has been built, to mock, sneer, vituperate."[34]

Whitaker's Populist Forum was intent on keeping white parental disgust toward public schools alive, bringing antibusing activists in Boston together with antitextbook activists in West Virginia to form what the spokesman for the group, Bob Hoy, called a coalition of "forgotten silent Americans."[35] They organized a march on Washington in support of a constitutional amendment banning school busing, in coalition with Restore Our Alienated Rights (ROAR), an antibusing group started in Boston in 1974 by the notorious antibusing activist Louise Day Hicks. The previous year the Boston antibusing protests had been violent, as white parents in South Boston, children in tow, threw rocks and bricks at a bus transporting black children from Roxbury to South Boston High School. A white parent at that protest complained to a reporter, "They let the niggers in."[36] Marching in Washington, Boston protesters carried signs that read "Southie Says Forced Busing Is Kidnapping."[37] They were joined by the Kanawha County antitextbook group Concerned Citizens, one of whom, Becky Hedrick, told *The Boston Globe* that they had joined the protest because "we realize the problems Boston has are the same as ours—parental control." Bob Hoy, Whitaker's partner in the short-lived Populist Forum, organized a press conference ahead of the march where Hicks called for a constitutional amendment banning busing, warning that "if Congress does not listen to the people, there will be no need to celebrate the Bicentennial. We will not celebrate until we are assured that our children will be free."[38] In *Conservative Digest,* Whitaker, identified by the magazine as a "populist leader," extolled the "persistence" of Boston's antibusing protesters and their commitment to the "special character" of their communities they were "fighting to preserve." Populists, he wrote, "know there is nothing 'un-American' about unique cultures within our country."[39]

Although Whitaker specialized in amplifying local conflicts nationally, he was hardly alone within the conservative movement and the Republican Party in his virulent opposition to busing. In testimony to a congressional committee in 1974, M. Stanton Evans, the Joseph McCarthy–defending conservative luminary[40] who at the time was the chairman of the American Conservative Union, blamed "federal functionaries and liberal interest groups" who promoted busing as necessary "to overcome the effects of historic discrimination and to bring about authentic 'integration,' allegedly mandated by the U.S. Constitution and the nation's civil rights laws." Evans coupled his outright derision of civil rights with a transparently malicious claim that black schoolchildren were actually better off in segregated schools—better off, Evans argued like any dedicated segregationist, with their own kind. The "educationists"—the conservative buzzword for the all-powerful, liberal education establishment—"became convinced and apparently convinced some of our federal judges that Negro children must be taken out of their homes and neighborhoods and placed in an 'artificial environment' created by the government, where they will be immersed as fully as possible in an altogether different culture," Evans told lawmakers. "The object is to break into the Negro family and culture pattern and remold black children according to the guidelines preferred by middle-class (and predominantly white) social planners who think they have a commission to tinker around with the psychic makeup of the human species."[41] This pretense of concern for black children—that compelling them to attend integrated schools constituted an unfair imposition of "white cultural values"—was a sleight of hand that instead exposed Evans's rejection of the linchpin of *Brown:* that separate was not equal.

While the battle over busing raged on, Whitaker sought to distill his experiences into a readable manifesto for the new right-wing populists. He would soon meet Rusher, the *National Review* publisher and self-described conservative Republican who believed conservatives like himself needed to be in coalition with populists—even though he didn't know any until he met Whitaker.[42] Rusher advised his establishment friends that they needed to pay attention to the new populist coalition of anti-abortion, anti-gay-rights, and antibusing activists. In 1975, Rusher had published his own effort toward a conservative-populist alliance, *The Making of a New Majority Party,* and had led a short-lived, but failed, effort to forge a third-party presidential ticket for the 1976 presidential campaign that would fuse traditional Republicans with George Wallace–style Democrats[43]— foreshadowing Trump's later success at hijacking the GOP ticket with his embrace of the religious right, rejection of Republican orthodoxies on free markets and foreign policy, and purported alliance with white working-class voters.

Weyrich was smitten with Rusher's analysis, particularly his identification of far-right, third-party candidates in the tumultuous 1968 and 1972 presidential elections as "forerunners of a major realignment in American politics."[44] He cited approvingly Rusher's argument about the "predictive importance" of the 1968 and 1972 third-party candidacies of George Wallace and Joseph Schmitz. Wallace, the segregationist former governor of Alabama, had blocked the integration of public schools and promised, in 1963, "segregation now, segregation tomorrow, segregation forever," becoming a hero to many in the New Right. Wallace publicly changed his position on segregation in a 1971 speech at the National Press Club, but this was, according to the historian Dan T. Carter, a nod to "changing political winds," and Wallace "remained as racially insensitive as ever."[45] Schmitz, a member of the conspiracist John Birch Society, was a former California state senator and U.S. congressman associated with Holocaust deniers,[46] and, like many on the New Right, he admired Joseph McCarthy.[47]

The one true "explosive force" in current politics, Weyrich maintained in a 1975 review of Rusher's book, "is the anti-establishment impulses of such ordinary citizens as the people of South Boston who want their own neighborhood schools, the men and women of West Virginia who have stood up against the establishment for their beliefs"—showing how New Right operatives like Weyrich continued to mine the Boston and West Virginia cases as evidence of an extemporaneous uprising of ordinary, fed-up Americans against patronizing elites. The "new establishment orthodoxy in the United States," Weyrich contended, "is now Liberalism."[48] And it was now the target of both mainstream conservatives and the "populist" New Right.

Rusher, the doyen of American conservatism who relished hobnobbing about opera, traveling to Europe, and fine dining with Peter Brimelow, also schemed about a populist uprising of working-class voters with Bob Whitaker. After becoming acquainted with Whitaker, he became intrigued with Whitaker's book in progress, which derided both the liberal and conservative "establishments." Whitaker, keen to meet in person, eagerly sought a meeting in Washington, D.C., to discuss the manuscript. At one point, Rusher suggested a meeting at the Metropolitan Club, the very heart of the exclusive establishment that Whitaker purported to rail against.[49] While the irony seemed lost on Rusher, he did recognize the tension between his loyalty to Buckley and his new friend's stoking of the "antiestablishment" mutiny. He gently warned Whitaker that he was "rather too hard on the 'conservative establishment,'" but at least they agreed that liberals "are running (and fast ruining), this country."[50] Whitaker's movement could offer the coalition Rusher had been looking for, and he offered to help find a publisher for his book.

The following year, in 1976, Whitaker published—with a glowing foreword from Rusher—his stunningly racist *A Plague on Both Your Houses*.[51] Rusher hailed the book as "a blockbuster," praising

Whitaker's comparison of the "liberal establishment" to both the "slavocracy" of the mid-eighteenth-century South and the robber barons of the early twentieth century. (Whitaker described the conservative establishment as "little more than the political shadow of liberalism.") Rusher wondered, in his foreword, whether liberals would dismiss the book with "a few of their verbal stink-bombs ('racist,' 'fascist')."[52] Despite this attempt at a preemptive refutation of such charges, what followed was page after page of racist invective masquerading as a defense of the common man. But to Rusher, Whitaker was the "real article," having just come off participating in the "populist" uprisings in Boston and Kanawha County.[53] Rusher used the national platform of his syndicated column to plug Whitaker's book and to proclaim him populism's "spokesman of the first rank."[54]

Whitaker carried over racist tropes about education to the pages of *Plague,* devoting a chapter to his opposition to busing. "The proposition that busing promotes brotherhood would be hilarious if it were not so cruel," he wrote. "The bused generation has learned first and foremost that the state is more powerful than they are, that the parents they looked up to cannot prevent anything the state wishes to do with or to their children." In fact, Whitaker argued in a bizarre twist, busing served only to confirm white students' racist views of blacks— because proximity to blacks served only to confirm all the white students' racist stereotypes about them. "In many schools, children raised in the ghetto are a terror," Whitaker wrote. "Hence, for impressionable young white minds, the black beast of the most virulent racist literature seems observed reality."[55]

Not surprisingly, then, Whitaker's quintessential populist candidate was the segregationist Wallace, whose appeal to the grassroots was, according to Whitaker, lost on both the liberal and conservative establishments.[56] *National Review* editor Buckley—his friend Rusher's friend and employer—"is as oblivious as the most devout liberal to the class Wallace represents," Whitaker wrote. Whitaker was so admiring of Wallace's racism, he didn't try to downplay it or couch it in euphemisms like states' rights. "Liberal suspicions that Wallaceite slogans" like states' rights "were code words for racist feelings may well have had some merit," Whitaker conceded.[57]

Whitaker was also well versed in the writings of other racists of his day, ones he believed deserved more admiration than they received in an academy that was teeming with "anti-white prejudices,"[58] where "Black militants qualify as professors and lecture at schools with no qualification but the outspoken demand that the students kill the taxpayers who pay for the schools," he wrote in *Plague*.[59] He praised the eugenicist William Shockley[60] and the controversial anthropologist Carleton Coon, calling Coon's *The Origin of Races* "one of the most important books of our age."[61] Coon's claim—that the "white race" developed hundreds of thousands of years before the "Negroid race," which accounted for the latter's "backwardness"— was widely rejected and denounced as blatantly racist within his field. But to Whitaker, Coon had a brilliant insight, one that would cause the entire civil rights experiment to crumble. After Coon's book came out, Whitaker concluded, liberals could no longer hope to prove "that beneath the skull of every man on earth there lies a western liberal mind, just waiting to be reached by liberal dogma and made part of a united, peaceful world."[62] Any movement for legal equality, Whitaker believed, was made futile by this "scientific" evidence of racial differences. Yet Whitaker complained despite this supposed evidence, it was whites who were persecuted and silenced: "white concern with racial survival" was "still taboo." As proof of his claim that whites might not survive as a race—a fixation that foreshadowed his emergence as a mastermind of the "white genocide" mantra—Whitaker, too, turned to Raspail's *The Camp of the Saints*, which showed that whites were "doomed to extinction through racial mixture."[63]

Rusher was one of the *Plague*'s biggest fans, keeping its theses alive for more than a decade in his nationally syndicated column. Viguerie might have believed that *Conservative Digest* was the "transmission belt" for New Right ideas, but Rusher happily helped those ideas ripple beyond a niche propaganda magazine's audience and onto the pages of America's local newspapers. In 1981, Rusher used Whitaker's book to support his endorsement of a New Right plan, hatched in the offices of Weyrich's think tanks, to stack the judiciary with conservative judges. "Concern with the growing power and alienation of the federal judiciary is a New Right preoccupation of long-standing," he wrote. "As the populist author Robert Whitaker shrewdly pointed out years ago, the Supreme Court in particular has historically served as the last bastion of dying establishments." The Court, Rusher wrote, "is running true to form today, as it shoves forced busing down the throat of a revolted America at the behest of a repudiated and outworn liberalism."[64] He cited Whitaker's "last bastion" claim again four years later, still litigating his discontent with "a narrow majority" of the Supreme Court that "continues to order forced busing,"[65] and again in 1990, aggrieved over how the liberals "have managed to continue imposing many of their views on a reluctant nation by discovering them hidden in previously unsuspected clauses of the Constitution."[66] Rusher used Whitaker's book repeatedly to generate support for a conservative takeover of the judiciary—a scheme now being carried out more comprehensively by Trump than by any of his predecessors, and that will likely be one of the New Right's most enduring imprints on American society.

After *Plague* was published, Whitaker's career continued apace, despite the book's pervasive racist invective, including explicit support for segregation and eugenics—or perhaps because it seemed so unremarkable in his circles. He went on to spend five years on Capitol Hill, landed a book deal to edit a collection of essays by leading New Right figures, and then, with Rusher's enthusiastic recommendation, secured a position in the Reagan administration, working in the Office of Management and Budget to shrink the size of the federal government.

In the late 1970s, Whitaker worked for two years as a staff assistant for Rep. John Ashbrook of Ohio, a longtime friend of Rusher's from their days working on Barry Goldwater's 1964 presidential campaign.[67] Ashbrook was one of a group of arch-conservative Republicans and a co-founder of the American Conservative Union, serving as its chairman from 1966 to 1971.[68] First elected to the House in 1960, Ashbrook voted against the Civil Rights Act of 1964 and had long disparaged and denigrated civil rights leader Martin Luther King, Jr., accusing him of preaching nonviolence but fomenting riots, maintaining Communist ties, and being "disloyal" to the United States. His lengthy conspiratorial diatribe was entered into the *Congressional Record* in 1967,[69] then was used again the year after King's assassination in an effort to force FBI director J. Edgar Hoover to release King's files. Ashbrook portrayed King as a shadowy outsider whose "cause is said to be civil rights," but "for one reason or another, however, very little is known about the real Martin Luther King."[70] Decades later, in 2011 and 2012, when Donald Trump was considering a presidential bid and Barack Obama was running for reelection, the real estate developer pressed a similarly sinister case against the first black president of the United States, baselessly claiming that Obama's birth certificate was fake, that his passport records were sealed, and that Obama was hiding his college applications and transcripts. "We don't know a thing about this guy," Trump told the Associated Press. "There are a lot of questions that are unanswered about our president."[71]

Ashbrook died suddenly of complications from a peptic ulcer in 1982 while mounting a campaign for Senate, challenging long-serving Ohio Democrat Howard Metzenbaum. More than two decades later, on his blog, Whitaker fomented conspiracy theories about his friend and former boss's death, suggesting that either a "mob" or a "Jewish" connection had caused his sudden demise. Even if "it does make me look like a conspiracy nut," Whitaker wrote, "it is my obligation to report this set of coincidences."[72]

Ashbrook has become part of the institutional legacy of the conservative movement. His namesake think tank, the John M. Ashbrook Center for Public Affairs, at Ashland University in Ohio, is part of the State Policy Network,[73] the group of think tanks that serve the American Legislative Exchange Council, the Weyrich brainchild that has radically reshaped law and policy to suit right-wing interests in state legislatures across the country. Ashbrook's biography at the center's website blandly notes his opposition to "unbridled national power with a resultant loss of individual freedom and local autonomy" and to "the expansion of federal aid to education and other New Deal and Great Society programs." It claims he had "a nationwide reputation as an intelligent, candid, and persuasive champion of the conservative cause."[74] In the years since Ashbrook's death, the conservative movement eventually determined to repurpose the King legacy to portray him as a middle-of-the-road promoter of a color-blind society, and therefore a hero to them, rather than as a secret Communist sympathizer. Through this change of strategy, the conservative movement manages to elide both King's groundbreaking radicalism and its own vilification of him.

When Whitaker worked in Ashbrook's congressional office, then for three years as a legislative associate for the House Committee on Education and Labor, on which Ashbrook served, he boasted that he was Ashbrook's "idea man," including on the Christian school tax-exempt issue. On his application for employment with the federal government, he claimed to have researched the IRS "attempt to use lower federal court to impose quotas on private schools, drafted amendment to reverse it, wrote floor speech, and coordinated legislative effort," an apparent reference to an amendment sponsored by Ashbrook that barred the IRS from using federal funds to implement the private school tax-exempt rule.[75] The same year Ashbrook died, 1982, Whitaker published *The New Right Papers*, a collection of essays he edited that would define the New Right—and presage the rise of the white nationalist Trump coalition.

The central thesis of *The New Right Papers* was that the Republican Party, while riding high on Reagan's election in the wake of Watergate and Jimmy Carter's presidency, still had work to do in building Rusher's and Whitaker's coalition of conservatives and right-wing white populists. Contributors included Weyrich, Rusher, direct mail guru and *Conservative Digest* publisher Richard Viguerie, and other right-wing figures, like the columnist and avowed white supremacist Sam Francis. Francis, a historian and prolific writer, came to Washington in 1977 to work as a national security and terrorism expert at the Heritage Foundation and would go on to become the intellectual godfather of the alt-right, inspiring the likes of Richard Spencer, Jared Taylor, and their followers. In his own essay in the book, Whitaker summed up the "social engineering" of the "establishment" as the implementation of "programs to achieve racial balance, 'progressive' education, the discrediting of traditional values and parental authority, and imposition of a new ideology and morality." The "social conservatives" of the New Right were motivated, he wrote, by their opposition to busing, "racial quotas," and immigration—and all these liberal policies would, he predicted, drive these social conservative voters out of both the Democratic and Republican Party establishments and into the arms of this new, unabashedly right-wing, populist movement.[76]

The other essays blended homages to middle America and beleaguered working-class white people with threats of violence if their prerogatives were not restored. Bob Hoy, Whitaker's partner in the antitextbook and antibusing wars, warned in his essay, "Lid on a Boiling Pot," that "nothing has contributed more to white populist disillusionment than the breathtaking hypocrisy and condescending arrogance shown by the establishment over the race issue," and that many populists, therefore, are "ready for violence."[77] He recalled his deathbed vigil for George Wallace with aides from the segregationist's failed presidential campaign, noting that their "despair" had "portended a more militant populism that would not confine itself to due process."[78]

That theme was similarly pressed by the future alt-right patron saint Sam Francis. The New Right, Francis wrote, roots its message "in perceived injustices, unrelieved exploitation by anonymous powers that be, a threatened future, and an insulted past." It is "therefore understandable," he concluded, "that some of its adherents sometimes fantasize that the cartridge box is a not unsatisfactory substitute for the ballot box."[79]

Francis's essay reads like a chilling prototype for the Trump

campaign more than thirty years down the road, including a com-
mendation for a nationalistic, strongman presidency to override the
courts, Congress, the media, and globalist elites. He derided the
"cosmopolitan ethic" of the "elites," who exhibit "open contempt" for
"the small town, the family, the neighborhood, the traditional class
identities and their relationships—as well as for authoritative and
disciplinary institutions—the army, police forces, parental authority,
and the disciplines of school and church." The New Right sought to
replace globalism with nationalism, which, Francis predicted, would
"probably replace the anti-Communism of the Old Right as a focus
of foreign policy." An imperial presidency—or "the adoption of the
Caesarist tactics"—would, he argued, "reflect the historical pattern
by which rising classes ally with an executive power to displace the
oligarchy that is entrenched in the intermediate bodies." The elite,
Francis concluded, is a "parasitical tumor on the body of Middle
America. These structures should be leveled or at least radically
reformed, and only the Presidency has the power and the resources
to begin the process and to mobilize popular support for it."[80]

After *The New Right Papers* was published, and following the loss
of his congressional position in the wake of Ashbrook's death, Whitaker was anxiously seeking a new perch from which to advance his
far-right ideas. Even though Whitaker had deemed the Reagan revolution "dangerously incomplete,"[81] Rusher recommended him to a
White House contact as a "highly intelligent and able man."[82] Whitaker was hired as a special assistant to Donald J. Devine, the head of
Reagan's Office of Management and Budget, who was known as the
"terrible swift sword of the civil service" because of his unrelenting
slashing of the federal workforce in the early 1980s, the class of
bureaucrats disdained by New Right writers like Whitaker and Francis as the "elites" holding down middle America. *The New York Times*
cited Whitaker's appointment as evidence of how conservatives in
Reagan's Washington were building up "a farm system, identifying
bright young people, sending them to Washington, planting them in
the Government and hoping that what sprouts is a perennial presence
here." Reagan's "greatest legacy," the *Times* noted, could be in aides

like Whitaker, "all but anonymous figures in the Federal bureaucracy," who "toil away with titles such as executive assistant, personal assistant, special assistant," and are "among the earliest links in a network of young conservatives that is only now emerging in Washington."[83]

Later, Whitaker spun off the Populist Forum into a new group he called Republican Action for the 90s, whose chief purpose was supporting the Senate candidacy in Louisiana of former Grand Wizard of the Knights of the Ku Klux Klan David Duke. Washington Republicans steered away, and so did Whitaker's old friends from the New Right. Still, Weyrich understood the Duke appeal.[84] About Duke's failed bid for Louisiana governor in 1990, Weyrich told the Heritage Foundation's influential *Policy Review* journal that Louisiana voters "knew about his sympathies for Hitler, his racist past, and his association with the Ku Klux Klan." But, he went on, Duke was "touching a chord and raising issues that people want to hear about and want dealt with." A "substantial number" of Louisiana voters, he said, "feel so alienated from the political establishment that they're willing to pick somebody as embarrassing and as scary as David Duke"—a candidate who, Weyrich said, raised important issues "of fundamental fairness and colorblindness in race relations, welfare and the destruction of families, unchecked crime."[85] In other words, as long as a white supremacist candidate didn't wear a white hood or a swastika, Weyrich could get behind his ideas that were matters of "fundamental fairness."

As Brimelow said of the present-day alt-right inhabiting the corners of official Washington, the New Right populist rebellion of the 1970s and '80s was also comfortably ensconced in the capital, at think tanks and government agencies—giving the right-wing populism of the New Right greater currency within the conservative movement, no matter how much "mainstream" conservatives chafed at its conspiratorial or racist excesses. Sam Francis, too, was one of these figures and was, like Brimelow, eventually banished from "respectable" conservative circles—but not until nearly twenty years after his arrival in Washington. At the Heritage Foundation, which he joined in 1977, he made major contributions to the policy recommendations in "Mandate for Leadership,"[86] a three-thousand-page New Right policy wish list delivered to Ronald Reagan shortly after he took office in 1981. In that document and others he authored at Heritage, and later as a Senate aide, Francis regularly called for increased FBI surveillance, including in the form of wiretaps and secret informants, of supposed internal threats, including "radical and New Left groups," as well as "clergymen, students, businessmen, entertainers, labor officials, journalists and government workers." Civil rights and civil liberties were inconsequential collateral damage to Francis, who called them "secondary to the requirements of national security and internal civil order."[87]

After his gig at Heritage, Francis, like Whitaker and Brimelow, decamped to Capitol Hill, joining the staff of Sen. John East of North Carolina, after his election in 1980. East was so far to the right that Jesse Helms, then the senior senator from the state and a notorious racist, was jokingly referred to as the state's liberal senator. From the Capitol, Francis continued to espouse his claims that an internal leftist (and often black) threat to the country required increased surveillance—positions East staunchly defended. After Frank Donner, a civil liberties advocate and expert on domestic surveillance, lambasted Francis's policy recommendations in *The Nation,* East entered Francis's verbose, bitter defense—longer than the original article—into the *Congressional Record*.[88]

In 1986, after East committed suicide, Francis joined the editorial page staff of the conservative *Washington Times,* became the deputy editorial page editor the following year, and was given his own column, which was also syndicated around the country, in 1991.[89] He was prolific. And in his columns, he openly revealed his racist views. He wrote supportively about Klansman David Duke and his quests for elective office, and he praised academics who were "building the case that intelligence is inherited and the races differ in it."[90]

He regularly backed the apartheid regime and its supporters in South Africa, complaining, in a 1992 column, that civil rights and democracy were being "rammed down their esophagus's [sic]."[91] He called *Brown v. Board of Education* "the most dangerous and destructive Supreme Court decision in American history"[92] and regularly railed against civil rights and notions of equality, making the now-familiar claim that white people in the United States were the real victims of racism. In 1992, when George H. W. Bush was president and supporting Head Start, which provides prekindergarten for children from low-income families, Francis called the program a "massive disaster" and an example of the "whole bloody mess of planned integration" and "multiculturalist and educationist chicken droppings." "You think exposing boondoggles like desegregation and Head Start means we'll abandon these programs and their exploded egalitarian assumptions?" Francis wrote. "Think again."[93]

Other Francis hobbyhorses were framed to inflame white readers by making them believe they would not be fairly treated by the criminal justice system. He repeatedly argued that racially motivated attacks against whites would not receive the same attention as crimes against blacks, and that if whites were criminal defendants, black jurors would not treat them fairly because of "Afro-racism." He complained that newspapers "have spilled gallons of ink to recount every detail about Rodney King"—a black motorist who was brutally beaten by white Los Angeles police officers in 1991—"and every other stage-prop martyr of Afro-racism" but, he charged, did not cover the murder of a white woman, Melissa McLauchlin, by a black man. White people, he concluded against all evidence, "no longer enjoy the same legal rights, the same protection of the laws, as non-whites."[94] The right to allege hate crimes, he wrote, was reserved only "for Certified Victims of Centuries of Oppression,"[95] and the category of crime was "mainly intended to drop a punitive hammer on white heterosexual males for what were supposed to be the characteristic sins of that wicked breed."[96] Whites who faced repercussions for expressing racist views were the victims of "the self-appointed Thought Gestapo," as Francis put it in a 1992 column defending Cincinnati Reds owner

Marge Schott after reports that she had called some of her players "million-dollar niggers" and talked about "Jew bastards" and "money-grubbing Jews."[97]

Any promotion of civil rights for black Americans seemed to enrage Francis, spurring him to inveigh that his readers were the victims of an out-of-control movement to subvert the legal system and overturn the tranquility of white people's lives. He called a 1993 settlement of a lawsuit alleging discrimination against black customers by the restaurant chain Denny's "a billion-dollar blackmail of Denny's by the NAACP and its legal goons."[98] He attacked the first female black U.S. senator, Carol Moseley Braun of Illinois, for her "whiny self-importance and the morbid obsessions she inflicts on herself and the rest of us," complaining that she "and her Afro-racist comrades, who use race and the fear of racism among the pale-face dweebs of the Senate to beat down and shut up anyone who would like to conserve the country's real heritage."[99]

In a 1994 foreword to a book published by the far-right anti-immigrant group the American Immigration Control Foundation, Francis wrote about "the immigration that is at the root of much of the anti-Western multiculturalist strategy and which provides a never-ending stream of constituents for multiculturalist energies and anti-American agendas." For immigration to be constrained, it was "necessary first to assert the existence, integrity, and legitimacy of the Western and American way of life—to assert, in other words, the legitimacy of a 'we' against the demands of a 'they.'"[100]

Francis finally earned a rebuke from his boss, *Washington Times* editor Wesley Pruden, after a 1995 column deriding the Southern Baptist Convention over a resolution condemning racism and slavery. Neither racism nor slavery, Francis argued, was a sin in the Bible—only after the Enlightenment "did a bastardized version of Christian ethics condemn slavery."[101] This statement might have seemed stunning to any reader not versed in the orthodoxies of the American right. But the claim that slavery is actually biblical had been made by other twentieth-century writers, most notably R. J. Rushdoony, the influential Christian Reconstructionist, who had worked with the New Right for years and who had appeared on the 1983 Council for National Policy education panel with Rev. Robert Billings.

Despite Francis's "biblical" defense of slavery, it wasn't until later that year, after conservative pundit Dinesh D'Souza reported on remarks Francis had made at a gathering of white nationalists, that Pruden fired him from the paper. (Although D'Souza was responsible for revealing Francis's speech to the white nationalist conference, D'Souza would later become one of the conservative movement's key purveyors of conspiratorial, racist attacks on Barack Obama.) Yet as with many of these instances of a far-right writer being banished from "respectable" conservatism, what turned out to be the last straw for Pruden did not diverge much from the typical fare in Francis's regular column and other writings. Francis had said, D'Souza reported, that whites must "reassert our identity and our solidarity, and we must do so in explicitly racial terms through the articulation of a racial consciousness as whites," and that the "civilization that we as whites created in Europe and America could not have developed apart from the genetic endowments of the creating people."[102] Piecing together these very same beliefs from Francis's collected works for the newspaper would not have been difficult to do, but speaking to an explicitly white nationalist group brought on banishment, as that would make it hard for the right to present itself to the broader public as a "respectable," "mainstream" movement of conservatives.

Even after Francis lost his perch at *The Washington Times,* he continued to be granted a platform through a syndicated column distributed by the Tribune Media Group and Creators Syndicate. He was close with the like-minded Pat Buchanan and advised his 1996 presidential campaign, wrote a column for the paleoconservative *Chronicles* magazine, and edited the white supremacist *Citizens' Informer,* the newsletter of the Council of Conservative Citizens (CCC), of which he was a prominent member. The CCC was formed in 1985 by leaders of the segregationist White Citizens Councils and drew well-known Republican politicians to some of its gatherings. In

2005, Francis wrote the group's statement of principles, which held that the United States was a "Christian" and "European" country, then laid out a racist laundry list. It opposed all "non-European" immigration and "all efforts to mix the races," including integration; and it favored the use of military force, if necessary, to end illegal immigration; American withdrawal from NAFTA; and an "America First" foreign policy, including opposition to "continued membership in NATO and similar outdated Cold War alliances."[103] Dylann Roof, who slaughtered nine black worshippers at Mother Emanuel Church in Charleston, South Carolina, in 2015, wrote before his massacre that the council's website had introduced him to "brutal black on White murders" that made him wonder "how could the news be blowing up the Trayvon Martin case while hundreds of these black on White murders got ignored?"[104] Decades before, Sam Francis had made those same claims about black-on-white crime repeatedly in his syndicated national column.

After leaving *The Washington Times,* Francis continued to be a known anti-immigrant voice on the right. In a 1996 appearance on *BorderLine,* the television show hosted by the anti-immigrant Federation for American Immigration Reform, and broadcast on Weyrich's National Empowerment Television network, Francis advanced a conspiracy theory that Mexican immigrants were building a fifth column in the United States, while they maintained a dual loyalty to Mexico. In an argument that foreshadowed the opening salvo of Trump's presidential campaign—that Mexico sent its criminals and rapists to immigrate to the United States—Francis said Mexico encourages "their proletariat, their unwanted citizens," and that by these immigrants having "dual citizenship," the Mexican government could "have it both ways, they get rid of people they don't want, their own countrymen, and at the same time, they create a political lobby in this country as a kind of bludgeon against the United States." He claimed that Americans "are really beginning to feel the pressure, from the crime, the economic displacement, the cultural displacement, that this wave of illegal aliens is bringing," and that the

Americans see this as comparable to Soviet and Nazi infiltration into the country in the 1930s "using ideological and ethnic loyalties to manipulate a political force inside our own government."[105]

Francis was no outlier of the New Right—he was its intellectual core. He might have been "banished" from *The Washington Times,* but he was hardly a distant cousin or even the crazy uncle. Francis and Paul Weyrich, according to alt-right financier Bill Regnery, who was friends with both men, were "similar in their political outlook." Regnery, initially at Francis's urging, would go on to bankroll the alt-right's attempts to institutionalize itself through "think tanks" like the National Policy Institute and the Charles Martel Society. He recalled to me that Weyrich, like Francis, "did not suffer fools gladly. He had a good mind." Regnery was "more simpatico" with Weyrich than nearly anyone else he knew in political Washington, many of whom he met through introductions by his uncle, the publisher Henry Regnery, in the 1960s. "I'm not going to put words in the mouth of a dead man," said Regnery, but "my sense is that Paul veered in my direction more and more." But Weyrich's "paymasters were movement types, so he had to be obviously careful about what he said. I'm sure the firing of Sam Francis was an object lesson for him if he needed one, which I doubt, he was sharp guy."[106] In 1990, Regnery's family charitable foundation, the Western Shade Cloth Foundation, gave a $168,000 grant to Weyrich's Free Congress Foundation.[107]

Regnery first met Francis in the late 1990s, at a gathering of eugenicists. Regnery recalled a day spent, with a nice lunch and dinner, at the Repository for Germinal Choice in Escondido, California, also known as the "Nobel sperm bank." The repository's founder, Robert Klark Graham, had used his fortune from his invention of shatterproof eyeglasses and contact lenses to fund the creation of a pool of sperm for white "super-kids," because he believed that "retrograde humans" were becoming more numerous than intelligent ones, and the population needed to be boosted by women choosing the sperm of intelligent white men.[108] The only known Nobel Prize winner to contribute to the sperm bank was the eugenicist William Shockley, who had won the prize for physics for his invention of the transistor, and was much admired by white nationalists—including Bob Whitaker. After meeting Francis at this daylong conference, Regnery kept up with his new friend through correspondence and the occasional lunch.

Unexpectedly, in 2004, Francis approached Regnery with an enticing offer: a funder, whom Francis knew well, "wanted to start a right wing public issues organization" and would provide a matching grant of $500,000 to form what would become the National Policy Institute (NPI)—the "think tank" that white nationalist Richard Spencer would later take over, using it as an incubator for putting an academic or intellectual sheen on white nationalist and white supremacist ideologies. The time frame was short, said Regnery, and he was able to raise only half that amount. "But I got the matching grant," Regnery remembered. "It was only through Sam's involvement with the contributor and his help in securing other funds that made NPI possible."[109] Regnery would not reveal the name of the funder, or the other attendees at the Repository for Germinal Choice gathering. Francis died suddenly just months after the pair founded the NPI, but he left a lasting imprint on what would become Spencer's project, and more broadly on the American right in the Trump era. Francis's books are regularly read and celebrated by the alt-right and by paleoconservatives like Pat Buchanan. They have even been unofficially and secretly given out to interns at mainstream conservative organizations like the Leadership Institute, a training ground for college students in conservative activism.[110]

Weyrich played another, more direct role in shaping the political rhetoric that Trump so successfully capitalized on in building his alt-right/Christian right bloc. The assault on "political correctness" and "cultural Marxism" was profoundly shaped by the work of Weyrich's Institute for Cultural Conservatism, a Free Congress Foundation project he launched in 1986, tapping a young Senate staffer with degrees from Dartmouth and Princeton, William S. Lind, to spearhead the project. The institute positioned itself as an influential counterweight to elitist academia, which had been hijacked by foreign, leftist intellectuals bent on destroying the Judeo-Christian traditions of the West, and the well-ordered moral society those traditions ensured. Weyrich's new project aspired to turn conservative intellectuals and think tanks away from their fixations with free market economics, and toward saving Western civilization from mortal cultural threats.

Weyrich sought to portray the new initiative as a salvific plan to rescue America from a decadent, debased culture. To spin it to the press, though, Weyrich would cast it as a moderate new trend in politics. In a splashy 1986 op-ed in *The Washington Post,* he called cultural conservatism "the most important political idea" of the era.[111] In this new era, conservatives would draw attention to their ideas not through loud antitextbook or antibusing protests in the streets but with white papers and essays extolling America's lost, virtuous past. Weyrich used his press savvy to push various versions of his cultural conservatism manifesto out to the media, encouraging his employees to have patience in selling the idea to reporters. Reporters would have to be "spoon-fed over and over again these ideas,"[112] according to an internal memo. He received flattering coverage in *The New York Times,* which suggested that the manifesto, with its pabulum calls for a government role in restoring imagined *Leave It to Beaver* mores, could be ushering in a new era of conservative compassion and service to others.[113]

The Institute for Cultural Conservatism positioned conservatives as victims of the left's machinations, robbed of their constitutional inheritance in their own country—particularly in its schools, which had been overrun by foreign ideologies, depriving those conservative white Christians of their right to an education steeped in their own "culture." No one, its 1987 manifesto, *Cultural Conservatism: Toward a New National Agenda,* charged, "shall be forced into a 'brave new world' in which the past is forcibly obliterated or distorted, whether by Maoist Red Guards in a 'cultural revolution' or by university professors who replace education with indoctrination and ideology."[114]

Yet Weyrich tried to spin this big new political idea in ways that departed from the racist roots of the New Right coalition. He sought to portray conservatives as a movement of color-blind, race-neutral traditionalists who merely wanted a return to a time and place—small towns in 1950s America—when everyone understood their role in the world, and no liberals or secularists were disturbing the peace. The Free Congress Foundation commissioned a poll that Weyrich and Lind claimed showed that even blacks believed they were better off and "happier" in the segregated 1950s than in the moral rot of the 1990s.[115]

But cultural conservatism's schmaltzy retrospectives of white Christian America proved less enduring as motivators for the American right than its attacks on various leftist bêtes noires. In an undated video produced by the Free Congress Foundation, *Political Correctness: The Dirty Little Secret*,[116] Lind is seen sitting in a chair, his sandy hair cropped short around his round, boyish face, a pipe in his hand, as if to evoke a professorial air, revealing the dark masterminds of a global campaign subversive to Western civilization. "The Frankfurt School, Marxist in origin, wants to create a cultural revolution against Western society," Lind says in the video, referring to the social theory institute formed in interwar Germany by a small group of intellectuals who, drawing on different streams of philosophy, developed the approach known as Critical Theory, which sought to understand structures and systems that can oppress human freedom and how to liberate people from them. Lind's conspiratorial characterizations have dark, genocidal roots: the intellectual historian Ben Alpers has called Lind's conception of cultural Marxism "explicitly anti-Semitic," and the historian Samuel Moyn has described the alt-right's revival of it "a version of the Judeobolshevik myth"—the conspiracy theory, promoted by the Nazis, that Communism was a nefarious Jewish plot to destroy Europe.[117]

Although some of the Frankfurt School theorists who were Jewish escaped Nazi Germany, Lind portrayed them not as victims of persecution or as thinkers who developed ideas for how to understand and combat persecution, but as evil conspirators plotting an overthrow of the western European order. Once the Frankfurt School was in the United States, Lind charged, it inserted itself as a fifth column here, as it "gradually shifted the focus of its work from destroying German society and culture to attacking the society and culture of its new place of refuge." Once again, the locus of the supposedly subversive leftist activity was the education system. "Through unremitting destructive criticism of every institution of Western society, they hope to bring that society down," Lind warned Free Congress Foundation viewers. "Critical theory is the basis for gay studies, black studies, women's studies, and various other 'studies' departments found on American university campuses today," he added derisively. "These departments are the home base of political correctness."[118] Over time, Lind took an even more extreme view, describing multiculturalism as, "quite simply, cultural treason,"[119] the aim of which was nothing short of "destroying Western culture and the Christian religion."[120]

Lind even wrote a futuristic novel, *Victoria*, set in 2050, imagining an America dramatically reconfigured by a bloody civil war triggered by those evil multiculturalist forces. In the introduction to an excerpt published in *The Washington Post* shortly after Timothy McVeigh's 1995 terrorist bombing of the Oklahoma City federal office building, the paper suggested that Lind's writings could offer insights into the motivations of apocalyptic militia movements, whose antigovernment views were "not restricted to isolated pockets of rural America but are also found in Washington." Lind's narrator writes from Maine, in the new nation of Victoria, which has been formed to revive Victorian mores from the ashes of the civil war; other New Englanders and upstate New Yorkers have joined Victoria, while New York City is absorbed by Puerto Rico, and a second confederacy has been established in the South. The narrator wistfully recalls the early 1960s, when "America was still the greatest nation on earth, the most powerful, the most productive, the freest, a place of safe homes, dutiful children in good schools, strong families and a hot lunch for orphans." But after all the social upheaval, by the 1990s, "the place had the stench of a Third World country. The cities were ravaged by punks, beggars and bums. Law applied only to the law-abiding. Schools had become daytime holding pens for illiterate young savages. Television brought the decadence of Weimar Berlin into every home." In Lind's Victoria, universities—whose promotion of multiculturalism he blamed for millions of deaths in the ensuing civil wars—were dismantled.[121]

Lind now lives in his hometown of Cleveland, Ohio—he once wrote that "Washington does not believe anything of importance can happen elsewhere, least of all in 'fly-over land' where most of Middle America lives"[122]—and in a nod to his homages to a past "retro" culture, he does not use email. His more recent writings vividly show the ideological trajectory from that nostalgic cultural conservatism to the dispossession tropes of the alt-right of the 2010s. After the violence at the white supremacist rally in Charlottesville, Virginia, in 2017, he wrote a blog post titled "The White Right Rises," praising "the rise of white political consciousness." He echoed alt-right conspiracy theories (also parroted by Trump and some right-wing Republicans in Congress) that the left caused the violence in Charlottesville while the far-right organizers of the rally were merely defending their cultural inheritance. Whites, he maintained, needed to be ready for the coming civil war. "Whites who rally against cultural Marxism, in defense of Confederate history or anything else from America's past, must be prepared for violence," he wrote. "If Southern whites want to win our second civil war, the war against cultural Marxism, they have to know their enemy and fight smart. The South cannot afford a second defeat."[123]

From Bob Whitaker to Sam Francis to William Lind to Donald Trump, the mythic "middle American radical" was honed not only as a political mascot but as a locus for voter resentment, a rallying cry for cultivating voters who believed that liberalism, pluralism, and civil rights had ripped their heritage and culture right out from under them. The history of the New Right—and its deep and pervasive opposition to civil rights, desegregation, immigration, and other efforts at ending race discrimination—has been largely forgotten or erased. But that history demonstrates, in multiple ways, how the New Right, and its calculated alliance with white evangelicals, foreshadowed the rise of Trump's coalition. The bloc behind Trump—

a combination of the religious right, white nationalists and their sympathizers, and more "traditional" Republicans—had been mapped out by Weyrich decades before, fusing the ideas of New Right ideologues like Rusher and Whitaker with the grassroots activism of conservative white evangelicals and antichoice Catholics. Over the years, the coalition yielded to societal pressure to reel in its overt racism and opposition to civil rights advances for black Americans.

But once Trump brought white nationalism out of the closet, the opposition to civil rights and multiculturalism as elitist ideas tyrannically imposed on white Americans were familiar not only to the hardcore white supremacists of the alt-right but to conservatives and paleoconservatives steeped in the same grievances. These voters still harbored resentments that their rights and standing in American society had been somehow diminished by the civil rights movement—and that the "mainstream" conservatism of the two Bush presidencies had not represented their interests, either. Trump didn't make an entirely new movement out of whole cloth. With his own televangelist gloss, he reactivated the fundamental driving force of the conservative movement in the second half of the twentieth century.

7

The Civil Rights Era Is Over

Although Reagan was the religious right's first presidential hero, the full promise of a theocratic presidency was left unfulfilled on his watch. His successor, George H. W. Bush, was a one-term disappointment for the religious right, leading to the election of Bill Clinton—a charming white southern Christian, but a Democrat whose presidency the religious right was determined to destroy. During this period, Weyrich's coalition began to see its influence grow, even when Republicans were out of power. The political machine he had played a key role in building—the echo chamber of Washington insiders meeting weekly to plot strategy on core issues, reinforced by expanding conservative media willing to repeat right-wing talking points, and a grassroots constituency eager to be mobilized by the latest secular outrage—had been realized. Yet despite presiding over this influential network, Weyrich was often publicly despondent about his movement's shortcomings. Even after the historic GOP takeover of the House in 1994, he despaired over whether the establishment was just exploiting the coalition, fueled by the religious right and other white voters disaffected by the expansion of civil rights for minorities, for its numbers, but then would ignore it when it came to policy making and Weyrich's mission to remake America. He still saw the "establishment" as a reluctant and unreliable ally.

After Clinton was reelected in 1996, Weyrich publicly brooded that party leaders were insufficiently grateful to their New Right base. "The Religious Right saved the Republicans, but some in the GOP have already drawn the long knives to further disassociate the party from issues of concern to social conservatives," he complained in the Heritage Foundation journal *Policy Review,* invoking a pungent reference that has been used to describe extrajudicial executions and political purges, including in Nazi Germany in 1934. Weyrich's indignation over the party's insufficient gratitude and even, he implied, outright hostility to its loyal base led him to a familiar ultimatum: "The Republican establishment risks precipitating a new party if they persist on alienating these conservatives."[1] But just as it had in the 1970s, the threat of a third party turned out to be empty—until 2016, when Trump all but created a third party by energizing the social conservatives first organized by Weyrich.

Weyrich didn't live to see it, but Trump was the Wallaceite candidate he and his New Right allies had dreamed of elevating with the support of the religious right. Before Trump, the circle of "New Right" and paleoconservatives like Pat Buchanan had been unsuccessful either in launching a third party or in nominating a Republican presidential candidate who fit the mold. Before Trump, Buchanan had twice—in 1992 and 1996—tried and failed to win the Republican nomination by giving voice to the New Right's "social issues"— which included not just abortion and LGBTQ rights but also immigration and race. Trump shaped the GOP more forcefully into the party of the New Right's dreams by waging a war of attrition on the party establishment of #NeverTrumpers who opposed his candidacy in the hope of preserving the customs and mores of mainstream Republicanism. Once Trump consolidated control, and the GOP's accession to him became complete, he was able to bring the GOP closer to the New Right's third-party vision than it had ever been in Weyrich's or Rusher's lifetimes.

As president, Trump has checked off box after box on Weyrich's long-unfulfilled wish list. He is unquestioningly responsive to the religious right's demands and a promoter of the white voters the New Right had convinced were a disenfranchised, forgotten majority, left behind as historically marginalized and disenfranchised groups increasingly attained legal rights rooted in the promise of America's founding documents. Much like the New Right, Trump has been a persistent antagonist to the values of a pluralistic democracy, and he is particularly opposed to advancing the civil rights of racial, ethnic, and sexual minorities, and to an independent judiciary protecting those rights.

As Trump's short-lived and beleaguered attorney general, Jeff Sessions proved himself to be a dutiful student of the Christian right's tactics to upend the law, in alignment with its ideology that conservative Christians were the ones whose civil rights truly needed protection. For guidance, Sessions turned to the leading experts at the Alliance Defending Freedom (ADF), the powerhouse Christian right legal advocacy organization that had battled for years to ban same-sex marriage and abortion, elevate expanded religious rights for conservative Christians, and erase the separation of church and state. The ADF was omnipresent in every one of these fights in court, and in the court of public opinion. Having interviewed its lawyers, watched them argue in court and to Congress, and witnessed the organization mushroom in size and reach, I saw the ADF gradually transform itself, along with its legal theories, into a preeminent player in the legal mainstream. By the time Trump took office, the ADF and its affiliated lawyers were positioned to segue into high-ranking political positions, be nominated to the federal bench, and play an integral role in shaping the policy of the U.S. government.

Much of the organization's raison d'être has been to cast Christians as the victims of LGBTQ rights. When the organization was founded in 1993, voters in Colorado had just approved Amendment 2, a ballot referendum that changed the state constitution to preempt state or local recognition of gay men, lesbians, or bisexuals as a protected class. But this attempt to block the advancement of civil rights drew an immediate court challenge, leading to the Supreme Court's 1996 ruling in *Romer v. Evans,* striking down Amendment 2 as an unconstitutional violation of the Equal Protection Clause. Alan Sears, a former Reagan administration lawyer and the ADF's first president, provided early signals of the future strategy, both rhetorical and legal, in his 2003 book *The Homosexual Agenda: Exposing the Principal Threat to Religious Freedom Today.* Sears argued that the legal challenge to Amendment 2 was proof that "radical homosexual activists and their allies are looking for any opportunity to attack and silence any church that takes a biblical stand with regard to homosexual behavior." The persecution that churches faced due to the "wrath of angry homosexual activists," Sears wrote, "is a snapshot of what will happen to the church in America." In 2006, I saw Sears tell the first Values Voter Summit that "the homosexual agenda and religious freedom are on a collision course." Perhaps he knew this because the organization he ran was making it so. The ADF, which today boasts an annual budget of nearly $50 million, has, more than any other Christian right organization, laid the groundwork for that draft executive order on religious freedom, leaked within the first two weeks of Trump's presidency, forecasting the Trump "religious freedom" agenda.

To the public, the ADF presents itself as a protector of religious freedom for all. But from 146 appellate and Supreme Court briefs that the organization's lawyers filed—all the briefs I could find in public databases and on its website—a strikingly different picture emerges. It focuses almost exclusively on cases involving the religious rights of Christians, including rights to pray and evangelize in public schools, rights to Christian prayers during legislative sessions, and the right of Christian social service providers and professionals to refuse service to LGBTQ clients—the very sort of refusals envisioned by the draft executive order. In the first Supreme Court term of Trump's presidency, the ADF won two important cases. In one, the Court ruled that enforcement of Colorado's nondiscrimination law—the type of law that *Romer v. Evans* made possible—against a baker who had refused to make a cake for a gay wedding violated his religious rights. In the other, the ADF won a challenge, brought on behalf of Christian "crisis pregnancy centers," against a California law that required them to inform patients about state programs offering free or low-cost access to abortion, contraception, and prenatal care. Both those cases involved claims by conservative Christian proprietors that state laws protecting LGBTQ and reproductive rights infringed on their religious and speech rights.

When Sears made his "collision course" remarks to the Values Voter Summit, Donald Trump was having an affair with porn star Stormy Daniels and joking with shock jock Howard Stern about being a sexual predator.[2] But ten years later, when Trump formalized his alliance with a thousand religious right leaders at that meeting in Manhattan, promising them he would get rid of the Johnson Amendment's ban on electioneering by churches and make it safe for them to say "Merry Christmas" again, he was actually agreeing to an agenda far broader and more threatening to the rights of millions of Americans. The Christian right's religious freedom agenda isn't just about holiday greetings and clergy endorsement of candidates. Most urgently in 2016, the leaders who met with Trump that day had spent the past eight years fighting some of the signature achievements of Barack Obama's presidency: the passage of the Affordable Care Act, particularly its regulation requiring that employer-sponsored health care plans include full coverage for contraception, and the rapid and historic expansion of LGBTQ rights.

Their oppression narrative, though, was exaggerated and misleading. During the Obama era, their religious objections were very frequently accommodated, both by the Obama administration and by the courts. After protests from the religious right, the Obama administration allowed houses of worship who claimed the Affordable Care Act's contraception coverage violated their conscience to exempt themselves from the requirement. When religious nonprofits also objected, the Obama administration created a procedure for the nonprofit to sign a form to shift the responsibility of providing the coverage to their insurance carrier. But for Obama's fervent opponents, even signing the form would cause a religious objector to participate in an immoral act and therefore violate their religious rights—a novel legal theory that Christian right legal advocates litigated for years afterward. Family-run businesses that had to comply with the contraception coverage requirement sued and won, in the Supreme Court's 2014 decision in *Burwell v. Hobby Lobby Stores,* the right to refuse to provide the coverage. *Hobby Lobby* opened a new legal door: although previously religious objectors had been granted exemptions if doing so did not infringe on anyone else's rights—in this case, the right to access the birth control coverage—the Court in that case signaled a trend allowing such infringements on third parties based on conservative Christian objections, including the objections of corporations, which now had religious rights of their own. Yet even in the face of these victories, Christian right legal advocates sought more. They turned once again to the state and local level, always fertile ground for personalizing the culture wars. By doing this, they could bring Alan Sears's "collision course" to life for the culture warriors at the grassroots, setting the stage for them to see Trump's promises to protect their religious liberty as a promise to save America—and Christianity—from ruin.

Throughout 2014 and 2015, lobbyists, working with a national network of Christian right state policy councils that push state legislatures to adopt conservative legislation, tried to get ever more expansive religious freedom bills passed, aimed at circumscribing marriage equality and thwarting other rights for LGBTQ people. In Kansas, for example, the state legislature in 2014 considered a bill that would have allowed "any individual or religious entity" to claim a religious exemption from having to "treat any marriage, domestic partnership, civil union, or similar arrangement as valid." Robert Noland, executive director of the Kansas Family Policy Council, testified that the bill was needed because "relatively recent developments in the area of homosexual marriage (the past 12 years or so) have quite literally turned thousands of years of religious and social mores on their heads."[3] The Kansas bill died in committee, and similar efforts in other states were also unsuccessful, stopped in their tracks by skeptical legislators or blocked by the courts. But these setbacks made Christian right legal advocates even more intent on finding new ways to "protect religious freedom." Just as activists had turned Kanawha County and Boston and Bob Jones University into culture war flashpoints in the 1970s, Houston, Texas, became one in the era of LGBTQ rights.

In May 2014, under the leadership of the city's first lesbian mayor, Annise Parker, the Houston City Council passed the Houston Equal Rights Ordinance (HERO), a comprehensive antidiscrimination law. HERO would have outlawed discrimination based not only on race, gender, age, and ethnicity but also on sexual orientation and gender identity. Jared Woodfill, a Houston lawyer and Republican political activist—and part of a tight-knit circle in Houston that attends the same megachurch, Second Baptist, as Dan Patrick, the state's powerful lieutenant governor—spearheaded the opposition. The church's senior pastor, Dr. Ed Young, used his pulpit to warn that the HERO bill would mean "we will be discriminated against," calling it a "totally deceptive" and "deadly" measure that "will carry our city further and further, further down the road of being totally, in my opinion, secular and godless."

Immediately after the HERO ordinance passed, Woodfill began seeking signatures on a petition to force a referendum vote on the measure. "The message was real simple," Woodfill recalled as we talked in his law office a few months after Trump was sworn in as president. "No men in women's bathrooms, showers or locker rooms. Period." If he could get a referendum on HERO on the ballot for Houston voters, he could mobilize a large coalition, he thought, by stoking disgust and outrage about lecherous men, masquerading as women, in women's and girls' bathrooms. With that singular focus, he could—and ultimately did—bring down the entire nondiscrimination law.

The city itself boosted Woodfill's prospects for victory when its attorneys made a critical misstep that allowed him to add fears about government oppression of Christians' religious freedom to his messaging—and to turn Houston's legal saga into a national cultural one. Woodfill had collected the required fifty thousand petition signatures to place HERO on a referendum, but after a review, city attorneys ruled thousands of them invalid, bringing the total number of signatures collected below the required minimum. Woodfill sued, and in the course of the lawsuit, the city subpoenaed records, including sermons, from five Houston pastors whose congregations had helped collect signatures. Although document requests are standard discovery procedure in litigation, the government request for the sermons was proof, to Christian-right activists who had spent years warning that the government aimed to "criminalize Christianity" in order to advance LGBTQ equality, that the state did indeed intend to muzzle churches. The ADF accused the city of "engaging in an inquisition." The city eventually modified the subpoenas, but it was too late to stop a national firestorm. "Houston, we have a problem" soon became a refrain of Christian right action alerts. ADF attorney Erik Stanley told a gathering of activists at a Houston megachurch that the subpoenas were "just one front in a rapidly developing conflict. The philosophy underlying this conflict is that sexual liberty trumps everything, including religious liberty." Family Research Council president Tony Perkins told Fox News' Megyn Kelly the subpoenas were about "political intimidation" and "unprecedented, and we've been hearing from pastors across the nation."[4] In November 2015, the referendum to reverse HERO passed, with 61 percent of Houstonians voting to eliminate it.

Despite the Houston victory, Christian right legal visionaries knew they could not stop the Supreme Court from ruling on marriage equality, and they could not anticipate all the ways the law could change in favor of LGBTQ rights. "Religious freedom," then, became their principal weapon in trying to blunt the impact of these historic changes. In the months before the Supreme Court's June 2015 *Obergefell* decision, Mike Johnson, a freshman legislator in the Louisiana House of Representatives and a former attorney at the ADF, introduced the Marriage and Conscience bill,[5] which would prohibit the state from "any adverse action against a person, wholly or partially, on the basis that such person acts in accordance with a religious belief or moral conviction about the institution of marriage."

I first met Johnson in 2007, when I interviewed him for a story about the ADF's ambitions to erase the separation of church and state. He told me then that Christians were increasingly experiencing "discrimination against particular viewpoints, even outright hostility" against, for example, students who hold anti-LGBTQ beliefs. Johnson described them as "kids who hold a Christian kind of world view who want to share Christian viewpoints or speech on campus, and they're being discriminated against because some people see that as intolerant, or however they characterize it." Johnson would go on to win a congressional seat from Louisiana and become a leading proponent of the Christian right's view of religious freedom in the House of Representatives. In 2015, he told his state legislative colleagues his bill was necessary because after the anticipated outcome of *Obergefell,* "a person cannot be given the equivalent of the death penalty" because of their opposition to same-sex marriage.[6]

To support Johnson's Louisiana bill, the Christian right's public relations machinery sprang into action. Once again, it used a template that had been honed for years: amplify a local incident to national importance by telling the stories of well-meaning conservatives besieged by a high-handed government prioritizing civil rights at their expense. At the Heritage Foundation's *Daily Signal,* Travis Weber, a policy expert from the Family Research Council, invoked a number of such local incidents. One had taken place in Washington State, where a florist ran afoul of the state's nondiscrimination law by refusing to "use her floral skills in support of a same-sex union." Barronelle Stutzman, the florist, "just doesn't want to be forced to violate her conscience," Weber wrote. But without a law like the one proposed in Louisiana—which would provide a religious override to antidiscrimination laws—"she is left at the mercy of the all-powerful state should it seek to coerce her to act against her beliefs."[7]

Johnson's legislative colleagues were unpersuaded, and the bill died in committee. But advocates at his former employer, the ADF, worked with then-governor Bobby Jindal to turn the text into an executive order, which he signed. (It was later rescinded by Jindal's Democratic successor, John Bel Edwards.)[8] Austin Nimocks, an

ADF attorney who had pushed for the Louisiana law, then turned to pressing Mississippi officials to adopt a similar executive order or law that would, he told them, "prevent state governments from discriminating against their citizens because of their views about or actions concerning marriage."[9] Weeks after the Supreme Court handed down its landmark decision in *Obergefell,* Mississippi lawmakers did just that, passing a sprawling law of unprecedented scope, allowing, among other things, religious objectors to refuse to serve or do business with people based on their sexual orientation, gender identity, or marital status, or even their engagement in premarital sex. Despite legal challenges to the law's constitutionality, the Supreme Court ultimately declined to hear the case, allowing it to stand. A years-long effort to enact a state law that could be used as a model for federal action had finally been realized. To civil rights advocates who had followed the twists and turns of the Mississippi law, Trump's draft religious freedom executive order circulating in the administration in early 2017 looked to be nearly a carbon copy.

Once Trump authorized Sessions in May 2017 to implement a religious freedom agenda, the ADF helped guide the attorney general. Following Trump's Rose Garden executive order, directing him to issue religious freedom guidance, Sessions delivered a closed-door speech to the group's conference on religious liberty in Dana Point, California. The attorney general of the United States promised the gathering of ADF attorneys that the guidance Trump commanded him to prepare would ensure that "religious Americans will be treated neither as an afterthought nor as a problem to be managed." He consulted with ADF attorneys while drafting the guidance, and the organization in turn praised the final document, which turned its once-marginal legal theories into the official policy of the U.S. government.[10] A few months later Sessions issued a twenty-five-page memo, "Federal Law Protections for Religious Liberty," outlining twenty principles that the ACLU called "a dangerously broad interpretation of religious freedom laws that will open the door to discrimination against LGBTQ people, women, and religious minorities."[11]

While expanding its protections of religious people with conservative political beliefs, Sessions's DOJ was also defending Trump's Muslim ban in court, and was unwinding one of the most critical tools of federal enforcement of racial minorities' civil rights. Under his watch, DOJ attorneys were instructed, when settling civil rights cases, not to enter into consent decrees, which had historically been used to ensure ongoing compliance with court orders to desegregate schools or to reform police departments that had systematically infringed on citizens' rights.[12] By diminishing its use of consent decrees, the department was relinquishing its own civil rights enforcement teeth. At the same time, it was ramping up its efforts to vindicate expanded, unprecedented rights for conservative Christians.

In his religious freedom guidance memo, Sessions adopted the framework of religious right ideologues: that the government, by enacting and enforcing civil rights laws, was backing Christians into a morally untenable corner. "Except in the narrowest circumstances," he wrote, "no one should be forced to choose between living out his or her faith and complying with the law." He directed agencies that religious observance and practice "should be reasonably accommodated in all government activity, including employment, contracting, and programming."[13] DOJ then began to lead the way for other federal agencies: it consulted with the ADF about its pending cases, choosing which ones would receive the support of the U.S. government. "We've provided information to people in the administration; people in the administration asked for information about our cases," Casey Mattox, director of the ADF's Center for Academic Freedom, told me.

DOJ then sought to intervene in an ADF case in Georgia, in which a student claimed that Georgia Gwinnett College had violated his rights to free speech and free exercise of religion when it asked him to stop preaching outside the school's designated free speech zones. DOJ argued that it was in the government's interest to "lend its voice" because the student's "First Amendment claims are intertwined with allegations of disparate treatment based on religion." In an even more unusual move, the department filed a friend of the court brief in a high-profile Supreme Court case, in which the ADF was representing Colorado baker Jack Phillips, owner of Masterpiece Cakeshop. Phillips refused to bake a cake for a gay couple's wedding, then claimed that state enforcement of a law barring discrimination based on sexual orientation violated his constitutional rights. After Phillips won the case—thanks to the Court adopting the ADF's argument that Colorado officials had exhibited a "hostility" to Phillips's religion—Sessions returned to speak to another ADF religious liberty conference. Referring to the "ordeal faced bravely by Jack Phillips," Sessions made clear whose civil rights the Trump DOJ was keen on vindicating. "People of faith are facing a new hostility," Sessions said. "Really, a bigoted ideology which is founded on animus towards people of faith."[14]

That same summer, DOJ's Religious Liberty Task Force—an initiative that had been envisioned in Trump's scuttled executive order—had its ceremonial launch in the Great Hall at the department's headquarters in Washington. There Sessions vividly laid out an existential threat, a "dangerous movement" that is "challenging and eroding our great tradition of religious freedom." This movement—which he did not further identify, though he seemed to refer to the LGBTQ rights movement or possibly secularism more broadly—"must be confronted and defeated." It was a stunning statement by the U.S. attorney general, who is charged with enforcing all the nation's laws and protecting the civil rights of all Americans. He signaled his embrace not only of the Christian right's narrative that Christianity was under threat by LGBTQ rights but also, more generally, that "the cultural climate in this country—and in the West more generally—has become less hospitable to people of faith." Americans are deeply concerned about these changes, Sessions maintained. But Trump had come to the rescue, Sessions said—they were no longer abandoned by their political leaders. "President Trump heard this concern" and was elected, in part, because of his commitment to protecting religious freedom. He had, after all, "declared we would say 'Merry Christmas' again." A "dangerous movement" posed a threat to religious people; Trump was the savior who would "defeat" it.[15]

Sessions's official Department of Justice guidance effectively gave federal agencies the leeway to create the same expansive religious exemptions envisioned by the draft executive order. By directing Sessions, a Christian right ally, to instruct federal agencies on how to protect religious freedom, Trump was greenlighting a radical transformation of the reviled "administrative state" from a tool of anti-Christian bureaucrats to the domain of heroic defenders of the religious freedom of Christians beaten down by eight years of Obama. His political appointees had their marching orders, and they were ready to carry them out in short order.

The Department of Health and Human Services (HHS) has been ground zero for many of these "religious freedom" and "conscience" initiatives. A sprawling agency of nearly eighty thousand employees and an annual budget in excess of one trillion dollars, it has a vast mandate related to health care and social services. It oversees a range of services that touch the life of nearly every American: Medicare and Medicaid, food and drug safety, disease control and prevention, health research and policy, refugee resettlement, adoption and foster care, substance abuse treatment, and much more. From the very outset of the Trump presidency, the administration began stacking the agency with political appointees who would prioritize restricting abortion and contraception access, scale back Obama-era efforts to protect LGBTQ rights, and broaden the ways in which social services providers—working with the agency as taxpayer-funded grantees and contractors—could refuse to refer clients for reproductive health care, to serve LGBTQ people or non-Christians—all in the name of protecting "religious freedom."

Like many federal agencies, HHS has an Office of Civil Rights (OCR), which is tasked with enforcing antidiscrimination, health privacy, and conscience laws and protecting access to health care for vulnerable groups. The conscience laws the office is charged with enforcing were enacted in the years after the Supreme Court's deci-sion in *Roe*. They include the 1973 Church Amendment, which requires federally funded health care facilities to allow providers to opt out of participating in abortion, sterilization, or other procedures to which they have religious or moral objections; the 1996 Coats-Snowe Amendment, which extends those same protections to medi-cal students and residents; and the 2004 Weldon Amendment, which extends these conscience exemptions related to abortion to a broader range of "health care entities."[16] Since these rules were enacted, only a handful of complaints have been filed with the HHS OCR, usually ending in settlements in which a particular health care worker was excused from having to participate in a procedure. But after the Wel-don Amendment's extension of abortion protections to that wider swath of "health care entities," as opposed to individual providers, Christian right legal advocates have sought to push the envelope. They have aimed to try to punish blue states for enacting laws that protected access to abortion, or guaranteed insurance coverage for it. And since the conscience laws condition federal funding—such as to a hospital—for violating a doctor's or nurse's conscience rights, these legal advocates reasoned, perhaps the federal hammer could be brought down on entire states, depriving them of critical federal funding from HHS, which covers a wide range of social welfare and safety net services like Medicare, Medicaid, food stamps, Head Start, and more.

Their first target, not surprisingly, was the big blue state of Cali-fornia. There state regulators had simply notified health insurers in the state of their obligation, under state law, to provide coverage for abortion. In 2014, Casey Mattox and Matthew Bowman, then both attorneys at ADF, together with an attorney from the Life Legal Defense Foundation, an antichoice advocacy group, brought a com-plaint to Obama's OCR, charging that the state had violated the con-science rights of six California churches and a Christian school by notifying their health insurance carriers of the abortion coverage rule.[17] But only the churches and school, not the health insurance companies, objected to the coverage—meaning that there wasn't a "health care entity" that had raised a conscience objection. Jocelyn Samuels, a seasoned civil rights attorney who was then the head of the OCR, found no violation. In her letter to the complainants closing the case after a two-year investigation, she also noted the possible unconstitutionality of finding a violation against an entire state, as the complainants had requested. A finding of a violation, she wrote, could require the government to cut off all funding to the state—crucial money it receives not only from HHS but also from the Departments of Education and Labor, which are funded in the same appropriations bill.[18] The remedy the complainants sought could have been catastrophic—for one of the bluest states in the nation.

Christian right advocates were furious with Samuels's decision. Mattox accused the Obama administration of "making a mockery of the law" and vowed that the ADF would "continue to defend churches from this clear violation of the 1st Amendment and federal law and call on Congress to hold HHS accountable." Speaking just days before the 2016 election at the Catholic Information Center, a hub for conservative Catholic Washington insiders, Bowman falsely accused Obama's OCR of trying to force all health care facilities, including Catholic hospitals, to perform abortions. "This is a serious issue about whether health care professionals, whether health care facilities will be able to practice medicine consistent with their beliefs," he said. Under "the view, apparently, of the HHS OCR, all women who are pregnant will have to have their babies delivered at abortion clinics. Because there will only be abortion clinics because all Catholic hospitals will be abortion clinics, everyone has to do abortions."[19] Before becoming a lawyer, Bowman had numerous run-ins with the law himself, stemming from his attempts to block women from entering abortion clinics and his participation in aggressive protests at various locations, including a high school, Senate office, and Disney World.[20] Under Trump, he served as deputy general counsel at HHS, where, among other duties, he provided legal advice to the OCR, and later became principal adviser to the OCR's director.

To lead the Office of Civil Rights in this new era of civil rights, Trump tapped Roger Severino, who had most recently been the director of the DeVos Center for Religion and Civil Society at the Heritage Foundation. Severino, a Harvard-educated lawyer, had also worked at the Becket Fund for Religious Liberty, the conservative legal advocacy firm that famously represented the Green family of Hobby Lobby craft stores, who challenged the HHS contraception coverage rule and won at the Supreme Court. In his high-visibility Heritage Foundation post, Severino all but auditioned to serve in a Republican administration keen on turning civil rights protections, particularly for LGBTQ people, upside down. After Mississippi governor Phil Bryant signed that state's "religious freedom" bill, Severino advanced the claim that Christians are the victims, cheering that Bryant had stood up to "liberal bullies." He described the law as "precise and balanced," even as it gave government clerks, universities, social service providers, landlords, doctors, bakers, photographers, florists, and private businesses the ability to legally discriminate against people based on their sexual orientation, gender identity, marital status, and more. To Severino, this meant that "religious adoption agencies can continue to operate by their conviction that every child they serve deserves to be placed with a married mom and dad," that wedding vendors "cannot be forced to use their talents to celebrate same-sex weddings if they cannot do so in good conscience," and that schools and businesses, "not bureaucrats, get to set their own bathroom, shower, and locker room policies."[21]

"For decades," he wrote on the Heritage Foundation website, "the left has attempted to raise sexual orientation and gender identity to special protected status through Congress." After Republican majorities blocked these efforts, Obama shifted gears to "issuing various edicts that misinterpret existing civil rights protections to include sexual orientation and gender identity," including his 2014 executive order that barred discrimination against LGBTQ people by federal contractors. When Trump signs executive orders, the Christian right cheers. But when Obama signed one, Severino charged he had "unilaterally elevated sexual orientation and gender identity to special status." He accused Obama of interpreting religious conscience protections "narrowly in order to make religious groups bend to the LGBT agenda," concluding that his administration had a "proven lack of respect for religious freedom" in its push to expand LGBTQ rights.[22]

Severino specifically derided the actions of the office he would later be appointed to lead. He attacked the Obama regulation known as Section 1557, protecting transgender patient rights, saying it posed a risk of "serious conflict with long-standing and widely accepted law and policies protecting conscience." Enforcement of Section 1557 became Severino's responsibility as head of the OCR—and the regulation was immediately slated for eradication.[23] Under Severino's leadership, the OCR also sought to reverse what he and other partisans contended was the Obama administration's insufficient protection of the "conscience" rights of opponents of abortion, such as Samuels's closure of the California case—moves that involved turning the office's priorities on their head.

Once installed at the OCR, Severino proceeded to hire staff from leading Christian right organizations who had track records of advocating for special religious protections for people who oppose abortion and LGBTQ rights, and against access to health care for women. As his chief of staff, he hired March Bell, whose previous appointments included serving as staff director and chief counsel for the Select Investigative Panel on Infant Lives, an investigative committee Republicans launched in 2015 in reaction to the Center for Medical Progress's deceptive Planned Parenthood videos—with the goal of ending all federal family planning funding for the organization.[24] From the Family Research Council came Mandi Ancalle, who had served as the organization's general counsel for government affairs, as a contract policy adviser. At the 2016 Values Voter Summit, Ancalle revealed that she was "working to generate a comprehensive list" of policy priorities for a potential Trump administration that included reviving the Bush-era conscience rule, rescinded by Obama, that gave health care workers religious exemptions from treating women, LGBTQ people, or others based on religious objections. She noted that the Family Research Council "wants to make sure that new regulations allow physicians not to care for transgender patients"—referring to the religious right's goal of eliminating the transgender protections in Section 1557.[25]

When Severino was first named to the post, twelve Democratic senators, led by Washington's Patty Murray, wrote to then–HHS secretary Tom Price, saying they were "deeply troubled" by the decision, citing Severino's "long history of making bigoted statements toward lesbian, gay, bisexual, and transgender people and attacking women's access to health care services and reproductive rights." Severino's "past statements, writings, and affiliations make him unqualified to lead an office whose purpose is to ensure that 'people have equal access and opportunities to participate in certain health care and human services programs without unlawful discrimination,'" they wrote.[26] But to Christian right legal pundits like Matthew Franck of the conservative think tank the Witherspoon Institute, Severino was "just the right person to correct the course of HHS's efforts at enforcing anti-discrimination principles in federal law" who would restore the OCR's "true mission"[27]—protecting the "conscience" of religious objectors. To Severino, it was "my honor to be a member of an Administration that is dedicated to religious freedom and of reining in the excesses of the administrative state to return it to its constitutional moorings," he told a Federalist Society gathering months after he assumed the helm of the OCR. "As the state tends to grow, religious liberty tends to shrink."[28] As he spoke—calling for a shrinking of government—he was looking to expand it, putting together an entirely new division within the OCR for the sole purpose of protecting "conscience" and "religious freedom."

On a bitter cold January day, about a year into the Trump presidency, at HHS headquarters, Christian right activists and agency employees—some stunned by the event but obliged to be on hand anyway—gathered in the Great Hall on the first floor of the brutalist federal building just blocks from the Capitol. The mood was festive; activists who had known and networked together for years were ebullient about their new political muscle in Trump's Washington. They had come to the invitation-only event to watch the formal announcement of a new Conscience and Religious Freedom Division within the agency's Office of Civil Rights. The new division was now, Severino told the crowd, "open for business."

Although the event was open to the media, it was designed more as a cheerleading session for Christian right ideologues than as an effort to inform the public. Reporters were cordoned off in the back of the room, away from both the speakers and the invited guests. Severino and nine other speakers—including HHS deputy secretary Eric Hargan, House majority leader Kevin McCarthy, Missouri congresswoman Vicky Hartzler, and Oklahoma senator James Lankford—gave prepared remarks, after which there was no question and answer session for the assembled media. They were instead instructed, by Charmaine Yoest, a longtime antichoice activist and former president of Americans United for Life, who was serving as an undersecretary for public affairs, to email any questions to Arina Grossu, a contractor on loan to the department from the Family Research Council. Grossu did not respond. Severino acted as the master of ceremonies and opened the festivities with a broadside against his predecessors at the agency, who had "not always been the best keeper" of religious freedom, "a civil right that deserves complete enforcement and respect."

Severino then turned to some historical analogies that served only to highlight his astonishing misapprehension of history and of civil rights. He recalled learning about religious conscience as a child, after seeing a photograph of shoe insoles that Nazis forced Jews to wear, with Hebrew words sewn into them, which would force the Jews to violate their conscience with every step they took. "It struck me as a child, then, the wrongness of that action," he said, calling it an "attack on their human dignity." (Never mind that the Nazis were burning and looting their homes and shipping Jews off like cattle to concentration camps and near certain extermination; the shoes were the real affront, apparently, to Severino.) He then segued to the Rev. Martin Luther King, Jr., and his "Letter from Birmingham Jail." King's famous letter provides regular fodder to contemporary Christian right activists—heirs to the earlier New Right influencers and politicians who spread conspiracy theories about him—as a cautionary tale about how the government oppresses Christians. But King was thrown in the Birmingham jail not because police in the Jim Crow South were antireligion but because segregationist law enforcement charged he had no right to protest segregation there. Severino's invocation of King's name and his famous letter awkwardly compared King's advocacy for basic human rights for black people—to be able to attend the same schools, eat in the same restaurants, drink from the same water fountains, vote, and be free from intimidation and violence by police and citizen posses—to someone angered that their health insurance policy covered abortion.

The division Severino is now leading will consider, as an appropriate penalty for providing or even talking about abortion, the elimination of all federal funding to an entire state, potentially stripping poor children and the elderly of health care and eliminating countless other services to citizens. The OCR has not yet taken such an extreme action—and as Samuels pointed out in her letter closing the 2014 California complaint, if it did, it would face immediate constitutional challenges. But Severino and his allies in outside advocacy groups actively encouraged people to file complaints seeking just such a remedy. "For eight years, former President Obama's administration turned a blind eye to these injustices, despite numerous federal laws protecting pro-life conscience rights," wrote David Christensen, the vice-president for governmental affairs at the Family Research Council, in an email to supporters. The email even suggested that Americans would be performing a civic duty by filing a complaint: "To stop these injustices, President Trump's administration needs pro-life Americans who have been directly harmed to file a complaint." The email then offered a tutorial on how to file a complaint.[29] By the summer of 2019, the division had received 1,300 complaints, retaining 784 of them to investigate for possible violations.

At the Conscience and Religious Freedom Division unveiling, Severino said he was launching the new division because of a "rise of complaints on religious freedom and conscience," as if the uptick had been spontaneous.[30] To Severino's predecessor Samuels, it looked like he was trying "to prioritize defending the rights of health care professionals to deny care" over "focusing on the goals of the civil rights laws to expand access to health coverage and to eliminate barriers for vulnerable people, communities that have been subjected to discrimination over time."[31]

The OCR was not the only division within the vast Department of Health and Human Services seeking to upend civil rights protections. The Administration for Children and Families (ACF) oversees, through its programs and contracts and grants with outside contractors and nonprofits, a panoply of essential services including foster care and migrant and refugee services to children and minors. The ACF is the HHS division that oversees the facilities in which children torn from their parents through Trump's family separation policy are detained. Yet this did not appear to upset Trump's allies in the Christian right, who were more focused on activities like that of Scott Lloyd, now the former head of the Office of Refugee Resettlement within the ACF, who tried to personally bar a teenager who had arrived in the United States as an unaccompanied minor from having an abortion. (He was not successful.) But Christian right partisans had other successes. Miracle Hill Ministries, a Christian foster care placement agency in South Carolina, obtained an exemption from having to comply with federal nondiscrimination laws after a direct appeal to ACF by the state's governor, Henry McMaster, a Trump ally, so that it could place foster children only with Protestant Christian families. Before McMaster's intervention, and ACF's agreement to give Miracle Hill the exemption, the placement agency was at risk of losing its state license because of its refusal to comply with the federal nondiscrimination law that required it to place children with families without regard to religion.[32] In 2019, the department set in motion the administrative process to enact a regulation expanding such an exemption to every religious adoption and foster care placement agency across the nation.

Beyond HHS, the Trump administration is engaged in a wide-ranging effort to elevate religious freedom for conservative Christians, and to scale back civil rights protections on the basis of sex, sexual orientation, gender identity, race, and more. At the Department of Education, Secretary Betsy DeVos rescinded Obama-era guidance, issued by the department's OCR, to public schools to allow transgender students to use the bathroom or locker room of their gender identity. She later announced her department would not even investigate any complaints by transgender students of discrimination—even though she knew about studies showing "alarming" levels of transgender youth attempting suicide.[33]

While Christian right allies in the Trump administration elevate the rights of conservative Christians to discriminate against others and to alter the way social services are provided across the country, under his watch countless civil rights protections on the basis of race are at risk of being scaled back or eliminated. Education secretary DeVos has also revoked an Obama-era initiative aimed at reducing proven racial disparities in school discipline,[34] which had put public schools on notice of their "obligations to avoid and redress racial discrimination in the administration of student discipline."[35] She has sought to roll back protections for minority students with disabilities.[36] Department of Housing and Urban Development officials halted implementation of an Obama-era rule that required localities to study and develop plans to reverse racial segregation in housing,[37] removed language promising inclusion and nondiscrimination from its mission statement,[38] and put on hold investigations into violations of the Fair Housing Act, which prohibits discrimination in housing.[39] At the Department of State, career staffers were ordered to scale back language in a global human rights report that historically had addressed women's rights, family planning, and abortion, as well as discussion of racial, ethnic, and sexual discrimination.[40] The Office of Fair Lending and Equal Opportunity, which investigated and enforced laws barring discrimination in lending at the Consumer Financial Protection Bureau, was stripped of those enforcement powers.[41] And in what might be the Trump administration's most chilling move showing its dereliction of the promise of civil rights laws to end discrimination and its effects, the Department of Justice signaled a government-wide retreat on pursuing any civil rights violations if there was no proof of discriminatory intent but only disparate impact on a protected class. If implemented, such a government-wide policy could strike a potentially fatal blow to redressing the deleterious effects of policies that, on their face, do not evince a discriminatory intent but have discriminatory effects—in housing, education, employment, banking, and more.[42]

These ambitions might have been lost to history had Merrick Garland been confirmed to the Supreme Court or had Hillary Clinton become president. As a Supreme Court justice, Garland would have given the liberal wing of the Court a 5–4 majority; a Clinton presidency would have, even with GOP control of both houses of Congress, continued the Obama legacy of making advances for civil rights. Even in the face of a recalcitrant Congress, Clinton could have, like Obama, pursued goals of equal rights at the agency level. But now religious right—and white nationalist—goals could be cemented with the Supreme Court's solid, dependable conservative majority, making the radical unwinding of the promise of civil rights and equality the law of the land for at least a generation. The Trump presidency put all these goals within reach. Majority Leader Mitch McConnell's smug audacity in refusing Garland even a hearing, along with Trump's brazenly false claims of a landslide victory giving him a mandate, together opened multiple entry points for the Christian right to turn back the clock on civil rights advances.

Trump had a deep well of talent from which to draw his political appointees to carry out the religious right's wishes. Christian right lawyers and policy makers, educated at colleges and law schools like Regent and Liberty universities, and trained at Christian right legal advocacy and policy organizations like the ADF, the Family Research Council, and the Heritage Foundation, were ready to accept political appointments at key agencies like the Departments of Justice, Health and Human Services, and Education. They came from the ranks of legal and policy organizations that had litigated cases on behalf of Christians who refused service to gay couples or contraception coverage for their employees, had lobbied state legislatures to oppose nondiscrimination legislation to protect the rights of LGBTQ people, and had pushed for "religious freedom" bills that would give those Christians the right to elevate their religious conscience over other people's rights. They were handpicked from networks of culture warriors who regularly argued in public, on the radio, on television, in op-eds, that these ideas were mainstream, casting conservative Christians as victims of—once again—"social engineering."

Their allies in the Federalist Society and the Judicial Crisis Network were primed to hand Trump an extensive list of ideologically like-minded judicial nominees and to wage multimillion-dollar dark money campaigns to get them confirmed. One of Trump's signature achievements for the conservative movement has been his compliant stacking of the federal judiciary with nominees who have espoused extreme right-wing views on race, LGBTQ rights, abortion, and religion and state issues. Trump's nominees to lifetime appointments in trial and appellate courts have alarmed civil rights advocates, especially as Majority Leader McConnell has jettisoned any Senate oversight role in favor of working with the president to erode an independent judiciary—a sweeping sabotage of the entire system of checks and balances. What's more, the overwhelming majority of Trump's judicial nominees are male and white. By the summer of 2019, 80 percent of his nominees confirmed to appellate judgeships, and 74 percent of his nominees confirmed to the trial court bench, were men, compared to 56 and 59 percent, respectively, for Obama's nominees. Eighty-six percent of his confirmed appellate nominees and 90 percent of his confirmed trial court choices were white, compared to Obama's appellate and trial court selections, who were 65 and 63 percent white respectively.[43]

Many of Trump's judges are skeptical of—if not outright hostile to—the legal structure protecting civil rights. Eleven Trump nominees refused to say during their confirmation hearings whether *Brown v. Board* was correctly decided.[44] Others have openly derided diversity and pluralism. Neomi Rao, whom the Senate confirmed to fill Brett Kavanaugh's seat on the powerful D.C. Circuit Court of Appeals after he was elevated to the Supreme Court, had written in a 1994 tirade against "the multicultural college campus" that the "multiculturalists are the self-appointed heirs of the civil rights movement," who promote "divisiveness not togetherness" as they "seek to undermine American culture."[45] Trump and his Senate allies, led by Majority Leader McConnell, have, according to the Leadership Conference on Civil and Human Rights, done "everything they can to reshape the federal judiciary to roll back our civil and human rights at record speed."[46] But for some conservatives, any opposition amounts to persecution of Christians. After it was reported that Trump judicial nominee Gordon Giampietro once wrote on a Catholic website that "calls for diversity" are "code for relaxed standards (moral and intellectual),"[47] Democrats achieved a rare success in blocking his nomination to the U.S. District Court for the Eastern District of Wisconsin. *The Federalist*, a conservative news and opinion site that is frequently a mouthpiece for the Trump administration, complained that "for the crime of publicly voicing the teachings of his faith, Giampietro will never sit on the federal bench."[48] Instead of women being the victims of sexism or black Americans the victims of racism, conservative Christians have become the victims of "political correctness."

The political machinery that has enabled Trump in what will likely be his most lasting assault on America's democratic institutions arose out of an organized conservative backlash to Reagan's failed 1987 Supreme Court nomination of Robert Bork. The former solicitor general under Richard Nixon was famous for his role in the Saturday Night Massacre, in which the president ordered the firing of the Watergate special prosecutor; Ronald Reagan later successfully nominated Bork to the U.S. Court of Appeals for the D.C. Circuit. Weyrich's Free Congress Foundation was on the front lines of the fight over Bork's Supreme Court nomination, but there was "insufficient organization of ideas and messaging on the conservative side of things compared to the left side," recalled Patrick McGuigan, a former Weyrich lieutenant who ran the Free Congress programs on the judiciary. McGuigan and another conservative activist, Daniel Casey, at the time the executive director of the American Conservative Union, were a two-man team leading the conservative support for Bork in the face of robust liberal opposition.[49] The dust jacket of *Ninth Justice,* a book McGuigan wrote with Weyrich's daughter Dawn, a meticulous retelling of every twist and turn in the Bork confirmation fight, describes McGuigan and Casey as "intensely Republican, devout Catholics, ardent admirers of the nominee—who understood from the first moment of the battle that they were involved in the most significant political confrontation of their lives."

This was war.

As much as the conservative mythology around Bork has portrayed him as a victim, his views on a number of issues were, even at the time, well outside the political and legal mainstream. Bork and his defenders maintained that his views were based not in animus but in his "originalist" view of the constitution. Whatever label was affixed to the Bork judicial ideology, his positions were shaped by his antipathy, shared with the New Right, to legal changes in the 1960s made to protect the rights of minorities and women. Bork had opposed the 1964 Civil Rights Act, which prohibited discrimination in public accommodations, writing prior to its passage that such protections were based on a "principle of unsurpassed ugliness." He rejected Supreme Court legal rulings that had found a constitutional right to privacy, the legal underpinning not only of *Roe v. Wade,* which struck down laws criminalizing abortion, but also *Griswold v. Connecticut,* an earlier case that invalidated state criminalization of the sale of contraceptives.[50] During Bork's confirmation hearings, Sen. Orrin Hatch asked him if any Supreme Court case had stirred more controversy and criticism than *Roe;* Bork, seemingly oblivious, identified *Brown v. Board,* a case that was most certainly not even remotely controversial by 1987.[51] Massachusetts Democrat Ted Kennedy, who led the Senate opposition to Bork, warned of the judge's view of America as "a land in which women would be forced into back-alley abortions, blacks would sit at segregated lunch counters," and "the doors of the federal courts would be shut on the fingers of millions of citizens for whom the judiciary is often the only protector of the individual rights that are the heart of our democracy."

Weyrich urged conservatives to show liberals "that they could not simply destroy conservative nominees en masse and get away with it."[52] He and other conservatives were determined to exploit the political tools available to them to create a judiciary that would reject the civil-rights-era consensus and to persuade the public that it was that consensus that was outside the mainstream, not conservative jurisprudence. They would convince their base that this new, scorched-earth strategy—using every financial, rhetorical, and parliamentary tool at their disposal to push through the most conservative judicial nominees over any objection of Democrats—was proof that the democratic process worked, because it was all done in defense of the base's "traditional" values and therefore represented the will of the people.

The high-stakes and very public Bork loss vividly evoked conservative resentments that the civil rights era had corrupted their cultural and social prerogatives and established future nominations to the nation's highest court as the ground on which America's culture wars would be fought. After the Bork nomination failed, in his stead, President Reagan nominated Anthony Kennedy, who would go on to author one of the most reviled Supreme Court opinions among American conservatives: *Lawrence v. Texas,* the 2003 decision that ruled criminal antisodomy laws unconstitutional—a ruling that created the legal building blocks for the decision, twelve years later, in *Obergefell v. Hodges,* striking down bans on same-sex marriage nationwide. Conservative activists were determined not only to prevent another Bork defeat and another insufficiently ideological pick like Kennedy but also to block future Democratic nominees at all costs. They worked for years to enhance the conservative political apparatus with organizations that could lobby Congress and wage battle in the court of public opinion in order to promote what conservative legal thinkers call "originalists" like Bork to combat what conservative activists deride as the courts' "judicial activism"—meaning the protection of the rights of historically unprotected groups.

During the Bork hearings, Dan Casey argued that "the American people should be outraged that the liberals are spending millions of dollars to try to buy a Supreme Court seat."[53] Today Casey—who

politely declined to speak with me when I called him in 2018, as
the Senate was gearing up for confirmation hearings for Brett Kavanaugh's Supreme Court nomination—is no longer with the American Conservative Union. Today he works nearly completely off the
public radar, quietly serving as president of the Judicial Crisis Network and other related organizations, the heart of a conservative
political operation created to prevent another Bork debacle, and
whose multimillion-dollar funding is shrouded in mystery.

Casey's Judicial Crisis Network is the top organization in a
multimillion-dollar dark-money advocacy campaign that grew out of
the conservative backlash to the failed Bork nomination.[54] Founded
after the 2004 presidential election as the Judicial Confirmation Network, to influence senators to confirm George W. Bush's nominees in
the newly Republican-controlled Senate, the organization developed
heavy-handed tactics to shape public opinion, state by state, to pressure red-state Democrats to vote for Bush nominees. After Obama was
elected, the group changed its name to the Judicial Crisis Network
(JCN) and worked to thwart the confirmation of his nominees; in
opposing Sonia Sotomayor's 2009 nomination to the Supreme Court,
the group called the future justice "a liberal judicial activist of the first
order who thinks her own personal political agenda is more important
than the law as written."[55] JCN's tactics did not stop either Sotomay-
or's or Elena Kagan's confirmations, but in 2016, the JCN spent
$7 million on ads successfully opposing Obama's nomination of Mer-
rick Garland to the Supreme Court. The ads ominously painted Garland as part of a villainous Obama power grab. Obama has "ignored
the Constitution for years," one of the ads said. "Now in his last days,
President Obama wants to add a liberal justice to the Supreme Court."
Targeted once again at voters in purple states with Democratic senators, the ads demanded that voters not let Obama and their senator
"stack the Supreme Court. Let the people decide."[56]

Despite the stakes, the public cannot find out where that money
came from, because there is no legal requirement that the identity of
the donor of a massive $17.9 million contribution to the group be
disclosed.[57] When Trump nominated Brett Kavanaugh to the high

court two years later, the JCN portrayed him as the regular person's choice, touting him as a "grand slam for conservatives" and warning Democrats that they should not succumb to "pressure from East Coast liberals."[58]

The mutual dependence between Trump and the religious right persists not in spite of his scandalous presidency but because of it. The movement desperately needed a savior; Trump was eager to oblige because of his bottomless need for a worshipful retinue. Trump and the religious right, then, are each essential to the other's success. For Trump, success is evading culpability for a dizzying mess of political and financial corruption, and carrying out his xenophobic goals of sealing the country from "invasions" of black and brown people. For the Christian right, success is flipping the script on civil rights, casting conservative Christians as the real victims of prejudice and discrimination, undermining the separation of church and state, and implementing a totalizing legal structure of "biblical" law. Their symbiotic relationship, in which Christian right leaders regularly glorify Trump, and Trump in turn gives them carte blanche to radically reshape law and policy, has brought the country closer to the Christian right's aspirations than it ever has been in the movement's history.

Trump has so advanced the Christian right's personnel and policy ambitions that it's unlikely the movement would be copacetic with turning back the clock when—and however—his presidency ends. But the turn toward increasingly theocratic and autocratic governance did not emerge solely from the peculiarities of the movement's relationship with Trump. Under the cover of protecting "Christian" values, the Christian right has enmeshed itself in the global wave of right-wing authoritarianism, and evinces admiration for the same nativist despots who have inspired the alt-right. Trump, then, is not the only exemplar for the new leadership that will turn back the clock on democracy and human rights. For the Christian right, America's future leaders also should be looking toward these foreign autocrats for inspiration.

8

The End of American Exceptionalism

The religious right and the alt-right are bonded together by shared grievances over a supposedly lost America in which Christians don't have to bake cakes for gay couples and white people don't have to bow to "multiculturalism" or "political correctness." But this fused political bloc does not actually long for a mythical past of the formerly "great" America that Trump idealized for them. Instead, it envisions a future in which America, and the hard-won values it codified over the past seven decades—desegregation and church-state separation by the Supreme Court; laws passed by Congress to protect the rights of minorities such as the Civil Rights Act, the Voting Rights Act, and the 1965 Immigration Act; the advance of rights for women and LGBTQ people—loses its standing as a moral and political leader in the world and is transformed into a nativist power that accords different rights to different groups of people, based on race, religion, and ethnicity. For the ideologues of this bloc, America has so lost its bearings that they must look now to leadership outside of the United States to lead it out of an abyss. Their shared target: modern, pluralistic liberal democracy that is led by what they would disparage as "globalists" who are destroying "Western civilization."

Once again Weyrich's career presaged the turn toward the post-Communist eastern bloc so evident in today's Trumpist right. In the late 1980s, when Communism's fall was on the horizon, and into the 1990s, Weyrich devoted considerable energy to recast the culture wars as a global endeavor. To Weyrich, an ardent anti-Communist, the fall of the Iron Curtain meant not just the end of a reviled ideology and totalitarian regimes but a chance for a "Christendom" that had fallen away to be reborn. America could well have some new allies, not just geopolitically but, more important, spiritually. "If the Judeo-Christian culture is to survive and renew itself," he wrote, "it needs to reunite—from California to a non-communist Russia."[1] In his revised culture war, Communists were replaced by "cultural Marxists" as the global enemy, which included a fifth column in the United States.

Alt-right funder Bill Regnery recalled to me having conversations about "what happens when the wall comes down," and he said that Weyrich "was involved in some overtures to right wingers, or those he perceived to be somewhat right wing, in Russia."[2] After the fall of Communism, Weyrich began making regular trips to Russia and the former Soviet states, training activists in organizing and campaign strategies he had honed in his years in American politics. Friends described him as "energized" and "having fun" in his travels there.[3] He backed the presidential campaign of Boris Yeltsin and later became a cheerleader of Vladimir Putin.

Weyrich and Institute for Cultural Conservatism director William Lind presented a new alliance with Russia as an essential component for saving "Christendom" from Islam. In a commentary on Weyrich's *Direct Line,* a program on his short-lived National Empowerment Television network, Lind argued that Russia "holds the West's—and Christendom's—vast open flank that faces east and south. If that flank collapses, we will soon find Islam once again at the gates of Vienna." Lind was invoking what has become a staple of Islamophobic demagoguery—that the

1683 battle between the Ottoman and the Holy Roman empires means that Christian Europeans should always be on the lookout for Muslim invasions and repel them. But for Lind, the Washington "establishment" failed to recognize Russia's critical strategic importance to the United States, in the context of what Lind believed was a third world war already in motion. "It is a war of Islam against everyone else," he argued, and "Russia is Christendom's most important barrier against Islam." Lind told a conference of U.S. and Russian policy makers, organized by the Free Congress Foundation in 2001, that "Holy Russia" should be "America's most important ally."[4]

The terrorist attacks of 9/11 only intensified these arguments. The Bush administration did make a strategic alliance with Putin's Russia to fight terrorism, but for Weyrich, this was not enough—he pushed for a spiritual alliance, too. He pressed, in his daily commentary posted on his website in 2002, for an expansion of the U.S.-Russia relationship so that the two countries "will become real partners and what was once Christendom will again be united." Putin, Weyrich acknowledged, "is not perfect," but all things considered, "I would much rather be dealing with a leader who proclaims that Russia should once again seek to be known as Holy Russia by returning to her Christian roots than with some of the ugly alternatives waiting in the wings."[5]

During the George W. Bush presidency, Weyrich's Free Congress Foundation continued to champion closer U.S.-Russian ties, NATO membership for Russia, and a celebration of Russia's embrace of its "Christian culture."[6] He scoffed at then–secretary of state Colin Powell for having "upbraided Putin for his seeming lack of concern for political and human rights." Putin, Weyrich believed, was the "iron fist" that Russians were looking for, even as he admitted that the Russian leader had eliminated his political opposition and taken over the media, hallmarks of a tightening autocratic grip. "Their system may not end up looking the way we would prefer," Weyrich wrote, minimizing these concerns, "but if we can count on Russia as an ally, why should we fret?" He urged U.S. policy makers to put pressure on Russia only privately and to continue to build an alliance with "Christian" Russia against Islam.[7]

In a signal of things to come, Weyrich was not alone among Republicans in pressing for closer ties to the Russian strongman. At Weyrich's 2002 conference aimed at bolstering this alliance in defense of "Christendom," Dana Rohrabacher, the California congressman who once served as a speechwriter in the Reagan White House, said that "Russia is terrific" and the two countries "are going to be best friends." Foreshadowing the rise of the anti-EU far right in Europe, and Trump's embrace of it, Rohrabacher declared the U.S. alliance with Europe to be "history." He even called for the elimination of NATO—a radical idea that Trump would resuscitate, to the dismay of European allies, more than a decade later.[8]

Weyrich's 2004 conference, this time held in a Senate office building, was framed as a debate over whether the United States should pressure Russia to uphold democratic institutions and values, in alignment with the long-standing, bipartisan foreign policy consensus. The conference, according to the Free Congress's promotional materials, would examine "whether the United States is too aggressive in urging Russia to adopt 'Democracy U.S.-style.'" It criticized a push in the House of Representatives to condition Russian participation in the G-8 on its voluntary adherence to "the norms and standards of democracy." (Russia would be expelled from the G-8 in 2014, after its invasion of Ukraine and annexation of Crimea; in 2018 Trump would stun the world when he called for letting Russia back in, even though "it may not be politically correct.") Back in 2004, Weyrich, too, had waved off concerns that Russia was flouting democratic norms, suggesting that instead of mimicking American democracy, perhaps Russia should be "permitted to find its own way."[9] Trump may have had other interests in forging closer ties with Putin—an interest, perhaps, in building a Trump Tower in Moscow, rather than zeal for a united Christendom—but Weyrich was an early visionary for the GOP right flank's growing appetite for authoritarianism abroad, even before Trump's brazen embrace of it.

• • •

Weyrich's political progeny have acted on these same impulses, building an increasingly global presence of right-wing Christians united against a supposedly decadent, sexualized, and diverse West. At the World Congress of Families in Chişinău, Moldova—where, in 2018, the American anti-abortion activist Thomas Jacobson praised Donald Trump to me as carrying out a "divine mandate"—this global alliance bent on weakening liberal democracy was on stark display. Inside Chişinău's Palace of the Republic, leading activists of the Christian and nativist right from the United States, Russia, and Europe mingled before entering the high-ceilinged ballroom for a morning of ceremony and speeches. Stoic young guards in elaborate military uniforms adorned with gold cords, red epaulets, and embroidered capes, some with bayonets in hand, lined the curving marble staircase and expansive foyer. As guests trickled into the ballroom, lined with lush, caramel velvet draperies and lit by ornate crystal chandeliers, they were treated to music by a live orchestra, dance performances by Moldovan women and girls in virginal white dresses, and videos projected onto a jumbo screen of joyous couples frolicking with their children in the verdant countryside. Over the course of the two-day conference, the ideal of an idyllic life of fertile rural families was exalted in speeches and reinforced in dances, posters, slide shows, videos, and song. It was relentlessly depicted as under assault by decadent liberalism—a global menace imposing "gender ideology," "aggressive feminism," and "death culture" on "the natural family."

Igor Dodon, then the Putin-aligned Moldovan president, made a grand entrance, accompanied by military pageantry, to deliver a grim speech in which he railed against "an anti-family ideology, which is artificially propagated all over the world." He called for a comprehensive national program in which the government would enlist the Orthodox Church, mass media, and civil society to jointly "promote family values in the society." He warned that any "festivals and other events that promote immoral principles"—referring to gay pride parades—could be outlawed.[10]

The theme of the 2018 conference was "Uniting East and West"—promoting the idea that the Cold War was long over, and that the United States and western European countries no longer faced the intractable ideological differences that once divided them from the Communist world. Instead, conservatives of the West must unite with their brethren in the former Soviet bloc in opposition to Western liberalism, particularly its emphasis on individual rights over that of the "natural family."

As became evident over the course of the weekend of speeches and glad-handing, "uniting east and west" was about Western social conservatives embracing the rising right-wing authoritarianism in Eastern countries as an antidote to what they claimed was the decadence and moral rot of the West. For them, liberal democracy was the root cause of that decline; greater authoritarianism was the answer.

This gaze eastward was an extraordinary shift for the American Christian right. Deeply woven into the movement's DNA was the idealization of divinely ordained, Christian America that was the leader of the free world against the forces of Communism and totalitarianism. But now, many in the Christian right believed that America had failed as a role model for the rest of the world—that liberalism, unrestrained, had fatally compromised American exceptionalism. American conservatives, then, needed to find new allies, not in secular liberal Europe but in the rising autocracies that were posing a threat to it. "Around the world there are those who don't wish for unity, who don't have the same vision of truth and of family," Brian Brown, the American president of the International Organization for the Family, the parent organization of the World Congress, said in his opening speech. Moldova, by contrast, was "blessed with a president that is willing to stand for truth." Brown assured the gathering that while "some in the U.S. and Western Europe continue to question this" and "some want to use the Russia investigation to divide us," these "attempts to muddy the water are attempts to stop us from creating unity around family." The World Congress of Families gathering had moved east, Brown said, because "we've been welcomed."[11]

For Brown, a forty-four-year-old father of nine who was raised in Orange County, California, as a "rock-ribbed anti-Communist" and served as the president of his College Republicans, looking to the former Soviet bloc for inspiration was an unexpected development. He told me in Chişinău that for his type of conservative, "the notion that, now, that Russia can be doing good things, it's a tough—it can be a tough turn." But to Brown, liberals had exploited human rights to undermine the "traditional" family, while Russia was upholding those traditions, in part by cracking down on the human rights of LGBTQ people. The idea that "same-sex marriage is a right is false in the first place," he told me. One of the central guiding principles of the World Congress of Families is that the Universal Declaration of Human Rights—the landmark 1948 document adopted by the United Nations in the wake of the horrors of World War II—was never intended to, in Brown's words, "undermine the rights of the family." For Brown, the rights of women to reproductive freedom, and of LGBTQ people to equality, are the primary examples of how this "false" human rights framework was a mortal threat to the "natural family."

Brown made his name in American politics by waging a years-long campaign against the legalization of same-sex marriage, as the president of the National Organization for Marriage, a post he still held alongside his international work. Seeing the writing on the wall, he began building an international movement against LGBTQ rights before the Supreme Court's landmark 2015 decision legalizing same-sex marriage. In the mid-2010s, as the United States was moving rapidly toward greater LGBTQ equality, Putin's Russia was stripping its LGBTQ citizens of rights. In 2012, the Duma instituted a hundred-year ban on gay pride parades.[12] In 2013, it passed a law outlawing gay "propaganda," the official purpose of which was "protecting children from information promoting the denial of traditional family values." The law drew condemnation across the world, as it outlawed LGBTQ advocacy and expression and resulted in greater social stigma to, hostility toward, and violence against LGBTQ Russians.[13]

In 2013, Brown traveled to Russia to support the law.[14] In a speech there, he worried aloud about trends in the United States toward legalizing same-sex marriage, and he pressed for a global movement of strong opposition to them. He predicted that his visit to Russia would "enable the development of this movement around the world. We will band together, we will defend our children and their normal civil rights. Every child should have the right to have normal parents: a father and a mother."[15]

The World Congress of Families' quest to create an international movement to defend "normal" families actually began in Russia, conceived in a Moscow apartment on a winter day in 1995,[16] when the American historian Allan Carlson met with Russian counterparts interested in his work. At the time, Carlson, a conservative Lutheran with a deep nostalgia for agrarian society, was the head of the Illinois-based Rockford Institute and a self-styled expert on family and demographic trends. The institute, founded in 1976 to "preserve the institutions of the Christian West: the family, the Church, and the rule of law; private property, free enterprise, and moral discipline; high standards of learning, art, and literature," was, until 2018, the publisher of *Chronicles* magazine, which the white supremacist website *American Renaissance* has called "an important but mostly forgotten forerunner of the Alt-Right."[17] Carlson is still a contributor, as is former Republican presidential candidate and conservative pundit Pat Buchanan. Carlson stepped down as president of the Rockford Institute in 1998 to lead the parent organization of the World Congress of Families (WCF). In a speech to the 2018 gathering in Moldova, he described that first meeting in Moscow as a discussion of trends in "plummeting marriage and fertility rates, rising out of wedlock births, and divorce" in post-Communist countries, in order to determine whether capitalism or Communism was the cause of demographic decline. The researchers' aim, said Carlson, was to discern whether these developments were the result of "the Marxist system" or "governments in the Western nations adhering to liberal capitalism."[18] Over its two-decade existence, the WCF had repeatedly warned that the West faces a "demographic winter,"[19] caused by a decline in white Christian fertility coupled with Muslim immigration. It also identified the culprit in this crisis: liberal democracy.

Carlson was largely unknown outside Christian right circles; he was neither a flashy televangelist nor a red-meat political activist but instead a prim academic given to dense disquisitions on family size and demographics, issuing dire warnings about the societal ills caused by secularization, urbanization, and family planning. While his name might not be recognizable even to the average rank-and-file Christian right activist, he was a prominent figure in influencing the movement's leading thinkers and in shaping Christian right policy priorities. Carlson and his colleagues at his academic journal, *The Family in America,* called federal funding of family planning "the U.S. War on Fertility"[20] and influenced efforts to strip Planned Parenthood of such funding, which became a top priority of the Trump administration. His 2012 book, *Godly Seed: American Evangelicals Confront Birth Control, 1873–1973,* detailed the history of evangelical support for family planning, portraying that as a dark period before they climbed on board with the Catholic-led movement against abortion and contraception. The book drew praise from Russell Moore, who described Carlson as "one of the world's foremost family-issues scholars," and the book as a necessary self-examination for contemporary evangelicals.[21]

By the time WCF held its fourth gathering in Warsaw, Poland, in 2007, organizers believed that a demographic crisis had descended across western Europe, as "plunging birthrates coincide with heavy immigration, primarily from Muslim lands," Carlson wrote that year. "Poland saved Europe before," he argued, "by lifting the Turkish siege of Vienna in 1683 and helping to demolish the Soviet empire three centuries later"[22]—a reference to an iconic historical moment in which Europeans defended the continent against an "invasion" from Muslim forces. Carlson's WCF was assembling the elements for the multipronged nationalism of the Trump era, blending hostility to immigrants, LGBTQ rights, and feminism with a full-throated defense of "traditional" cultures, civilization, and heritage that is under siege.

Carlson's words portended nearly precisely a speech President Trump would give in Warsaw ten years later—a speech considered by his nationalist admirers as one of his best. To the chants of "Donald Trump, Donald Trump" from the Polish crowd, the American president enlisted the Poles in a common battle to save Europe. "Just as Poland could not be broken, I declare today for the world to hear that the West will never, ever be broken," he said. "Our values will prevail. Our people will thrive. And our civilization will triumph."[23] But when someone like Carlson, or Trump, or Steve Bannon, who openly advocated for an alliance between the alt-right and Christian right, talks about saving "the West" or "Western civilization," they're not talking about the values of the Enlightenment that made Western democracies possible. Quite the contrary: those are the values they intend to destroy—battling right alongside the autocrats in Putin's orbit of Russia and the former Soviet bloc.

In the twelve years since its 2007 Warsaw conference, and as right-wing authoritarian populism began sweeping across Europe in the wake of the 2008 financial crisis, the WCF continued to set its sights eastward. In 2013, the organization began planning to hold its big event for 2014 at the Kremlin; Larry Jacobs, then the group's managing director, told an American Christian radio program that Russia's antigay "propaganda" law was "a great idea and the rest of Europe is going the other way, legalizing LGBT propaganda."[24] After Russia's 2014 invasion of Ukraine and annexation of Crimea, the Obama administration imposed a series of sanctions on individuals in or connected to the Russian government for actions that "undermine democratic processes and institutions in Ukraine; threaten its peace, security, stability, sovereignty, and territorial integrity; and contribute to the misappropriation of its assets."[25] In the wake of the sanctions, the WCF suspended planning for the conference but praised Russia for having "taken a leadership role to advance the natural family" at a time when "Western governments are moving backward to a pagan worldview."[26] Although the WCF decided it would not officially sponsor the conference, which took place in Moscow despite the sanctions, it sent representatives—and continued to work with sanctioned individuals from Russia. Brian Brown was among the Americans attending the Moscow gathering.

Just one year later, in 2015, the WCF was back with a showy U.S.-based event, an expansive meeting in Salt Lake City featuring many luminaries of the American Christian right and leading Republican Party figures.[27] Salt Lake City was followed by congresses hosted by far-right nationalists and Putin allies. The 2016 conference was held in Tbilisi, Georgia, chaired by an American-educated CEO of a Moscow-based private equity firm, Levan Vasadze, a major figure in the Georgian nativist scene.[28] The WCF advertised the location as crucial, arguing that Georgia's "traditional family-based culture is besieged by sexual radicals in the West, including the EU, U.S. State Department under the current administration and leftist NGOs supported by George Soros."[29]

Brown's forays into Russia paid off for building relationships that blossomed for the WCF. He befriended rising stars and Putin allies of Europe's far right, including Moldova's Dodon, Hungarian prime minister Viktor Orbán, and Matteo Salvini, the charismatic leader of Italy's far-right populist Lega (League) party, who was the country's deputy prime minister from 2017 until 2019. Orbán hosted the WCF in 2017 in Budapest, and Salvini hosted it in Verona in 2019, five months before he was ousted from Italy's parliament following a political upheaval orchestrated by his rivals on the right and the left.

In Chişinău in 2018, the audience was welcomed by Yelena Mizulina, known as Putin's "morality crusader" who, in the guise of "protecting" children, had been the force behind the 2013 antigay law that Brown supported. She was the deputy of the state Duma when Russia invaded Ukraine in 2014 and was among the Russian officials sanctioned by the Obama administration. To the Moldova gathering, Mizulina, her blond hair pulled back in a tight, severe bun, hailed the WCF's prescience in seeing the "threat," back in the 1990s, to "family values." She proceeded to depict LGBTQ and reproductive rights as "anti-human values" that are based on "hatred" and "destroy happiness and life." Have you ever seen, Mizulina asked, "a happy woman who has had an abortion" or a happy man "who gives away his biological material?"[30]

For some at the World Congress in Moldova, that destruction of happiness and life had already been accomplished. Valery Alexeev, the president of a Russian foundation that purports to advance "the unity of Orthodox Christian nations," claimed in a speech that the U.S. election in 2016 showed that "the liberal democratic model is exhausted everywhere" and concluded the "liberal project is dead." Levan Vasadze, who had chaired the 2016 World Congress in Tbilisi, gripped the audience with a speech, delivered in nearly flawless English, in which he urged the assembled to reject urbanization because it was destroying the family. "This is a new kind of human who lives in a small cage of concrete which is called the apartment; in that cage of concrete, the functions of a man and a woman are identical," he said. "The family function is to go to the refrigerator, take something out of the refrigerator, and then open the smart phone, and stare into it. Same function for a man and a woman. And as a result, you have continuous erosion of differences between a man and a woman." When men and women no longer know their respective places, he went on, "why shouldn't a man wear high heels and a skirt and women wear men's clothes?" If people want "to save our cultures, if we want to multiply, if we want to come back to normality, we need to come back to the beauty of our lands." Vasadze urged conference attendees to return to the countryside, where families could better multiply and thus save the "great cultures" of countries such as Moldova, Georgia, or France.

Vasadze is an acolyte of the neofascist Russian philosopher Aleksandr Dugin, a favorite of the American far right who argues that the three chief ideologies of the twentieth century—communism, fascism, and liberalism—are all defunct and must be replaced with a fourth political theory, emerging from Russia and rooted in "tradition." (Dugin's book, *The Fourth Political Theory*, is widely read by the American alt-right.) Dugin, who also was barred from traveling to the United States because of sanctions imposed by the Obama administration for his role in fomenting instability in Ukraine,[31] was solicited in 2015 by an American white supremacist, Preston Wiginton, to deliver a speech by video to a gathering at Texas A&M University.[32] Wiginton, a fifty-two-year-old white supremacist who had enrolled at the university, briefly, in his forties, was relatively unknown at the time. But he later achieved a dubious national notoriety when he arranged, the following year, for Richard Spencer to speak at the College Station campus, drawing intense protests. Wiginton had long-standing ties to the Russian far right. In 2007, he had traveled to Russia, where he told attendees at a far-right anti-immigrant rally in Moscow, "I'm taking my hat off as a sign of respect for your strong identity in ethnicity, nation, and race." The crowd raised their arms in the Nazi salute and chanted "white power" in English as Wiginton, in Russian, proclaimed, "glory to Russia."[33] The title of Dugin's speech, when Wiginton brought him to Texas A&M, was "American Liberalism Must Be Destroyed."[34]

Vasadze, the Georgian "pro-family" activist, shares Dugin's anti-Americanism. In 2017, he attended a Dugin-sponsored gathering in Chişinău, where he called Dugin "a great philosopher" and argued that "liberalism kills more people than fascism and communism" because of its tolerance for abortion. *Egalité,*" Vasadze said, using the French word for equality, "is the biggest lie of liberalism brought upon the planet, and when liberalism dies, this nonsense of *egalité*— not that we're all equal before God, but we should be equalized, forcefully—will stay on the planet."

Vasadze's allies in the American Christian right have given him space to espouse his views to American audiences. When Vasadze chaired the 2016 World Congress of Families conference in Tbilisi, he was interviewed on the Christian Broadcasting Network and asked whether, a quarter century after the fall of Communism, Georgians still viewed America as "that shining city on a hill." The "city on a hill" phrase comes from the New Testament, in Jesus's Sermon on the Mount, in which he tells his disciples, "You are the light of the world. A city set on a hill cannot be hidden." The phrase is deeply woven into the religious right's mythology of America as a Christian nation; Ronald Reagan, the religious right's first presidential icon, transformed it into a triumphalist, Christian nationalist slogan. Reagan first started using the phrase in 1969, when he was governor of California,[35] adding a theatrical "shining" modifier to it in a speech to the Conservative Political Action Conference in 1974.[36] Six years later, running for president and enlisting the support of the brand-new Christian right organizations like the Moral Majority, Reagan used "shining city on a hill" regularly in campaign speeches and made it the centerpiece of the final speech of his campaign.[37] It became one of the most recognized catchphrases of American exceptionalism.

By asking the question, the CBN correspondent gave Vasadze a wide opening in which to promote the narrative that it is actually the eastern, former Communist bloc whose "tradition" and "faith" and "culture" will save the West. "Look, when we grew up in Soviet Union, we longed for the West," he said, and for the "light" that was freedom of speech, free enterprise, and private property. Only now, he said, "in our quest towards the West, we sometimes hardly recognize it, because sometimes we feel like freedom of speech is much more under danger in the West than in our parts of the world. You can no longer freely express your opinion about what's shameful"—homosexuality—"and what is disgraceful, and you are crucified for that."[38] The West is no longer the protector of "freedom" to the nativist, natalist right, because the West has spent too much time protecting the rights of marginalized people at the rightists' expense. America, then, is no longer leading the way, and has been displaced by Russia and its allies in the authoritarian factions on the rise in Europe.

Over the course of Obama's two terms, the Christian right, increasingly vividly, portrayed his tenure as a deep, possibly fatal blow to America's status as a moral leader in the world. Primed by conspiracy theories about Obama's place of birth, his race, and his religion, from the outset many in the movement were ready to believe that this interloper president was poised to eviscerate their freedom and crush Christianity. His every move as president—real and imagined—was fodder for these superstitions.

As much as Obama made deliberate efforts to prove his friendliness to religion, the Christian right leadership was intent on portraying him as hostile to it—particularly to Christianity. During his 2008 campaign, Obama hired a faith outreach director who made direct overtures to evangelical leaders, and as president he maintained, with some modifications, the White House Office of Faith-Based Initiatives that had been launched by his predecessor, George W. Bush, renaming it the White House Office of Faith-Based and Neighborhood Partnerships. Obama resisted calls from advocates for the separation of church and state to eliminate some of the Bush office's most troublesome policies that were favored by the religious right, such as the policy that permitted taxpayer-funded religious nonprofits that provide social services to refuse to hire candidates who did not meet their religious requirements. He carried over his campaign's outreach to evangelical and Catholic leaders.

But none of this mattered after the passage of his signature legislative accomplishment, the Patient Protection and Affordable Care Act. From the start, Obama's adversaries on the religious right—from officials of the Catholic Church to leaders of antichoice organizations to evangelical celebrities—portrayed Obamacare as a socialist takeover that would force taxpayers to pay for coverage of abortion services. That was not true, but it proved a potent talking point, priming the base for outrage when the Obama administration, in early 2012, finalized a regulation under the act requiring employer-sponsored health plans to cover contraception without a copay. Even after the Obama administration exempted houses of worship from the requirement and offered religious nonprofits an "accommodation" that permitted them to opt out by signing a form that would put the onus of coverage on their insurers, the regulation triggered a series of overheated, Republican-led congressional hearings, activist protests, and years of protracted litigation.

The contraception coverage requirement was just one facet of a multipronged campaign against a number of "grave threats" to religious liberty, a spokesman for the U.S. Conference of Catholic Bishops warned in a congressional hearing in 2011, one in a series of hearings led by Republicans intended to depict the Obama administration as "overreaching" and "trampling" on the rights of Christians.[39] The owners of a family-run chain of arts and crafts stores, Hobby Lobby, became national heroes to the religious right when they took their case against the contraception coverage all the way to the Supreme Court, winning, in 2014, a corporate exemption from the requirement.

But throughout 2014, as federal courts were striking down bans on same-sex marriage and a Supreme Court ruling making marriage equality legal nationwide seemed inevitable, the Christian right was already panicking and summoning its foot soldiers to the trenches. In May 2015, Kelly Shackelford, a lawyer for Christian right causes, told a gathering of the Council for National Policy, an important, agenda-setting umbrella group for the conservative movement, that a Supreme Court ruling legalizing same-sex marriage "is going to be a direct attack" on religious freedom. Ryan Anderson, an opponent of LGBTQ rights at the Heritage Foundation, put activists on notice that such a ruling would require the same unbounded commitment to undoing a liberal trend that the Court's 1973 decision in *Roe v. Wade* triggered on abortion.[40]

The battle cry to culture warriors was not just to combat the rising tide of LGBTQ rights or contraception coverage; it was to defend the divine place America held among nations that they believed was rapidly being erased. America was losing its "city on a hill" status. While his family's case was winding its way through the courts, David Green, patriarch of the Hobby Lobby family, portrayed the contraception requirement as evidence that America's status as a godly nation rooted in biblical principles was falling away. "If there's any hope for our government, it will be via Christians declaring that our foundation is in going to God's Word to define our laws," Green wrote in 2013. "This is how we began as a nation and, if we hope to once again be a 'city on a hill,' it's what we must return to."[41] Mathew Staver, a prominent lawyer for the Christian right who once served as the dean of the law school at Jerry Falwell's Liberty University, attacked Obama's promotion of LGBTQ rights both at home and internationally, accusing his administration of "actively proliferating homosexuality around the world."[42] On his radio program, *Faith and Freedom,* in July 2014, Staver bemoaned that "America used to be the shining city on the hill, the example for other nations to follow," but "now it's the example of what not to follow."[43]

While Reagan had urged Americans to take pride in America as a "shining city on a hill," reveling in how the rest of the world would turn its gaze to us as a beacon of freedom, Trump groused that the rest of the world was "laughing at us" and vowed in his inaugural address to put an end to the "American carnage." For Trump's coalition, the Obama era had marked the end of American exceptionalism—and making the country great again would require some new sources of inspiration.

Even before Trump, activists like Staver were looking to other examples of leadership. Other countries, Staver noted in another radio broadcast in January 2014, are "reaffirming marriage as one man and one woman" and "rejecting this radicalized homosexual agenda."[44] Among the countries Staver cited was Russia, where, under Putin's leadership, the anti-LGBTQ legislation and rhetoric was alarming human rights advocates. Staver subsequently tried to backtrack on his praise for Russia, claiming that he "has never supported" anti-LGBTQ laws in Russia but only expressed "opposition to the Obama administration for using the State Department funding to force countries to change their laws on abortion or marriage."[45] But his radio co-host, the lawyer and pundit Matt Barber, had even more explicit praise for Russia, saying in that same 2014 broadcast in which they discussed the Russian "propaganda" law, "We are going to stop this homosexual activist propaganda from corrupting children in our nation and we need to see that right here in the United States."[46]

Staver and Barber weren't the only figures cheering Putin's moves as necessary to keep children safe, even as hate violence against LGBTQ Russians was on the rise.[47] "VLADIMIR PUTIN SIGNS BILL PROTECTING CHILDREN FROM HOMOSEXUAL PROPAGANDA," read the headline in *LifeSiteNews,* a popular outlet for anti-abortion news.[48] "I hope that the United States will learn some lessons, quite frankly, from Russia," Janice Shaw Crouse, a fellow at the Beverly LaHaye Institute, a think tank affiliated with the Christian right group Concerned Women for America, told *BuzzFeed*.[49] Pat Buchanan, who shares affinities with both the Christian right and the alt-right, has praised Putin for "trying to re-establish the Orthodox Church as the moral compass of the nation it had been for 1,000 years before Russia fell captive to the atheistic and pagan ideology of Marxism." Buchanan admired Putin's declaration that Christianity was "a turning point in the fate of our fatherland, made it an inseparable part of the Christian civilization and helped turn it into one of the largest world powers"—words that he complained we would not hear from "Barack Hussein Obama."[50] In the summer of 2013, even American conservatives who didn't fully support Putin commended the way they believed he stood for Christian morality more than Obama's America did. Rod Dreher, a blogger for *The American Conservative*, wrote that he "agree[d] with Pat Buchanan when he says that Vladimir Putin's Russia is defending traditional Christian moral standards and actual Christians more than America is."[51]

At the time, Putin was portraying his anti-LGBTQ moves as necessary measures to protect and defend Russian "identity," which he tied to religion and morality. "We can see how many of the Euro-Atlantic countries are actually rejecting their roots, including the Christian values that constitute the basis of Western civilisation," he said in a 2013 speech. "They are denying moral principles and all traditional identities: national, cultural, religious and even sexual." He decried "the excesses of political correctness" that have led to people in Europe being "embarrassed or afraid to talk about their religious affiliations," and holidays being "abolished or even called something different; their essence is hidden away, as is their moral foundation." One might see this as Putin's own crusade against an imagined war on Christmas—and Christians. And in an obvious jab at Obama, he blamed unspecified "people" who are "aggressively trying to export this model all over the world. I am convinced that this opens a direct path to degradation and primitivism, resulting in a profound demographic and moral crisis."[52]

In speaking in these terms—that "political correctness" was stripping Russia of its national identity and therefore threatening its demographic and moral future—Putin was directly aligning with the ideology of the American Christian right and World Congress of Families. When Orbán hosted the WCF in 2017, Brown and other organizers were unbothered by the autocratic turn Hungary had taken under his watch and even portrayed those changes as something the United States should emulate. In an early 2017 cover story in *Chronicles,* Allan Carlson questioned whether America could still be a "City on a Hill—With Transgender Toilets?" He praised Orbán's "pro-family" policies, arguing "if we want to make America great again," we should follow his lead.[53] But while Carlson was starstruck, human rights groups, pro-democracy activists, the European Union, and the pre-Trump foreign policy establishment in the United States had been sounding alarms that the powerful central European leader was not only undermining democracy in his own country but developing a template for what he infamously touted, in a 2014 speech, as "illiberal" democracy across Europe.[54]

Since gaining power in 2010, Orbán has moved to control the media, redraw voting districts to advantage his party in future elections, and erode the power of an independent judiciary.[55] He demonized immigrants and asylum-seekers and closed Hungary's borders to migrants. But most significant to Orbán's admirers in the American Christian right were the constitutional reforms put in place in 2011 by his far-right Fidesz Party–controlled parliament—changes that were made, according to Human Rights Watch, while "civil society and opposition groups in Hungary were largely excluded from the process." The reforms created a "right to life" from the moment of conception and defined marriage as the union of a man and a woman. In 2013, Hungary further amended its constitution to define heterosexual "marriage and parent-child relationships" as "the basis of the family."[56] Fidesz's and Orbán's subsequent election victory in 2014 was criticized by the U.S. State Department as having been the result of moves he made to blur "the separation between a ruling party and the state." In 2015, Orbán was the first foreign leader to endorse Trump's presidential candidacy, later citing the commitment of "this resolute American presidential candidate" to abandoning "the policy of exporting democracy."[57] Orbán was reelected in 2018 after campaigning against "migrant invasions" that he claimed Hungarians opposed because they didn't want their "own color, traditions and national culture to be mixed by others."[58]

Orbán, who has cultivated a growing relationship with Trump, became emboldened to further flout his critics after receiving an unequivocal endorsement from the American president and his allies for his moves to strangle democracy in Hungary. In Orbán's speech at the 2017 WCF gathering, he claimed Hungary was experiencing declining fertility rates, and he rejected any suggestion of solving the problem through immigration, because Hungary would rather see a "renewal of our own resources."[59] After his 2018 reelection, which Trump cheered, Orbán moved quickly to suppress NGOs that received foreign funding and provided assistance to migrants. In a speech that year, Orbán cemented his vision of Hungary as a "Christian" democracy, presenting himself as the political and spiritual leader of "a new constitutional order based on national and Christian foundations." He specifically rejected the western European norms of human rights and equality in favor of his own "illiberal" governance. "Thirty years ago we thought that Europe was our future," he said. "Today we believe that we are Europe's future."[60]

In 2018, Tony Perkins, the influential president of the Family Research Council, which is an official partner of the WCF, praised Orbán on his radio program as "a strong conservative that has championed biblical values in Hungary."[61] The notion that Orbán was protecting "biblical" values superseded any concern about his evisceration of democratic institutions. In Chişinău, Brian Brown waved away worries about Orbán's actions—which include efforts to undermine an independent judiciary. For Brown, the American judiciary was crushing freedom, while Orbán's Hungary was promoting it. The legalization of same-sex marriage in the United States had been decided by the Supreme Court—"forced from above," Brown contended—but in Hungary it was put to a voter referendum. Hungary, then, "allowed

their people to speak on this," Brown told me. "It is absolutely absurd
to say that Hungary is not a participatory democracy."[62] That is precisely how authoritarians deceptively portray their "illiberal" democracies as democratic. They can dismantle democratic institutions
such as a free press, independent judiciary, and robust civil society,
and they can compromise election integrity—while still ostentatiously
holding elections in which the people vote. In the 2018 Russian election, Putin won 77 percent of the vote.[63] In spite of warnings to Trump
by his national security team not to congratulate the Russian strongman,[64] Trump did congratulate Putin, just as he congratulated Orbán
when he won reelection for a third term.

Peter Sprigg, a fellow with the Family Research Council who represented the group in Moldova, also downplayed concerns about
Orbán's autocratic moves. As the speeches and panels wrapped up in
Chişinău, Sprigg was exuberant about the conference's impact. Perhaps the most important result of such conferences, he told me, was
"exchanging business cards and forming relationships. I know we've
had people that I've met at events like this, when they come to Washington come visit us at Family Research Council, and we'll have a
chance to [have] more in-depth discussion." Sprigg, a major figure in
the Christian right's anti-LGBTQ advocacy circles, also seemed
unmoved by criticism of Orbán's antidemocratic moves. "It seems like
the Western media likes to focus on some of these sort of procedural
things and doesn't focus on the things—like he [Orbán] talks about
defending Western civilization rooted in Christianity," Sprigg said. "I
mean, that's where we see we have common cause with him."[65]

These "procedural things" that Sprigg minimized are the very
norms that are essential to a functioning democracy, including
upholding the rule of law, maintaining separation of powers, an independent judiciary, and a free press—all vital foundations that Trump
has attacked as president. These are not mere "procedural" niceties;
they are the institutions and norms required to hold the powerful
accountable and protect the rights of those lacking political power or
majority status. Without them, democracy can quickly backslide into

autocracy or kleptocracy or an ethnonationalist state—even if the people go out and cast ballots in elections. When a crucial part of the American polity shares more values with foreign autocrats than with their domestic political adversaries, American democracy is in a state of emergency. If an autocrat's gesture of a shared "Christian" heritage is more meaningful than the U.S. Constitution, the sirens are blaring.

For David Barton, a former Republican Party official and consultant, and longtime promoter of a revisionist history that the Founders intended America to be a "Christian nation," Poland is the new model. According to the U.S. pro-democracy watchdog organization Freedom House, Poland's ruling Law and Justice Party has "appropriated a vocabulary similar to that of Fidesz" and "embarked on a course of change that places it solidly in the illiberal camp, with many of the initiatives mirroring those enacted by Fidesz in Hungary."[66] But after a 2018 visit, Barton rhapsodized on his radio program that Poland is "a Christian nation in the old school sense of the word."[67] He did not address Poland's illiberal turns, characterizing "progressive media" as "always portray[ing] Poland as kind of backward people." In this he found a way to further malign the "progressive media" as enemies of the Christian values he claims to now share with Poland. "It's the same way they treat Christians in America," he said.[68]

Blaming the media or European Union elites for criticism of rising autocrats like Orbán is becoming increasingly common for the Christian right.[69] In 2017, the Heritage Foundation published a column that portrayed Orbán as having been "vilified in the mainstream media and formally rebuked by the EU" for opposing "the EU's overly permissive migrant policy" and fighting against George Soros's influence.[70] Hungary, the Christian Broadcasting Network claimed the following year, "has been treated like a pariah in the Western media over its position on open borders, but Hungary's leaders are smart enough to know that their national values will never please the global Left."[71] Even Chuck Norris, the martial arts actor and pop culture hero to the Christian right, has boasted of his "bromance" with the prime minister after spending a day with Orbán, who drove Norris and his wife for a personal tour of Budapest.[72]

The common cause is driven, at its core, by a shared rejection of liberal democracy—even hopes for its downfall. "There are great experiments in post-liberal political and economic life occurring right now in real places," Allan Carlson wrote in 2018, "in Poland's Law and Justice Party; in the Hungary of Prime Minister Viktor Orbán; and—yes—in the land of the Great Russians led by Vladimir Putin."

Carlson's long-standing gaze eastward, and toward Putin in particular, mirrors that of the white nationalists of the alt-right, who would become the most enthusiastic promoters of Trump's dalliances with Putin. Their own admiration for Putin predates Trump's. Back in 2008, the anti-Semitic, white nationalist journal *Occidental Quarterly* and its website *Occidental Observer* were marginal publications known mostly, outside of their small readership, to researchers at the Southern Poverty Law Center and the Anti-Defamation League. That year the journal's editor, Kevin MacDonald, a tenured professor of evolutionary psychology at California State University at Long Beach, was formally rebuked by his university colleagues, through the university's academic senate. The body passed a resolution that contained a detailed denunciation of MacDonald's repeated support for a white ethnostate and his extensive writings portraying Jews as a threat to white survival. The academic body, the resolution read, "firmly and unequivocally disassociates itself from the anti-Semitic and white ethnocentric views he has expressed."[73] MacDonald ended up taking an early retirement from teaching but continued to write for and edit *Occidental Quarterly* and *Occidental Observer*.

Launched in 2001, MacDonald's journal has positioned itself as the defender of "the cultural, ethnic, and racial interests of Western European peoples." It operates under the tax-exempt status of the Charles Martel Society, a nonprofit founded by William H. Regnery II, the alt-right funder and member of the dynastic family behind conservatism's most influential book publishing empire, Regnery Publishing. Founded in 1947, the firm published the iconic books of the conservative movement, including William F. Buckley's *God and Man at Yale* and Russell Kirk's *The Conservative Mind*. Today it is part of the Salem Media Group, a conservative Christian media conglomerate that has long dominated Christian talk radio. Regnery Publishing is also responsible for many of the books that have infused contemporary politics with right-wing calumnies and conspiracy theories, such as *Unfit for Command*, co-authored by conspiracy theorist Jerome Corsi, which promoted the smear that 2004 Democratic presidential nominee John Kerry had abandoned troops under his command in Vietnam. The company helped make Ann Coulter a media celebrity by repeatedly catapulting her to the top of the *New York Times* best-seller list. In 2002, it published the anti-immigrant book *Invasion*, by conservative media personality Michelle Malkin, and two years later it published her defense of the Japanese internment as a model for how the United States should address terrorism.[74] In 2017, it published conservative pundit Dinesh D'Souza's best-selling *The Big Lie: Exposing the Nazi Roots of the American Left*. It then announced it was boycotting the *Times* best-seller list because, the company alleged, it had exhibited a bias against conservative books—all evidence to the contrary.[75]

William H. Regnery II, the family member who worked with Sam Francis to found the National Policy Institute, though, was too extreme even for these circles. He is the nephew of Henry Regnery, founder of the publishing powerhouse, and the grandson of William H. Regnery, one of the founders of the America First Committee, whose spokesman, the aviator and Nazi sympathizer Charles Lindbergh, helped popularize the group's opposition to America's intervention in World War II. The younger Regnery, known as Bill and now in his seventies, was expelled from mainstream conservative circles in 2006, he has said, because "my infractions of orthodoxy involved delving into group differences and cognitive heritability"[76]— quite a euphemism for racism.

At the National Policy Institute conference just after Trump was elected in November 2016, at which Spencer notoriously elicited the Nazi salutes during his speech, Bill Regnery told me, over coffee in the deserted food court of the Ronald Reagan Building, that he felt "a real sense of dispossession" because the country was no longer "90 percent white." He rejected the label "white supremacist"—and defended himself by making racist claims about genetic differences in intelligence. "If you are a white supremacist, all other races are inferior," he told me. He offered "proof" that he didn't believe "all other races are inferior" by going on to claim that Ashkenazi Jews—of which I am one, he made certain to point out—have "an average IQ of 115," while "we whites have an average IQ of 100."

Regnery's Charles Martel Society, which has described itself as "the intellectual home of Western Nationalism,"[77] is named for the medieval Frankish military leader who defeated an Islamic army in the Battle of Tours in 732, a historical marker frequently invoked by the contemporary anti-Muslim right as emblematic of a "European" or "Christian" victory over what they portray now as invading hordes of Muslim migrants. The alt-right is not alone in its admiration for Martel. Michele Bachmann, the former Republican member of Congress and presidential candidate who, since leaving public office, has built another career as a Trump supporter and prolific motivational speaker to Christian right groups, marked the 1281st anniversary of the victory at Tours at the 2013 Values Voter Summit. "That day changed the course of history," she said. "For 100 years the Islamic marauders had won battle after battle after battle and were moving their fear and their tyranny across the world." But Martel's troops "literally stood shoulder to shoulder with their shields up and their javelins pointed, and they won that decisive battle, and Charlemagne became the father of modern Europe, and Christian Europe and the values of Christian Europe prevailed and ultimately led to those same immigrants coming to the United States and creating this magnificent country."[78] One would not likely find Bachmann, a staunch Christian Zionist, at an alt-right conference standing alongside Richard Spencer overseeing Nazi salutes or cheering one of

MacDonald's unrepentant anti-Semitic speeches. But her lionizing of Martel as a civilization-defining hero is just one example of how these movements share a common ideology about a superior "western culture" or "western civilization" and their role in saving it from intruders.

In the years before Trump came on the scene, MacDonald was one of white nationalism's top intellectuals. His racist and anti-Semitic articles and books deeply influenced the burgeoning alt-right, gaining attention on hard-core neo-Nazi websites as well as in the movement's pseudo-intellectual circles. As Trump's campaign was electrifying the alt-right in the latter half of 2015, MacDonald was gaining notoriety, among watchers of the rising alt-right, for cheering the candidate's "revolution" to "restore a White America." After Trump's campaign unveiled his hard-line immigration policy that August, MacDonald's magazine endorsed his candidacy. "I don't think we ever did before," MacDonald told me, of the endorsement.[79] Once-fringe figures like MacDonald were suddenly a vital part of the American political conversation. When Donald Trump, Jr., retweeted a MacDonald tweet disparaging Hillary Clinton as politically corrupt, it signaled to the alt-right that their leaders were gaining an unprecedented sort of traction.[80] Trump's ongoing refusal to rebuke or distance himself from the far-right figures who were supporting his campaign bolstered their belief that he was helping transition them—or at least their ideas—into the mainstream.

Trump wasn't explicitly identifying himself as part of the alt-right or as a white nationalist, something that MacDonald thought was a wise political strategy, he told me during the campaign. For MacDonald, Trump was activating a quiescent alt-right base without explicitly coming out as alt-right, something the movement's leading lights, including Peter Brimelow and MacDonald himself, knew from experience could be a career-ending, or at least career-altering, move. But for MacDonald, it didn't matter whether Trump proclaimed himself a fellow traveler. "A lot of his policy issues are the same as things that we've advocated," he told me. Those policy issues extended beyond the obvious, like immigration, and included Trump's abrupt rejection of the long-standing, bipartisan foreign policy consensus on America's role in promoting the growth of democracy in the former Soviet bloc by bolstering civil society and the strength of democratic institutions.

Although MacDonald had never endorsed an American presidential candidate before Trump, he harbored great admiration for a foreign politician—Vladimir Putin. In 2008, just after the Russian invasion of neighboring Georgia, MacDonald enthused on *Occidental Observer*, "Russia stands out among the white-majority societies of the world because it is not dominated by elites bent on managing the dissolution of the peoples and culture that created them." Russia had drawn the ire of the George W. Bush administration for its invasion of its neighbor, an act of aggression that Bush characterized as "bullying and intimidation."[81] But for MacDonald, Russia was acting heroically, by flexing its nationalist muscle and sticking its finger in the eye of the West. "Nationalism in a white country—a frightening prospect indeed for Western elites," he wrote. But the "good news," he went on, "is that Russian nationalism is real."[82]

MacDonald was particularly taken with Russia's ultranationalist Rodina (Motherland) Party and a flagrantly xenophobic ad it had run on Russian television in 2005. The ad featured a party leader, Dmitry Rogozin, and another party member in a park. Near them, a Russian woman is pushing a baby carriage, and some darker-skinned men—in the ad, actors—dispose of melon rinds in her path. Rogozin demands that the men pick up their trash. His companion belligerently queries whether they even understand Russian. When the men fail to respond, the ad closes with the words, "Let's clean our city of garbage!" across the screen.[83] The ad was seen as an unambiguous attack on Azerbaijanis and other ethnic groups from former Soviet republics, recognizable to Russian television viewers because some of them sold melons from street stands in the Russian capital. The ad set off a diplomatic skirmish and led to a court ruling banning Rodina from that year's election for Moscow's city duma, for inciting ethnic hatred.[84]

Writing about Russian nationalism in 2008, MacDonald was

impressed that Rogozin, in spite of this history, remained a powerful figure in Russian politics. "If an American or European politician were associated with such a video," MacDonald wrote, "he or she would be condemned to the extremist fringe of political life, with no chance whatever of obtaining power or influence." But not even he could have anticipated, nearly a decade before Trump's successful Russian-backed presidential campaign, an American politician's ability to similarly evade repercussions for his xenophobia, and for his incitements by tweet, campaign rally, and advertisements. Yet in the Russia MacDonald so admired, in 2008, three years after the xenophobic ad, Putin appointed Rogozin ambassador to NATO, just before Russia began escalating its military conflict with Georgia.

The appointment of a xenophobic nationalist to represent Russia to NATO was widely seen as another sign of Putin's increasingly confrontational stance toward the West.[85] But MacDonald saw it as another sign of Russia's embrace of white nationalism. "Rogozin has been elevated to an important, high-profile foreign policy position," he wrote, "where he can express his nationalist views to NATO, whose actions have been a sore point with Russian nationalists for years." Rogozin would later go on to serve in President Putin's cabinet, as deputy prime minister, including during the crisis in Ukraine.

In 2018, a decade after MacDonald extolled his white nationalism, Putin appointed Rogozin to a new post, as head of Russia's space agency Roscosmos. It was, undoubtedly, a provocative move, since Rogozin was under U.S. government sanctions for his role in the 2014 Russian annexation of Crimea. Roscosmos's American counterpart, NASA, has relied on the Russian agency to travel to the international space station since the retirement of the U.S. space shuttle in 2011. When Rogozin was sanctioned by the Obama administration, he tweeted, "After analyzing the sanctions against our space industry I suggest the US delivers its astronauts to the ISS [international space station] with a trampoline."

Not unexpectedly, then, when Jim Bridenstine, a former naval pilot and Christian right favorite as a congressman from Oklahoma,[86] who had narrowly won Senate confirmation to be the top administrator of NASA, invited Rogozin for an early 2019 visit to the space agency headquarters in Houston, it set off a diplomatic firestorm. Not only did the American diplomatic community see Rogozin as a hardened nationalist with a xenophobic—and also homophobic—past, he also had a history of anti-American, anti-West statements. In 2012, he wrote that the West would "fall under the weight of Islamic State and gays." In June 2018, to allow Bridenstine to interact with Rogozin, the Treasury Department granted permission for the pair to engage in space-related issues.[87] "Wow" and "appalling" were the reactions of seasoned foreign policy professionals in Washington because of Rogozin's history and his sanctions status.[88] Bridenstine ultimately rescinded the invitation, but the relationship wasn't finished: Bridenstine, who had visited Rogozin in Moscow in October 2018,[89] spoke with him by phone about the prospect of another visit to the Russian capital. Because the phone call took place during the government shutdown of late 2018–early 2019, NASA claimed not to have a readout of the call, the industry news site *Space News* reported. The agency retweeted Roscosmos's Russian-language tweet about the call and referred the American press to the Russian space agency's account of the conversation. Rogozin went on Russian television and claimed that the reason his Houston trip had been canceled was because a "second American civil war" was underway.[90]

Trump's candidacy and presidency brought closer ties with Russia into a new and sinister focus, given the influence that the Russian president exerted on the election of 2016. But in embracing Moscow, Trump was not articulating a new idea for many leading thinkers of his new political coalition—he just elevated it to a global conversation. The white nationalist admiration for Putin began during the George W. Bush era, expressed as a hostile reaction to Bush's neoconservative foreign policy and openness to immigration. The antipathy to Bush's foreign policy grew out of the movement's affinity for isolationism, a theme pressed on Republicans by Pat Buchanan and his fellow paleoconservatives when he ran unsuccessfully for the Republican presidential nomination in 1992 and 1996. The alt-right and its precursors, like Buchanan, persisted in this isolationism despite the failure of his presidential ambitions, particularly in opposition to Bush's war in Iraq. But this faction of the conservative movement was largely sidelined, in part because of the immense power of the Christian right within conservatism, and the convergence of its priorities in the Middle East with those of conservative foreign policy hawks. The Christian right was one of the top cheerleaders for the Iraq War, which it saw as part of an existential battle to defend both America and Israel from "radical Islam."

In the decade before Trump entered the presidential race, it would have seemed impossible that the openly anti-Semitic and isolationist alt-right would have found itself in the Trump camp with the Christian Zionists of the Christian right. After all, the Christian Zionists' support for Israel and a militaristic foreign policy is anathema to the anti-Semitic and isolationist alt-right. But both movements, with their shared hostility to pluralism and democratic values, found a common antagonist in the first black American president. Barack Obama's presidency—and the right's stoking of conspiracy theories questioning his place of birth and citizenship, his supposed Muslim faith, his imagined Communist links—brought the alt-right and Christian right together in support of Donald Trump and the new nationalist right.

The Christian right, driven by what it claimed was the undermining of Christian values during the Obama era, began looking toward the very same autocrats who had captivated the alt-right. These political figures were also using "family values" such as opposition to abortion and LGBTQ rights as a means to merge Christian nationalism with ethnic nationalism, creating a potent bloc against European Union "elites." These two parts of the bloc were further drawn together by the migrant crisis that escalated in 2015, which was caused, the alt-right claimed, by the needless wars in the Middle East launched by their ideological enemy, the neoconservatives. Because many of the migrants were from Muslim countries, the situation seemed to embody long-standing conspiracy theories in the Christian right about invasions of the West by Muslim hordes. For both the Christian right and the alt-right, the reaction of Europe's xenophobes to an influx of refugees and asylum seekers served as a template for what Trump portrayed as an "invasion" on the U.S. southern border.

Both the alt-right and Christian right claim to be saving "Western civilization" or "the Judeo-Christian West." But what those slogans really mean is that America and the western European countries that dominate the European Union are already dead, having succumbed to "globalists" and "political correctness." What both the Christian right and the white nationalist right are looking toward now—with or without Trump—is a new locus of power in the world, one defined by a rejection of the hard-won and fragile American values of democracy and human rights, and by an exaltation of authoritarian natalism, xenophobia, and homophobia.

9

The Undrained Swamp Loves an Autocrat

Although Trump is frequently portrayed as bumbling or misspeaking in defense of authoritarianism, seeming missteps or bizarre asides, such as his claim to have exchanged "beautiful love letters" and fallen "in love" with North Korean dictator Kim Jong-un, are not isolated blunders. Despite his attempts to be seen as bringing fresh thinking to outdated foreign policy, his description of the European Union as a "foe," and NATO as an "obsolete" relic that should be discarded,[1] are not the harmless pronouncements of an outsider, renegade president shaking up the wonks of the "deep state." Nor is his affinity for Putin a consequence simply of his business ties to Russia, or his lust to see its hacked Hillary Clinton emails arrayed in public view. Trump means it. But he did not invent these changes. He is less a leader than a vehicle for a global assault on democratic institutions and human rights, assaults that began in Washington well before he became president, in the seamy world of unscrupulous political strategists and lobbyists—the denizens of the swamp that Trump had disingenuously promised to drain.

For decades, Republicans had turned to Arthur J. Finkelstein, a top political strategist known for his precision polling and messaging, and for advising clients that a winning message was one that would "polarize the electorate."[2] Finkelstein, who died in 2017, was gay, although that did not appear to diminish the mutual affection between him and the Republican Party. Some of Finkelstein's many protégés, affectionately known as "Arthur's kids," ended up in the orbit of the Trump campaign. These Trump allies included self-identified "dirty trickster" and Trump adviser Roger Stone, who in 2019 was convicted for obstruction and lying to investigators in the Russia probe, and campaign pollster Tony Fabrizio, who has claimed he urged Trump to contest Michigan and Wisconsin late in the campaign, a strategy credited with tipping the election in his favor.[3] Paul Manafort, Trump's onetime campaign manager and now a convicted felon, had used Finkelstein's attack strategy as far back as 1996 while working on Bob Dole's presidential campaign against Bill Clinton. These tactics, according to a campaign trail dispatch in *Newsweek,* "boiled down to a single sentence that employed Finkelstein's favorite pejorative term: 'Clinton is a liberal.'"[4]

American political strategists have not confined their activities to the United States; they have exported this disdain for liberalism around the world, and in Europe they have aided the rise of right-wing-populist, anti–European Union, anti-NATO autocrats. In 2008, Finkelstein set off for Budapest to become a political consultant for Viktor Orbán's Fidesz Party.[5] At the time, Orbán had been out of power for six years, after serving one term as prime minister during the years following Hungary's 1999 admission into NATO. In 2010, two years after retaining Finkelstein, Orbán ran again and won. Although Hungary had been a member of the European Union since 2004, Orbán promptly began a coordinated assault on his country's democratic institutions, in direct contravention of the EU political order. The Fidesz-controlled parliament enacted a law requiring media organizations to register with a governmental body appointed by the ruling party, drawing criticism from human rights NGOs and the European Union.[6] Over the objection of civil society

advocates and opposition groups, the parliament enacted a new constitution eroding checks and balances, enshrining a "right to life"
from the moment of conception, and defining marriage as between a
man and a woman. After ignoring EU pleas for the constitution to be
withdrawn,[7] Fidesz further consolidated its grip on power, passing
laws redrawing parliamentary districts and shifting the process for
determining allocation of seats in the parliament, in order to make it
easier for the party to win future elections.[8] It later limited the power
of the constitutional court, lowered the retirement age for judges so
the court could be stacked with loyalists, and restricted political
campaigns' press outreach to state-run media.[9] When Fidesz and
Orbán scored another resounding victory in the 2014 elections, the
Organization for Security and Cooperation in Europe (OSCE)—
another transnational democracy-promoting organization in the
crosshairs of Europe's far-right nationalists—charged that "a number
of factors provided undue advantage" to Fidesz, including "the manner in which a large number of changes to the legal framework were
passed, restrictive campaign regulations, biased media coverage, and
the blurring of the separation between a ruling party and the state."[10]
Barack Obama's State Department, in its annual human rights report
for Hungary that year, made note of the OSCE criticism, as well as
"serious governmental and law enforcement actions against civil
society organizations, continued curtailment of media pluralism,"
and "the systematic erosion of the rule of law, checks and balances,
democratic institutions, and transparency, and of increased intimidation of independent societal voices."[11]

  In undertaking a coordinated assault on democratic institutions
that would become a model for other European autocrats, Orbán
was not only directly snubbing the EU, of which Hungary had only
recently become a member. He was also sticking his finger in the eye
of the established, bipartisan American foreign policy consensus.
During his first turn in office, when Hungary was a new NATO
member, Orbán had run into trouble with George W. Bush's State
Department, too. The Bush administration applied diplomatic pressure on Budapest at moments when Orbán departed from bedrock

NATO commitments to democracy, human rights, and the rule of law. Heather Conley, who served as deputy assistant secretary of state in the Bureau for European and Eurasian Affairs under Bush, recalled that after 9/11, Orbán was "openly flirting" with anti-Semitism, including blaming Jews for the attacks. After American diplomats confronted him privately to no avail, the State Department cleared the ambassador to give a speech, Conley told me, something she characterized as "one of the first big warnings" to a new NATO ally to send a strong message that "these values, they're important to us. We subscribe to them, and we'll work hard privately to get to the right place, but if you didn't get to the right place privately, we're going to have to say something."[12] Orbán went on to lose his bid for reelection in 2002—something Conley said he blamed on the United States. Less than a decade later, under Finkelstein's tutelage, he returned to power. Finkelstein masterminded a campaign that cast Hungary as a victim suffering at the hands of the United States, the United Nations, and other purveyors of Western liberal democracy. Since the 2015 refugee crisis, Orbán has defined his rule with his rhetorical and legal assaults on immigrants and refugees. Finkelstein was behind the anti-immigration billboards that have proliferated in Hungary over the past decade.[13]

While advising European autocrats, Finkelstein kept a close eye on U.S. politics—and on Trump. During a rare public appearance in 2011, at the Cevro Institute,[14] a university in Prague, the famously reclusive Finkelstein provided insights into the divisive campaign strategy he used on behalf of Orbán and other politicians across the continent. That strategy, he said, was crafted to respond to world events, particularly the global financial crisis of 2008, and the Arab Spring that spread across the Middle East two years later. Starry-eyed Westerners, Finkelstein intimated, believe grassroots protests, like the Arab Spring, that sought to bring down dictatorships, would result in "more freedom in the world." But to Finkelstein, who was always looking for the points of division, these rebellions against autocratic regimes would ultimately produce "stronger not weaker governments" and "stronger not weaker personalities." That was because, he concluded, xenophobic and nationalist parties in Europe and even the United States used the refugee crisis that unspooled from war, violence, and unrest in the Middle East to sow anti-Muslim and anti-immigrant hate. "Anti-Muslim parties become important in developing coalitions for their governments," he said, with a message of "they're taking our jobs. They're taking away our way of life." In the United States, Finkelstein said, the scapegoats were Mexicans— "not even all Hispanics, the Mexicans." The targeting of one group to hate and to blame for all failures, he went on, was "creating an energy source around which these movements take place." This growing appetite for strongmen, he further predicted, would lead to Trump's rise. "I don't know if anybody here is watching Donald Trump in the United States," he gushed, "but it's mind-boggling, it's just pure personality."[15] When Trump announced his candidacy four years later, just as Finkelstein had forecast, he scapegoated Mexican immigrants directly, calling them rapists and criminals.

The most important political point for an aspiring political strategist to remember, according to Finkelstein, was that because "no one knows anything about anything," a consultant's job was to tell people what they should know and "make it interesting." He recalled a favorite commercial he crafted for an Albanian client, featuring pictures of his opponent, a sumo wrestler, and a kangaroo, juxtaposed together. The ad's punch line was these three figures had one thing in common—they knew nothing about Albania. Finkelstein reveled in his opponent's anger over the spot, a reaction that played right into Finkelstein's hands. After the opponent protested, "everybody wanted to see the commercial," ensuring its wider reach. To see the impact of this same vapid political strategy in the United States, one need look no further than Trump's Twitter feed, where he can dictate the course of a day's news coverage with a false, misleading, racist, sexist, or simply insipid tweet. Distracting people from what really does matter—and steering them into thinking meaningless conflict is what matters—is the point. Meanwhile, democracy is in tatters.

As Finkelstein hinted in his Prague speech, the machinations that would culminate in Trumpism were already underway by 2011, when

Trump seriously contemplated running against Obama and spent his time promoting his birther conspiracy theory about the president. But Trump's decision not to run in that cycle didn't put the Finkelstein machinery in the deep freeze. Just after the 2012 election, Finkelstein disciple Manafort, who would go on to serve as Trump's campaign chairman, was representing Ukraine's strongman, Putin-backed President Viktor Yanukovych. (Manafort's 2018 convictions on tax evasion and bank fraud stemmed from money he was paid for his work in Ukraine.) In an early 2013 memo he prepared for Yanukovych, Manafort argued that changes in the Republican-controlled House of Representatives created an opportunity to "expand relationships, open minds, and demonstrate to the global community that Ukraine is a modern democracy." In fact, the opposite was true: Yanukovych, a notoriously corrupt Putin ally, would, the following year, violently crush pro-democracy demonstrations in Kyiv that were triggered by his refusal to enter into an agreement that would bring his country closer to the EU. Just a year after Manafort plotted how he would sanitize Yanukovych in Washington as a democratic leader, the Ukrainian strongman was overthrown, fleeing to exile in Russia. After he was deposed, Ukrainian citizens discovered that Yanukovych's official, taxpayer-funded residence was a lavish $100 million estate known as Mezhyhirya, featuring a five-story Finnish palace, a private zoo, a restaurant in a replica of a Spanish galleon, gilded toilets, dozens of luxury cars, a tennis court, a bowling alley, and an underground shooting range. Ukrainian citizens sought, unsuccessfully, to turn it into a Museum of Corruption. In 2019, a Ukrainian court convicted Yanukovych of treason in absentia;[16] he remains in exile in Russia.

But back in the swamp of 2013, Manafort assured his client Yanukovych, in a memorandum that was disclosed in his 2018 criminal tax fraud trial, that his "US consultants team has already been active" in implementing a strategy, called "Engage Ukraine," in order "to deepen the relationships between the two countries, and focus on major policy initiatives of significance to both countries."[17] In particular, Manafort noted, Yanukovych had a dependable congressional ally whom the House Republican leadership had just installed in a powerful position: Putin ally Dana Rohrabacher, who had a decade earlier, at Paul Weyrich's Russia conference, touted closer U.S. ties with Russia. The thirteen-term Orange County Republican had just been named chair of the Europe and Eurasia Subcommittee of the House Foreign Affairs Committee by the House leadership. Rohrabacher, Manafort assured his client, is "a good appointment for Ukraine and will be open minded about key policy issues." In contrast, Manafort noted, the Human Rights and Democracy Subcommittee will "seek to pressure the VY Government," and therefore "the best block of its actions is to have the pertinent SubCommittee on Europe take more positive stands. This is the strategy we are building." Manafort's strategy was to latch onto a friendly subcommittee chair—Rohrabacher—to neutralize any effort by other subcommittees that might pose problems for Yanukovych's consolidation of power. In 2014, a month after Yanukovych was deposed, Rohrabacher was one of just nineteen House members to vote against a bill funding aid to Ukraine and sanctioning Russia for its invasion of Ukraine and annexation of Crimea.[18]

Rohrabacher lost his reelection bid in the blue wave midterms of 2018 that hit his Orange County particularly hard, but he helped pave the way for Trump's dalliances with Russia; he is known among human rights advocates as being pro-Putin before Trump made it cool.[19] According to the indictment of accused Russian spy Maria Butina, she planned to meet with "a U.S. Congressman" during a Rohrabacher visit to Russia in August 2015.[20] Rohrabacher has admitted that he is the lawmaker referenced.[21] The following year, in April 2016, he met in Russia with lawyer Natalia Veselnitskaya, where she reportedly supplied him with the same talking points she later gave Trump campaign officials in their notorious June 2016 meeting in Trump Tower.[22]

Rohrabacher was one of Capitol Hill's early fans of Orbán as well. Given Putin's influence over Orbán, "these are not separate things to think about—the Russian influence and Hungarian influence," Kim Lane Scheppele, a Hungary expert at the Woodrow Wilson School at Princeton,[23] told me. Orbán, Scheppele says, is "Putin's pet."[24]

Rohrabacher's embrace of Orbán advanced as Orbán's attacks on democracy were becoming increasingly disquieting to the Obama administration. In a 2014 speech, Orbán claimed liberal values "embody corruption, sex and violence"; predicted that the successful nations of the future would reject these values and draw inspiration instead from Russia, China, or Turkey; and claimed that nongovernmental organizations working on building up civil society were actually "paid political activists who are attempting to enforce foreign interests here in Hungary."[25] The speech forecast Orbán's escalating moves to close Hungary's borders to migrants and refugees, silence political opposition, stifle a free press, erode the independence of the judiciary, and scapegoat supposed outsiders as conspirators against Hungary's sovereignty and "Christian" heritage.[26] That year on the Senate floor, Trump nemesis Sen. John McCain, the Arizona Republican, called Orbán "a neofascist dictator getting in bed with Vladimir Putin"[27] and accused him of "practicing the same kinds of antidemocratic practices" as the Russian president.[28]

The Obama administration shared McCain's worries. Sarah Sewall, who served as undersecretary of state for civilian security, democracy, and human rights from 2014 until Obama left office, told me that over that period, "anti-Semitic statements and policies, repression of speech and restrictions on civil society, [and] demonization of Americans who were promoting liberal values" by Orbán and his ruling Fidesz Party were becoming "more public, more entrenched, more concerning." Sewall said it then "became necessary to become more pointed in our criticism of these policies. And it became necessary to have uncomfortable conversations, privately"—conversations she viewed as "consistent with long-standing bipartisan American foreign policy principles." Doing so, said Sewall, seemed "a self-evident proposition" for the United States and was "entirely consistent with the history of American foreign policy, certainly through my lifetime."[29]

Trump did not even nominate a candidate to fill Sewall's former post at the State Department until nineteen months into his presidency. When he finally nominated Marshall Billingslea, a former official in the George W. Bush Defense Department, in August 2018, twenty-one human rights NGOs objected because he lacked the background in human rights, development, and refugee policy that recent Democratic and Republican administrations had required of appointees to that position. Worse, as a DoD official, Billingslea had endorsed "the use of interrogation methods that amounted to torture or other cruel, inhuman, or degrading treatment," according to the letter the NGOs sent to senators.[30] After his nomination failed because the Senate took no action on it, Trump renominated him.[31]

The Trump administration's first human rights report for Hungary, issued in April 2018, used far more tepid language than the reports prepared during the Obama era, which had warned of "systematic erosion of the rule of law; potential violations of international humanitarian law; weakening of checks and balances, democratic institutions, and transparency; and intimidation of independent societal voices" since Orbán regained power in 2010. Trump's report blandly described "the most serious human rights issues" as "allegations of" media consolidation, criminal penalties for libel, restrictions on NGOs, political corruption, growing anti-Semitism, and mistreatment of migrants. But, it concluded, "impunity for human rights abuses was not widespread."[32] Trump made an enthusiastic call to Orbán to congratulate him on the formation of his new government following his April 2018 reelection victory. "Both leaders agreed on the need for strong national borders," the White House said, and "pledged to keep United States–Hungary relations strong."[33]

Just two months later, on World Refugee Day, the Hungarian parliament demonstrated just the kind of impunity that Trump's State Department had claimed was "not widespread": it passed a law criminalizing NGO aid to refugees and migrants. Human Rights Watch (HRW) described the law as an attempt to silence critics of "the country's despicable treatment of asylum seekers and migrants at its border, to block their access to asylum, and to punish those who show solidarity with asylum seekers." The law's final passage on World Refugee Day showed the Hungarian government's "contempt for human rights values," HRW said, then called on the European

Parliament to suspend Hungary's voting rights.[34] Neither the White House nor the State Department issued any statements condemning the passage of the NGO law, which came just as the United States was facing its own human rights crisis—the separation of thousands of children from their refugee parents at the southern border, the product of one of the Trump administration's cruelest anti-immigrant initiatives. The image of caged migrants at the border had precedent; the previous year Orbán's government had set up detention camps for migrants at its border with Serbia.[35]

Since then the Trump administration has only further solidified its relationship with Orbán and has even aided his attacks on a free press—the sort of thing about which Trump often daydreams aloud. Under pressure by pro-Orbán Republicans in Congress, the State Department ended a government-sponsored program supporting media outlets engaged in "fact-based" reporting in Hungary.[36] After meeting with the prime minister in Budapest, energy secretary Rick Perry tweeted a photograph of the pair in a warm handshake, saying he hoped it "can mark the beginning of an even closer relationship between the U.S. & Hungary."[37] The meeting was not covered in the U.S. press. Orbán's office boasted, "Hungarian-US relations are excellent," highlighting how the two countries "confirmed that historical traditions and Christian roots must also play an important role in modern governance."[38]

After the Bush and Obama State Departments scolded him, Orbán, like Yanukovych, declined to engage the U.S. government's diplomatic establishment and instead shifted his efforts to the more malleable environs of K Street. When countries "are getting in trouble on human rights, rule of law, the governance direction of the country," said Conley, the former Bush State Department official, the countries "flood Washington with funding" to lobbyists and think tanks to soften the story or make it go away. "Instead of [us] fixing the problem," she said, "they fix us." Less than two months after Orbán declared Hungary an "illiberal" democracy in July 2014, his government signed a contract with a Washington lobbyist to craft "political messages" to deliver to the administration, Congress, and the media, in order to "have an influence on political decision making."[39]

Orbán's goal, in working with Washington insiders, was to get "the foreign policy world that could make life miserable for Hungary to think that he was just an ordinary conservative government," said Scheppele, a "garden variety conservative state besieged by liberals." Orbán, Scheppele said, knew this approach had the potential to win him instant sympathy with the American right. To aid in that image crafting, Orbán's government hired Connie Mack IV, a former Republican congressman from Florida who, after serving four terms in the House, lost a 2012 bid for the Senate seat once held by his father, Connie Mack III. Both Mack and his father had used Finkelstein as a paid consultant for their campaigns, and the younger Mack has described him as "a friend" to whom he has turned often for advice.[40] One of the founding members of the House's hard-line Freedom Caucus, Mack IV served on the Foreign Affairs Committee but had an otherwise unremarkable tenure.[41] One of his best-known legislative proposals was the dubious "Mack Penny Plan" to balance the budget by cutting one penny out of every dollar the government spent.[42] His failed Senate run was hampered by allegations of barroom brawls and incidents of road rage, which his campaign tried unsuccessfully to portray as the distant escapades of an exuberant youth.[43] The Democratic incumbent, Bill Nelson, defeated him handily.

Following his Senate loss, Mack traded in an ineffectual political career for a profitable turn as a lobbyist. After signing the contract with the Hungarian government, Mack quickly catapulted to the top of the revolving-door profiteers, becoming one of the five most highly paid foreign agents in 2015, when he pulled in over a million dollars.[44] Trump campaign national security adviser J. D. Gordon— a former Pentagon spokesperson who himself went on to cultivate ties with Budapest—described Mack to me as "a very effective and influential ally."[45]

Mack, as Manafort had planned to do, worked Rohrabacher and other members of his subcommittee. In October 2015, the U.S. ambassador to Hungary, Colleen Bell, in keeping with the bipartisan approach to Orbán since the George W. Bush era, condemned Orbán's "words of intolerance and xenophobic characterizations of refugees—some of the world's most vulnerable people—as invaders and antagonists" and called on Hungary "to come up with a comprehensive, practical, and compassionate solution to this crisis."[46] A few weeks later Rohrabacher convened a hearing on the "growing refugee crisis" in Europe, where he commended the Orbán regime and condemned his own government. During his opening statement, Rohrabacher paused to thank Hungary's then–ambassador to the United States, Réka Szemerkényi, for attending the event, and to praise Hungary as a "tremendous friend and asset to the peace and stability of the world.

"I am personally upset," Rohrabacher added, "that our administration has sought to find out and try to complain about every little thing they disagree with, with Hungary. Hungary has every right to set their own policies, and I am pleased that Hungary has a track record of doing good things with the United States."[47] Scheppele, who attended the hearing, could not believe she witnessed "a member of the U.S. Congress literally read the script of the Hungarian government in a congressional hearing"—a script that resonated with Trump's team, too.

Just as Trump dismissed the conclusions of U.S. intelligence agencies, he also dismissed the conclusions of the diplomatic establishment—that is, the establishment as it was before he began remaking it in the service of a global antidemocratic agenda. Obama's State Department had been publicly critical of the Hungarian government's mistreatment of immigrants and its systematic erosion of democratic institutions like a free press and an independent judiciary. But for the Trump campaign, these warnings about Hungary's assault on democratic norms did not stop its overtures to Budapest. Ambassador Szemerkényi attended the Republican National Convention in July 2016, where she praised Rudy Giuliani's "fiery and impassioned" speech on the convention floor, in which he attacked Hillary Clinton for supporting "open borders" and pledged that Trump would secure them. After the convention, Trump campaign adviser Carter Page traveled to Budapest at Szemerkényi's invitation, he later told congressional investigators, for a private meeting with Jeno Megyesy, a top Orbán adviser.[48] The Trump campaign's senior foreign policy adviser, his future attorney general, Jeff Sessions, sent Szemerkényi a warm letter at the height of the campaign, accepting an invitation to the Hungarian embassy in Washington. In his letter, Sessions embraced the Hungarian government's propaganda, describing Hungary as "a global beacon for the power of freedom, democracy, and human rights," in direct disagreement with the conclusions of his own country's government.

The mutual embrace between the Trump campaign and Budapest persisted throughout the Trump transition. In December 2016, Gordon, the Trump campaign adviser, gave a speech at a Budapest think tank, where, he later told me, he focused on NATO. "I stressed that all twenty-eight NATO member nations should spend the agreed upon two percent of GDP on defense," he said, and that "our allies need to do more for collective security. That includes securing their own borders, a shared challenge in the USA."

The *Budapest Business Journal* had a different take on Gordon's message, reading it much more explicitly as a mind-meld between Trump and Orbán. The newspaper reported that Gordon expressed admiration and respect for Orbán "and what he is doing to make Hungary great again," describing him as "one of the best world leaders" who "understands the threats from open borders." Trump and Orbán, Gordon predicted, "will be good friends."[49] Gordon, speaking to the now-defunct *Budapest Beacon*—one of the many Hungarian news outlets forced to close under the weight of Orbán's assaults on press freedom[50]—said that over the summer "a close friend who served as Hungarian Ambassador" had sent him a link to Orbán's endorsement of Trump, who, Gordon said, was "delighted."[51]

Szemerkényi became an even more visible presence and, measured by her social media posts, was proud of her many encounters in Trump's orbit. She tweeted about a preinaugural event at the Trump Hotel where she "gained insights" from Trump's short-lived national security adviser Michael Flynn, who later pleaded guilty to lying to investigators and became a cooperating witness in the special counsel's probe into Russian interference in the 2016 election. The Hungarian embassy hosted a postinaugural party, where Szemerkényi posted a photograph of herself with Gordon, the campaign adviser, and Rep. Devin Nunes, the California Republican who has been a dutiful Trump ally and was at the time the chairman of the House Intelligence Committee. She later attended an event at Mar-a-Lago and posted a photograph of herself with Trump and his wife, Melania; less than a month into Trump's term, she tweeted that it had been "a tremendous honor" to have met with Trump three times since his election. Szemerkényi was eventually recalled by Orbán, but Washington-Budapest ties continued to grow.

After Trump took office, Mack maintained regular contacts with members of Congress and their staffs, conservative think tanks such as the Heritage Foundation, and even the White House—with Vice President Mike Pence, national security adviser John Bolton, and White House adviser Sebastian Gorka, who left his post after coming under scrutiny for his ties to Nazi and anti-Semitic political organizations in his native Hungary.[52] (Gorka has denied these ties and remains an ardent and often churlish Trump defender in conservative media.) Mack distributes a newsletter, *Hungary Insights,* which includes frequent reminders of Orbán's early support for Trump and roundups of positive news coverage of Orbán, such as his friendly relationship with Israeli prime minister Benjamin Netanyahu. In his newsletter, Mack does not mention that Orbán foments anti-Semitism with his attacks on Hungarian-American pro-democracy philanthropist George Soros. He has encouraged American lawmakers to believe that Orbán is the bellwether not just of Hungarian but of broader European public opinion. In April 2018, in advance of another Rohrabacher hearing on mass migration in Europe, Mack sent Rohrabacher a packet of materials, which Rohrabacher entered into the *Congressional Record,* that included a letter from the new Hungarian ambassador to the United

States, László Szabó, arguing that "public sentiment in Europe is largely on Hungary's side" on the issue of migration.

Mack has also spun his Hungarian client as fellow traveler to American conservatives in right-wing media. In a November 2017 appearance on *Blunt Force Truth,* hosted by former *Love Connection–*host-turned-conservative-podcaster Chuck Woolery, Mack complained that Orbán was being unfairly maligned by career officials inside the State Department who were still loyal to Obama and Soros. Orbán has engaged in sustained and blatantly anti-Semitic attacks on the philanthropist, scapegoating him as a shadowy enemy outsider responsible for migration undermining Hungary's national and "Christian" identity, to the point that Soros-funded NGOs were forced to leave Hungary in 2018.[53] But Mack portrayed Orbán as the victim of Soros. "I wish our State Department would treat him more like a friend and an ally," Mack told Woolery, "instead of some of these underlings attacking him for things that George Soros is making up."[54]

Hungarian officials continue to be a presence in Trump's Washington, helping craft the conservative portrayal of U.S. and Hungarian interests as aligned against the liberal, Soros-backed enemy. Hungarian foreign minister Péter Szijjártó has met with Secretary of State Mike Pompeo and has attacked previous American efforts to promote democracy and human rights in addresses to American conservatives. "These kinds of open attempts to interfere in domestic politics issues should not be applied," he said at a 2017 appearance at the Heritage Foundation, "and I really do hope will not be part of our relationship in the future, if we have respect mutually for each other." The promotional materials for that event touted the "many similarities" shared by Trump and Orbán "on important policy issues," forecasting that "a new episode" in relations between the two countries could begin after "years of one-sided criticism" of Hungary.

The Trumpian fascination with Orbán is far from an isolated dalliance. Republican lawmakers, before Trump, had for years sidled up to Europe's far-right nativists and Islamophobes, sometimes giving fringe figures greater prominence and laying the groundwork for the American president's imprimatur to further elevate their global standing. In April 2015, Steve King, the Iowa Republican congressman known for his white supremacist sympathies, invited Geert Wilders, the founder of the Netherlands' far-right Freedom Party, to speak to the Conservative Opportunity Society, a group of House Republicans first launched by Newt Gingrich that still hosts a weekly breakfast gathering of House Republicans that King chairs. King remains the head of this agenda-setting group, even after the Republican congressional leadership stripped him of his committee assignments after his comments questioning why white supremacism was offensive in a January 2019 *New York Times* interview. His regular breakfasts draw prominent speakers, including Trump administration officials—one of many signals that despite King's overt racism, he remains an admired figure within party and activist circles; after he lost his committee posts, religious right leaders came to his defense, claiming he had been the victim of an "outrageous misquote" by the "liberal media."

Back at that 2015 meeting, Wilders, one of the world's most notorious Islamophobes and fresh off delivering a speech to Germany's explicitly anti-Muslim Pegida Party, called on his American friends to join his bigoted campaign against Islam—and liberal democracy. "Our duty is clear," he told the American lawmakers. "In order to solve the problem, we have to stop mass immigration to the West from Islamic countries. And we have to get rid of the cultural relativism."[55] Although the breakfast took place behind closed doors, King was eager to publicly depict it as a top-level meeting at which Wilders was an esteemed guest. "Geert Wilders speaking now before Members of Congress & national security experts," he tweeted. "Islam will not assimilate. Western culture is superior." The next day Congressman King called a press conference on the Capitol grounds to amplify Wilders's message, where he was flanked by fellow Republican congressmen Louie Gohmert of Texas and Scott Perry of Pennsylvania.[56] "It's important for us to expand and build our networks across the ocean, and to tie together the anchor which is Western

Civilization," he said. Other Republicans took note; Wilders later attended the 2016 Republican National Convention as the invited guest of the Tennessee Republican Party. At a strange bedfellows soiree hosted by former *Breitbart* editor and alt-right inciter Milo Yiannopoulos and a group of gay Republicans, young white men in MAGA hats chanted "Geert Geert Geert" and "Trump Trump Trump" as Wilders called for an end to "political correctness" and demanded that we "de-Islamize our societies." He accused political leaders in Europe and the United States of "abandoning us" but predicted that "parties like Mr. Trump, like my party, all over Europe, from France to Germany, from Austria to Italy, they are winning."[57]

As he pledged he would during his visit with Wilders in April 2015, King continued to build bonds with the European far right. That November, with the presidential primary campaigns in full swing, and just after Rohrabacher held his pro-Hungary hearing, King made a solo trip to Europe on official business of the House Judiciary Committee, on which he served—an irregular journey given that official committee business typically requires a bipartisan delegation. "6000 migrants/day transit through here at Adasevci, Serbia. From as far as Pakistan, mostly young Muslim males," King tweeted. Then from Sid, Serbia, he tweeted another apocryphal claim: "Trains bound 4 Croatia-Slovenia-Austria then Germany. 1000 people per train. 6 trains per day. No end." He had nothing but praise for Hungary's installation of a border fence, which, he claimed, had worked to keep out refugees.

During the same period when King was cultivating relationships with the European far right, 2016 GOP presidential hopefuls were aggressively seeking his support, given his status as a kingmaker in Iowa's caucuses. King ultimately endorsed Ted Cruz as the "candidate whom God will use to restore the soul of America." In a measure of King's influence in the party, Cruz embraced the endorsement, saying he was "beyond honored" to receive it from "one of the few truly principled men" in Washington.[58]

King continued to travel solo on official congressional business— including to France, Finland, and Austria, where he met with leaders of the far-right, Putin-backed Freedom Party.[59] The party, which was founded in 1956 by a former SS officer, has recently regained formal political power. For the first time in more than a decade, following elections in 2017, it became part of a coalition government, and Heinz-Christian Strache, the party's chair, became the country's vice-chancellor.[60] "This is the beginning of a good friendship," King said to Freedom Party leader Norbert Hofer in a party video posted on the party's website in October 2016. King's trip to Vienna was followed by a Freedom Party visit to the United States, shortly before the election. A delegation of party members traveled to New York, Washington, and North Carolina for "a multitude of conversations," according to a party newspaper.

Later—the day before Trump was inaugurated—Strache boasted on social media of his high-level Washington meetings. "Excellent talks in Washington D.C. at the International Republican Club of Capitol Hill with Congressman Steve King and [former Minnesota congresswoman] Michele Bachmann," Strache wrote on his Facebook page. Szemerkényi was also on hand, along with Rep. Marsha Blackburn, the Tennessee Republican who later won a Senate seat in the 2018 midterms, "and other US congressmen," according to Strache's post.

The GOP's embrace of authoritarians has extended to volatile regions like the Balkans, where right-wing nationalism led to genocide and other war crimes in the wars of the 1990s. In 2016, Macedonian prime minister Nikola Gruevski of the far-right VMRO Party was forced out amid widespread corruption scandals; later that year, running to regain power, he joined Orbán's demagogic call for "de-Soros-ization."[61] Gruevski, who had turned Macedonia in an increasingly corrupt and authoritarian direction over the course of his ten-year reign,[62] had been indicted in a wiretapping scheme to spy on over twenty thousand people, including journalists, members of the political opposition, and civil society advocates. At the time, the Obama State Department condemned "the inflammatory rhetoric from some political leaders which gives license to attacks on democratic institutions" and called on political leaders to "stop unwarranted attacks, respect the democratic process, and allow the formation of a credible, stable government committed to the rule of law, accountability, and fundamental freedoms."[63]

But three days before Trump's inauguration, Sen. Mike Lee, the influential Utah Republican, took a very different stance, writing an angry letter to Jess Baily, the U.S. ambassador to Macedonia, complaining that "I have received credible reports that, over the past few years, the US mission to Macedonia has actively intervened in the party politics of Macedonia, as well as in the shaping of its media environment and civil society, often favoring groups of one political persuasion over another." This was, Lee contended, "highly problematic."[64] Two months later Lee followed up with another letter, to Secretary of State Rex Tillerson, specifically attacking Soros-linked programs funded by the U.S. Agency for International Development that he claimed "push a progressive agenda and reinvigorate the political left." He further demanded an investigation into "all funds associated with promoting democracy and governance." That letter, which mimicked a pamphlet distributed on Capitol Hill by a VMRO-backed Macedonian group called Stop Operation Soros,[65] was signed by five of Lee's Republican Senate colleagues: James Inhofe of Oklahoma, Thom Tillis of North Carolina, David Perdue of Georgia, Bill Cassidy of Louisiana, and Ted Cruz of Texas.[66] Some of the most powerful members of the Republican Party were flexing their muscle in support of the demonization of Soros, and against American promotion of democratic values, at a time when regional experts and pro-democracy advocates were becoming increasingly concerned about a resurgence of right-wing nationalism.

Ambassador Baily told a Macedonian television station that the embassy had responded to the lawmakers' inquiries, though in keeping with State Department protocol, the embassy would not release that response publicly. But in defending the embassy's bolstering of the institutions of civil society, he made clear that he wasn't going to be daunted by the lawmakers' complaints. "What we support is helping build the institutions of a healthy democracy," he said. "That includes engagement by citizens in their affairs, and it includes media and other things."[67]

Senator Lee, though, continued to portray the VMRO and "conservative" countries like Poland as victims of leftist scheming. In March 2017, at a Heritage Foundation event, Lee, emboldened in the Trump era to launch a verbal assault on American democratic values, argued that under Obama, American diplomacy "took a decidedly leftist turn," taking up the "pet causes of a privileged global elite" such as abortion and "alternative family structures"—a reference to the Obama administration's support for LGBTQ rights around the world. At the Heritage event, Lee sounded more like an Alex Jones–style conspiracy theorist than a sitting U.S. senator whom President Trump had considered for a seat on the Supreme Court. To Lee, America under Obama was not promoting democracy but was participating in an insidious, anti-American plot. American efforts to bolster democratic institutions in fledgling democracies were, according to Lee, "the substance of a global re-education campaign, funded by American taxpayers, from whom they were hidden under the guise of innocuous sounding program titles like 'democracy assistance,' 'government transparency,' and 'human-rights.'"[68]

The campaign to prop up Macedonia's right wing received another considerable boost from the echo chamber of conservative media, when the conservative *American Spectator* published a series of articles on the Balkans,[69] and other conservative outlets including Fox,[70] *Breitbart*,[71] and *The Daily Caller*,[72] as well as Russian state media outlets *RT*[73] and *Sputnik*,[74] chimed in. The same month that Lee spoke at Heritage, the *Spectator* described "small but mighty Macedonia" as "the mouse that roared this year, declaring war on George Soros, 86, and his U.S. government handmaidens, who, incredibly, have financed a left-wing agenda to divide the nation and bring a socialist-Muslim coalition to power." The article further portrayed this religious war as one that would make Russia more attractive to Macedonian Christians than America, with its fallen version of Christianity. The article deemed U.S. goals in the region "so unsavory to the majority Orthodox population" that many Macedonians "are beginning to look toward Russia as a more sympathetic—not to mention Christian—ally."[75]

In May 2017, after months of political turmoil in Macedonia and as the formation of a new government approached, House Judiciary Committee chairman Bob Goodlatte led a congressional delegation that included King and Trump ally Matt Gaetz of Florida to Skopje, Macedonia's capital.[76] The *Spectator*'s coverage cast the trip as an "urgent mission" as "evidence mounts that Obama-era favoritism continues—to the detriment of citizens, local institutions, and regional stability."[77] State-run media quoted extensively from the *Spectator*'s coverage of the trip.

The support from American conservatives for VMRO's campaign was no coincidence. A 2017 investigation by the Organized Crime and Corruption Reporting Project, a transnational consortium of investigative journalists, found that between 2015 and 2017, VMRO had engaged in a concerted lobbying campaign in Washington, which "prompted U.S. conservatives to join in on an anti-Soros line of attack favored by Russia and Europe's authoritarian nationalists."[78] Even after VMRO lost power when a new coalition government formed in 2017, American conservatives kept up the fight, garnering coverage on Fox News of their anti-Soros campaigns in the Balkans. In order to keep a tale of liberal perfidy alive, the right-wing government watchdog group Judicial Watch continued to press for releases of documents from the State Department and USAID under the Freedom of Information Act in search of proof that the "U.S. government has quietly spent millions of taxpayer dollars to destabilize the democratically elected, center-right government in Macedonia by colluding with left-wing billionaire philanthropist George Soros."[79] By filing a Freedom of Information Act request, then blasting out a press release about it, Judicial Watch was able to push a bogus but cleverly crafted conspiracy theory that the U.S. government's efforts to promote democracy in the Balkans were actually an antidemocratic, Soros-funded attack on a "conservative" government—a narrative familiar to American conservative activists who had been primed to believe their own "conservative" president was the victim of conniving leftists carrying out a "witch hunt" while Soros paid protesters to trick the public into thinking that the president faced opposition. That way a far-right government—like the VMRO in Macedonia, or the GOP under Trump—was painted as moderate, and any efforts to bring it in line with democratic norms was portrayed as a shadowy, extreme leftist plot.

Over the course of Obama's presidency, the entire framework of protecting human rights came under attack, as the historic expansion of LGBTQ rights and Obama's efforts to protect reproductive rights in the United States and abroad terrified the American Christian right. Through conferences like the World Congress of Families, and at events at major think tanks like the Heritage Foundation, conservatives increasingly sought to mobilize their followers by conflating those rights with human rights as a whole, turning what was once a bedrock principle of America's post–World War II alliances in Europe into a suspicious phrase suggestive of a nefarious plot to steal away the rights of conservative Christians. Abortion, "gender ideology," and "alternative family structures" are presented as outrageous and even dangerous expansions of this leftist agenda.

Secretary of State Mike Pompeo, who is venerated on the Christian right, has given an official seal of approval to this approach. After the State Department welcomed Christian right notables to its July 2018 first annual Ministerial to Advance Religious Freedom, members of Congress, conservative activists, and conservative scholars were energized by what they saw as an official elevation of their own "religious freedom" over reviled "human rights." At a Heritage Foundation panel discussion following the ministerial, panelists assailed what they called "human rights inflation." The expansion of human rights to women and LGBTQ people, panelists complained, put religious freedom even more at risk. "The activist left," said Benjamin Bull, a leading Christian right attorney, was using "newly manufactured human rights to crush" what he called "traditional human rights" and "natural rights." Christians' rights are "traditional" and "natural." LGBTQ rights were, to these activists, "newly manufactured" and therefore to be relegated to lower status.[80]

Officials from far-right parties in Europe have seized on these issues as their point of entry to form alliances with Republican law-makers in their ambitions to undermine institutions created to pro-mote civil society and democracy in post–World War II Europe. At the World Congress of Families in Moldova in September 2018, Claudio D'Amico, a pro-Putin official with Italy's far-right League Party and a special adviser to Matteo Salvini, then Italy's far-right populist deputy prime minister and interior minister, shared how he initiated a "family" lunch at the Organization for Security and Coop-eration in Europe (OSCE), the intergovernmental body that pro-motes human rights, fair elections, and civil society within its fifty-seven member states. He did so, D'Amico said, after finding a "very bad situation" within the organization because of the "strong majority" of liberals who supported LGBTQ rights. Levan Vasadze, the Georgian venture capitalist who had told the conference attend-ees they needed to abandon urbanization so they could better "mul-tiply," helped him organize the lunch. D'Amico described his activities during a panel on "political strategies" at Chișinău's Radis-son Blu Hotel, alongside Radoš Pejović, a representative of Serbia's far-right DVERI Party, and Robert Siedlecki, a "pro-marriage" activist from the United States. Siedlecki had previously served in the George W. Bush administration and hoped to get federal funding from the Trump administration for his "innovative" Christian coun-seling program that he claimed kept married couples together. Like other speakers at the conference who worried that not enough peo-ple were getting or staying married, he claimed that married people had "better and more frequent" sex.[81] He told me that his hopes for getting federal funding were bolstered by knowing that he now had allies inside the Department of Health and Human Services and because "the Trump administration's clearly more friendly to this stuff."[82]

D'Amico had already held "family" lunches for far-right party members, on the sidelines of OSCE's parliamentary assembly, three times, first in Tbilisi in 2016, then in Minsk in 2017, and in 2018 in Berlin. After the panel at the Radisson Blu, he told me representatives have hailed from Russia and from other far-right parties such as Hungary's Fidesz, Austria's Freedom Party, Germany's Alternative for Germany, Switzerland's Christian Democrat Party, Sweden's Swedish Democrats—and the Republican Party. Members in attendance in 2017, he said, included King and, in 2018, Rep. Chris Smith of New Jersey, who had strong ties to the U.S. Christian right and the anti-choice movement. "Family" issues were "like the bridge or the glue" in bringing together countries that might otherwise be at odds with one another, like Russia and the United States, D'Amico said in an interview. "If this will happen, Russia and United States to find the agreement on the issue where they have problems between them, I would be very happy. Very happy."[83]

But "family issues" are less a bridge than cover for further anti-democratic ambitions. In the interview, D'Amico likened immigration to Italy to a "disease" or a "fever" that his country needed to treat; he wanted pro-natalist policies to encourage Italians to have bigger families, rather than accepting immigrants and refugees from Africa. He criticized a judge overseeing a criminal case against Matteo Salvini, who, as Italy's interior minister, was charged with kidnapping after he blocked 177 refugees aboard a coast guard ship from disembarking and entering the country. D'Amico called the case an "inquisition" and lamented that Italy's separation of powers barred Salvini from simply firing the judge.[84] A politician aspiring to erase separation of powers and undermine an independent judiciary is a grave warning sign to a democracy, as is the vilification and scapegoating of outsiders or ethnic minorities. Yet warning signs of "illiberal" democracy as envisioned by Orbán, D'Amico, and Trump are becoming increasingly commonplace. After the Ninth Circuit Court of Appeals ruled that Trump could not, by executive order, bar asylum seekers from crossing the U.S. border, Trump complained that the court was "very unfair," threatening, "We're going to have to look at that." With Majority Leader McConnell's help, Trump was well on his way to reshaping that court to his satisfaction.[85]

Before Trump's presidency, career diplomatic hands and political appointees with regional expertise would have served as a check on congressmen staging show hearings on the Hill, and on lawmakers jetting to Europe to meet with political parties founded by Nazis. But under Trump, the purposeful neglect of the State Department, which began under his first secretary of state, Rex Tillerson, has created a dangerous void—a dereliction that burst out in the open during the 2019 impeachment hearings into Trump's machinations in Ukraine. Just three months after being confirmed, Tillerson signaled to State Department employees that promoting human rights and democracy abroad could often create an "obstacle" to advancing American interests,[86] thereby casually upending the foreign policy establishment. Even after replacing Tillerson with CIA director Mike Pompeo, Trump continued to eviscerate the apparatus of the State Department, especially its functions dedicated to the protection and promotion of democracy and human rights. A U.S. government infrastructure that once had the capacity to stand up to the growing alliance between the European far right and the American right, rooted in shared antipathy to these values, is withering, and the important work it has done, unnoticed by most Americans during less turbulent times, is at risk of being devalued and discarded. Midway through his presidency, Trump had yet to name a nominee for fifty senior posts within the State Department, nearly a third of the total political posts requiring Senate confirmation. Trump's base of Christian right and nativist supporters not only doesn't care—it actively cheerleads the denigration of democracy and human rights, the rise of autocrats whipping up the grievances of right-wing populists, and disdain for what America once was.

Beyond Europe and the former Soviet bloc, the Christian right has backed Trump's growing far-right alliances. In Brazil, the fascist president elected in 2018, Jair Bolsonaro, is fluent in speaking the religious language familiar to American evangelicals. By comparison to Russia, Italy, Hungary, and Moldova, religion and politics in Brazil have followed a far more familiar path, as the political clout of its expanding evangelical and Pentecostal population has grown, surpassing even that of Catholics. When Bolsonaro—now known as "the Trump of the tropics"—was elected, Trump predicted that he and the Brazilian strongman would have "a fantastic working relationship" because of their "many views that are similar."[87]

On cue, just a few months later, Trump invited Bolsonaro for an official White House visit, flouting worldwide condemnation of the new Brazilian president's endorsements of extrajudicial killings and torture, calls for shooting or jailing political enemies, threats to media critical of him, and aspirations to stack the Brazilian supreme court with judges whose views align with his. He has said he would rather his son die in an accident than be gay, and he has called refugees "scum of the earth."[88] At the White House, though, Trump suggested that Brazil become a major non-NATO ally, or "maybe a NATO ally." As a non-European country, Brazil would not be eligible to become a NATO member and could only become a "partner" to the alliance, despite Trump's obtuse aspirations.[89] But "major non-NATO ally" is a designation that would afford Brazil preferential access to U.S. defense research and programs, and perhaps more important, it would place an American imprimatur on Brazil's sudden fascist turn. If Trump cannot dispense with NATO entirely, as he has publicly wished to, he can take a page from Putin's playbook—and try to undermine it from within.

Trump receives no pushback from his base, in part because Bolsonaro's religious appeals have given him hero status, as he uses religious language simultaneously to present himself as a protector of freedom and to denigrate his liberal adversaries—a playbook similar to the one used by his American evangelical admirers. During his White House visit, Bolsonaro described the two countries as bonded together in a shared commitment to "the guarantee of liberty, respect for the traditional family, the fear of God our creator, against gender identity, political correctness and fake news." Following his appearance with Trump, this new strongman alliance was sanctified during a gathering at Blair House, the historic presidential guest quarters, with about a dozen Christian right leaders. Pat Robertson, the chief of the Trump-cheerleading Christian Broadcasting Network, prayed

for "the anointing of the Holy Spirit" to descend upon Bolsonaro;
CBN aired footage of him gripping the hands of assembled leaders
in prayer. "Lord, uphold him. Protect him from evil. And, use him
mightily in years to come," Robertson implored.[90] Bolsonaro gave an
exclusive interview to the network, which praised his and Trump's
commitment to "biblical values" and made note of Bolsonaro's middle name: "Messias," Portuguese for "Messiah."[91] Religion, though, is
just a cover for the endgame: the extinction of the democratic institutions built in the wake of World War II and during the Cold War,
all meant to protect human rights and prevent another resurgence of
totalitarianism and the human devastation that comes with it.

All the bureaucratic and policy changes are driven not by Trump
acting alone but by a profound rightward ideological shift within the
Republican Party. "I think there is certainly affinity with the Hungarian government's view, I would say, the Austrian government's view,
increasingly the Italian government's view," said Heather Conley, the
former Bush official who has witnessed her party evolve ever rightward. It's an affinity, she said, with anti-immigrant rhetoric and policy and with the claim that the right must "vigorously defend the
conservatives, the traditional values against the decadence of a Western social agenda."[92]

Trump did not devise these changes alone. But he has become
the forceful role model making them the new cornerstone of the
Republican Party. The Republican base now exhibits a reflexive
antipathy to "globalists" and "liberalism," thanks not only to Trump,
but to the groundwork laid by right-wing lawmakers, lobbyists, consultants, media, and think tanks, all of which eased Trump's path to
power. Undermining institutions like NATO, the EU, the OSCE,
and even the State Department is a deliberate dismantling of what
former Trump strategist Steve Bannon derided, in a speech at a
Budapest think tank, as "this humanitarian expeditionary force that
they"—referring to "global elites"— "can send everywhere to be the
global cop for their rules-based order."[93] In the new, Trump-led
Republican era, "humanitarian" is not an accolade but an epithet.

10

The Assault on Reality

T rump's assault on human rights and the rule of law depends on far more than his supporters cheerleading his strongman moves or looking the other way as he eviscerates democratic institutions. It requires an affirmative buy-in to his alternative reality, where facts are fake news, the press is the enemy of the people, Democratic lawmakers are traitors, and only devout Christians know the real "truth," whether from their proof-texting of the Bible or in their claimed prophecies from God. Trump—as will anyone following in his footsteps—benefits from a prodigious infrastructure decades in the making, including networks of churches, advocacy organizations, charismatic televangelists, and Christian media, all of which have converged to maintain a fervent audience primed to be politically activated by the relentless chaos sown by Trump and his allies. The havoc is the point: while the rest of the public is whipsawed and overwhelmed, Trump's loyal followers see their divine leader as a victim beset by enemies from multiple directions, and see themselves as spiritual warriors called by God to protect him.

By activating every obscure corner of evangelical culture, Trump has elevated every obedient foot soldier into a critical cog in his totalizing strongman politics.

Editors, colleagues, and even readers often ask me whether a particular religious right figure is powerful or influential, worthy of news coverage or even any attention at all. Clearly some figures are more influential than others, either because they have bigger churches, larger television and conference audiences, and best-selling books, or because they are especially close to presidents or other elected officials. But under Trump—the televangelism president—the doors of the Oval Office have been opened to pastors and religious leaders, and televangelists in particular, in unprecedented ways. These meetings are not mere photo ops, so often the approach of George H. W. and George W. Bush that irked Christian right leaders as trivial gestures. In the Trump presidency, Christian right leaders routinely boast that they attend high-level meetings, and that the White House seeks their counsel on important matters of policy, from religious freedom to prison reform to Israel. These leaders, in turn, have become accomplices in Trump's assault on the truth.

The White House's open door policy, and the frequency with which Christian right leaders are welcomed for meetings both ceremonial and highly political, has not only boosted the celebrity of the Christian right leaders who have been brought into the presidential circle. Proximity has also multiplied the ways that Trump's lies and conspiracy theories become the reality of the followers of these Trump allies. In that alternate, conspiratorial reality, any scrutiny of Trump or his inner circle is cast as a plot, deeply rooted in "fake news," George Soros–funded protesters, Clinton family machinations, or even Satan, to bring down God's chosen leader of the United States of America. The religious leaders close to the Trump White House assist in his assault on reality by immersing their followers at church, on television, and online into a universe disassociated from reality and severed from even the most basic facts. Their alternative universe is instead permeated with narratives about how Christians and Trump are under attack, and about how only Trump's heroic defense of their religious freedom saves them from the onslaught of godless secularism.

Trump has consistently used these Christian right supporters as a shield against news coverage that exposes his wrongdoing, potentially threatening his presidency. In July 2017, just three days after *The New York Times* broke the explosive story that Paul Manafort, Donald Trump, Jr., and Jared Kushner had met in Trump Tower with a Russian lawyer who they believed had "dirt" on Hillary during the presidential campaign,[1] Johnnie Moore, an evangelical public relations professional who served as the spokesman for Trump's evangelical advisory board, tweeted a photograph of Trump in the Oval Office, sitting at his desk, with Moore, Paula White, the televangelist Rodney Howard-Browne, and Browne's wife, Adonica, standing behind him. "Really wonderful visit with @POTUS and @VP after an all day meeting w/evangelical leaders & the WH Office of Public Liaison, Y'day," Moore wrote.[2] Three hours later Moore tweeted another photo, this one showing the back of Trump's head as he was surrounded by people laying hands on him, Pence nearby, his face bowed in prayer. "Such an honor to pray within the Oval Office for @POTUS & @VP," Moore tweeted.[3]

The second photo instantly went viral on social media; TV and print media promptly picked it up. Suddenly the news cycle was about Trump's Oval Office apostles, not the *Times* story about the Trump Tower meeting that was one of the first big public insights into what "collusion" with Russia might have looked like. But the intense focus on the photo, and the secular media's astonishment at the practice of laying on hands, especially in the White House, was a boon for Trump's allies. It allowed Trump's evangelical supporters to tout their high-level access and at the same time berate the media for portraying their sincere religious activity as peculiar and for even raising questions about church-state separation. The viral photo was a win-win: evangelicals were so vital and valued to the president that he sought their prayers. The media reaction was proof that evangelicals, along with their anointed leader, were being unfairly targeted by what Steve Bannon had called "the opposition party."[4]

This was not the first time Trump's evangelicals performed a prayerful rapid response to a damning news story. In October 2016, just after the *Access Hollywood* tape broke, at least three influential evangelical pastors, who all had Trump's cell phone number, called the candidate to offer him prayer and friendship, according to Moore. They were, Moore told me, "forgiving."[5] Moore, a veteran in evangelical circles after working in the administration at Liberty University for more than a decade, and then as chief of staff for reality television (and *Apprentice*) producer Mark Burnett, is a smooth-talking flack skilled at translating aspects of evangelicalism that appear eccentric to outsiders. I met him the day after those White House meetings but before he tweeted out the photos, in Crystal City, a Washington suburb packed with drab office buildings and hotels, where he was scheduled to deliver a speech to a gathering of conservative high school students. When talking one on one, Moore strains to present himself as an earnest believer who has accidentally fallen into politics but wishes he could rise above it.

Pastors, Moore insisted, are not as political as portrayed in the media, "but most of these guys, every single day, they help people through life weddings and funerals and counseling preaching and teaching." That, he said, is what they do for Trump. At the moment of the *Access Hollywood* tape (which happened to be released just weeks before the presidential election many evangelicals viewed as pivotal for Supreme Court nominations and more), "they weren't advancing a political agenda; they were pastors. And, by the way, the number one thing I think that this informal group, which is—maybe it'll be formal at some point—but this group, the number one thing they've done for the president, the vice president, and various members of the administration, they prayed for them. There are no big stories about that." A few hours later, Moore changed that supposed lack of coverage with his tweet; the story of the Oval Office prayer was suddenly all over the news.

The night before, I had seen Pastor Howard-Browne, whose

wife's dark blue fingernails are front and center on Trump's back in Moore's viral Twitter photo, preaching at the final night of the "Celebrate America" revival he held that week at the Daughters of the American Revolution Constitution Hall just a few blocks from the White House.[6] Howard-Browne, an immigrant from South Africa now based in Tampa, Florida, is known as the "Holy Ghost Bartender," notorious for his role in promoting "holy laughter" gifts— a faction of a charismatic revival in which uncontrollable laughing and even animal sounds are seen as a sign of divine utterances, like speaking in tongues or prophesying. At his revivals and at his River Church, congregants typically break out in clamorous laughter or even barking sounds. He is a close friend of Paula White, who has said that early in her career, when she was a struggling preacher, before she had a television show or a large following, he and his wife "really helped break the spirit of poverty" in her own life. "There's only a handful of people in my life that I can say it's because of these people that God used to launch me into strategic places, and two of those people are Pastor Rodney and Adonica Howard-Browne," White told his congregation a week after Trump's inauguration, where she had delivered the invocation. "Had God not used you, then we would never be here, because 15 years ago, I received a phone call from now-President Trump"—the call that launched the friendship that brought the televangelist into the highest echelons of political power in the world. Without Rodney and Adonica, she told their congregation, "I could have never fulfilled the assignment God gave to me," in which God told her to "speak the word of the Lord" with Trump. Turning to Howard-Browne, she added, "Your obedience and Pastor Adonica's obedience unlocked in me a gift that set me before our president and unlocked many things."[7]

Just hours after having prayed with Trump in the Oval Office, Howard-Browne was onstage at Constitution Hall casting out demons and slaying people in the spirit. I was in the crowd as Pastor Rodney pushed his hand on people's foreheads; as they collapsed toward the floor, filled with the holy spirit, ushers rushed to catch them. "Pick this lady up," Howard-Browne ordered the ushers, pointing to a woman in the front row, rocking on the floor and laughing, as people were hooting and shouting. "Looks like she's been drinking. But she's not drinking the stuff you think. She's drinking new wine," said Howard-Browne. "I'm talking about the holy ghost." Amid the intensity, the shouting, and the laughing, Howard-Browne didn't mention Trump specifically, but he boasted that politicians always wanted to come around to his church at election time. And he claimed to know of divine intervention right there in the nation's capital. He shouted that he saw "the fire of God coming upon the White House, upon the Executive Branch, upon the Congress, upon the Senate, upon the Supreme Court, upon the FBI, upon the CIA, upon the NSA, upon every realm of government, upon the IRS. My God, shake the IRS."[8]

Howard-Browne was an enthusiastic Trump backer during the 2016 campaign, attending the Republican National Convention as a guest of the Hawaii Republican delegation and tweeting a photograph of himself with Trump campaign manager Paul Manafort, who was "doing such a stellar job."[9] Three days before the election, he delivered the invocation at a Florida campaign rally, where he was introduced by Florida attorney general Pam Bondi and where he prayed that "total confusion would be wrought in the camp of the enemy."[10] On Christian radio, Howard-Browne has explained his endorsement of Trump as necessary because "he's a threat to the New World Order and the one-world government." During the campaign, he defended Trump's immigration stance: "he's been labeled by the left as a racist and Hitler—something that they even use in the U.K. against Nigel Farage and UKIP for the same reasons." He blamed this on the fact that "too many Americans are liberals when it comes to the way they lean because of the media and the education system and how they've been dumbed down."[11] He left no conspiracy theory untouched in his explanations of why Christians should vote for Trump. "If people don't understand about the private central banking system of the last two hundred years started by the Rothschilds, if they don't understand that this is the Luciferian structure of the globe," he said on a radio program during the GOP primary, "here comes a man who does not need anybody's money, who's not interested in anybody's money, because he's self-funded, and he comes out of the blue, he controls the media, basically, with two billion dollars' worth of free advertising, which irritates them, but the American people have watched him, when he's said to people 'You're fired.' They love that. They love the outspokenness." The country, he said, had been taken over by the "globalist" agenda, which was "why millions of illegals are let into the country, and they all become dependent on the government, so they can all then vote and ultimately to change the Constitution," after which the government would "go house to house and disarm the American people."[12]

The Sunday before Christmas 2016, I saw Howard-Browne preach at his Tampa church as he filled the sanctuary with people, many of whom appeared destitute, upon the promise of a toy give-away after the service was over. After the service was over, people lined up on the hot blacktop parking lot to receive a toy distributed from trucks. Later that day Howard-Browne and his wife, according to their social media, flew to Mar-a-Lago, Trump's private resort, where he posted about the lavish setting and meeting the president-elect.[13] He later told his congregation, "We got to stay at his house for two days, and we went to the Christmas party on the eighteenth of December."[14] Howard-Browne had just returned from Ukraine, where he had preached at a Kyiv revival. He later became an enthusiastic backer of Trump's debunked conspiracy theory, reprised during his impeachment hearings, that Ukraine, not Russia, meddled in the 2016 election on behalf of Hillary Clinton. As early as July 2017, when Trump tweeted about "Ukrainian efforts to sabotage Trump campaign" and "quietly working to boost Clinton," Howard-Browne retweeted it with the comment, "That's a fact ...... I was in the Ukraine and know the story ..... they were working with Crooked Hillary #Fact."[15] At other times, he boasted of having met with Ukrainian government officials who "asked me to get a message to the President Elects office, offering deep apologies for their involvement in backing and funding #CrookedHillary #fact #truenews."[16]

For Howard-Browne, the Oval Office photo was an opportunity to talk more about his connections to Trump and his friend Paula White; on Instagram he posted a photograph of himself, his wife, and White "talking strategy" at the Trump Hotel in Washington.[17] In a video he posted online, Howard-Browne, sitting at a desk with a framed photograph of himself with Trump pointed toward the camera, described how on that pivotal day, a group of pastors was escorted to the Oval Office, where they engaged in "a radical prayer" against "every evil attack" on Trump. But "the Communist News Network didn't like it," Howard-Browne complained, using his favored term for CNN, "they said it was really freaky that we were laying hands on the president."

"I'm not really worried about that," Howard-Browne told his congregation the following Sunday, "because I am a full-blown radical Pentecostal who believes in laying on of hands, casting out devils, and praying for the sick, and we believe in prosperity, all of those things." The president "gets" you, Howard-Browne was telling his Pentecostal audience, even though the media mocks you.[18] Recounting the story to his congregation, Howard-Browne claimed his phone had "been ringing off the hook," but he "wasn't going to do any interviews with the mainscream media." He did, though, agree to interviews with the Christian Broadcasting Network and *Fox & Friends*, clips he played during the service. CBN asked him how Trump was handling "the press amidst the nonstop Russia mania." Confidently, Howard-Browne replied, "he's always handled pressure," adding that "it energizes him, he seemed totally relaxed." Howard-Browne assured the CBN audience that despite what the other media told you, "It was not Russia that put President Trump in the White House, it was the American people." On *Fox & Friends*, he promised, "I just prayed for his protection, really, because I realized the attack against our president, to take him out, so we just prayed for him," referring to a conspiracy theory Howard-Browne spread, including on Alex Jones's *InfoWars* program, that a member of Congress warned him there was a "physical" plot to "take out" Trump.[19]

When I met Howard-Browne a year later, he was signing copies of his conspiratorial new book, *The Killing of Uncle Sam,* at a predominantly black church in Prince George's County, Maryland, just outside the capital.[20] He insisted the book was "nonpartisan" but said it would explain why Trump got elected. Trump, Howard-Browne told me in a hushed voice, did not even know that he was being used by God as a "temporary reprieve" to hold off "one world government, one world system, the Anti-Christ." Had Trump not won, he said, there would have been "open borders" and "the North American Union," a "one-world government," and more wars, because terrorism was "funded out of America" by "the cabal" that "took over education, they took over the seminaries, they took over the media." Spinning his dizzying mishmash of conspiracy theories, Howard-Browne noted that he did not know whether Trump was a Christian, but "all I can tell you from my observation, does he pray, I don't know, he doesn't talk Christian, he's a playboy, who—he does his own thing." But in that now-famous Oval Office meeting, "he stood behind me, and we said, we'll pray for you, and he said, that would be great. And then we talked for twenty minutes and then he said—he said, 'Who is going to pray.' So he brought it up."[21] So maybe even if he wasn't a Christian, he would at least receive the prayers of Christians.

Howard-Browne has repeated some of the most venal, worn conspiracy theories about Jews—such as about the Rothschilds controlling the banking system and world events. Yet he was not only welcomed in the White House and kept up to date via its email briefing sent to evangelical leaders, he was also invited specifically for an evangelical strategy meeting about White House policy on Israel.[22] The meeting, which took place in early March 2019, was intended to assuage evangelical leaders in the wake of reports that Jared Kushner was negotiating a peace deal that would include a Palestinian state with a capital in East Jerusalem, something that hard-line Christian Zionists had long opposed. Also present at the off-the-record "listening session" with Trump's Middle East envoy Jason Greenblatt were Lance Wallnau and Paula White, as well as the televangelist John Hagee, a leading Christian Zionist who teaches that Christian support for Israel is part of God's plan for the second coming of Jesus, and Joel Rosenberg, the author of numerous books about the end times.[23] In 2008, Sen. John McCain, then the presumptive Republican presidential nominee, renounced Hagee's endorsement and distanced himself from the televangelist as a result of his anti-Catholic comments, as well as a sermon in which he claimed that God sent Hitler to set off the chain of events that would lead to the Jews fulfilling biblical prophecy by establishing the State of Israel. Despite the McCain denunciation, Hagee has remained a celebrated figure in Christian Zionist circles—and is consulted on matters of Israel policy by the Trump White House.

While they claim to "love the Jewish people" as evidenced by their support for Israel, Trump's evangelical allies regularly spread anti-Semitic conspiracy theories about billionaire philanthropist George Soros, who has backed pro-democracy institutions and civil society building across the globe—the very same conspiracy theories spread about Soros by the nationalist far-right in Europe and by white nationalists in the United States. Trump-aligned Republican and Christian right leaders have blamed Soros for, among other things, orchestrating a campaign against Supreme Court nominee (and now Justice) Brett Kavanaugh, for running a "shadow party" on behalf of Barack Obama, for carrying out a "deadly" agenda, for promoting "open borders and lawless 'sanctuary' cities increasing drugs, disease, crime, gangs and terrorism," for paying protesters to incite racial violence, and even possibly for being the anti-Christ. This conspiracy-mongering about Soros persisted even after he was the target of a pipe bomb, sent by a Trump fan in Florida, Cesar Syroc, who had, among other bizarre conspiracies, claimed Soros paid the Parkland shooting survivor and gun control activist David Hogg to fake the massacre. Trump himself has targeted Soros: he tweeted that the women who confronted Sen. Jeff Flake about sexual assault in a Senate elevator during the Kavanaugh hearings were "paid for by Soros and others,"[24] and he has tried to lend credence to a debunked—but widely disseminated in conservative circles—claim that Soros paid for a caravan of refugees to travel to the United States from Honduras.[25]

Two days after Syroc left the pipe bomb in Soros's mailbox, the charismatic publishing giant Stephen Strang wrote in a column that while he did not believe that Soros was the Antichrist, "it's obvious he operates in the spirit of the Antichrist," because "Soros funds many of the attacks on conservative, biblical values. The media tries to make it seem as though the many liberal protests we're seeing nowadays are spontaneous." But, Strang went on, in a claim regularly made by white nationalists, and which I heard repeated at a neo-Nazi rally in Harrisburg, Pennsylvania, days before the 2016 election, "there's strong reason to believe that many of these protesters are paid to come and stir up trouble. Rich socialists like Soros know that if they can manage to disrupt society with chaos, good and decent people will cave into liberal demands and give way to the left-ist agenda."[26]

Putin had led the way in the anti-Soros backlash in Europe, first cracking down on Soros-funded NGOs in the summer of 2015, putting them on a "patriotic stop list," then ultimately labeling them "undesirable in Russia." Putin's ally Orbán—who earlier in his career himself received funding from Soros's Open Society Foundation—in October 2015, at the height of the refugee crisis, declared war on Soros, saying he "maintains and finances the European human rights activism which encourages the refugees."[27] Orbán quickly recognized that the election of Trump, whom he had endorsed, would help his cause, predicting a month after Trump's election that "in every country, they will want to displace Soros," and "in the coming year, Soros and his forces will be squeezed out."[28] Three years later Howard-Browne claimed to have visited a Pentecostal church in Budapest, which had "single-handedly kicked George Soros out of Hungary," a claim amplified by Strang on his podcast and in his newsletter.[29]

With his expanding relationships with evangelical and Pentecostal figures, Trump has been building a defensive line of protection against revelations about the avalanche of criminality and corruption that are engulfing his administration, using conspiracy theories to stoke panics of a secularist attack on Christianity. In turn, white evangelical voters have bought into the manufactured, Trumpian reality perpetuated by the evangelical leaders whose standing Trump has elevated in order to ensure their ongoing support. And it has worked: after special counsel Robert Mueller wrapped up his investigation of the Trump campaign's possible coordination with Russia, and of Trump's possible obstruction of justice relating to the investigation, white evangelical voters, more than any other demographic, remained convinced that he had done nothing wrong. Seventy-seven percent of them told pollsters they did not believe Trump had obstructed justice, and 67 percent believed Trump had been telling the public the truth about the investigation. In contrast, a majority of all American adults—58 percent—believed Trump had lied.[30]

Other Republican candidates and presidents have courted the religious right, televangelists in particular, elevating their status despite scandals and rhetoric that offended other key constituencies. Most critically, these candidates extended legitimacy to their claims to know of God's plans and prophecies and the power to carry them out. But no previous Republican candidate or president sought the evangelical embrace to support their autocratic impulses, or to broadcast a claim that he is God's anointed, a leader of unparalleled divinity and authority. No previous Republican candidate or president has embraced, perpetuated, and enabled such a staggering exhibition of lies and conspiracy theories and used his bully pulpit to denigrate his perceived enemies.

Trump has succeeded in captivating white evangelical voters not just because he has befriended certain high-level leaders in the evangelical world. He has succeeded because there is virtually no leader in the evangelical world he wouldn't welcome by his side—as long as that leader pledged allegiance to him. Out in the world, the foot soldiers of the Christian right, in seeking out prophets and apostles and teachers and preachers, don't follow just one evangelist, or even a few. Through television, conferences, books, and social media, evangelicals absorb the teachings and writings of a wide variety of figures. I've lost count of the conversations I've had with people—at churches, at conferences, even standing in line at a pro-Trump church service the day before he was inaugurated—discussing all the teachers they've learned from. It's like a buffet meal, and the offerings of pro-Trump propaganda are vast.

Trump will not always be president, but he has elevated the conspiracy theory to a new high status in American politics. His evangelical allies, in turn, promote conspiracy theories about Trump the strongman, a fearless, anointed leader who is laboring heroically to save the Christian nation despite threats from socialism, the deep state, or George Soros. In return for their veneration, the life raft his presidency needs daily, Trump has given the Christian right new life, has spared them a Hillary Clinton presidency and a more liberal Supreme Court, and has given them unprecedented free rein in his administration and a defining role in the government of the United States. He's the leader they've been waiting for—the one who has been prophesied—who will affirm their authority as long as they accede to his. And they were there for him when he needed them most—to be his shield against impeachment—armed not only with all of their adulation, but with the escalating and ever-evolving set of conspiracy theories that became the president's only defense.

And God Will Smite the Impeachers

By the time congressional Democrats officially launched their impeachment inquiry in late September 2019, Trump's evangelical enablers had in place an immovable protective fortress of compliant Christian media, solicitous Republican lawmakers, dedicated political foot soldiers, and fervent prayer warriors who literally believed they were shielding Trump from satanic forces bent on his downfall. Seemingly no new piece of damning evidence could erode the enthusiasm of Trump partisans. That the proceedings themselves were, bit by bit, exposing a dangerous, self-serving plot by the president and his cronies was only proof, to Trump's evangelical loyalists, that Democrats, disappointed that the Mueller investigation had failed to end Trump's presidency, were only manufacturing new ways to mount a "coup."

It is far too facile an explanation to pin this devotion solely on a personality cult around Trump. The conditions that first brought him to power and, later, led to a nearly complete Republican capitulation to his whims were set in motion by two religious and political transformations of the 1970s: the sprawling political and ideological infrastructure Paul Weyrich built in the wake of Watergate, and the proliferation of televangelism and its marriage to Republican politics. At this critical moment in American history, when the democratic experiment hangs in the balance, this totalizing political and religious culture, rooted in a white Christian nationalist political ideology, was tailor-made to go to the mat for Trump.

For Trump's white evangelical supporters, defending him became indistinguishable from defending white Christian America. As the impeachment probe was heating up and its findings were beginning to be made public, Robert Jeffress's confidence in Trump's evangelical backing remained unshakable. On October 29, 2019, twenty-five evangelical leaders, many of whom were part of the regular gathering of faith leaders at the White House, including top figures like the Family Research Council's Tony Perkins and the Faith and Freedom Coalition's Ralph Reed, met with Trump in the Roosevelt Room. Once again, they prayed with him, and afterward, Johnnie Moore again pushed out reverential photographs on social media.[1] The day after the meeting, Jeffress, who also attended, told me, "I think just the whole basis of the impeachment is flawed." He argued that "the American people have a right to know" whether Ukraine had "undue influence" over Joe Biden, just as Americans wanted to know whether Russia had undue influence over Trump—even though this supposed Ukrainian influence was nothing more than a conspiracy theory spread by Trump and his allies, and Russian interference in the 2016 election had been established by U.S. intelligence agencies. But more important to Jeffress than the particulars of the impeachment inquiry was "a war for the soul of our nation," in which evangelical voters are the shock troops. "I think most evangelicals believe this impeachment is an attempt to overthrow the 2016 election and therefore negate the votes of millions of evangelical Christians," he said. To many evangelicals, Jeffress maintained, "this is a war between good and evil. They see Donald Trump is the warrior in that battle between good and evil and they're not about to abandon him over some trumped-up impeachment charges."[2]

Trump's willingness to stack the courts and federal agencies with Christian right loyalists, and to give them full authority to transform a secular liberal democracy into a Christian nationalist autocracy, has produced more gratitude for his presidency than for the presidency of any other Republican since the advent of the modern Christian right. And movement leaders know they have Weyrich to thank for his vision of a government led by right-wing Christian ideologues trained in the network of think tanks and advocacy organizations that had been his brainchild. The annual Values Voter Summit, held in October 2019, kicked off the day after Lev Parnas and Igor Fruman, associates of Trump's personal lawyer Rudy Giuliani in his Ukrainian dealings, were arrested at Dulles Airport and charged with felony violation of U.S. campaign finance laws. But this news was of no concern to the values voters; instead, speakers were reminding attendees of the unprecedented power Trump had delivered to them. "I was thinking about the late Paul Weyrich, who used to say, 'Personnel is policy,'" Perkins told the audience as he introduced Alex Azar, the health and human services secretary, whose department has been ground zero for the implementation of Christian right policy priorities. "What makes the difference in this administration," said Perkins, "is that we're not on the outside looking in, we are on the inside working out."[3] In a fund-raising email two weeks later, Perkins described impeachment as a "virus" and accused "the Left" of having been unable to produce "a single legitimate charge against President Donald J. Trump!" It was therefore time, Perkins wrote, "for America's Christians and conservatives to use our combined clout and put a stop to this political attack tearing our nation apart."[4]

That combined clout includes, crucially, the network of televangelists and self-proclaimed prophets who have backed Trump with an unparalleled fervor. In mid-October, less than a month into the House Democrats' formal impeachment inquiry, Jim Bakker, the televangelist and convicted felon, was on the set of his television program filmed in front of a studio audience at his Morningside USA complex in Blue Eye, Missouri, an isolated village of fewer than two hundred people in the Ozark Mountains. As he waited for the crew to prepare the set for taping, the seventy-nine-year-old Bakker stepped out from behind the semicircular desk where he conducts

interviews with his evangelical celebrity guests who make the pil-
grimage from all over the country, and from which he evangelizes his
strident support for Trump and warns of coming riots and race wars.
This day, Bakker had an additional, important message for the roughly
one hundred people who had come to watch that day's taping, though
he was mindful of delivering it only after making certain the cameras
were not rolling. God, he said, is "sending judgment." God, Bakker
continued to applause and *yeses* and murmurs of affirmation from
the audience, "anointed your president." Any opponent of Trump's,
then, risks God's wrath, including, Bakker said, "that man" who
"would vex my soul when he was on TV, spewing against the president." That morning, the news had broken of the unexpected death
of Elijah Cummings, the Democratic congressman and chair of the
House Oversight Committee. Cummings, the son of Baptist preachers, was a civil rights hero who had a lifelong scar on his face, the
result of being attacked by a white mob when, as an eleven-year-old
child, he integrated a Baltimore city swimming pool.[5]

Bakker would not be offering any prayers or condolences for the
storied lawmaker. Instead, Bakker expressed satisfaction that "one of
the number one enemies of our president fell dead last night. A man
who insists on impeaching the president of the United States, he fell
dead."[6]

Bakker then returned to his seat behind the desk as the crew and
his co-host Mondo De La Vega anticipated the arrival of that day's
featured guest, Anne Graham Lotz, the daughter of the legendary
evangelist and spiritual adviser to presidents, the late Billy Graham.
Lotz was a featured celebrity for the Prophetic Encounter Conference Bakker was hosting that week, and was there to promote her
new book, *Jesus in Me*, and patter with Bakker about the news of the
day. Bakker spoke of the role Lotz's family—particularly her father
and brother, Franklin, heir to his father's empire and a vociferous
Trump defender—played in his rehabilitation in prison, and in helping him to reinvent himself in this isolated spiritual garrison, where
Bakker's loyal followers live in the condos built above the television
studio or are pressed to buy a new house atop "Prayer Mountain."

Bakker described his prison visits from Billy and Franklin Graham, the Bibles they sent him, their help with his transition to life on the outside, the chicken dinner at the Graham family home, the meal at a Red Lobster with Franklin. "I just want people to know the Grahams touched my life," said Bakker. Lotz replied, "What makes you unique in a world of sinners is that you are so honest, and you're humble about it."[7]

Bakker was also eager to promote others' prophecies about Trump's anointing, and featured the evangelist Jeremiah Johnson, author of a self-published book entitled *Trump, 2019, & Beyond*. In the book, Johnson claims, among other things, that he received a vision, in early 2018, of "Donald Trump's right hand that began to turn into an IRON FIST." He also says he saw in this vision "the liberal agenda gasping for breath as the Trump agenda (the iron fist) squeezes and suffocates its opponents." Johnson warned, "The attacks, plots, and plans against him will become more and more bizarre in the days ahead," and that Christians should continue to pray for him "and for the purposes of God to be manifested through his life and presidency."[8]

Bakker may seem like an aging relic of the 1980s televangelist scandals, consigned to a remote outpost after his spectacular fall from grace three decades ago. But his rehabilitation is a cautionary tale that suggests why Trump's white evangelical supporters continue to rally around him. Back in the 1980s, Bakker's fall had begun, in part, after revelations of an affair with his secretary, Jessica Hahn, and hush money payments he made to her became public. In 1989, a federal jury in North Carolina convicted him on twenty-four counts of fraud and conspiracy stemming from charges that he conned followers out of $158 million by hawking worthless "partnerships" in his Heritage USA vacation compound for one thousand dollars apiece. According to Associated Press coverage of the trial, Bakker's defense attorney called fifty followers as character witnesses to the witness stand, and many "acknowledged under cross-examination that no facts that came up in the trial could alter their view of Bakker." Some Bakker supporters accused Judge Robert Potter, the

Reagan appointee who presided over the case, of bias.[9] Thirty years later, Bakker compared himself to Trump. He told the influential magazine and book publisher Stephen Strang in 2019 that he has "so much in common" with the president because, like him, Trump "had every agency of government trying to destroy him."[10]

Since his return to televangelism, Bakker has been embraced and promoted by top evangelical names, including, in the Trump era, the president's personal pastor, Paula White. The week before the Prophetic Encounter Conference during which Bakker celebrated what he believed to be God's judgment on Elijah Cummings, White had been to Morningside to promote her new book, *Something Greater: Finding Triumph Over Trials*, which details her eighteen-year friendship with the president. Bakker was delighted that the president's closest spiritual adviser had graced his studio with her presence. During the Prophetic Encounter Conference, Bakker solicited donations from the studio audience and television viewers for "the voice of the prophets" outreach, for which he claimed he needed a million dollars. For one thousand dollars, he said, donors would get a membership card and their picture in a photo album just like Paula White, who he says was the first one to make a thousand-dollar donation. He proudly showed the audience the album with White's photograph in it.

White's book tour turned out to be just as much a tour promoting Trump, coming as the Democrats' official impeachment inquiry was getting underway. Two weeks after her appearance at Morningside, she was back preaching at her friend Rodney Howard-Browne's church in Tampa, Florida, where she once again detailed how she and Trump had met, and the "supernatural miracle" that led to her acquisition of a condo in Trump Tower. "Did I ever think he was going to be president?" White asked. "No. But God gave me an assignment" and she followed "a divine instruction."[11]

In the midst of the impeachment turmoil, Trump appointed White the head of his Faith and Opportunity Initiative—Trump's reinvention of George W. Bush's White House Office of Faith-Based and Community Initiatives. The televangelist had no experience in government or policy making, but she did have plenty of experience portraying Trump as a divinely anointed figure under attack by satanic forces. On November 5, 2019, White told supporters during a conference call hosted by the One Voice Prayer Movement, which she launched with other Trump allies during the frenzied fall of Trump's showdown with House Democrats, that they needed to pray "to deliver our president from any snare, any trap, any setup of the enemy." This omnipresent enemy, although formidable, could be vanquished, in White's telling, by two powerful forces: Jesus and Trump. White thanked God that "the blood of Jesus is superior, so any persons, entities, that are aligned against President Trump, the will of God, against the mantle that he would carry against him as president, that it would be exposed and dealt with and overturned in Jesus's name."[12]

As much as White and Bakker seem like televangelism caricatures, the divine appointments and judgments they claim to discern are echoed throughout the evangelical world, and help form the grassroots shield for Trump against impeachment. At the Values Voter Summit in 2019, I met Carly Eli, who very much wanted to talk with me about the visions she had received from God about Trump and the "hedge of protection" God had placed on him. Eli counsels—not unlike Bakker—that in the Book of Psalms, God warns not to come against his anointed ones. She compares Trump to David, the biblical king. "David had so many enemies, but they never touched him because God's hand was on David," she said. "And he was crowned as a king on top of it."

Eli, a diminutive woman with long brown hair, thick mascara, and red lipstick, was dressed in a blue suit with a rhinestone lapel pin that spelled out the words "How can I pray for you?" She wants to show me her Bible, with its color-coded Post-its—purple for verses dealing with obedience, blue for salvation, red for judgment, and yellow for end times. She waves off news coverage of impeachment as "distractions," and is focused more on visions she says she has received from God about Trump—that she saw him and Rudy Giuliani on an inauguration platform as early as September 2015, that she saw God place a crown on Trump's head twice, signaling to her that he will serve two terms. "I fear for anyone that comes against this man," Eli said. She brought up the "hedge of protection" again, and began to laugh. "It's so beautiful. I say, you go, Lord, you go. It's amazing. It's amazing."[13]

And so an untold number of Trump's evangelical supporters believe that God has anointed him, God will protect him, and God will smite his enemies. However his presidency ends, the fundamental damage it has inflicted on our democracy will not be healed overnight. His "base" is not an accident of his unconventional foray into politics, or a quirk of this particular political moment. The vast majority of white evangelicals are all in with Trump because he has given them political power and allowed them to carry out a Christian supremacist agenda, inextricably intertwined with his administration's white nationalist agenda. Conspiracy theories and lies about the core of our democracy—separation of powers, a free and independent press, and the dedication of public servants—run rampant through their print and social media, podcasts, and television programs. The depth and durability of their fervor have disproven the mantra "the religious right is dead" again and again—and their ability to sustain a presidency in the face of unprecedented scandal is the most compelling evidence against that mantra yet.

Trump's white evangelical supporters make up an army of partisans decades in the making, and they will not quietly retreat in the face of defeat.

ACKNOWLEDGMENTS

I had the great fortune of having as my editor Mark Warren, who fully embraced my vision for this book and pressed me at every turn to excel at achieving it. Mark immersed himself in my reporting, and pushed and prodded me to tell more stories, to make more arguments, to bring the reader with me. Mark: thank you for your insight, inspiration, and confidence in me. Thanks also to Chayenne Skeete and the entire Random House team, who all worked so hard on every step of production and presentation.

I never would have written *Unholy* if Stuart Krichevsky, exemplary literary agent, had not emailed me one day in early 2017. I cannot say enough about Stuart's dedication and advocacy on my behalf, his astute understanding of my work, and the care and attention he devotes to his clients. Thanks also to all of his colleagues, especially the discerning Laura Usselman.

I am indebted to Esther Kaplan, my visionary editor at Type Investigations, where I am a reporting fellow, and which has made so much of my investigative journalism possible. Many thanks to my other colleagues at Type, Taya Kitman, Sarah Blustain, David

Neiwert, Joe Conason, and Kristine Bruch; to its team of current and former editors, interns, researchers, and fact-checkers extraordinaire: Jaime Longoria, Richard Salame, Kalen Goodluck, Evan Malmgren, Naomi Gordon-Loebl, Jayati Vora, Jasper Craven, Jake Bittle, Queen Arsem-O'Malley, and Darya Marchenkova. Thanks to Julia Herrnböck for her invaluable research on American lawmakers and the Austrian and German far right. I've also had the privilege of working with outstanding editors at Type Investigations' publishing partners— Richard Kim, Lauren Kelley, Sean Woods, Nick Baumann, Clara Jeffery, Mark Follman, Bob Moser, Sasha Belenky, Ellis Jones, Nona Willis-Aronowitz, and John Light. Thank you also to Rachel Dry for asking me to write about Trump and evangelicals in 2016, to Mike Madden, Michelle Boorstein, and Sarah Pulliam-Bailey for asking me to write about Trump and religion, and to Greg Sargent, Paul Waldman, Ruth Marcus, and James Downie for the opportunity to write for The Plum Line. I'm also incredibly lucky to have many colleagues and friends—exceptional journalists and scholars—I have turned to while writing this book for insight, expertise, and encouragement: Anthea Butler, Adele Stan, Peter Montgomery, Kathryn Joyce, Lisa Goldman, Jerome Copulsky, Martyn Oliver, Evan Berry, Jeff Sharlet, Julie Ingersoll, Ed Kilgore, and Janet Reitman. Thanks also to the invaluable librarians and archivists who helped with research at the Library of Congress, the University of Wyoming, the George Washington University, the University of California, Berkeley, Brigham Young University, and Yale University. I also am grateful to Christopher Buckley for granting permission for me to review portions of his father's papers.

To my beloved family: you are simply the best. To my dear friends, neighbors, and dog-helpers: a million thankful and flaming emojis to you. To all the people who daily protect and defend democracy through their work, service, activism, or art: persist. It all matters.

ARCHIVES

MSS 176; American Conservative Union (ACU) records, L. Tom Perry Special Collections, Harold B. Lee Library, Brigham Young University

William F. Buckley Papers, Accession Number 2001-M-066, Yale University

Federation for American Immigration Reform (FAIR) Papers, Special Collections Research Center, The George Washington University

People for the American Way Collection of Conservative Political Ephemera, BANC MSS 2010/152, Bancroft Library, University of California, Berkeley

William Rusher Papers, Manuscript Division, Library of Congress

Paul M. Weyrich Papers, Collection no. 10138, American Heritage Center, University of Wyoming

Paul M. Weyrich Scrapbooks, Paul M. Weyrich Papers, Manuscript Division, Library of Congress

NOTES

INTRODUCTION

1. "Welcome," Weyrich Lunch, https://www.weyrichlunch.com/.
2. "Paul Weyrich to Be Honored at Tribute in Washington, D.C. for His Life, Work and Service," *Standard Newswire,* September 9, 2008, http://www.standardnewswire.com/news/266063320.html.
3. "A Salute to Paul Weyrich" (video), 2008, https://www.youtube.com /watch?v=x_FEWUyDSoI.
4. "Q&A with Paul Weyrich" (transcript), C-SPAN, March 22, 2005, https://www.c-span.org/video/transcript/?id=7958.

1 The Blueprint for an Assault on Civil Rights

1. Sarah Posner, "Leaked Draft of Trump's Religious Freedom Order Reveals Sweeping Plans to Legalize Discrimination," *Nation,* February 1, 2017, https://www.thenation.com/article/leaked-draft-of -trumps-religious-freedom-order-reveals-sweeping-plans-to-legalize -discrimination/.
2. Ryan T. Anderson, "Mr. President: Don't Cave to Liberal Fearmongering. Protect Religious Freedom," *Daily Signal,* February 2, 2017,

https://www.dailysignal.com/2017/02/02/mr-president-dont-cave-to
-liberal-fearmongering-protect-religious-freedom/.

3. Council for National Policy to President Donald Trump, March 1,
2017, http://files.constantcontact.com/2438cc3e001/b3d4b1e1
-6f27-4002-90d1-9a3a1fba3904.pdf?ver=1488490366000.

4. Sarah Posner, "Religious Right Leaders Blast Trump's Order as a
Betrayal," *Nation,* May 5, 2017, https://www.thenation.com/article
/religious-right-leaders-blast-trumps-order-as-a-betrayal/.

5. Rep. Warren Davidson et al. to President Donald Trump, April 5,
2017, https://www.scribd.com/document/346168978/Letter-to
-President-Trump-on-Religious-Liberty.

6. "National Day of Prayer" (video), Jack Graham Vimeo, https://
vimeo.com/216033652.

7. "President Trump Signs the Executive Order on Promoting Free
Speech and Religious Liberty" (video), White House, May 4, 2017,
https://www.youtube.com/watch?v=5n3L75jpUlg.

8. Posner, "Religious Right Leaders Blast Trump's Order."

2　God's Strongman

1. Ralph Reed, remarks to Congressional Town Hall, Faith and
Freedom Coalition Road to Majority Conference, Capitol Visitors'
Center, Washington, D.C., June 27, 2019.

2. *Washington Post*–ABC News Poll, January 21–24, 2019, *Washington Post,* February 8, 2019, https://www.washingtonpost.com
/page/2010-2019/WashingtonPost/2019/01/28/National-Politics
/Polling/question_21174.xml.

3. Johnnie Moore, interview by author, July 11, 2017.

4. Moore interview; Rodney Howard-Browne and Paula White-Cain,
"Winter Camp Meeting" (video), River Church, Tampa, Fla., January 27, 2017, https://www.youtube.com/watch?v=U9-oVEakQvw.

5. "Paula White Today Trump" (video), April 29, 2008, https://www
.youtube.com/watch?time_continue=7&v=EqcZ5NcnGYk.

6. David Barstow, Susanne Craig, and Russ Buettner, "Trump Engaged
in Suspect Tax Schemes as He Reaped Riches from His Father,"
New York Times, October 2, 2018, https://www.nytimes.com
/interactive/2018/10/02/us/politics/donald-trump-tax-schemes-fred
-trump.html.

7. Sen. Charles Grassley to Randy and Paula White, November 5, 2007, https://www.finance.senate.gov/imo/media/doc/prg110607a .pdf.

8. Senate Finance Committee, "Minority Staff Review of Without Walls International Church, Paula White Ministries," January 5, 2011, https://www.finance.senate.gov/imo/media/doc/WWIC%20 Whites%2001-05-11.pdf.

9. Theresa Pattara and Sean Barnett to Sen. Charles Grassley, memo regarding "Review of Media-Based Ministries," January 6, 2011, p. 54, https://www.finance.senate.gov/imo/media/doc/SFC%20 Staff%20Memo%20to%20Grassley%20re%20Ministries%2001-06 -11%20FINAL.pdf.

10. Brian Tashman, "Pat Robertson: Multiple Sclerosis Is 'Demonic' and Can Be Healed Once Rebuked," *Right Wing Watch,* March 29, 2017, http://www.rightwingwatch.org/post/pat-robertson-multiple -sclerosis-is-demonic-and-can-be-healed-once-rebuked/.

11. Brian Tashman, "Pat Robertson: Black Families Were Better Off in the 1930s," *Right Wing Watch,* November 8, 2016, http://www .rightwingwatch.org/post/pat-robertson-black-families-were-better -off-in-the-1930s/.

12. David Brody, interview by author, May 31, 2016.

13. David Brody, *The Brody File,* CBN News, April 12, 2011, http:// www1.cbn.com/cbnnews/shows/brodyfileepisodes/103376.

14. David Brody, "Only on *The Brody File:* Donald Trump to Meet with Group of Christian Pastors," CBN News, May 11, 2011, http://www1.cbn.com/thebrodyfile/archive/2011/05/11/only-on-the -brody-file-trump-to-meet-with-group.

15. Rodney Howard-Browne and Paula White-Cain, "Winter Camp Meeting" (video), River Church, Tampa, Fla., January 27, 2017, https://www.youtube.com/watch?v=U9-oVEakQvw.

16. Jerry Falwell, Jr., interview by author, June 22, 2016.

17. Recording of meeting provided by #NeverTrump source.

18. Republican Party Platform 2016, p. 11, https://prod-cdn-static.gop .com/static/home/data/platform.pdf.

19. Ralph Reed, speech to "Life of the Party" luncheon, Cleveland, Ohio, July 19, 2016.

20. Brendan Fischer, "Destroying the Johnson Amendment: How Allowing Charities to Spend on Politics Would Flood the Swamp

That President Trump Promised to Drain," *Campaign Legal Center,* August 13, 2018, http://www.campaignlegalcenter.org/sites/default /files/Johnson%20Amendment%20White%20Paper_0.pdf.

21. Stephen Strang, *God and Donald Trump* (Lake Mary, Fla.: Charisma House, 2017).

22. Jared Woodfill, interview by author, May 4, 2017.

23. Edward-Isaac Dovere, "Tony Perkins: Trump Gets a 'Mulligan' on Life, Stormy Daniels," *Politico,* January 23, 2018, https://www .politico.com/magazine/story/2018/01/23/tony-perkins-evangelicals -donald-trump-stormy-daniels-216498.

24. Laurie Goodstein, "Conservative Christian Leader Accuses Repub- licans of Betrayal," *New York Times,* February 12, 1998, https://www .nytimes.com/1998/02/12/us/conservative-christian-leader-accuses -republicans-of-betrayal.html.

25. David D. Kirkpatrick, "Christian Conservatives Consider Third- Party Effort," *New York Times,* September 30, 2007, https://the caucus.blogs.nytimes.com/2007/09/30/christan-conservatives-consider -third-party-effort/.

26. Rachael Bade and Christopher Cadelago, "Trump's Pit Bulls on Capitol Hill," *Politico,* July 27, 2010, https://www.politico.com /story/2018/07/27/jordan-meadows-trump-allies-congress-745121.

27. "Watchmen 2018: Rep. Mark Meadows" (video), Watchmen Pastors, June 5, 2018, https://www.youtube.com/watch?v= FWjQ5HeqiWg.

28. Vicki Stahl, interview by author, September 21, 2018.

29. Lance Wallnau, speech to Values Voter Summit, Washington, D.C., September 21, 2018.

30. Lance Wallnau, "My Unusual Saturday with Trump," Facebook post, October 12, 2015, https://www.facebook.com/LanceWallnau /posts/10153701097479936.

31. "Mission and Vision," Global Life Campaign, n.d., https://www .globallifecampaign.com/wwwgloballifecampaigncom-c1ppg.

32. Thomas Jacobson, interview by author, September 14, 2018.

33. Sarah Posner, "How One Evangelical Family Is Reshaping Politics, Law and Religious Research," *Washington Post*, November 17, 2017, https://www.washingtonpost.com/outlook/how-one-evangelical -family-is-reshaping-politics-law-and-religious-research/2017/11 /16/ba043b8e-b998-11e7-a908-a3470754bbb9_story.html.

34. Elizabeth Dias, "Inside Evangelical Leaders' Private White House Dinner," *Time*, May 4, 2017, http://time.com/4766485/national-day -prayer-white-house-dinner/.

35. "Watchmen 2018: Mike Pence" (video), Watchmen Pastors, June 5, 2018, https://www.youtube.com/watch?v=8IY8Rr-NrGM.

3   Race Rules

1. "Pete Buttigieg Uses Border to Slam Republicans' Christian 'Hypocrisy,'" Fox News, June 29, 2019, https://video.foxnews.com /v/6053803719001/#sp=show-clips.

2. Robert Jeffress, interview by author, October 7, 2011.

3. Jon Greenberg, "Trump's Pants on Fire Tweet That Blacks Killed 81% of White Homicide Victims," *Politifact,* November 23, 2015, https://www.politifact.com/truth-o-meter/statements/2015/nov/23 /donald-trump/trump-tweet-blacks-white-homicide-victims/.

4. "O'Reilly Confronts Trump on Retweeting Inaccurate Stats About Black Murder Rate," Fox News Insider, November 23, 2015, https://insider.foxnews.com/2015/11/23/bill-oreilly -confronts-donald-trump-about-retweeting-inaccurate-statistics -about-black.

5. Jennifer Agiesta, "Trump Dominates GOP Field Heading into 2016," CNN.com, December 24, 2015, https://www.cnn.com /2015/12/23/politics/donald-trump-ted-cruz-cnn-orc-poll/index .html.

6. Katie Zezima and Tom Hamburger, "Ted Cruz Huddles with Faith Leaders at Ranch of Super PAC Donor," *Washington Post*, December 29, 2015, https://www.washingtonpost.com/news/post-politics /wp/2015/12/29/ted-cruz-huddles-with-faith-leaders-in-texas/.

7. "White Nationalist Pays for Radio Airtime and Robocalls to Promote Donald Trump in Iowa" (press release), American Freedom Party, January 9, 2016, http://american3rdposition.com/nationalist-pays -radio-airtime-robocalls-promote-donald-trump/.

8. Sarah Posner and David Neiwert, "How Trump Took Hate Groups Mainstream," *Mother Jones*, October 14, 2016, https://www.mother jones.com/politics/2016/10/donald-trump-hate-groups-neo-nazi -white-supremacist-racism/.

9. Sarah Posner, "Baptist Blogger Who Discovered Land Plagiarism Says Investigation Is 'Unprecedented,'" *Religion Dispatches,*

April 23, 2012, http://religiondispatches.org/baptist-blogger-who
-discovered-land-plagiarism-says-investigation-is-unprecedented/.

10. Aaron Weaver, interview by author, April 23, 2012.

11. Tiffany Stanley, "The Culture Warrior in Winter: Richard
Land's Fall and the End of the Old Religious Right," *National Journal,* July 12, 2014, https://static1.squarespace.com
/static/56ae81a03c44d810c6717b8c/t/590a48c8e58c6287a4282b
fc/1493846218239/The+Culture+Warrior+in+Winter.pdf.

12. Michelle Boorstein, "An Interview with Russell Moore of the
Southern Baptist Convention," *Washington Post,* July 18, 2013,
https://www.washingtonpost.com/local/an-interview-with-russell
-moore-of-the-southern-baptist-convention/2013/07/18/40957c32
-ef2a-11e2-bed3-b9b6fe264871_story.html.

13. "Transcript: Eric Garner and the Case for Justice," Ethics and
Religious Liberty Commission, December 3, 2014, https://erlc.com
/resource-library/articles/transcript-eric-garner-and-the-case-for
-justice.

14. Russell Moore, "The Cross and the Confederate Flag," June 19,
2015, https://www.russellmoore.com/2015/06/19/the-cross-and-the
-confederate-flag/.

15. *Washington Post*–ABC News Poll, July 16–19, 2015, *Washington
Post,* July 20, 2015, https://www.washingtonpost.com/page/2010
-2019/WashingtonPost/2015/07/20/National-Politics/Polling
/question_15822.xml.

16. Russell Moore, "What Will Matter to Evangelicals in 2016,"
Wall Street Journal, February 5, 2015, https://www.wsj.com
/articles/russell-moore-what-will-matter-to-evangelicals-in-2016
-1423179343.

17. Michael Gerson, "The Trump Evangelicals Have Lost Their Gag
Reflex," *Washington Post,* January 22, 2018, https://www.washington
post.com/opinions/the-trump-evangelicals-have-lost-their-gag
-reflex/2018/01/22/761d1174-ffa8-11e7-bb03-722769454f82_story
.html.

18. Russell Moore, "Have Evangelicals Who Support Trump Lost
Their Values?," *New York Times,* September 17, 2015, https://www
.nytimes.com/2015/09/17/opinion/have-evangelicals-who-support
-trump-lost-their-values.html.

19. Jerry Falwell, Jr., interview by author, May 31, 2016.

20. Donald Trump, tweet, May 9, 2016, https://twitter.com/real
     DonaldTrump/status/729613336191586304.

21. Todd Littleton, interview by author, February 2, 2016.

22. Russell Moore, "A White Church No More," *New York Times,*
     May 6, 2016, https://www.nytimes.com/2016/05/06/opinion/a-white
     -church-no-more.html.

23. Posner and Neiwert, "How Trump Took Hate Groups Mainstream."

24. Jared Taylor, interview by author, August 24, 2016.

25. "Trump Campaign Announces Evangelical Executive Advisory
     Board," campaign press release, June 21, 2016, http://www.p2016
     .org/trump/trump062116evangelical.html.

26. Eric Metaxas, interview by author, June 24, 2016.

27. Richard Spencer, interview by author, July 19, 2016.

28. Drew Magary, "What the Duck?," *GQ,* December 18, 2013, https://
     www.gq.com/story/duck-dynasty-phil-robertson.

29. "'Duck Dynasty' Phil Robertson to Receive Andrew Breitbart First
     Amendment Award at CPAC,'" *Breitbart News,* February 17, 2015,
     https://www.breitbart.com/entertainment/2015/02/17/duck-dynasty
     -phil-robertson-to-receive-andrew-breitbart-first-amendment-award
     -at-cpac/.

30. Steve Bannon, interview by author, July 21, 2016; and Sarah Posner,
     "How Donald Trump's New Campaign Chief Created an Online
     Haven for White Nationalists," *Mother Jones,* August 22, 2016,
     https://www.motherjones.com/politics/2016/08/stephen-bannon
     -donald-trump-alt-right-breitbart-news/.

31. Ibid.

32. Steve Bannon, interview by author, July 21, 2016.

33. Cathy Burke, "Tony Perkins: I Will Be Voting for Trump," *News-
     max,* July 21, 2016, https://www.newsmax.com/politics/tony
     -perkins-endorsement-donald-trump-rnc/2016/07/21/id/739935/.

34. Steven K. Bannon, speech to Values Voter Summit (video), Octo-
     ber 14, 2017, https://www.c-span.org/video/?435688-1/steve
     -bannon-addresses-values-voter-summit&start=NaN.

35. Ian Lovett, "Baptist Figure Faces Backlash over His Criticism of
     Donald Trump," *Wall Street Journal,* December 19, 2016, https://
     www.wsj.com/articles/baptist-figure-faces-backlash-over-his
     -criticism-of-donald-trump-1482162791.

36. Tom Gjelten, "Evangelical Leader Under Attack for Criticizing Trump Supporters," NPR, December 20, 2016, https://www.npr.org/2016/12/20/506248119/anti-trump-evangelical-faces-backlash.

37. Russell Moore, "Election Year Thoughts at Christmastime," December 19, 2016, https://www.russellmoore.com/2016/12/19/election-thoughts-christmastime/.

38. "Open Letter to President Trump from Religious Leaders," October 2, 2017, https://web.archive.org/web/20171002221620/https://www.unifyingleadership.org/.

39. Sarah Pulliam Bailey, "Trump's 'Shithole' Comments Have Enraged Many. But Some Evangelical Leaders Still Back Him," *Washington Post,* January 12, 2018, https://www.washingtonpost.com/news/acts-of-faith/wp/2018/01/12/trumps-shithole-comments-have-enraged-many-but-some-evangelical-leaders-still-back-him/?utm_term=.a4f36da63c88.

40. POTUS Shield, https://www.potusshield.com/mission.

41. Frank Amedia, interview by author, May 23, 2016.

42. "District of Columbia Results," *New York Times,* n.d., https://www.nytimes.com/elections/2016/results/district-of-columbia.

43. Frank Amedia, sermon, Chevy Chase Baptist Church, Washington, D.C., November 3, 2018.

44. Lance Wallnau, Facebook Live, https://www.facebook.com/wallnau/videos/10210025887819501/.

45. Michael Cohen, interview by author, August 31, 2016; Sarah Posner, "Trump 'Diversity' Advisers Push Conspiracy Theories and Fringe Ideas About Minorities," *Mother Jones,* September 3, 2016, https://www.motherjones.com/politics/2016/09/trump-black-latino-voters-national-diversity-coalition/.

46. Ibid.

47. Emily Jane Fox, "Michael Cohen Says Trump Repeatedly Used Racist Language Before His Presidency," *Vanity Fair,* November 2, 2018, https://www.vanityfair.com/news/2018/11/michael-cohen-trump-racist-language.

48. Frank Amedia, interview by author, November 5, 2018.

49. "Addressing the Spirit of Racism," Kenneth Copeland Ministries, November 1, 2018, http://kcm.org/watch/tv-broadcast/addressing-the-spirit-racism?type=371&tags=All&speaker=All&result_page=1.

50. "'These Children Are Being Trafficked, We Must Have Stricter

Border Laws': Pastor Paula White Tours Migrant Detention Facility," CBN News, July 9, 2018, http://www1.cbn.com/cbnnews /national-security/2018/july/these-children-are-being-trafficked-we -must-have-stricter-border-laws-pastor-paula-white-tours-migrant -detention-facility.

51. Ibid.

52. Matthew Soerens, "The Baby in the Manger and at the Border: What Paula White Gets Wrong," *World Relief*, July 16, 2018, https://worldrelief.org/blog/the-baby-in-the-manger-and-at-the -border.

53. "Illegal Immigrant Could Not Be Messiah, Trump's Religious Adviser Says," *RT*, July 11, 2018, https://www.rt.com/usa/432740 -illegal-immigrant-not-messiah/.

54. Paula White-Cain, "Jesus, Immigration, and My Critics," *Christian Post*, July 18, 2018, https://www.christianpost.com/voice/jesus -immigration-my-critics-paula-white-cain.html.

4   The Alt-Right Out in the Open

1. Craig Timberg, Karla Adam, and Michael Kranish, "Bannon Oversaw Cambridge Analytica's Collection of Facebook Data, According to Former Employee," *Washington Post*, March 20, 2018, https:// www.washingtonpost.com/politics/bannon-oversaw-cambridge -analyticas-collection-of-facebook-data-according-to-former -employee/2018/03/20/8fb369a6-2c55-11c8-b0b0-f706877db618 _story.html.

2. "Exposed: Undercover Secrets of Trump's Data Firm," Channel 4 News, March 20, 2018, https://www.channel4.com/news/exposed -undercover-secrets-of-donald-trump-data-firm-cambridge -analytica.

3. "The Philosophy of Race Realism," *American Renaissance*, n.d., https://www.amren.com/about/issues/.

4. "Transcript: Hillary Clinton's Full Remarks in Reno, Nevada," *Politico*, August 25, 2016, https://www.politico.com/story/2016/08 /transcript-hillary-clinton-alt-right-reno-227419.

5. Jared Taylor, interview by author, August 24, 2016.

6. Richard Spencer, "What Is the Alt-Right?," Washington, D.C., September 9, 2016; see also Sarah Posner, "Meet the Alt-Right 'Spokesman' Who's Thrilled with Trump's Rise," *Rolling Stone*, October 18,

2016, https://www.rollingstone.com/politics/politics-features/meet-the-alt-right-spokesman-whos-thrilled-with-trumps-rise-129588/.

7. Andrew Lawler, "How a Child Born More Than 400 Years Ago Became a Symbol of White Nationalism," *Washington Post,* May 24, 2018, https://www.washingtonpost.com/news/made-by-history/wp/2018/05/24/how-a-child-born-more-than-400-years-ago-became-a-symbol-of-white-nationalism/.

8. "What Is Immigrant Mass Murder Syndrome?," *VDare.com,* July 30, 2016, https://vdare.com/articles/what-is-immigrant-mass-murder-syndrome.

9. Peter Brimelow, interview by author, September 9, 2016.

10. Geoffrey Kabaservice, "The Syndicate," *New Republic,* August 27, 2012, https://newrepublic.com/article/106505/william-rusher-national-review-david-frisk.

11. National Empowerment Television, *BorderLine* #39, "Immigration History and the 1965 Act" (video), October 21, 1996, in FAIR Records, Boxes 142 and 143.

12. Rod Dreher, "America's Camp of the Saints Problem," *American Conservative,* October 22, 2018, https://www.theamericanconservative.com/dreher/america-camp-of-the-saints-problem-migrant-caravan/.

13. Paul Blumenthal and J. M. Rieger, "This Stunningly Racist French Novel Is How Steve Bannon Explains the World," *HuffPost,* March 4, 2017, https://www.huffingtonpost.com/entry/steve-bannon-camp-of-the-saints-immigration_us_58b75206e4b0284854b3dc03.

14. Eliana Johnson and Eli Stokols, "What Steve Bannon Wants You to Read," *Politico,* February 7, 2017, https://www.politico.com/magazine/story/2017/02/steve-bannon-books-reading-list-214745.

15. James Hohmann, "The Daily 202: Five Books to Understand Stephen K. Bannon," *Washington Post,* February 7, 2017, https://www.washingtonpost.com/news/powerpost/paloma/daily-202/2017/02/07/daily-202-five-books-to-understand-stephen-k-bannon/58991fd7e9b69b1406c75c93/.

16. Peter Brimelow to William Rusher, March 7, 1978, in Rusher Papers, Box 12, Folder 5.

17. Rusher to Brimelow, March 17, 1978, ibid.

18. "Enoch Powell's 'Rivers of Blood' Speech," *Telegraph,* November 6,

2007, https://www.telegraph.co.uk/comment/3643823/Enoch
-Powells-Rivers-of-Blood-speech.html.

19. Peter Brimelow, "Editor Peter Brimelow on Enoch Powell, a Double
    April Prophet—and Why You Should Give to VDARE.com NOW!,"
    VDare.com, April 19, 2018, https://vdare.com/posts/editor-peter
    -brimelow-on-enoch-powell-a-double-april-prophet-and-why-you
    -should-give-to-vdare-com-now.

20. Peter Brimelow, résumé, in Rusher Papers, Box 12, Folder 5.

21. Rupert Murdoch to William F. Buckley, Jr., March 5, 1986, in
    Rusher Papers, Box 12, Folder 5.

22. Peter Brimelow, "Time to Rethink Immigration?," *National Review,*
    June 22, 1992.

23. Peter Brimelow, *Alien Nation: Common Sense About America's Im-
    migration Disaster* (New York: Random House, 1995), pp. 10–11.

24. Reed Ueda, "Natterings of a Neo-Nativist," *Wall Street Journal,*
    April 18, 1995.

25. William F. Buckley to Peter Brimelow, April 24, 1995, in Buckley
    Papers, Box 1, Folder 13.

26. Brimelow to author, September 24, 2019.

27. Peter Brimelow, "William F. Buckley, Jr., RIP—Sort Of," *VDare.com,*
    February 28, 2008, https://vdare.com/articles/william-f-buckley-jr
    -rip-sort-of.

28. Peter Brimelow, "The Great Immigration Debate," *VDare.com,*
    March 27, 2007, https://vdare.com/articles/the-great-immigration
    -debate; Richard Spencer, interview by author, February 13, 2018.

29. Palmer Stacy and John Vinson, "The Great Betrayal," American
    Immigration Control Foundation, https://www.aicfoundation.com
    /books/Great-Betrayal_Palmer-Stacy.pdf.

30. Eugene Kiely, Robert Farley, and D'Angelo Gore, "FactChecking
    Trump's National Emergency Remarks," FactCheck.org, February 15,
    2019, https://www.factcheck.org/2019/02/factchecking-trumps
    -national-emergency-remarks/.

31. "Chain Migration by the Numbers," White House, January 24, 2018,
    https://www.whitehouse.gov/articles/chain-migration-numbers/.

32. Richard Spencer, interview by author, February 13, 2018.

33. Donald Trump, tweet, July 14, 2019, https://twitter.com/real
    DonaldTrump/status/1150381395078000643.

34. Richard Spencer, interview by author, February 13, 2018.

35. Ibid.

36. Robert Costa, "Trump Speechwriter Fired amid Scrutiny of Appearance with White Nationalists," *Washington Post,* August 19, 2018, https://www.washingtonpost.com/politics/trump-speechwriter-fired-amid-scrutiny-of-appearance-with-white-nationalists/2018/08/19/f5051b52-a3eb-11e8-a656-943eefab5daf_story.html; "Annual Report to Congress on White House Office Personnel," White House, June 29, 2018, https://www.whitehouse.gov/wp-content/uploads/2018/06/07012018-report-final.pdf.

37. Paul Gottfried, "An Old Paleocon Sets the Record Straight," *American Conservative,* February 1, 2018, https://www.theamericanconservative.com/articles/an-old-paleocon-sets-the-record-straight/.

38. Paul Gottfried, "Don't Call Me the 'Godfather' of Those Alt-Right Neo-Nazis. I'm Jewish," *National Post,* April 17, 2018, https://nationalpost.com/opinion/paul-gottfried-dont-call-me-the-godfather-of-those-alt-right-neo-nazis-im-jewish.

39. Philip Oltermann, "Heidegger's 'Black Notebooks' Reveal Antisemitism at Core of His Philosophy," *Guardian,* March 12, 2014, https://www.theguardian.com/books/2014/mar/13/martin-heidegger-black-notebooks-reveal-nazi-ideology-antisemitism.

40. "Intelligentsia and the Right" (manuscript), https://www.documentcloud.org/documents/4780191-Intelligentsia-and-the-Right.html.

41. Robert Wright and Darren Beattie, "The Wright Show" (video), Bloggingheads.tv, June 7, 2017, https://bloggingheads.tv/videos/46401. At around the 5:30 mark, Beattie says he has supported Trump since July 2015.

42. Likhitha Butchireddygari, "Professor Who Predicted Trump's Win Explains How He Knew, What Comes Next," *Duke Chronicle,* November 11, 2016, https://www.dukechronicle.com/article/2016/11/professor-who-predicted-trumps-win-explains-how-he-knew-what-comes-next.

43. James Kirkpatrick, "Trump Caves to 'Enemy of the People'—Time to Show Loyalty to Those Loyal to Him," *VDare.com,* August 20, 2018, https://vdare.com/articles/trump-caves-to-enemy-of-the-people-time-to-show-loyalty-to-those-loyal-to-him.

44. Lisa Rein, "Don't Condemn White Nationalists, Veterans Affairs' Diversity Chief Was Told After Charlottesville, Emails Show," *Washington Post,* December 5, 2018, https://www.washingtonpost.com

/politics/dont-condemn-white-nationalists-veterans-affairs-diversity
-chief-was-told-after-charlottesville-emails-show/2018/12/05
/fbff66ce-f41d-11e8-aeea-b85fd44449f5_story.html.

45.   Andrew Kaczynski, "Trump Appointee Carl Higbie Resigns as
      Public Face of Agency That Runs Americorps After KFile Review
      of Racist, Sexist, Anti-Muslim and Anti-LGBT Comments on the
      Radio," CNN.com, January 19, 2018, https://edition.cnn
      .com/2018/01/18/politics/kfile-carl-higbie-on-the-radio/index
      .html.

46.   Andrew Kaczynski, Chris Massie, and Nathan McDermott, "Home-
      land Security's Head of Community Outreach Once Said Blacks
      Turned Cities to 'Slums' with 'Laziness, Drug Use and Sexual Pro-
      miscuity,'" CNN.com, November 16, 2017, https://www.cnn
      .com/2017/11/16/politics/kfile-jamie-johnson-dhs/index.html;
      Noah Lanard, "DHS Official Who Made Islamophobic Comments
      Resigns. Another Remains in a Senior Role," *Mother Jones*, No-
      vember 17, 2017, https://www.motherjones.com/politics/2017/11
      /dhs-official-who-made-islamophobic-comments-resigns-another
      -remains-in-a-senior-role/.

47.   Michael Edison Hayden, "Stephen Miller's Affinity for White
      Nationalism Revealed in Leaked Emails," Southern Poverty Law
      Center, November 12, 2019, https://www.splcenter.org/hate
      watch/2019/11/12/stephen-millers-affinity-white-nationalism
      -revealed-leaked-emails.

48.   Robert Costa, "Trump Adviser Larry Kudlow Hosted Publisher of
      White Nationalists at His Home," *Washington Post*, August 21,
      2018, https://www.washingtonpost.com/politics/trump-adviser
      -larry-kudlow-hosted-publisher-of-white-nationalists-at-his
      -home/2018/08/21/f418a76c-a55e-11e8-8fac-12e98c13528d_story
      .html.

49.   Peter Brimelow, "Jared Taylor and Peter Brimelow: Let's Put a Cherry
      on Top of the Trump Immigration Plan!," *VDare.com*, August 27,
      2015, https://vdare.com/articles/jared-taylor-and-peter-brimelow-let
      -s-put-a-cherry-on-top-of-the-trump-immigration-plan.

50.   Brimelow, *Alien Nation*, pp. 3–4.

51.   Peter Brimelow, "Larry Kudlow: A Piebald Pill?," *VDare.com*, March
      15, 2018, https://vdare.com/posts/larry-kudlow-a-piebald-pill.

52.   Peter Brimelow, "Brimelow on Krugman, 1998—Selected Reflec-
      tions of a 'Hot Economist,'" *VDare.com*, August 22, 2018, https://

vdare.com/articles/brimelow-on-krugman-1998-selected-reflections
-of-a-hot-economist.

53. Alice B. Lloyd, "Going Rogue at CPAC: Mona Charen Slams
Sexist Hypocrisy and Racism at CPAC; Calls Invitation of Le Pen
a 'Disgrace,'" *Weekly Standard,* February 24, 2018, https://www
.weeklystandard.com/alice-b-lloyd/going-rogue-at-cpac-mona
-charen-slams-sexist-hypocrisy-and-racism-at-cpac-calls-invitation
-of-le-pen-a-disgrace.

54. Alice Ollstein, "CPAC Official: It Was Wrong to Elect Former RNC
Chair 'Because He's a Black Guy,'" *Talking Points Memo,* February
24, 2018, https://talkingpointsmemo.com/news/cpac-official-it-was
-wrong-to-elect-former-rnc-chair-because-hes-a-black-guy.

55. Lloyd, "Going Rogue at CPAC."

56. Ibid.

57. Emily Jashinsky, "Email Reveals CPAC Talking Points on Its Most
Controversial Speakers," *Washington Examiner,* February 22, 2018,
https://www.washingtonexaminer.com/email-reveals-cpac-talking
-points-on-its-most-controversial-speakers.

58. Adam Nossiter, "'Let Them Call You Racists': Bannon's Pep Talk to
National Front," *New York Times,* March 10, 2018, https://www.ny
times.com/2018/03/10/world/europe/steve-bannon-france-national
-front.html.

59. Brathovd identified his employer as the Army National Guard
in campaign finance disclosures for a $55.14 donation he
made to the Trump campaign in August 2016. "Schedule
A-P, Itemized Receipts," https://docquery.fec.gov/cgi-bin/fecimg
/?201906289150412758.

60. Chris Schiano and Dan Feidt, "Richard Spencer's Bodyguard 'Caerulus Rex' Exposed as Member of National Guard," Unicorn Riot,
October 17, 2017, https://unicornriot.ninja/2017/richard-spencers
-bodyguard-caerulus-rex-exposed-member-national-guard/.

61. Kevin Rawlinson, "Merkel Condemns Xenophobic Riots After
Killing of German Man," *Guardian,* August 27, 2018, https://www
.theguardian.com/world/2018/aug/27/germany-xenophobic-riots
-chemnitz-far-right-pegida.

62. "How the Alternative for Germany Has Transformed the Country,"
Der Spiegel, September 21, 2018, http://www.spiegel.de/international
/germany/how-the-alternative-for-germany-has-transformed
-the-country-a-1227360.html.

63. "AfD: What You Need to Know About Germany's Far-Right Party," DW.com, n.d., https://www.dw.com/en/afd-what-you-need-to-know-about-germanys-far-right-party/a-37208199.

64. Ibid.

65. E.g., George Hawley, "The Alt-Right's Moment Has Come and Gone," *American Conservative,* December 6, 2018, https://www.theamericanconservative.com/articles/the-alt-rights-moment-has-come-and-gone/.

66. Anton Shekhovtsov, *Russia and the Western Far Right* (New York: Routledge, 2018), p. xxiii.

67. Richard Spencer, interview by author, August 12, 2017.

68. "Conservatives, Gun Control, and China," *AltRight Politics* (podcast), February 26, 2018, https://www.spreaker.com/user/altright/february-26-conservatives-gun-control-an.

5   The Origin Myths of the Christian Right

1. Weyrich Scrapbooks, Box 3, Folder 9.

2. Paul M. Weyrich, "Blue Collar or Blue Blood?: The New Right Compared with the Old Right," in Robert W. Whitaker, ed., *The New Right Papers* (New York: St. Martin's Press, 1982), p. 53.

3. "Nixon Abortion Statement," *New York Times,* April 4, 1971, p. 28, https://www.nytimes.com/1971/04/04/archives/nixon-abortion-statement.html.

4. Paul M. Weyrich, "President's Surprise," *Wanderer,* April 17, 1971, in Weyrich Scrapbooks, Box 4, Folder 3.

5. Paul M. Weyrich to Raymond Smith, April 29, 1971, ibid., emphasis in original.

6. Charlie Savage, "On Nixon Tapes, Ambivalence over Abortion, Not Watergate," *New York Times,* June 23, 2009, https://www.nytimes.com/2009/06/24/us/politics/24nixon.html.

7. Paul M. Weyrich to Bishop Thomas Welsh, December 8, 1975, in Weyrich Papers, Box 1, Folder 11.

8. Paul Weyrich to Frank Walton, Ed Feulner, Tom Cantrell, Dick Thompson, and George Archibald, January 20, 1976, in Weyrich Papers, Box 1, Folder 14.

9. David Roach, "How Southern Baptists Became Pro-Life," *Baptist Press,* January 16, 2015, http://www.bpnews.net/44055/how-southern-baptists-became-prolife.

10. R. Albert Mohler, "Roe v. Wade Anniversary: How Abortion Became an Evangelical Issue," *On Faith,* January 22, 2013, http://cathnews usa.com/2013/01/roe-v-wade-anniversary-how-abortion-became -an-evangelical-issue/.

11. "Interview: Frank Schaeffer," *God in America,* PBS, October 23, 2009, http://www.pbs.org/godinamerica/interviews/frank-schaeffer .html#3.

12. "Resolution on Abortion, Norfolk, Virginia—1976," Southern Baptist Convention, http://www.sbc.net/resolutions/15/resolution-on -abortion.

13. "Resolution on Abortion, Kansas City, Missouri—1977," Southern Baptist Convention, http://www.sbc.net/resolutions/16/resolution -on-abortion.

14. "Resolution on Abortion, St. Louis, Missouri—1980," Southern Baptist Convention, http://www.sbc.net/resolutions/19/resolution -on-abortion.

15. Macel Falwell, *Jerry Falwell: His Life and Legacy* (New York: Howard Books, 2008), p. 107.

16. Richard Viguerie and David Franke, *America's Right Turn: How Conservatives Used New and Alternative Media to Take Power* (Chicago: Bonus Books, 2004), p. 132.

17. Peter Applebome, "Jerry Falwell, Moral Majority Founder, Dies at 73," *New York Times,* May 16, 2007, https://www.nytimes .com/2007/05/16/obituaries/16falwell.html.

18. Frances FitzGerald, "A Disciplined, Charging Army," *New Yorker,* May 18, 1981, https://www.newyorker.com/magazine/1981/05/18 /a-disciplined-charging-army.

19. Susan Friend Harding, *The Book of Jerry Falwell: Fundamentalist Language and Politics* (Princeton, N.J.: Princeton University Press, 2000), p. 303n5; see also Michael Lienesch, "Right-Wing Religion: Christian Conservatism as a Political Movement," *Political Science Quarterly* 97, no. 3 (1982): 403–25, esp. 409, doi:10.2307/2149992.

20. Matthew Avery Sutton, *Jerry Falwell and the Rise of the Religious Right: A Brief History with Documents* (Boston: Bedford/St. Martin's, 2013), p. 12.

21. William Martin, *With God on Our Side: The Rise of the Religious Right in America* (New York: Broadway, 1996) p. 69; Beverly Gage, "What an Uncensored Letter to M.L.K. Reveals," *New*

York Times Magazine, November 11, 2004, https://www.nytimes
.com/2014/11/16/magazine/what-an-uncensored-letter-to-mlk
-reveals.html.

22. Sutton, *Jerry Falwell,* pp. 57–58.

23. Falwell, *His Life and Legacy,* pp. 96, 108.

24. Sutton, *Jerry Falwell,* p. 13.

25. FitzGerald, "Disciplined, Charging Army."

26. Michelle Jaconi and Gregory Wallace, "CNN's Gut Check for August 27, 2013," CNN.com, August 27, 2013, http://politicalticker
.blogs.cnn.com/2013/08/27/cnns-gut-check-for-august-27-2013/;
"Falwell Opposes MLK Day in 1983" (video), https://www.youtube
.com/watch?v=lcQbzZMW2Vo.

27. Kristine Phillips, "In the Latest JFK Files: The FBI's Ugly Analysis on Martin Luther King Jr., Filled with Falsehoods," *Washington Post,* November 4, 2017, https://www.washingtonpost.com/news/retropolis
/wp/2017/11/04/in-the-latest-jfk-files-the-fbis-ugly-analysis-on
-martin-luther-king-jr-filled-with-falsehoods/; Beverly Gage, "What an Uncensored Letter to M.L.K. Reveals," *New York Times Magazine,* November 11, 2014, https://www.nytimes.com/2014/11/16
/magazine/what-an-uncensored-letter-to-mlk-reveals.html.

28. Weyrich, "Blue Collar or Blue Blood?," p. 52.

29. Howard Phillips, ed., *The New Right at Harvard* (Vienna, Va.: Conservative Caucus, 1983), p. 19.

30. Nancy L. Cohen, "Why America Never Had Universal Child Care," *New Republic,* April 24, 2013, https://newrepublic.com/article
/113009/child-care-america-was-very-close-universal-day-care.

31. Phillips, *New Right at Harvard,* p. 21.

32. Randall Balmer, *Thy Kingdom Come* (New York: Basic Books, 2006), p. 16.

33. Martin, *With God on Their Side,* p. 173. Weyrich blamed the intervention on President Jimmy Carter, but the IRS enforcement action started during the Nixon and Ford administrations. Activists like Weyrich, mindful that evangelicals could be drawn to the born-again Democratic president, took pains to blame him for the actions of his predecessors. Carter's own special assistant for religious affairs, Robert Maddox, a Southern Baptist minister, later recalled religious right campaign literature "always painting Reagan as the paragon of Christian virtue and Jimmy Carter as kind of the

antichrist" being "mailed extensively" during the 1980 presidential campaign. Dr. Robert Maddox, interview by Marie Allen, December 8, 1980, p. 15, Jimmy Carter Presidential Library, https://www .jimmycarterlibrary.gov/assets/documents/oral_histories/exit _interviews/Maddox.pdf.

34.   Randall Balmer to author, February 8, 2017.

35.   Daniel K. Williams, *God's Own Party* (New York: Oxford University Press, 2010), p. 170.

36.   James S. Hirsch, *Willie Mays: The Life, the Legend* (New York: Simon & Schuster, 2011), p. 67.

37.   Danny Walsch, "20 Years Ago, North Street School All Black," *Daily Mail* (Hagerstown, Md.), May 17, 1974, p. 3.

38.   *Public Education: 1964 Staff Report, Submitted to the United States Commission on Civil Rights,* October 1964, p. 127, https://www2 .law.umaryland.edu/marshall/usccr/documents/cr12ed82964.pdf.

39.   Cei Richardson, "New School Aims to Put 'Christ in Every Course,'" *Morning Herald* (Hagerstown, Md.), November 25, 1968, p. 16.

40.   Dr. Robert J. Billings, "Morals Without God?" (letter to the editor), *Morning Herald* (Hagerstown, Md.), April 12, 1969, p. 6.

41.   "New High School Gets New Principal" (advertisement), *Times* (Munster, Ind.), January 16, 1970, p. 23.

42.   "Hyles-Anderson College Opens August 21!" (advertisement), *Times* (Munster, Ind.), July 21, 1972, p. 43.

43.   John Fea, "Hundreds of Sex Abuse Allegations Found in Fundamentalist Baptist Churches," *The Way of Improvement Leads Home* blog, December 9, 2018, https://thewayofimprovement.com/2018/12/09 /hundreds-of-sex-abuse-allegations-found-in-fundamentalist-baptist -churches/.

44.   Sarah Smith, "Hundreds of Sex Abuse Allegations Found in Fundamental Baptist Churches Across U.S.," *Fort Worth Star-Telegram,* December 9, 2018, https://www.star-telegram.com/entertainment /living/religion/article222576310.html.

45.   Jack Hyles, "Some Strange Bedfellows" (sermon), text and audio, https://www.jackhyleslibrary.com/jack-hyles-sermon-strange -bedfellows/#; for date see "Jack Hyles Sermons: 1968–1970," https://www.jackhyleslibrary.com/sermons/audio-sermons-1968 -1970-fbch/.

46. Jack Hyles, "Your Child" (sermon), text and audio, https://www
     .jackhyleslibrary.com/jack-hyles-sermon-child/.

47. Jack Hyles, "The Youth and the Yoke" (sermon), text and audio,
     https://www.jackhyleslibrary.com/jack-hyles-sermon-youth-yoke/.

48. Andy Grimm, "Ex-Pastor of Hammond Megachurch Gets 12 Years
     in Sex Case," *Chicago Tribune*, March 21, 2013, https://www
     .chicagotribune.com/news/ct-xpm-2013-03-21-ct-met-megachurch
     -pastor-sentencing-20130321-story.html.

49. Smith, "Hundreds of Sex Abuse Allegations."

50. Dr. Robert J. Billings, *A Guide to the Christian School* (Crown
     Point, Ind.: Hyles-Anderson, 1971), pp. 46, 50–51.

51. Woody Register, "Clarksville 'Mill' Gave Education Assistant PhD,"
     Tennessean, April 9, 1981.

52. *Green v. Kennedy*, 309 F. Supp. 1127 (D.D.C. 1970).

53. *Bob Jones University v. United States*, 461 U.S. 574 (1983).

54. *Green v. Connally*, 330 F. Supp. 1150 (D.D.C. 1971).

55. "Rev. Rul. 71-447, 1971-2 C.B. 230," https://www.irs.gov/pub/irs
     -tege/rr71-447.pdf; *Green v. Connally*, 330 F. Supp. 1150 (D.D.C.
     1971).

56. "A Special Word from the President," *Faith and Family*, September–
     October 1975, p. 23.

57. *Bob Jones University v. United States*, 461 U.S. 574 (1983).

58. Charles R. Babcock, "School Tax Status: Old Issue Was Heated
     Up by Courts in 1978," *Washington Post*, January 25, 1982, https://
     www.washingtonpost.com/archive/politics/1982/01/25/school-tax
     -status-old-issue-was-heated-up-by-courts-in-1978/195023fa-d9b2
     -42a9-8ce3-43dd6e37b3d5/.

59. Paul Weyrich, "Long Live the Religious Right," Free Congress
     Foundation, December 18, 2001.

60. Paul Weyrich to Robert Billings, June 1, 1978, in Weyrich Papers,
     Box 3, Folder 5.

61. Ibid.

62. Frances FitzGerald, *The Evangelicals: The Struggle to Shape Ameri-
     ca* (New York: Simon and Schuster, 2017), p. 304.

63. Babcock, "School Tax Status."

64. "Proposed Revenue Procedure on Private Tax Exempt Schools," 43

Fed. Reg. 37296, August 22, 1978, http://cdn.loc.gov/service/ll
/fedreg/fr043/fr043163/fr043163.pdf.

65. Robert J. Billings to IRS Commissioner Jerome Kurtz, September 12,
1978, 43 *Fed. Reg.*, August 22, 1978, http://digitalcollections
.library.cmu.edu/awweb/awarchive?type=file&item=597356.

66. Paul M. Weyrich to IRS Commissioner Jerome Kurtz, September
15, 1978, Weyrich Papers, Box 3, Folder 8.

67. Dudley Clendinen, "Rev. Falwell Inspires Evangelical Vote," *New
York Times,* August 20, 1980, https://timesmachine.nytimes.com
/timesmachine/1980/08/20/111170654.html?pageNumber=43.

68. Robert Billings, statement at ACU News Conference, October 30,
1978, in ACU Papers, Box 79, Folder 14.

69. Jerome Kurtz to Philip Crane, October 20, 1978, in ACU Papers,
Box 80, Folder 1.

70. *The Voice of Christian and Jewish Dissenters in America, U.S. Internal Revenue Service Hearings on Proposed "Discrimination" Tax Controls Over Christian, Jewish, and Secular Private Schools, December 5,
6, 7, 8, 1978* (Washington, D.C.: Piedmont Press, 1982), p. 141.

71. Charlie Green, "Church vs. State Debate Hits IRS Tax-Exempt
Rule," *Star Press* (Muncie, Ind.), December 7, 1978, p. 30.

72. James P. Turner, statement before the Committee on Ways and
Means Subcommittee on Oversight House of Representatives Con-
cerning Proposed IRS Procedures on Tax-Exempt Private Schools,
February 22, 1979, in ACU Papers, Box 80, Folder 1.

73. Philip M. Crane, statement before the House Ways and Means
Oversight Subcommittee, Hearings on IRS Proposed Regulations,
February 22, 1979, in ACU Papers, Box 80, Folder 1.

74. "Christian Lobbyist at the Congress," *Journal-Champion* 1, no. 23
(March 23, 1979), p. 1, https://digitalcommons.liberty.edu/cgi/view
content.cgi?article=1028&context=paper_78_80.

75. Ibid.

76. Philip M. Crane, "Power Grab Threatens Private Schools," ibid.,
p. 2.

77. Tim LaHaye, "Church-Related Schools Save Taxpayers $30 Billion,"
Journal Champion 1, no. 24 (April 6, 1979), p. 2, https://digital
commons.liberty.edu/cgi/viewcontent.cgi?article=1029&context=paper
_78_80.

78. "What Can Christian Schools Accomplish?" (editorial), *Journal-Champion* 1, no. 21 (February 23, 1979), p. 2, https://core.ac.uk/download/pdf/58823951.pdf.

79. "A Personal Message from Dr. Jerry Falwell," *Journal-Champion* 1, no. 25 (April 20, 1979), p. 5, https://digitalcommons.liberty.edu/cgi/viewcontent.cgi?article=1030&context=paper_78_80.

80. Williams, *God's Own Party*, p. 164.

81. Ibid., p. 189.

82. Joseph Crespino, *In Search of Another Country: Mississippi and the Conservative Counterrevolution* (Princeton, N.J.: Princeton University Press, 2007), p. 256.

83. Charles R. Babcock, "Segregated Private Schools," *Washington Post*, February 20, 1982, https://www.washingtonpost.com/archive/politics/1982/02/20/segregated-private-schools/7f813725-bfb8-43da-936a-e389019b4271/; Stuart R. Taylor, "Reagan Tax Exemption Bill Assailed," *New York Times*, February 2, 1982, https://www.nytimes.com/1982/02/02/us/reagan-tax-exemption-bill-assailed.html.

84. Sandra Sugawara, "Prince Edward Academy Regains Tax-Exempt Status," *Washington Post*, October 10, 1985, https://www.washingtonpost.com/archive/politics/1985/10/10/prince-edward-academy-regains-tax-exempt-status/0d605888-2d39-49bd-8658-43ef409b2646/.

85. Marlene Cimons, "Dual School Systems in the South Thrive," *Los Angeles Times*, March 1, 1982.

86. "Exclusive to the JTA: Former Moral Majority Official Is Author of Speech Deploring Erosion of 'Christian Values,'" Jewish Telegraphic Agency, January 24, 1985, https://www.jta.org/1985/01/24/archive/exclusive-to-the-jta-former-moral-majority-official-is-author-of-speech-deploring-erosion-of-christ.

87. "Council for National Policy Board of Governors Meeting" (booklet), January 23–24, 1983, in Weyrich Papers, Box 36, Folder 23.

88. Sarah Posner, "How a Fringe Theocratic Movement Helped Shape the Religious Right As We Know It," *Religion Dispatches*, August 6, 2015, http://religiondispatches.org/how-a-fringe-theocratic-movement-helped-shape-the-religious-right-as-we-know-it/.

89.   Pete Earley, "Article Called 'Inappropriate,'" *Washington Post,* June 13, 1983, https://www.washingtonpost.com/archive/politics /1983/06/13/article-called-inappropriate/80ddcf96-46b6-4795 -8c6c-c25ad5c4389b/.

90.   "U.S. Apology to Jewish Group," Associated Press, February 14, 1985, https://www.nytimes.com/1985/02/14/us/us-apology-to -jewish-group.html; "Exclusive to the JTA: Former Moral Majority Official Is Author of Speech Deploring Erosion of 'Christian Values,'" Jewish Telegraphic Agency, January 24, 1985, https://www.jta .org/1985/01/24/archive/exclusive-to-the-jta-former-moral-majority -official-is-author-of-speech-deploring-erosion-of-christ.

6   The New Right and Racism

1.   Robert Billings, "Private Education vs. Government Edict" (synopsis of remarks), in ACU Papers, Box 8, Folder 5.

2.   M. Stanton Evans, "Constitutional Amendment Against Forced Busing by the American Conservative Union," in ACU Papers, Box 77, Folder 17.

3.   "The Mantra," Bob Whitaker Online, http://www.robertwwhitaker .com/mantra/.

4.   "Arkansas Racist Billboard Part of White Supremacist Strategy," ADL, October 13, 2013, https://www.adl.org/blog/arkansas-racist -billboard-part-of-white-supremacist-strategy.

5.   "Down the Rabbit Hole with Horus the Avenger" (podcast), Counter-Currents Radio, March 24, 2012, https://www.counter -currents.com/2012/03/horus-the-avenger/.

6.   "What Is White Rabbit Radio All About?," White Rabbit Radio, n.d., https://whiterabbitradio.net/about-3.

7.   Ryan Lenz, "Bob Whitaker, Author of the Racist 'Mantra' on White Genocide, Has Died," Southern Poverty Law Center, June 7, 2017, https://www.splcenter.org/hatewatch/2017/06/07/bob-whitaker -author-racist-mantra-white-genocide-has-died.

8.   Laura, "American Freedom Party Launches Telephone Campaign in Idaho," Whitaker Online, August 3, 2015, http://www.whitaker online.org/blog/2015/08/03/american-freedom-party-launches -telephone-campaign-in-idaho/.

9.   James Edwards, "Bob Whitaker Has Passed Away," June 7, 2017, http://www.thepoliticalcesspool.org/jamesedwards/bob-whitaker -has-passed-away/.

10. Spencer J. Quinn, "Robert Whitaker Remembered," Counter-Currents Publishing, June 2017, https://www.counter-currents.com/2017/06/robert-whitaker-remembered/.

11. David Duke, tweet, June 8, 2017, https://twitter.com/DrDavidDuke/status/872853707637043200.

12. Nancy MacLean, *Democracy in Chains: The Deep History of the Radical Right's Stealth Plan for America* (New York: Viking 2017), p. 79.

13. Ibid., pp. 55–56.

14. Leo Casey, "When Privatization Means Segregation: Setting the Record Straight on School Vouchers," *Dissent,* August 9, 2017, https://www.dissentmagazine.org/online_articles/private-school-vouchers-racist-history-milton-friedman-betsy-devos.

15. MacLean, *Democracy in Chains*, pp. 65–73.

16. For Whitaker's employment history, see Whitaker SF-171, in Rusher Papers, Box 97, Folder 2.

17. National Education Association (NEA), Teacher Rights Division, *Inquiry Report, Kanawha County, West Virginia, A Textbook Study in Cultural Conflict* (Washington, D.C.: NEA, 1975), pp. 40–41.

18. Carol Mason, *Reading Appalachia from Left to Right: Conservatives and the 1974 Kanawha County Textbook Controversy* (Ithaca, N.Y.: Cornell University Press, 2009), p. 47.

19. NEA, *Inquiry Report,* p. 44.

20. Mason, *Reading Appalachia*, p. 46.

21. Ibid., pp. 48–49.

22. NEA, *Inquiry Report*, pp. 42–43.

23. Ibid., p. 44.

24. Ibid., p. 20.

25. Ibid., p. 50.

26. Ibid., p. 48.

27. Kay Michael, "Here's New Texts Process," *Sunday Gazette-Mail* (Charleston, W.V.), December 15, 1974, p. 18a.

28. Mason, *Reading Appalachia*, pp. 121–25.

29. "Book Battle Stirs Again," UPI, in *Raleigh Register* (Beckley, W.V.), November 29, 1974.

30. Richard Viguerie and David Franke, *America's Right Turn: How*

Conservatives Used New and Alternative Media to Take Power (Chicago: Bonus Books, 2004), p. 257.

31. Elmer L. Rumminger, "You Shall Not Do This to My Child!," *Faith and Family,* January–February 1975.

32. James T. McKenna, "The Textbook Revolt in West Virginia," *Conservative Digest,* June 1975.

33. B. Drummond Ayres, Jr., "School Critics Press Drive for Old Values," *New York Times,* July 25, 1975, https://www.nytimes.com/1975/07/25/archives/school-critics-press-drive-for-old-values-school-critics-press.html.

34. Paul Weyrich, statement to Republican Platform Committee, August 10, 1976, Kansas City, Mo., Weyrich Scrapbooks, Box 6, Folder 1.

35. Richard Starnes, "Text, Busing Foe Union Sought," *Pittsburgh Press,* March 19, 1975.

36. Bruce Gellerman, "Busing Left Deep Scars on Boston, Its Students," WBUR, September 5, 2014, https://www.wbur.org/news/2014/09/05/boston-busing-effects.

37. Marilyn Morgan, "Roaring for Rights: Women and Boston's Anti-Busing Movement," Archives and Public History at UMass Boston, March 18, 2017, http://www.archivespublichistory.org/?p=1555.

38. Walter Robinson, "Mrs. Hicks Leads Hub Group," *Boston Globe,* March 19, 1975.

39. Robert W. Whitaker, "When the Busing Had to Stop," *Conservative Digest,* July 1975, p. 29; "What Do You Mean . . . Populist?" *Conservative Digest,* July 1975, p. 41.

40. Adam Clymer, "M. Stanton Evans, Who Helped Shape Conservative Movement, Is Dead at 80," *New York Times,* March 3, 2015, https://www.nytimes.com/2015/03/04/us/m-stanton-evans-pioneer-of-conservative-movement-dies-at-80.html.

41. M. Stanton Evans, "Busing, The Final Failure," statement to the Subcommittee on Constitutional Rights, Senate Committee on the Judiciary, February 1974, in ACU Papers, Box 77, Folder 17.

42. William Rusher, foreword to Robert W. Whitaker, *A Plague on Both Your Houses* (New York: R. B. Luce, 1976), p. ix.

43. Sam Rosenfeld, *The Polarizers: Postwar Architects of Our Partisan Era* (Chicago: University of Chicago Press, 2018), pp. 189–90.

44. Elaine Hartman to Sheed and Ward, Inc., June 4, 1975, in Weyrich Papers, Box 1, Folder 6.

45. Dan T. Carter, *The Politics of Rage: George Wallace, the Origins of the New Conservatism, and the Transformation of American Politics* (Baton Rouge: Louisiana State University Press, 2000), p. 417.

46. Mark Weber, "John Schmitz, RIP," *Journal of Historical Review* 19, no. 6 (2000), p. 28, http://vho.org/GB/Journals/JHR/19/6/Weber28 .html.

47. One of Schmitz's sons, Joseph, was a foreign policy adviser to Trump's 2016 presidential campaign and came under scrutiny for anti-Semitism and Holocaust denial, charges he denied. Marisa Taylor and William Douglas, "Trump Adviser Accused of Making Anti-Semitic Remarks," McClatchy News, August 18, 2016, https://www.mcclatchydc.com/news/politics-government/election /article96421087.html.

48. Elaine Hartman to Sheed and Ward, Inc., June 4, 1975, in Weyrich Papers, Box 1, Folder 6.

49. William Rusher to Robert Whitaker, May 8, 1985, in Rusher Papers, Box 96, Folder 13.

50. Rusher to Whitaker, March 4, 1975, ibid.

51. Whitaker, *Plague*.

52. Ibid., p. xii.

53. Ibid., p. x.

54. William Rusher, "New Voice in Our National Dialogue," *Muncie Evening Press*, July 6, 1976, p. 4.

55. Whitaker, *Plague*, p. 142.

56. Ibid., p. 170.

57. Ibid., p. 32.

58. Ibid., p. 37.

59. Ibid., p. 11.

60. Ibid., p. 115.

61. Ibid., p. 121.

62. Ibid., p. 122.

63. Ibid., p. 119.

64. William Rusher, "New Right Looks at the Courts," *Salina Journal*, November 2, 1981.

65. William Rusher, "Emotions Mixed When Mathias Steps Down," *Index-Journal,* November 29, 1985.

66. William Rusher, "What Judge Souter Will Be Up Against," *Beatrice* (Neb.) *Daily Sun,* August 7, 1990.

67. William Rusher, "John Ashbrook, R.I.P.," *National Review,* May 14, 1982, reprinted at https://ashbrook.org/about/john-ashbrook/nr -ashbrook-rip/.

68. Ashbrook Center, State Policy Network, https://spn.org/organization /ashbrook-center/.

69. David L. Chappell, *Waking from the Dream: The Struggle for Civil Rights in the Shadow of Martin Luther King, Jr.* (New York: Random House, 2014), pp. 14–15.

70. *Congressional Record,* June 2, 1969, pp. 14428–29.

71. Beth Fouhy, "Trump: Obama Wasn't Qualified for Ivy League," NBC News, April 26, 2011, http://www.nbcnews.com/id/42762170 /ns/politics-more_politics/t/trump-obama-wasnt-qualified-ivy -league/#.XI_QSM9KifU.

72. Bob Whitaker, "The Mysterious Death of Senator John Ashbrook," Whitaker Online, June 1, 2004, http://www.whitakeronline.org /blog/2004/06/01/the-mysterious-death-of-senator-john-ashbrook/.

73. Ashbrook Center, State Policy Network, https://spn.org/organization /ashbrook-center/.

74. "Who Was John Ashbrook?" https://ashbrook.org/about/john -ashbrook/.

75. Whitaker SF-171, in Rusher Papers, Box 97, Folder 2.

76. Robert Whitaker, foreword to Whitaker, *New Right Papers,* pp. xv, xix.

77. Robert J. Hoy, "Lid on a Boiling Pot," ibid., pp. 98, 103.

78. Ibid., p. 94.

79. Samuel T. Francis, "Message from Mars: The Social Politics of the New Right," ibid., p. 66.

80. Ibid., pp. 69–81.

81. Whitaker foreword, ibid., p. xi.

82. Rusher to John Shrote, December 20, 1981, in Rusher Papers, Box 97, Folder 2.

83. David Shribman, ". . . And Recruit for the Government," *New York*

Times, October 12, 1983, https://www.nytimes.com/1983/10/12/us
/and-recruit-for-the-government.html.

84. Republican Action for the 90s, "David Duke in Washington" and
"GOP Senators Shun Duke," People for the American Way Collection of Conservative Political Ephemera, Box 64, Folder 38.

85. Adam Meyerson, "Conscience of a Cultural Conservative: Paul M.
Weyrich on the Politics of Character in Russia and America," *Policy
Review* 59 (Winter 1992), pp. 13–14.

86. Michael Brendan Dougherty, "The Castaway," America's Future Foundation, January 14, 2007, https://americasfuture.org/the-castaway/.

87. Frank Donner, "Rounding Up the Usual Suspects," *Nation,* August
7–14, 1982, pp. 110–11.

88. "A Reply to Frank Donner," *Congressional Record,* September 9,
1982, pp. 23084–87.

89. "Sam Francis, Columnist, 57, Dies," *Washington Times,* February 16, 2005, https://www.washingtontimes.com/news/2005
/feb/16/20050216-111354-3083r/.

90. Samuel Francis, "Race, IQ, and the Government," syndicated in
Elko (Nev.) *Daily Free Press,* November 9, 1994, p. 2.

91. Samuel Francis, "Cramming Civil Rights Down a Nation's Throat,"
Tennessean, March 25, 1992, p. 75.

92. Joe Holley, "Conservative Writer Samuel T. Francis," *Washington
Post,* February 26, 2005, https://www.washingtonpost.com/archive
/local/2005/02/26/conservative-writer-samuel-t-francis/8f0d59be
-94fe-43ec-93ce-0d24676cb608/.

93. Samuel Francis, "Head Start Doesn't Work," *Central New Jersey
Home News,* January 29, 1992, p. 7.

94. Samuel Francis, "Civil Rights Double Standard," *Elko* (Nev.) *Daily
Free Press,* October 30, 1993, p. 2.

95. Samuel Francis, "No Hate Here," *Elko* (Nev.) *Daily Free Press,* February 22, 1995, p. 2.

96. Samuel Francis, "Learning to Hate Hate Crimes," *Elko* (Nev.) *Daily
Free Press,* May 14, 1994, p. 2.

97. Samuel Francis, "Marge Schott and the Thought Police," *Central
New Jersey Home News,* December 10, 1992, p. 12.

98. Samuel Francis, "Racial Extortion," *Elko* (Nev.) *Daily Free Press,*
July 24, 1993, p. 2.

99. Samuel Francis, "I'm Black! I'm Black!," *Elko* (Nev.) *Daily Free Press,* August 10, 1993, p. 2.

100. Samuel Francis, foreword to William R. Hawkins, *Importing Revolution* (Monterey, Va.: American Immigration Control Foundation, 1994), p. ix.

101. Samuel Francis, "A Radical Split From Its Church Traditions," *Washington Times* column, syndicated in *Bismarck Tribune,* June 28, 1995, p. 4.

102. Howard Kurtz, "Washington Times Clips Its Right Wing," *Washington Post,* October 19, 1995, https://www.washingtonpost.com /archive/lifestyle/1995/10/19/washington-times-clips-its-right-wing /dd009c93-883b-446c-bbbf-94c0a0570a1a/.

103. Samuel Francis, "Statement of Principles," Council of Conservative Citizens, http://conservative-headlines.org/statement-of-principles/.

104. "Dylann Roof's Manifesto Is Fluent in White Nationalist Ideology," Southern Poverty Law Center, June 21, 2015, https://www.spl center.org/hatewatch/2015/06/20/dylann-roofs-manifesto-fluent-white -nationalist-ideology.

105. "U.S. and Mexico Relations," *BorderLine* no. 15, April 22, 1996, in FAIR Records.

106. Bill Regnery, interview by author, March 8, 2018.

107. Western Shade Cloth Foundation Form 990, 1990.

108. David Plotz, "The Genius Generation," *Guardian,* April 15, 2004, https://www.theguardian.com/science/2004/apr/15/science.higher education.

109. Regnery interview, March 8, 2018.

110. Jeremiah Bannister, interview by author, March 6, 2018.

111. Paul Weyrich, "The Cultural Right's Hot New Agenda," *Washington Post,* May 4, 1986, https://www.washingtonpost.com/archive /opinions/1986/05/04/the-cultural-rights-hot-new-agenda/34ad9580 -9d17-4b1e-a2a7-31782eed6ddd/.

112. "Plan to Launch Cultural Conservatism II," n.d., in Weyrich Papers, Box 16, Folder 29.

113. E. J. Dionne, "A Conservative Call for Compassion," *New York Times,* November 30, 1987, https://www.nytimes.com/1987/11/30 /us/a-conservative-call-for-compassion.html.

114. Institute for Cultural Conservatism, *Cultural Conservatism: Toward a New National Agenda* (Alexandria, Va.: Free Congress Foundation, 1987), pp. 134–35.

115. "Study Shows Americans Now Seek Old Values, Simpler Times," February 27, 1992, in Weyrich Papers, Box 16, Folder 29.

116. *The Dirty Little Secret* was the original subtitle—see https://www .splcenter.org/fighting-hate/intelligence-report/2003/cultural -marxism-catching—although the title was later changed to "A History of Political Correctness."

117. Ben Alpers, "A Far-Right Anti-Semitic Conspiracy Theory Becomes a Mainstream Irritable Gesture," Society for U.S. Intellectual History, December 1, 2018, https://s-usih.org/2018/12/a-far-right-anti -semitic-conspiracy-theory-becomes-a-mainstream-irritable-gesture/; Samuel Moyn, "The Alt-Right's Favorite Meme Is 100 Years Old," *New York Times,* November 13, 2018, https://www.nytimes .com/2018/11/13/opinion/cultural-marxism-anti-semitism.html.

118. "The History of Political Correctness" (video), Free Congress Foundation, https://www.youtube.com/watch?v=EjaBpVzOohs&t=1s.

119. William S. Lind, "Is Multiculturalism a Threat to the National Security of the United States?," Free Congress Foundation (archived), December 31, 2001, https://web.archive.org/web/20030802022815 /http://freecongress.org/commentaries/2002/020103BL.asp.

120. William S. Lind, "Next Conservatism #15: What Is Cultural Marxism?," Free Congress Foundation (archived), October 25, 2005, https://web.archive.org/web/20051128170201/http://www.free congress.org/commentaries/2005/051025.asp.

121. William S. Lind, "Understanding Oklahoma," *Washington Post,* April 30, 1995, https://www.washingtonpost.com/archive /opinions/1995/04/30/understanding-oklahoma/a03eb6e2-14df-434a -b6cb-d355aaf5f587/.

122. William S. Lind, "New Strategy for Culture War Already in Place: A Reply to Philip Gold," March 26, 2002, Free Congress Foundation (archived), https://web.archive.org/web/20051128182628/http:// www.freecongress.org/commentaries/2002/020326WL.asp.

123. William S. Lind, "The White Right Rises," *Traditional Right,* August 23, 2017, https://www.traditionalright.com/the-white-right-rises/.

7   The Civil Rights Era Is Over

1. Paul M. Weyrich, "Triumphs and Traps: What's Ahead for Conservatives," *Policy Review,* January 1, 1997, https://www.hoover.org /research/triumphs-and-traps-whats-ahead-conservatives#top.

2. Tierney McAfee, "A New Wife, Baby and Two Alleged Mistresses: Inside Donald Trump's World in 2006," *People,* March 7, 2018, https://people.com/politics/donald-trump-life-2006-stormy-daniels-affair/.

3. Sarah Posner, "Wave of New State Bills: Religious Freedom or License to Discriminate?," *Al Jazeera America,* February 7, 2014, http://america.aljazeera.com/articles/2014/2/7/wave-of-new-statebills religiousfreedomorlicensetodiscriminate.html.

4. "Tony Perkins on The Kelly File—Houston Pastors Asked to Turn In Sermons" (video), October 15, 2014, https://www.youtube.com/watch?v=_MzbildkSZg.

5. "Bossier Legislator Files 'Marriage and Conscience Act,'" *Shreveport* (La.) *Times,* April 3, 2015, http://www.shreveporttimes.com/story/news/local/2015/04/03/bossier-legislator-mike-johnson-marriage-conscience-act/25249197/.

6. Louisiana House of Representatives, Civil Law and Procedure, May 19, 2015, http://house.louisiana.gov/H_Video/VideoArchivePlayer.aspx?v=house/2015/may/0519_15_CL.

7. Travis Weber, "Why Do We Need Louisiana's Marriage and Conscience Act? Ask Indiana Pizza Owners," *Daily Signal,* April 13, 2015, https://www.dailysignal.com/2015/04/13/why-do-we-need-louisianas-marriage-and-conscience-act-ask-indiana-pizza-owners/.

8. "Gov. Edwards Signs Non-discrimination Executive Order; Rescinds Marriage and Conscience Executive Order," Governor of Louisiana, April 13, 2016, http://gov.louisiana.gov/news/gov-edwards-signs-nondiscrimination-executive-order.

9. Roberta A. Kaplan, Declaration in Opposition to Defendants Bryant's and Davis's Motion to Stay Preliminary Injunction Pending Appeal, *Barber v. Bryant,* U.S. District Court for the Southern District of Mississippi, Northern Division, Civ. No. 3:16:cv-417-CWR-LRA, filed July 20, 2016, pp. 4–5, exhibit G.

10. Sarah Posner, "The Christian Legal Army Behind 'Masterpiece Cakeshop,'" *Nation,* January 1–8, 2018, https://www.thenation.com/article/the-christian-legal-army-behind-masterpiece-cakeshop/.

11. "ACLU Statement on Department of Justice Licensing Discrimination in the Name of Religion," ACLU, October 6, 2017, https://www.aclu.org/news/aclu-statement-department-justice-licensing-discrimination-name-religion.

12. Jessica Huseman and Annie Waldman, "Trump Administration

Quietly Rolls Back Civil Rights Efforts Across Federal Government," *ProPublica,* June 15, 2017, https://www.propublica.org /article/trump-administration-rolls-back-civil-rights-efforts-federal -government.

13. Jeff Sessions, Memorandum for All Executive Departments and Agencies, October 6, 2017, https://www.justice.gov/opa/press -release/file/1001891/download.

14. "Attorney General Jeff Sessions Delivers Remarks at the Alliance Defending Freedom's Summit on Religious Liberty," Department of Justice, August 8, 2018, https://www.justice.gov/opa/speech /attorney-general-jeff-sessions-delivers-remarks-alliance-defending -freedoms-summit.

15. "U.S. Department of Justice Summit 'Religious Liberty: Our First Freedom and Why It Matters,'" July 30, 2018, Main Hall, Department of Justice, Washington, D.C. Attorney General Jeff Sessions's remarks as prepared for delivery are available at https://www .justice.gov/opa/speech/attorney-general-sessions-delivers-remarks -department-justice-s-religious-liberty-summit.

16. Sarah Posner, "Illinois Ordered a Doctor to Tell Women Where to Get Abortions. Now He Wants the Whole State to Suffer," *HuffPost,* January 28, 2018, https://www.huffpost.com/entry/gallant-trump -conscience-protections-trump_n_5a66635fe4b0e5630072babd.

17. Complaint for Discrimination in Violation of Federal Conscience Protections, filed with Department of Health and Human Services Office of Civil Rights by the Life Legal Defense Foundation et al., October 9, 2014, http://www.adfmedia.org/files/Calif ChurchesComplaint.pdf.

18. Jocelyn Samuels to Catherine W. Short et al., June 21, 2016, http:// www.adfmedia.org/files/CDMHCInvestigationClosureLetter.pdf.

19. "The Changing Face of Health Care and the 2016 Election" (video), event held at Catholic Information Center, November 2, 2016, https://www.youtube.com/watch?v=FV5X-sRK25o.

20. Hannah Levintova, "Two Decades Ago, He Blocked Abortion Clinics and Dodged Police. Now He's Helping Wage Trump's War on Reproductive Rights," *Mother Jones,* February 22, 2019, https://www.motherjones.com/politics/2019/02/matt-bowman-hhs -abortion-arrest-record-clinic-protests/.

21. Roger Severino, "Gov. Bryant Stands Up to Liberal Bullying, Signs Mississippi Religious Freedom Bill," *Daily Signal,* April 5, 2016,

https://www.dailysignal.com/2016/04/05/gov-bryant-stands-up-to
-liberal-bullying-and-enacts-mississippi-religious-freedom-bill/.

22. Roger Severino and Melanie Israel, "Obama Threatens to Veto
Military Bill Because It Protects Religious Groups," *Daily Signal,*
October 27, 2016, https://www.dailysignal.com/2016/10/27/obama
-threatens-to-veto-military-bill-because-it-protects-religious-groups/.

23. Dan Diamond, "HHS Nearing Plan to Roll Back Transgender
Protections," *Politico,* April 24, 2019, https://www.politico.com
/story/2019/04/24/hhs-transgender-1379336?.

24. "Blackburn Names Staff Director to Select Investigative Panel on
Infant Lives" (press release), November 17, 2015, https://web
.archive.org/web/20181228162006/https://energycommerce.house
.gov/news/press-release/blackburn-names-staff-director-select
-investigative-panel-infant-lives/.

25. Miranda Blue, "FRC's Agenda for President Trump's First 100
Days: Roll Back LGBT and Reproductive Rights," *Right Wing
Watch,* September 12, 2016, http://www.rightwingwatch.org/post
/frcs-agenda-for-president-trumps-first-100-days-roll-back-lgbt
-reproductive-rights/.

26. Sen. Patty Murray et al. to Secretary Tom Price, April 10, 2017,
http://www.washingtonblade.com/content/files/2017/04/041017
-SIGNED-Senate-Letter-to-Price-on-HHS-OCR-Director-Severino
-Appointment.pdf.

27. Matt Hadro, "New HHS Official Has Strong Background in Religious Freedom, Civil Rights," Catholic News Agency, March 28,
2017, https://www.catholicnewsagency.com/news/new-hhs-official
-has-strong-background-in-religious-freedom-civil-rights-99302.

28. "The Administrative State and Religious Freedom" (video),
Federalist Society, November 18, 2017, https://www.youtube.com
/watch?v=h9GRnQSYKNk.

29. "Were You Subject to Conscience Rights Violations?," Family Research Council Action Alert, January 9, 2018.

30. Posner, "Illinois Ordered a Doctor to Tell Women Where to Get
Abortions."

31. Jocelyn Samuels, interview by author, January 18, 2018.

32. Sarah Posner, "South Carolina Sought an Exemption to Allow a
Foster-Care Agency to Discriminate Against Non-Christians,"
Nation, June 15, 2018, https://www.thenation.com/article/south
-carolina-sought-exemption-allow-foster-care-agency-discriminate

-non-christians/; Emanuella Grinberg, "South Carolina Foster Care Providers Can Reject People Who Don't Share Their Religious Beliefs," CNN.com, January 23, 2019, https://www .cnn.com/2019/01/23/politics/south-carolina-religious-freedom -nondiscrimination-waiver-hhs/index.html?no-st=1554998079.

33.   Matt Shuham, "DeVos: We Knew of Potential Harms When We Rolled Back Transgender Protections," *Talking Points Memo,* April 10, 2019, https://talkingpointsmemo.com/news/devos-we-rolled -back-transgender-student-guidelines-despite-effects-of-harassment.

34.   Laura Meckler, "Betsy DeVos Panel Rejects Obama-Era Effort to Reduce Discrimination in School Discipline," *Washington Post,* December 10, 2018, https://www.washingtonpost.com/local/education /betsy-devos-school-safety-panel-takes-aim-at-obamas-discipline -guidance/2018/12/10/7e515700-f6b6-11e8-8c9a-860ce2a8148f _story.html.

35.   Joint "Dear Colleague" letter, Department of Justice and Department of Education, January 8, 2014, https://www2.ed.gov/about /offices/list/ocr/letters/colleague-201401-title-vi.html.

36.   Valerie Strauss, "DeVos Moves to Delay Obama-Era Rule on Minority Special-Education Students," *Washington Post,* February 26, 2018, https://www.washingtonpost.com/news/answer-sheet /wp/2018/02/26/devos-delaying-obama-era-rule-on-minority-special -education-students/.

37.   Emily Badger and John Eligon, "Trump Administration Postpones an Obama Fair-Housing Rule," *New York Times,* January 4, 2018, https://www.nytimes.com/2018/01/04/upshot/trump-delays-hud -fair-housing-obama-rule.html.

38.   Amanda Terkel, "Ben Carson Removes Anti-Discrimination Language from HUD Mission Statement," *HuffPost,* March 7, 2018, https://www.huffpost.com/entry/hud-mission-statement_n_5a9f5db 0e4b002df2c5ec617.

39.   Glenn Thrush, "Under Ben Carson, HUD Scales Back Fair Housing Enforcement," *New York Times,* March 28, 2018, https:// www.nytimes.com/2018/03/28/us/ben-carson-hud-fair-housing -discrimination.html.

40.   Nahal Toosi, "State Department Report Will Trim Language on Women's Rights, Discrimination," *Politico,* February 21, 2018, https://www.politico.com/story/2018/02/21/department-women -rights-abortion-420361?lo=ap_e1.

41.   Renae Merle, "Trump Administration Strips Consumer Watchdog
      Office of Enforcement Powers in Lending Discrimination Cases,"
      Washington Post, February 1, 2018, https://www.washingtonpost
      .com/news/business/wp/2018/02/01/trump-administration-strips
      -consumer-watchdog-office-of-enforcement-powers-against
      -financial-firms-in-lending-discrimination-cases/.

42.   Laura Meckler and Devlin Barrett, "Trump Administration Con-
      siders Rollback of Anti-Discrimination Rules," *Washington Post,*
      January 3, 2019, https://www.washingtonpost.com/local/education
      /trump-administration-considers-rollback-of-anti-discrimination
      -rules/2019/01/02/f96347ea-046d-11e9-b5df-5d3874f1ac36_story
      .html.

43.   Igor Bobic and Alexis Arnold, "Trump's Largely White and Male
      Appellate Judges, in One Photo," *HuffPost,* August 5, 2019, https://
      www.huffpost.com/entry/trump-judges-white-male-nominees_n_5d
      484719e4b0acb57fd05ec3.

44.   Sherrilyn A. Ifill to Sens. Mitch McConnell and Charles Schumer,
      July 30, 2019, https://www.naacpldf.org/wp-content/uploads
      /2019_07_30_19-Nominees-Opposition-FINAL.pdf.

45.   Alliance for Justice, *Neomi Rao Background Report,* citing Neomi
      M. Rao, "How the Diversity Game Is Played," *Washington Times,*
      July 17, 1994, https://www.afj.org/our-work/nominees/neomi-rao.

46.   "Extremist Judicial Re-Nominations Signal Continued Attack on
      Civil Rights," Leadership Conference on Civil and Human Rights,
      January 22, 2019, https://civilrights.org/2019/01/22/extremist
      -judicial-re-nominations-signal-continued-attack-on-civil-rights/.

47.   Zoe Tillman, "One of Trump's Judicial Nominees Once Wrote That
      Diversity Is 'Code for Relaxed Standards,'" *BuzzFeed News,* Febru-
      ary 15, 2018, https://www.buzzfeednews.com/article/zoetillman
      /one-of-trumps-judicial-nominees-once-wrote-that-diversity.

48.   Rick Esenberg and Anthony LoCoco, "Democrats Take Down
      Another Judicial Nominee Simply Because He's a Christian,"
      Federalist, February 22, 2019, https://thefederalist.com/2019/02/22
      /democrats-take-another-judicial-nominee-simply-hes-christian/.

49.   Patrick McGuigan, interview by author, August 2, 2018.

50.   Jeffrey Toobin, "Postscript: Robert Bork, 1927–2012," *New Yorker,*
      December 19, 2012, https://www.newyorker.com/news/news-desk
      /postscript-robert-bork-1927-2012.

51.   Linda Greenhouse, "Robert Bork's Tragedy," *New York Times,* Janu-

ary 9, 2013, https://opinionator.blogs.nytimes.com/2013/01/09
/robert-borks-tragedy/.

52. Adam Meyerson, "Conscience of a Cultural Conservative: Paul M.
Weyrich on the Politics of Character in Russia and America," *Policy
Review* 59 (Winter 1992), p. 8.

53. Sarah Posner, "The 'Anti-Catholic' Playbook," *Nation,* September 5, 2018, https://www.thenation.com/article/the-anti-catholic
-playbook/.

54. Ibid.

55. Ibid.

56. "Last Days" (video), Judicial Crisis Network, March 23, 2016,
https://www.youtube.com/watch?v=stJkA9z27sg; "Merrick Garland
60-Second Ad" (video), Judicial Crisis Network, March 23, 2016,
https://www.youtube.com/watch?v=MNVLvgbJ1Lo.

57. Margaret Sessa-Hawkins and Andrew Perez, "Dark Money Group
Received Massive Donation in Fight Against Obama's Supreme
Court Nominee," Maplight.org, October 24, 2017, https://maplight
.org/story/dark-money-group-received-massive-donation-in-fight
-against-obamas-supreme-court-nominee/.

58. Posner, "'Anti-Catholic' Playbook."

8   The End of American Exceptionalism

1. Paul Weyrich, "A New Conservative Agenda," *Baltimore Evening
Sun,* May 16, 1990.

2. Bill Regnery, interview by author, March 8, 2018.

3. Ed Feulner, "The Glimmer of Freedom," *Delta Democrat Times*
(Greenville, Miss.), September 10, 1990.

4. Paul M. Weyrich, "Conferences Aim to Strengthen U.S.-Russia
Relations," Weyrich Free Congress Foundation (archived), May 15,
2001, https://web.archive.org/web/20030724205112/http://www
.freecongress.org/commentaries/2001/010515PWfcc.asp.

5. Paul M. Weyrich, "Our Old Enemy May Become Our Newest
Friend," Free Congress Foundation (archived), October 22, 2001,
https://web.archive.org/web/20030821082253/http://freecongress
.org/commentaries/2001/011022PWfcc.asp.

6. William S. Lind, "Only One New NATO Member Makes Sense:
Russia," Free Congress Foundation (archived), April 25, 2002,

https://web.archive.org/web/20030813020824/http://freecongress
.org/commentaries/2002/020425WL.asp.

7. Paul M. Weyrich, "A Promising Post-Soviet Russia," Free Congress Foundation (archived), February 23, 2004, https://web
.archive.org/web/20041222004542/http://www.freecongress.org:80
/commentaries/040223pw.asp.

8. Matt Bivens, "Love and Infatuation at Russia Forum,"
Moscow Times, May 13, 2002, https://web.archive.org
/web/20180318214743/http://old.themoscowtimes.com/sitemap
/free/2002/5/article/love-and-infatuation-at-russia-forum/246616
.html.

9. "Noted Conservative Leader to Address World Russian Forum.
Paul M. Weyrich, 'Russian Democracy: An American Copy or
Uniquely Russian?,'" April 27, 2004, https://web.archive.org
/web/20040604003107/http://www.freecongress.org:80/media
/040426.asp.

10. President Igor Dodon, speech at Chişinău, Moldova, September 14,
2018, official English translation at http://www.presedinte.md/eng
/discursuri/d-i-s-c-u-r-s-u-l-presedintelui-republicii-moldova-igor
-dodon-la-congresul-mondial-al-familiilor-chisinau-14-16
-septembrie-2018.

11. Brian Brown, closing speech at World Congress of Families,
Chişinău, Moldova, September 15, 2018.

12. "Gay Parades Banned in Moscow for 100 Years," BBC News, August 17, 2012, https://www.bbc.com/news/world-europe-19293465.

13. Michael Garcia Bochenek and Kyle Knight, "Russia: 'Gay Propaganda' Law Endangers Children," Human Rights Watch, December 11,
2018, https://www.hrw.org/news/2018/12/12/russia-gay-propaganda
-law-endangers-children.

14. Miranda Blue, "Globalizing Homophobia, Part 2: 'Today the Whole
World Is Looking at Russia,'" *Right Wing Watch,* October 3, 2013,
http://www.rightwingwatch.org/post/globalizing-homophobia-part-2
-today-the-whole-world-is-looking-at-russia/.

15. Ibid.

16. Emily Belz, "An Ally at Arm's Length?," *World,* March 15, 2017,
https://world.wng.org/2017/03/an_ally_at_arm_s_length.

17. Peter Bradley, "Chronicling *Chronicles,*" *American Renaissance,* March
10, 2017, https://www.amren.com/features/2017/03/chronicles
-magazine-paleoconservatism-alt-right-donald-trump-pat-buchanan/.

18. Allan Carlson, speech to World Congress of Families, Chişinău, Moldova, September 14, 2018.

19. Kathryn Joyce, "Missing: The 'Right' Babies," *Nation,* March 3, 2008, https://www.thenation.com/issue/march-3-2008/.

20. "Defunding Planned Parenthood Is Only Part of the Story" (press release), Howard Center for Family, Religion, and Society, February 24, 2011, http://christiannewswire.com/news/5964316318.html.

21. Allan Carlson, *Godly Seed: American Evangelicals Confront Birth Control, 1873–1973* (New Brunswick, N.J.: Transaction, 2012). Moore's blurb is on the back jacket.

22. Allan Carlson, "The World Congress of Families," *Human Events,* March 22, 2007, https://humanevents.com/2007/03/22/the-world -congress-of-families/.

23. President Donald Trump, "Remarks to the People of Poland," Warsaw, July 6, 2017, https://www.whitehouse.gov/briefings-statements /remarks-president-trump-people-poland/.

24. Brian Tashman, "World Congress of Families Praises Russian Laws 'Preventing' Gays from 'Corrupting Children,'" *Right Wing Watch,* June 3, 2013, http://www.rightwingwatch.org/post/world-congress -of-families-praises-russian-laws-preventing-gays-from-corrupting -children/.

25. Office of the Press Secretary, "Fact Sheet: Ukraine-Related Sanctions," White House, March 17, 2014, https://obamawhitehouse .archives.gov/the-press-office/2014/03/17/fact-sheet-ukraine-related -sanctions.

26. "Planning for World Congress of Families VIII Suspended" (press release), World Congress of Families, March 25, 2014, http://www .christiannewswire.com/news/372773850.html.

27. "World Congress of Families IX—Our First Congress in the United States," *World Congress of Families News* 8, no. 5 (September–October 2015), http://54.165.152.74/worldcongress.org/files /1214/4476/1824/WCF_News_Sept_Oct_2015.pdf; "World Congress of Families IX Schedule October 27–30, 2015," https:// web.archive.org/web/20160322015945/http://wcf9.org/schedule/.

28. Julia Siân Williams, "Emory Abroad," *Emory Magazine,* Spring 2009, http://www.emory.edu/EMORY_MAGAZINE/2009/spring /abroad.html; "Levan S. Vasadze, Chairman, Prometheus Capital Partners," *Bloomberg,* n.d., https://www.bloomberg.com/profiles /people/4329980-levan-s-vasadze; Ghia Nodia, "Nativists Versus

Global Liberalism in Georgia," Carnegie Europe, October 4, 2018, https://carnegieeurope.eu/2018/10/04/nativists-versus-global-liberalism-in-georgia-pub-77376.

29. *World Congress of Families News* 9, no. 2 (February–March 2016).

30. Yelena Mizulina, speech to World Congress of Families, Chişinău, Moldova, September 14, 2018.

31. "Treasury Announces New Designations of Ukrainian Separatists and Their Russian Supporters" (press release), U.S. Department of the Treasury, March 11, 2015, https://www.treasury.gov/press-center/press-releases/pages/jl9993.aspx.

32. Matthew Watkins, "'Strongest Skinhead' Helped Arrange Richard Spencer Speech at Texas A&M," *Fort Worth Star-Telegram,* December 1, 2016, https://www.star-telegram.com/news/state/texas/article118219408.html.

33. Mansur Mirovalev, "Thousands of Russian Nationalists Stage Anti-Immigrant March in Moscow," *Seattle Times,* November 4, 2007, https://www.seattletimes.com/nation-world/thousands-of-russian-nationalists-stage-anti-immigrant-march-in-moscow/.

34. Aleksandr Dugin, "American Liberalism Must Be Destroyed" (video), speech at Texas A&M University, April 29, 2015, https://www.youtube.com/watch?v=y2NcpWI6iJk.

35. Daniel T. Rodgers, *As a City on a Hill* (Princeton, N.J.: Princeton University Press, 2018), p. 236.

36. Philip Gorski, *American Covenant* (Princeton, N.J.: Princeton University Press, 2017), p. 178.

37. Ronald Reagan, "Election Eve Address: A Vision for America," November 3, 1980, Reagan Presidential Library and Museum, https://www.reaganlibrary.gov/11-3-80.

38. "Levan Vasadze on Georgia's Demographic Time Bomb" (video), CBN News, May 10, 2016, https://www.youtube.com/watch?v=UyYk1GotQYg.

39. William E. Lori, testimony on behalf of U.S. Conference of Catholic Bishops Before the Judiciary Committee, House of Representatives, Subcommittee on the Constitution, October 26, 2011, http://usccb.org/issues-and-action/religious-liberty/upload/lori-testimony-on-religious-freedom-2011-10-26.pdf; "HHS and the Catholic Church: Examining the Politicization of Grants," Hearing Before the Committee on Oversight and Government Reform, House of Representatives, December 1, 2011, https://www.govinfo.gov

/content/pkg/CHRG-112hhrg73939/pdf/CHRG-112hhrg73939
.pdf, video at https://www.youtube.com/watch?v=XjjR0qtDidA;
"Lines Crossed: Separation of Church and State. Has the Obama
Administration Trampled on Freedom of Religion and Freedom of
Conscience?," Hearing Before the Committee on Oversight and
Government Reform, House of Representatives, February 16, 2012,
https://www.govinfo.gov/content/pkg/CHRG-112hhrg73614/pdf
/CHRG-112hhrg73614.pdf, video at https://www.youtube.com
/watch?v=9nJRUxj-HUY; "Executive Overreach: The HHS Mandate Versus Religious Liberty," Hearing Before the House Judiciary
Committee, February 28, 2012, https://www.govinfo.gov/content
/pkg/CHRG-112hhrg73101/pdf/CHRG-112hhrg73101.pdf, video at
https://www.youtube.com/watch?v=4QzESvF3OrM.

40. "The Fight to Preserve Marriage" (panel discussion), Council for
National Policy, May 16, 2015, https://cfnp.org/wp-content
/uploads/2018/04/Marriage-Panel.pdf.

41. David Green, "Our Fight for Religious Freedom," *Charisma,* n.d.,
https://www.charismamag.com/life/culture/17693-our-fight-for
-religious-freedom.

42. "Croatia Passes Constitutional Amendment Affirming Natural Marriage" (press release), Liberty Counsel, December 9, 2013, https://
lc.org/newsroom/details/croatia-passes-constitutional-amendment
-affirming-natural-marriage-1.

43. Miranda Blue, "Mat Staver: LGBT Equality Means America No
Longer 'Shining City on the Hill,'" *Right Wing Watch,* August 1,
2014, http://www.rightwingwatch.org/post/mat-staver-lgbt-equality
-means-america-no-longer-shining-city-on-the-hill/.

44. Kyle Mantyla, "Barber and Staver Want to See Russian-Like Anti-
Gay Laws 'Right Here in the United States,'" *Right Wing Watch,*
January 22, 2014, http://www.rightwingwatch.org/post/barber
-staver-want-to-see-russian-like-anti-gay-laws-right-here-in-the
-united-states/.

45. "Rebutting Right Wing Watch's 'Ten Horrific Things Kim Davis's Attorney Has Said About Gay People,'" Liberty Counsel, https://lc.org
/PDFs/Rebuttal-of-RWW-article.pdf.

46. Mantyla, "Barber and Staver."

47. "License to Harm: Violence and Harassment against LGBT
People and Activists in Russia," Human Rights Watch, December 15, 2014, https://www.hrw.org/report/2014/12/15/license-harm

/violence-and-harassment-against-lgbt-people-and-activists
-russia#.

48. Hilary White, "Vladimir Putin Signs Bill Protecting Children from
     Homosexual Propaganda," *LifeSite News,* July 1, 2013, https://www
     .lifesitenews.com/news/vladimir-putin-signs-bill-protecting-children
     -from-homosexual-propaganda.

49. J. Lester Feder, "Leading Conservative Group Withdraws from
     'Pro-Life Olympics' in Moscow over Russian Invasion of Ukraine,"
     BuzzFeed News, March 11, 2014, https://www.buzzfeednews.com
     /article/lesterfeder/leading-conservative-group-withdraws-from-pro
     -life-olympics.

50. Patrick J. Buchanan, "Culture War Goes Global," *American Con-
     servative,* August 13, 2013, https://www.theamericanconservative
     .com/2013/08/13/culture-war-goes-global/.

51. Rod Dreher, "1.5 Cheers for Putin," *American Conservative,* August
     13, 2013, https://www.theamericanconservative.com/dreher/1-5
     -cheers-for-putin/comment-page-1/.

52. Meeting of the Valdai International Discussion Club, President of
     Russia, September 19, 2013, http://en.kremlin.ru/events/president
     /news/19243.

53. Allan C. Carlson, "A City on a Hill—with Transgender Toilets?,"
     Chronicles, March 2017, p. 11.

54. "The Rise of 'Illiberal Democracy,'" Freedom House, n.d., https://
     freedomhouse.org/report/modern-authoritarianism-illiberal
     -democracies.

55. Ibid.; "Hungary: Media Law Endangers Press Freedom," Human
     Rights Watch, January 7, 2011, https://www.hrw.org/news
     /2011/01/07/hungary-media-law-endangers-press-freedom.

56. Kester Eddy, Peter Spiegel, and Neil Buckley, "Alarm Rises as Hun-
     gary Defiant on Law," *Financial Times,* March 11, 2013, https://
     www.ft.com/content/6a5bc73c-8a4f-11e2-bf79-00144feabdc0.

57. Viktor Orbán, speech at the 27th Bálványos Summer Open Univer-
     sity and Student Camp, July 26, 2016, https://www.kormany.hu
     /en/the-prime-minister/the-prime-minister-s-speeches/viktor-orban
     -s-presentation-at-the-27h-balvanyos-summer-open-university-and
     -student-camp.

58. Pablo Gorondi, "UN Human Rights Chief Stands By Criticism of
     Hungary Leader," Associated Press, March 6, 2018, https://www
     .apnews.com/2940ace1847d43deb15bffc04d70b0ae.

59. Peter Sprigg, "Budapest Family Summit Explores Ways to Revitalize the Family," FRC blog, May 30, 2017, https://frcblog.com/2017/05/budapest-family-summit-explores-ways-revitalize-family/.

60. Viktor Orbán, speech at the 29th Bálványos Summer Open University and Student Camp, July 29, 2018, https://www.kormany.hu/en/the-prime-minister/the-prime-minister-s-speeches/prime-minister-viktor-orban-s-speech-at-the-29th-balvanyos-summer-open-university-and-student-camp.

61. *Washington Watch with Tony Perkins,* February 15, 2018, https://afr.net/podcasts/washington-watch/2018/february/rep-jim-banks-peter-sprigg-zoltan-kovacs-randy-wilson/.

62. Brian Brown, interview by author, September 15, 2018.

63. Anton Troianovski, "Putin's Reelection Takes Him One Step Closer to Becoming Russian Leader for Life," *Washington Post,* March 19, 2018, https://www.washingtonpost.com/world/europe/putins-reelection-takes-him-one-step-closer-to-becoming-russian-leader-for-life/2018/03/19/880cd0a2-2af7-11e8-8dc9-3b51e028b845_story.html.

64. Carol D. Leonnig, David Nakamura, and Josh Dawsey, "Trump's National Security Advisers Warned Him Not to Congratulate Putin. He Did It Anyway," *Washington Post,* March 20, 2018, https://www.washingtonpost.com/politics/trumps-national-security-advisers-warned-him-not-to-congratulate-putin-he-did-it-anyway/2018/03/20/22738ebc-2c68-11e8-8ad6-fbc50284fce8_story.html.

65. Peter Sprigg, interview by author, September 15, 2018.

66. "The Rise of 'Illiberal Democracy,'" Freedom House, n.d., https://freedomhouse.org/report/modern-authoritarianism-illiberal-democracies.

67. "Poland Has Risen Strong After World War II Because of Their Christian Heritage," Wallbuilders Live!, April 13, 2017, https://wallbuilderslive.com/poland-risen-strong-world-war-ii-christian-heritage/.

68. Ibid.

69. David R. Sands, "'Natural Ally': Hungary Leads Fight Against Anti-U.S. 'Hysteria' in Europe," *Washington Times,* May 31, 2018, https://www.washingtontimes.com/news/2018/may/31/hungary-natural-ally-trump-pompeo-peter-szijjarto-/; Austin Ruse, "Hungarian Leader Rallies Christians, Gives EU Elites Indigestion," Center

for Family and Human Rights, August 2, 2018, https://c-fam.org /friday_fax/hungarian-leader-rallies-christians-gives-eu-elites -indigestion/.

70. Mike Gonzalez and Maiya Clark, "Why This European Leader Is Embracing the Trump Presidency," Heritage Foundation, July 21, 2017, https://www.heritage.org/europe/commentary/why-european -leader-embracing-the-trump-presidency.

71. Dale Hurd, "Hungarian Foreign Minister: We Are Fed Up with 'Politically Correct, Hypocritical' European Union," CBN News, October 9, 2018, https://www1.cbn.com/cbnnews/world/2018 /october/hungarian-foreign-minister-we-are-fed-up-with-politically -correct-hypocritical-european-union.

72. Chuck Norris, "My Bromance with the Hungarian Prime Minister," WND, December 2, 2018, https://www.wnd.com/2018/12/my -bromance-with-the-hungarian-prime-minister/.

73. "Statement on Dr. Kevin MacDonald's Work," Academic Senate, California State University, Long Beach, May 5, 2008, http://web .csulb.edu/divisions/aa/grad_undergrad/senate/resolutions /StatementonDr.KevinMacDonald.html.

74. Michelle Malkin, *Invasion: How America Still Welcomes Terrorists, Criminals, and Other Foreign Menaces to Our Shores* (Washington, D.C.: Regnery, 2002); Michelle Malkin, *In Defense of Internment: The Case for Racial Profiling in World War II and the War on Terror* (Washington, D.C.: Regnery, 2004).

75. Callum Borchers and Kevin Uhrmacher, "Why a Conservative Book Publisher's Protest of the *New York Times* Bestsellers List Is Just a Stunt," *Washington Post,* September 6, 2017, https://www.washington post.com/news/the-fix/wp/2017/09/06/why-a-conservative-book -publishers-protest-of-the-new-york-times-bestsellers-list-is-just-a-stunt/.

76. William H. Regnery, "The Richwine Atrocity: How Come Only the Left Retrieves Its Wounded?," *VDare.com,* May 29, 2013, https:// vdare.com/articles/the-richwine-atrocity-how-come-only-the-left -retrieves-its-wounded.

77. Charles Martel Society, Form 990, Return of Organization Exempt from Income Tax, 2001, https://projects.propublica .org/nonprofits/display_990/364397594/2002_09_EO%2F36 -4397594_990_200112.

78. Michele Bachmann, speech to Values Voter Summit, Washington, D.C., October 11, 2013.

79. Kevin MacDonald, interview by author, August 24, 2016.

80. Sarah Posner and David Neiwert, "How Trump Took Hate Groups Mainstream," *Mother Jones,* October 14, 2016, https://www.mother jones.com/politics/2016/10/donald-trump-hate-groups-neo-nazi -white-supremacist-racism/.

81. Ellen Barry and Graham Bowley, "Rice Presses for Pullout as Georgia Signs Cease-Fire," *New York Times,* August 15, 2008, https:// www.nytimes.com/2008/08/16/world/europe/16prexy.html.

82. Kevin MacDonald, "The Specter of Russian Nationalism," *Occidental Observer,* August 23, 2008, https://www.theoccidentalobserver .net/2008/08/23/the-specter-of-russian-nationalism/.

83. Tom Parfitt, "'Racist' Russian TV Advert Investigated," *Guardian,* November 10, 2005, https://www.theguardian.com/world/2005 /nov/10/russia.tomparfitt.

84. Victor Yasmann, "Russia: The Moscow City Duma Election— a Case of Managed Democracy," Radio Free Europe/Radio Liberty, December 2, 2005, https://www.rferl.org/a/1063465.html.

85. "Putin Picks Dmitry Rogozin, a Leading Nationalist, to Be NATO Envoy," *New York Times,* January 10, 2008, https://www.nytimes .com/2008/01/10/world/europe/10iht-russia.4.9135955.html.

86. "NASA Chief Finds Space for Faith," *Tony Perkins' Washington Update,* April 18, 2019, https://www.frc.org/updatearticle/20190418 /nasa-chief.

87. Bettina Inclan to William Gerstenmaier et al., Updated Draft Statement RE: Rogozin's Visit, January 4, 2019, obtained via Freedom of Information Act request.

88. Ben Schreckinger, "'Wow': NASA Startles with Invitation to Sanctioned Russian," *Politico,* January 1, 2019, https://www.politico .com/story/2019/01/01/nasa-sanctioned-russian-nationalist-1076621.

89. Jim Bridenstine, tweet, https://twitter.com/jimbridenstine/status /1050225260828680193.

90. Jeff Foust, "Bridenstine and Rogozin Speak by Phone After Canceled Visit," *Space News,* January 15, 2019, https://spacenews.com /bridenstine-and-rogozin-speak-by-phone-after-cancelled-visit/.

9   The Undrained Swamp Loves an Autocrat

1. Susan B. Glasser, "How Trump Made War on Angela Merkel and Europe," *New Yorker,* December 24 and 31, 2018, https://www

.newyorker.com/magazine/2018/12/24/how-trump-made-war-on
-angela-merkel-and-europe.

2. "Don't Look Now," *Newsweek,* November 17, 1996, https://www
    .newsweek.com/dont-look-now-176396.

3. Craig Shirley, "Not Just Good at National Politics, but the Best,"
    National Review, January 26, 2017, https://www.nationalreview
    .com/2017/01/arthur-finkelstein-republican-political-consultant
    -strategit-conservative-libertarian/; "Don't Look Now," *Newsweek,*
    November 17, 1996; Tony Fabrizio, "Trump's Road to the White
    House," *Frontline,* PBS, http://apps.frontline.org/trumps-road
    -whitehouse-frontline-interviews/transcript/tony-fabrizio.html.

4. "Don't Look Now," *Newsweek,* November 17, 1996.

5. Paul Lendvai, *Orbán: Hungary's Strongman* (New York: Oxford Uni-
    versity Press, 2017), p. 244.

6. "Hungary: Media Law Endangers Press Freedom," Human Rights
    Watch, January 7, 2011, https://www.hrw.org/news/2011/01/07
    /hungary-media-law-endangers-press-freedom.

7. "Hungary: New Constitution Enshrines Discrimination," Hu-
    man Rights Watch, April 19, 2011, https://www.hrw.org
    /news/2011/04/19/hungary-new-constitution-enshrines
    -discrimination.

8. "Freedom in the World 2015," report on Hungary, Freedom House,
    https://freedomhouse.org/report/freedom-world/2015/hungary.

9. "Q&A: Hungary's Controversial Constitutional Changes," BBC,
    March 11, 2013, https://www.bbc.com/news/world-europe
    -21748878.

10. "Although Parliamentary Elections in Hungary Offered Voters a
    Diverse Choice, Ruling Party Enjoyed Undue Advantage, Say Inter-
    national Observers," OSCE Newsroom, April 7, 2014, https://www
    .osce.org/odihr/elections/117200.

11. "Hungary 2014 Human Rights Report," U.S. State Department,
    https://2009-2017.state.gov/documents/organization/236744.pdf.

12. Heather Conley, interview by author, July 3, 2018.

13. Sarah Posner, "Right Makes Might," *New Republic,* March 25,
    2019, https://newrepublic.com/article/153276/republicans
    -congress-courted-nativist-authoritarian-leaders.

14. "Hostem CEVRO Institut Fora byl americký specialista na politické
    kampaně Arthur Finkelstein—Fotogalerie," May 16, 2011, http://

cevroinstitut.cz/cs/akce/hostem-cevro-institut-fora-byl-americky
-specialista-na-politicke-kampane-arthur-finkelstein-fotogalerie/.

15. "CEVRO Institut Forum / Arthur Finkelstein / English" (video),
https://www.youtube.com/watch?v=IfCBpCBOECU (at about
25:30 mark).

16. Andrew Roth, "Ukraine's Ex-President Viktor Yanukovych Found
Guilty of Treason," *Guardian,* January 25, 2019, https://www
.theguardian.com/world/2019/jan/25/ukraine-ex-president-viktor
-yanukovych-found-guilty-of-treason.

17. Paul J. Manafort to President Viktor F. Yanukovych, February 19,
2013, exhibit to Motion in Limine, filed July 26, 2018, *U.S.A. v.
Manafort,* Case No. 1:18-cr-00083, U.S. District Court for the
Eastern District of Virginia, https://www.documentcloud.org
/documents/4619185-U.S.A-v-Manafort-Motion-in-Limine-Exs
-Part7.html.

18. "Final Vote Results for Roll Call 148," House Clerk, March 27,
2014, http://clerk.house.gov/evs/2014/roll148.xml#N; Jonathan
Weisman, "Kremlin Finds a Defender in Congress," *New York
Times,* March 28, 2014, https://www.nytimes.com/2014/03/29/us
/politics/kremlin-finds-a-defender-in-congress.html.

19. Andrew Stroehlein, interview by author, June 20, 2018.

20. Affidavit in Support of an Application for a Criminal Complaint,
*In the Matter of an Application for Criminal Complaint for Mariia
Butina, also known as Maria Butina,* U.S. District Court for the
District of Columbia, https://www.justice.gov/opa/press-release
/file/1080766/download, p. 9.

21. Kyle Cheney, "Rep. Rohrabacher: Indictment of NRA-linked
Russian Is 'Stupid,'" *Politico,* July 17, 2017, https://www.politico
.com/story/2018/07/17/rohrabacher-russia-nra-indictment-butina
-726306.

22. Sharon LaFraniere and Andrew E. Kramer, "Talking Points Brought
to Trump Tower Meeting Were Shared with Kremlin," *New York
Times,* October 27, 2017, https://www.nytimes.com/2017/10/27/us
/politics/trump-tower-veselnitskaya-russia.html.

23. Kim Lane Scheppele, interview by author, June 15, 2018.

24. Ibid.

25. Viktor Orbán, speech at the 25th Bálványos Summer Free University and Student Camp, July 30, 2014, Website of the Hungarian
Government, https://www.kormany.hu/en/the-prime-minister/the

-prime-minister-s-speeches/prime-minister-viktor-orban-s-speech-at
-the-25th-balvanyos-summer-free-university-and-student-camp.

26. "The Rise of 'Illiberal Democracy,'" Freedom House, n.d., https://
freedomhouse.org/report/modern-authoritarianism-illiberal
-democracies.

27. "McCain Sparks U.S.-Hungary Diplomatic Row over Orban,"
BBC, December 3, 2014, https://www.bbc.com/news/world
-europe-30318898.

28. Executive Session, *Congressional Record* 160, no. 145 (Senate—
December 2, 2014), https://www.congress.gov/congressional
-record/2014/12/2/senate-section/article/s6240-2.

29. Sarah Sewall, interview by author, June 25, 2018.

30. "Groups Oppose Billingslea Nomination to State Department Role,"
Human Rights Watch, November 28, 2018, https://www.hrw.org
/news/2018/11/28/groups-oppose-billingslea-nomination-state
-department-role.

31. "Nominations Sent to the Senate," White House, January 16, 2019,
https://www.whitehouse.gov/briefings-statements/nominations-sent
-senate/.

32. "2017 Country Reports on Human Rights Practices," April 20,
2018, Hungary, U.S. State Department, https://www.state.gov
/reports/2017-country-reports-on-human-rights-practices/hungary/.

33. White House, "Readout of President Donald J. Trump's Call with
Prime Minister Viktor Orban of Hungary" (press release), June 16,
2018.

34. Todor Gardos, "Hungary Tries to Stop Asylum Seekers with New
Law," Human Rights Watch, June 22, 2018, https://www.hrw.org
/news/2018/06/22/hungary-tries-stop-asylum-seekers-new-law.

35. Patrick Wintour, "Hungary to Detain All Asylum Seekers in Con-
tainer Camps," *Guardian*, March 7, 2017, https://www.theguardian
.com/world/2017/mar/07/-hungary-to-detain-all-asylum-seekers-in
-container-camps.

36. Reuters, "U.S. Launches Media Fund for Hungary to Aid Press
Freedom," November 13, 2017, https://www.reuters.com/article
/us-hungary-us-media/u-s-launches-media-fund-for-hungary-to-aid
-press-freedom-idUSKBN1DD21C; "State Department Scraps Fund
for Hungarian Media," *Hungary Journal,* July 22, 2018, https://the
hungaryjournal.com/2018/07/22/state-department-scraps-fund-for
-hungarian-media/.

37. Secretary Rick Perry, tweet, https://twitter.com/SecretaryPerry
     /status/1062515961134223360.

38. The Prime Minister, "Hungarian-U.S. Relations Are Excellent,"
     Website of the Hungarian Government, November 14, 2018,
     http://www.kormany.hu/en/the-prime-minister/news/hungarian-us
     -relations-are-excellent.

39. Exhibit B to Registration Statement of SLI Group, https://www.fara
     .gov/docs/6259-Exhibit-AB-20141205-2.pdf.

40. "Exclusive Interview with Lobbyist Connie Mack IV, the Hungarian
     Government's Washington D.C. Advocate," *Hungary Today,* Decem-
     ber 13, 2016, https://hungarytoday.hu/exclusive-interview-lobbyist
     -connie-mack-iv-orban-governments-d-c-advocate-86547/.

41. Perry Stein, "Meet Connie Mack IV, the Republican Scion Who
     Could Take Down Florida's Last Democratic Holdout," *New Repub-
     lic,* August 13, 2012, https://newrepublic.com/article/106121/meet
     -connie-mack-iv-the-republican-scion-who-could-take-down-floridas
     -last-d.

42. Amy Sherman, "Connie Mack IV Says Cutting One Penny Out of
     Every Federal Dollar Would Quickly Balance the Budget," *Politifact,*
     July 5, 2012, http://www.politifact.com/florida/statements/2012
     /jul/05/connie-mack/connie-mack-says-cutting-one-penny-out
     -every-/.

43. Brendan Farrington, "Rep. Mack's Past Tussles an Issue in Senate
     Race," Associated Press, March 12, 2012, https://news.yahoo.com
     /news/rep-macks-past-tussles-issue-senate-race-172227461.html.

44. Joseph J. Schatz and Benjamin Oreskes, "Want to Be a 'Foreign
     Agent?' Serve in Congress First," *Politico,* October 2, 2016, https://
     www.politico.com/story/2016/10/congress-foreign-lobbying-228982.

45. J. D. Gordon to author, June 27, 2018.

46. Ambassador Colleen Bell, "'We Will Build a Stronger Bridge,'"
     speech at Corvinus University, *Budapest Beacon,* October 29,
     2015, https://budapestbeacon.com/we-will-build-a-stronger-bridge
     -ambassador-colleen-bells-speech-at-corvinus-university/.

47. "Challenge to Europe: The Growing Refugee Crisis," Hearing Be-
     fore the Subcommittee on Europe, Eurasia, and Emerging Threats,
     House Committee on Foreign Affairs, November 4, 2015, https://
     docs.house.gov/meetings/FA/FA14/20151104/104162/HHRG-114
     -FA14-Transcript-20151104.pdf.

48. Heather A. Conley and Charles Gati, "Trump Loves a Strongman,
     so of Course He Fawns over Hungary's Viktor Orban," *Washington
     Post,* May 25, 2018, https://www.washingtonpost.com/outlook
     /trump-loves-a-strongman-so-of-course-he-fawns-over-hungarys
     -viktor-orban/2018/05/25/a10bff28-5f64-11e8-a4a4-c070ef53f315
     _story.html; Carter Page, Testimony to U.S. House of Representa-
     tives, Permanent Select Committee on Intelligence, November 2,
     2017, https://www.lawfareblog.com/document-carter-page-house
     -intelligence-committee-hearing-transcript.

49. Christian Keszthelyi, "Trump Adviser: Orbán Aims to 'Make Hun-
     gary Great Again,'" *Budapest Business Journal,* December 2, 2016,
     https://bbj.hu/politics/trump-adviser-Orbán-aims-to-make-hungary
     -great-again-_125690.

50. Attila Mong, "Independent Journalists in Hungary Brace for Tough
     Times in Next Orbán Term," Committee to Protect Journalists,
     May 7, 2018, https://cpj.org/blog/2018/05/independent-journalists
     -in-hungary-brace-for-tough.php.

51. Lili Bayer, "J. D. Gordon Expects US-Hungarian Relations to Reach
     New Heights Under Trump Administration," *Budapest Beacon,*
     December 18, 2016, https://budapestbeacon.com/j-d-gordon
     -expects-us-hungarian-relations-to-reach-new-high-under-trump
     -administration/.

52. Lili Bayer, "Exclusive: Controversial Trump Aide Sebastian Gorka
     Backed Violent Anti-Semitic Militia," *Forward,* April 3, 2017,
     https://forward.com/news/national/367937/exclusive-controversial
     -trump-aide-sebastian-gorka-backed-violent-anti-semi/; Lili Bayer,
     "Exclusive: Senior Trump Aide Forged Key Ties to Anti-Semitic
     Groups in Hungary," *Forward,* February 24, 2017, https://forward
     .com/news/national/364085/sebastian-gorka-trump-aide-forged-key
     -ties-to-anti-semitic-groups-in-hunga/.

53. Marc Santora, "Soros Foundations Leaving Hungary Under Gov-
     ernment Pressure," *New York Times*, May 15, 2018, https://www
     .nytimes.com/2018/05/15/world/europe/soros-philanthropy-hungary
     -viktor-orban.html.

54. "Holding Government Accountable—An Interview with Rep. Con-
     nie Mack—Episode 281" (audio), Blunt Force Truth, n.d., https://
     bluntforcetruth.com/holding-government-accountable-an-interview
     -with-rep-connie-mack-episode-281/.

55. Geert Wilders, speech to U.S. Congressmen, Conservative Op-
     portunity Society, Washington, D.C., April 29, 2015, https://

www.geertwilders.nl/index.php/94-english/1921-speech-us
-congressman-29042015.

56. Rep. Steve King, "Congressman Steve King Press Conference with
Geert Wilders 'Fighting Radical Islam'" (video), press conference
with Geert Wilders, May 1, 2015, https://www.youtube.com
/watch?v=PPe__MzOdDE&t=110s.

57. Geert Wilders, speech at "Wake Up!" party, Cleveland, Ohio, July
19, 2016.

58. Ted Cruz, Facebook post, November 16, 2015, https://www.face
book.com/tedcruzpage/videos/congressman-steve-king-endorses
-ted/10153706639522464/.

59. "Cossacks and Flowers as Putin Dances at Austrian Minister's
Wedding," Reuters, August 18, 2018, https://www.reuters.com
/article/us-russia-austria-putin/cossacks-and-flowers-as-putin
-dances-at-austrian-ministers-wedding-idUSKBN1L30GP.

60. Nicola Slawson, "Austrian President Approves Far-Right Freedom
Party Joining Coalition Government," *Guardian,* December 16,
2017, https://www.theguardian.com/world/2017/dec/16/austrian
-president-approves-far-right-freedom-party-role-in-coalition
-government.

61. Goran Buldioski, "Balkan Conspiracy Theories Come to Capitol Hill," *Foreign Policy,* March 28, 2017, https://foreignpolicy
.com/2017/03/28/soros-gop-letter-open-society-macedonia
-albania/.

62. See, e.g., Aleksandar Dimishkovski, "Macedonia Has New Government, but Rocky Road Ahead," *New York Times,* June 1, 2017,
https://www.nytimes.com/2017/06/01/world/europe/macedonia
-zoran-zaev-election.html.

63. John Kirby, Daily Press Briefing (transcript), U.S. State Department, December 20, 2016.

64. "Lee Letter Seeks Accountability for US Ambassador in Macedonia" (press release), Office of Sen. Mike Lee, January 17,
2017, https://www.lee.senate.gov/public/index.cfm/press
-releases?ID=09FD00EC-5CA9-4FD4-8A18-03EE674
A592A.

65. Buldioski, "Balkan Conspiracy Theories."

66. Sens. Mike Lee and James Inhofe to Secretary of State Rex
Tillerson, March 14, 2017, https://www.scribd.com/document
/341866712/Lee-Inhofe-Letter-to-Secretary-Tillerson.

67. Ambassador Jess Baily, interview by Sitel TV, U.S. Embassy in North Macedonia, February 18, 2017, https://mk.usembassy.gov /ambassador-jess-bailys-interview-sitel-tv/.

68. "Diplomatic and Foreign Assistance Reforms for the Trump Era: The Negative Impact of Obama Policies on U.S. Interests," Heritage Foundation, April 25, 2017, https://www.heritage.org/event /diplomatic-and-foreign-assistance-reforms-the-trump-era-the -negative-impact-obama-policies-us; Sen. Mike Lee, "America First Diplomacy" (speech), April 25, 2017, https://www.lee.senate.gov /public/index.cfm/2017/4/america-first-diplomacy.

69. Victor Gaetan, "Macedonia to George Soros and USAID: Go Away," *American Spectator,* March 14, 2017, https://spectator.org /macedonia-to-george-soros-and-usaid-go-away/; Victor Gaetan, "George Soros's Contributions to a Cannabis Hotbed," *American Spectator,* April 18, 2017, https://spectator.org/george-soross -contributions-to-a-cannabis-hotbed/; Victor Gaetan, "Greece: George Soros' Trojan Horse Against Europe," *American Spectator,* May 24, 2017, https://spectator.org/greece-george-soros-trojan -horse-against-europe/.

70. E.g., "Report Alleges George Soros Is Meddling in Foreign Affairs" (video), Fox News, February 14, 2017, http://video.foxnews .com/v/5322951942001/?#sp=show-clips; Brooke Singman, "George Soros Battles $10B Lawsuit, Familiar Charges of Wielding Political Influence," Fox News, May 5, 2017, http://www.foxnews .com/world/2017/05/05/george-soros-battles-10b-lawsuit-familiar -charges-wielding-political-influence.html; "Obama Administration Meddled in Foreign Elections: Judicial Watch," Fox News, May 21, 2018, https://www.foxbusiness.com/politics/obama-administration -meddled-in-foreign-elections-judicial-watch.

71. John Hayward, "Chilimanov: Far-Left 'Soros Army' Invades Conservative Macedonia, Contributes to Migrant Crisis with U.S. Taxpayer Support," *Breitbart,* February 17, 2017, https://www.breitbart .com/radio/2017/02/17/chilimanov-far-left-soros-army-invades -conservative-macedonia-contributes-migrant-crisis-u-s-taxpayer -support/; Lee Stranahan, "Congressmen Call for Probe into Macedonian Soros Involvement," *Breitbart,* February 27, 2017, https:// www.breitbart.com/big-government/2017/02/27/congressmen-call -for-probe-into-macedonian-soros-involvement/; Tom Fitton, "Fitton: Judicial Watch Sues for More George Soros Documents," *Breitbart,* April 12, 2018, https://www.breitbart.com/obama/2018/04/12 /fitton-judicial-watch-sues-for-more-george-soros-documents/.

72.   Wes Martin, "Macedonia and USA Must Defeat Their Enemies—
       Let's Start with George Soros," *Daily Caller,* January 24, 2017,
       http://dailycaller.com/2017/01/24/macedonia-and-usa-must-defeat
       -their-enemies-lets-start-with-george-soros/; Alex Pfeiffer, "U.S.
       Interfered in Macedonia's Political Process, Documents Show,"
       Daily Caller, March 26, 2017, http://dailycaller.com/2017/03/26
       /u-s-interfered-in-macedonias-political-process-documents-show/;
       Peter Hasson, "Leaked Docs Show How Soros Spends Big to Keep
       Populists Out of Power in Europe," *Daily Caller,* April 5, 2017,
       http://dailycaller.com/2017/04/05/leaked-docs-show-how-soros
       -spends-big-to-keep-populists-out-of-power-in-europe/.

73.   "'Stop Operation Soros' Movement Begins in Macedonia," *RT,*
       January 19, 2017, https://www.rt.com/news/374241-stop-operation
       -soros-movement-macedonia/; "Senators Ask Tillerson to Probe US
       'Fomenting Unrest' in Other Countries," *RT,* March 15,
       2017, https://www.rt.com/usa/380886-senators-meddling-albania
       -macedonia/; "State Dept Sued Over Funding Soros Operations in
       Macedonia," *RT,* April 19, 2017, https://www.rt.com/usa/385333
       -state-department-soros-macedonia/.

74.   "State Dept. Receives Senator's Letter on US Meddling in For-
       eign States' Affairs," *Sputnik News,* March 16, 2017, https://
       sputniknews.com/us/201703161051628844-state-dept-letter-us
       -meddling/; "Senators' Letter to Tillerson Start of New Campaign
       to Break with Obama's Legacy," *Sputnik News,* March 17, 2017,
       https://sputniknews.com/us/201703171051672792-senators
       -campaign-end-obama-era/; "Senators Call for Probe into US Assault
       on Traditional Values in Other Nations," *Sputnik News,* March 18,
       2017, https://sputniknews.com/us/201703181051713199-senators
       -probe-us-assault-traditional-values/; "US Senators Challenge
       Trump to Probe Obama's Regime-Change Plots—Ex-Diplomat,"
       Sputnik News, March 18, 2017, https://sputniknews.com
       /us/201703181051711485-senators-trump-regime-change/.

75.   Victor Gaetan, "Macedonia to George Soros and USAID: Go
       Away," *American Spectator,* March 24, 2017, https://spectator.org
       /macedonia-to-george-soros-and-usaid-go-away/.

76.   "Report of Expenditures for Official Foreign Travel, Expended
       Between Apr. 1 and June 30, 2017," Committee on the Judiciary,
       House of Representatives, *Congressional Record,* August 29, 2017,
       p. H6626, https://www.congress.gov/crec/2017/08/29/CREC-2017
       -08-29-pt1-PgH6619-7.pdf.

77. Victor Gaetan, "Anti-U.S. Backlash in the Balkan Caldron," *American Spectator,* May 8, 2017, https://spectator.org/anti-u-s-backlash -in-the-balkan-caldron/.

78. Aubrey Belford and Saska Cvetkovska, "How Macedonia's Scandal-Plagued Nationalists Lobbied America's Right and Pulled Them into an Anti-Soros Crusade," Organized Crime and Corruption Reporting Project, June 13, 2017, https://www.occrp.org/en/spooks andspin/how-macedonias-scandal-plagued-nationalists-lobbied -americas-right-and-pulled-them-into-an-anti-soros-crusade/; Buldioski, "Balkan Conspiracy Theories."

79. Judicial Watch, emails, April 20, 21, and 27, 2017; May 31, 2017; June 2, 2017; April 4, 5, and 6, 2018; see "U.S. Gives Soros Groups Millions to Destabilize Macedonia's Conservative Govt.," Judicial Watch website, February 28, 2017, https://www.judicialwatch.org /corruption-chronicles/u-s-gives-soros-groups-millions-destabilize -macedonias-conservative-govt/.

80. "How to Protect International Religious Freedom from the Politicization of Human Rights," panel discussion at Heritage Foundation, Washington, D.C., July 26, 2018, available at https://www .heritage.org/event/how-protect-international-religious-freedom-the -politicization-human-rights.

81. "Political Strategies" panel at World Congress of Families, Chişinău, Moldova, September 14, 2018.

82. Robert Siedlecki, interview by author, September 14, 2018.

83. Claudio D'Amico, interview by author, September 14, 2018.

84. Ibid.

85. Ben Feuer, "Thanks to Trump, the Liberal 9th Circuit Is No Longer Liberal," *Washington Post,* February 28, 2019, https://www.washington post.com/outlook/2019/02/28/thanks-trump-liberal-ninth-circuit -is-no-longer-liberal/.

86. Ted Piccone, "Tillerson Says Goodbye to Human Rights Diplomacy," Brookings, May 5, 2017, https://www.brookings.edu/blog /order-from-chaos/2017/05/05/tillerson-says-goodbye-to-human -rights-diplomacy/.

87. Bryan Harris and Aime Williams, "Donald Trump and Jair Bolsonaro Heap Praise on Each Other," *Financial Times,* March 19, 2019, https://www.ft.com/content/dbf5e4e0-4a74-11e9-bbc9 -6917dce3dc62.

88. "Brazil: An Urgent Call to Protect Rights," Human Rights Watch,

October 28, 2018, https://www.hrw.org/news/2018/10/28/brazil
-urgent-call-protect-rights.

89. "Enlargement," North Atlantic Treaty Organization, February 15,
2019, https://www.nato.int/cps/en/natolive/topics_49212.htm.

90. Amber C. Strong, "'Lord, Uphold Him. Protect Him From Evil':
CBN's Pat Robertson Prays for Brazilian President Bolsonaro at
Meeting with Evangelical Leaders," CBN News, March 19, 2019,
http://www1.cbn.com/cbnnews/us/2019/march/lord-uphold-him
-protect-him-from-evil-s-pat-robertson-prays-for-brazilian-president
-bolsonaro-at-meeting-with-evangelical-leaders.

91. George Thomas, "'We Are God-Fearing Men': Brazil's President a
Friend to Trump and Biblical Values," CBN News, March 20, 2019,
http://www1.cbn.com/cbnnews/us/2019/march/exclusive-interview
-we-are-god-fearing-men-brazils-president-is-a-friend-to-president
-trump-and-biblical-values.

92. Heather Conley, interview by author, July 3, 2018.

93. "Stephen K. Bannon: 'Trump "Amerika az első" politikája és hatása
Közép-Európára'" (video), May 24, 2018, https://www.youtube.com
/watch?v=hQIkyLS_aR4&feature=youtu.be.

10   The Assault on Reality

1. Jo Becker, Matt Apuzzo, and Adam Goldman, "Trump Team Met
With Lawyer Linked to Kremlin During Campaign," New York
Times, July 8, 2017, https://www.nytimes.com/2017/07/08/us
/politics/trump-russia-kushner-manafort.html.

2. Johnnie Moore, tweet, July 11, 2017, https://twitter.com/JohnnieM
/status/884900134441582593.

3. Johnnie Moore, tweet, July 11, 2017, https://twitter.com/johnniem
/status/884942560439009281.

4. Aidan Quigley, "Trump Aide Bannon Calls Media the 'Opposition
Party,'" Politico, January 26, 2017, https://www.politico.com/story
/2017/01/steve-bannon-attacks-media-opposition-party-234235.

5. Johnnie Moore, interview by author, July 11, 2017.

6. "Celebrate America," Revival Ministries International, https://www
.revival.com/e/Celebrate-America.

7. Rodney Howard-Browne and Paula White-Cain, "Winter Camp
Meeting" (video), River Church, Tampa, Fla., January 27, 2017,
https://www.youtube.com/watch?v=U9-oVEakQvw.

8. "Celebrate America," DAR Constitution Hall, Washington, D.C., July 10, 2017.

9. Rodney Howard-Browne, tweet, July 18, 2016, https://twitter.com /rhowardbrowne/status/755081719020224512.

10. Rodney Howard-Browne and Adonica Howard-Browne, Facebook post, November 5, 2016, https://www.facebook.com/rodneyadonica howardbrowne/videos/i-had-the-privilege-of-opening-in-prayer-at -the-donald-trump-rally-held-at-the-f/10154665803882438/.

11. Brian Tashman, "Televangelist: Donald Trump Will Save Us From Antichrist," *Right Wing Watch,* March 17, 2016, http://www.right wingwatch.org/post/televangelist-donald-trump-will-save-us-from -antichrist/.

12. "Pastor Rodney Howard Browne—Should Christians Back Trump?" (audio), *Sheila Zilinsky Show,* April 4, 2016, https://www .podomatic.com/podcasts/sheilazilinsky/episodes/2016-04 -04T19_27_47-07_00.

13. Rodney Howard-Browne, Instagram post, December 19, 2016, https://www.instagram.com/p/BONoy8Ihp5Z/; Rodney Howard- Browne and Adonica Howard-Browne, Facebook post, December 19, 2016, https://www.facebook.com/rodneyadonicahowardbrowne /posts/10154810498767438.

14. Rodney Howard-Browne and Paula White-Cain, "Winter Camp Meeting" (video), River Church, Tampa, Fla., January 27, 2017, https://www.youtube.com/watch?v=U9-oVEakQvw.

15. Rodney Howard-Browne, tweet, July 25, 2017, https://twitter.com /rhowardbrowne/status/889911530887761925.

16. Rodney Howard-Browne, tweet, November 8, 2017, https://twitter .com/rhowardbrowne/status/928485266322583553.

17. Rodney Howard-Browne, Instagram post, July 13, 2017, https://www .instagram.com/p/BWe0xTHlEJF/?taken-by=rodney howardbrowne&hl=en.

18. Rodney Howard-Browne, "Praying for the President—What Really Happened at the White House" (video), July 13, 2017, https://www .youtube.com/watch?v=fy5SABdmu7g.

19. Rodney Howard-Browne, sermon at River Church (video), July 16, 2017, https://www.youtube.com/watch?v=mQFp6KL-zuk.

20. Rodney Howard-Browne and Paul L. Williams, *The Killing of Uncle Sam* (Tampa, Fla.: River, 2018).

21. Rodney Howard-Browne, interview by author, October 30, 2018.

22. "Last Thursday, my wife and I were invited to the White House to be a part of a faith leaders round table discussion about Israel. It was an amazing day with amazing people." Revival Ministries e-news, March 15, 2019.

23. Barak Ravid, "White House Working to Reassure Evangelicals on Middle East Peace Plan," *Axios,* March 9, 2019, https://www.axios .com/trump-kushner-middle-east-peace-plan-evangelicals-5337c4f7 -0f91-489c-baad-7799f63baed7.html; Samuel Smith, "Evangeli- cals Voice Concerns with Trump's Israeli-Palestinian Peace Plan at White House," *Christian Post,* March 13, 2019, https://www .christianpost.com/news/evangelicals-voice-concerns-with-trumps -israeli-palestinian-peace-plan-at-white-house.html; Jessilyn Lan- caster, "John Hagee, Jentezen Franklin, Paula White Cain, Lance Wallnau Stand for Israel at the White House," *Charisma News,* March 7, 2019, https://www.charismanews.com/opinion/standing -with-israel/75485-john-hagee-jentezen-franklin-paula-white-stand -for-israel-at-the-white-house.

24. President Donald Trump, tweet, October 5, 2018, https://twitter .com/realDonaldTrump/status/1048196883464818688.

25. Brett Samuels, "Trump: 'I Wouldn't Be Surprised' If Soros Were Paying for Migrant Caravan," *Hill,* October 31, 2018, https://the hill.com/homenews/administration/414171-trump-i-wouldnt-be -surprised-if-soros-were-paying-for-migrant-caravan.

26. Stephen Strang, "George Soros May Not Be the Antichrist, but the Antichrist Spirit Is Certainly at Work," *Charisma News,* October 24, 2018, https://www.charismanews.com/opinion/73727-george-soros -may-not-be-the-antichrist-but-the-antichrist-spirit-is-certainly-at -work.

27. Paul Lendvai, *Orbán* (New York: Oxford University Press, 2017), pp. 23, 207–9.

28. Andrew Byrne, "Orbán Takes Aim at Soros and Hungarian NGOs," *Financial Times,* January 13, 2017, https://www.ft.com /content/20d291f8-d87b-11e6-944b-e7eb37a6aa8e.

29. Stephen Strang, "Power of God Falls on Church That 'Singlehand- edly Kicked George Soros Out of Hungary,'" *Strang Report,* April 23, 2019, https://charismamail.com/ga/webviews/4-998331-32-27105 -28150-69437-61aab73652.

30. *"Washington Post–ABC News Poll, April 22–25, 2019," Wash-*

ington Post, April 29, 2019, https://www.washingtonpost.com
/politics/polling/washington-postabc-news-poll-april-2225
/2019/04/29/1b9300e4-6855-11e9-a698-2a8f808c9cfb_page
.html.

EPILOGUE   And God Will Smite the Impeachers

1. Johnnie Moore, tweet, October 31, 2019, https://twitter.com
    /JohnnieM/status/1189975313478017024.

2. Robert Jeffress, interview with author, October 30, 2019.

3. Tony Perkins, remarks to Values Voter Summit, October 11, 2019,
    Washington, D.C.

4. FRC Action Alert, "Stand Against Impeachment," October 23,
    2019.

5. Gillian Brockell, "A White Mob Attacked Elijah Cummings for In-
    tegrating a Swimming Pool. He Was 11," *Washington Post*, October
    17, 2019, https://www.washingtonpost.com/history/2019/10/17
    /white-mob-attacked-elijah-cummings-integrating-swimming-pool
    -he-was/.

6. Remarks by Jim Bakker, Morningside USA, Blue Eye, Missouri,
    October 17, 2019.

7. Jim Bakker interview with Anne Graham Lotz, Morningside USA,
    Blue Eye, Missouri, October 17, 2019.

8. Jeremiah Johnson, *Trump, 2019, & Beyond* (independently pub-
    lished, 2019), pp. 43, 45–46.

9. Associated Press, "Prosecution Built Clear Case Against Bakker,
    Observers Say," October 8, 1989, available at https://www
    .tulsaworld.com/news/prosecution-built-clear-case-against-bakker
    -observers-say/article_451dfd99-5eac-58b6-9932-27adb0dc41a2
    .html.

10. Stephen Strang, "Jim Bakker: Government Agencies Go After
    Trump Like They Went After Me," *Charisma News,* May 29, 2019,
    https://www.charismanews.com/opinion/76557-jim-bakker
    -government-agencies-go-after-trump-like-they-went-after-me.

11. "Fall MLC: There Is a Sound," October 20, 2019, available at
    https://www.youtube.com/watch?v=qkqsau2AqDo.

12. One Voice Prayer Movement conference call, November 5, 2019.

13. Carly Eli, interview with author, October 11, 2019.

INDEX

White, Paula, 7, 16–19, 21, 24–25, 35, 65, 67, 71–73, 248, 250, 253–54, 264–65
White, Randy, 18
White Citizens Councils, 50, 150
"white dispossession" theory, 54, 75
"white genocide" theory, 45, 54, 129, 140, 210
White House Office of Faith-Based Initiatives, 202, 264
white nationalists, xvii, 7, 10, 37–38, 54, 56, 58, 69–70, 74–78, 82, 85–86, 88–89, 91, 96, 130, 150, 153, 158, 181, 210, 213, 215, 260
White Rabbit podcast, 129
"White Right Rises, The" (Lind), 157
white supremacists, xiii, 28, 42, 43–44, 53, 69, 74, 129–30, 195, 200, 212, 234
Wiginton, Preston, 200
Wilders, Geert, 94, 234–35
Wilks, Farris, 44
Wisconsin, 57, 220
Witherspoon Institute, 176
women's rights, xvii–xviii, 8, 10, 14–15, 75, 156, 180
Wood, Nell, 133
Woodfill, Jared, 24–25, 165–66
Woolery, Chuck, 233

World Congress of Families (WCF), 195–99, 207, 240
2007 (Warsaw), 196–97
2014 (Moscow), 197–98
2015 (Salt Lake City), 198
2016 (Georgia), 198–200
2017 (Budapest), 198, 206–7
2018 (Moldova), 34, 192–95, 198–99, 207–8, 241
2019 (Italy), 198
World Refugee Day, 227
World Relief, 72
Wuco, Frank, 91
Wylie, Christopher, 75

xenophobia, 28, 49, 51, 59, 93, 187, 214, 215, 218

Yanukovych, Viktor, 224–25, 228
Yeltsin, Boris, 189
Yoest, Charmaine, 177
Youcis, Emily, 58
Young, Ed, 165
"You Shall Not Do This to My Child!" (Bob Jones University report), 134
Youth for Tomorrow, 71–72
Youth for Western Civilization, 93
YouTube, 42, 67
Zimmerman, George, 48, 49

ABOUT THE AUTHOR

SARAH POSNER is a reporting fellow with Type Investigations. Her investigative reporting has appeared in *Rolling Stone, The Nation, Mother Jones, The New Republic, Huff-Post, VICE,* and *Talking Points Memo.* Her coverage and analysis of politics and religion have appeared in *The New York Times, The Washington Post, The American Prospect, Politico,* and many other outlets. She graduated from Wesleyan University and has a law degree from the University of Virginia. Her story "How Trump Took Hate Groups Mainstream," published before the 2016 election, won a Sidney Award from the Sidney Hillman Foundation.

sarahposner.com
Twitter: @sarahposner

ABOUT THE TYPE

This book was set in Fairfield, the first typeface from the hand of the distinguished American artist and engraver Rudolph Ruzicka (1883–1978). Ruzicka was born in Bohemia (in the present-day Czech Republic) and came to America in 1894. He set up his own shop, devoted to wood engraving and printing, in New York in 1913 after a varied career working as a wood engraver, in photoengraving and banknote printing plants, and as an art director and freelance artist. He designed and illustrated many books, and was the creator of a considerable list of individual prints—wood engravings, line engravings on copper, and aquatints.